SHAKESPEARE'S WORKPLACE

Essays on Shakespearean Theatre

Shakespeare was easily the most inventive writer using the English language. His plays give us intricacies of vocabulary and usage that have enriched us immeasurably. This book provides a series of analytical essays on the marginalia relating to the plays. Each of them is a searching and authoritative account, packed with details, of some of the more peculiar conditions under which Shakespeare and his peers composed their playbooks. Among the essays are two completely new contributions. Altogether they reveal fresh details about the input of the playing companies, playhouses, individual players and even their controller, the Revels Office, to the complex fragments that we now have of the Shakespearean world. Gurr examines Shakespeare's own choice between playwriting and poetry, the requirements of working in a playhouse that wraps itself around the stage, and its impact on the creation of such figures as Henry V, Shylock, Isabella, King Lear and Coriolanus.

ANDREW GURR is Professor Emeritus at the University of Reading, and for the past thirty years has been the first Director of Research in London for Shakespeare's Globe Theatre. His books on the subject of theatre history include *The Shakespearean Stage 1574–1642* (1992), now in its fourth edition, *The Shakespearean Playing Companies* (1996), *Playgoing in Shakespeare's London* (Cambridge, 2004), *Staging in Shakespeare's Theatres* with Mariko Ichikawa (2000), *The Shakespeare Company 1594–1642* (2010), and *Shakespeare's Opposites: The Admiral's Company 1594–1625* (2012). He has also edited the New Cambridge Shakespeare's *King Richard II* (1984) and *King Henry V* (1992).

CAMBRIDGE
UNIVERSITY PRESS

University Printing House, Cambridge CB2 8BS, United Kingdom

One Liberty Plaza, 20th Floor, New York, NY 10006, USA

477 Williamstown Road, Port Melbourne, VIC 3207, Australia

4843/24, 2nd Floor, Ansari Road, Daryaganj, Delhi - 110002, India

79 Anson Road, #06-04/06, Singapore 079906

Cambridge University Press is part of the University of Cambridge.

It furthers the University's mission by disseminating knowledge in the pursuit of education, learning, and research at the highest international levels of excellence.

www.cambridge.org
Information on this title: www.cambridge.org/9781107167841
DOI: 10.1017/9781316716755

© Andrew Gurr 2017

This publication is in copyright. Subject to statutory exception and to the provisions of relevant collective licensing agreements, no reproduction of any part may take place without the written permission of Cambridge University Press.

First published 2017

Printed in the United States of America by Sheridan Books, Inc.

A catalogue record for this publication is available from the British Library

ISBN 978-1-107-16784-1 Hardback

Cambridge University Press has no responsibility for the persistence or accuracy of URLs for external or third-party internet websites referred to in this publication, and does not guarantee that any content on such websites is, or will remain, accurate or appropriate.

SHAKESPEARE'S WORKPLACE
Essays on Shakespearean Theatre

ANDREW GURR
University of Reading, Emeritus

CAMBRIDGE
UNIVERSITY PRESS

'The cause is in my will'.
Julius Caesar, 2.2.71

Contents

Illustrations   *page* ix
Acknowledgements   x
Note on the Text   xi

1. Introduction   1
2. Henry Carey's Peculiar Letter   10
3. Venues on the Verges: London's Theatre Government between 1594 and 1614   37
4. Three Reluctant Patrons and Early Shakespeare   60
5. The Great Divide of 1594   78
6. The Choice between Plays and Poems   99
7. Accommodating the Revels Office   115
8. The War of 1614–1618: Jacobean Absolutism, Local Authority, and a Crisis of Overproduction   130
9. Metatheatre and the Fear of Playing   145
10. Why was the Globe Round?   167
11. The General and the Caviar: Learned Audiences in the Early Theatre   181
12. Headless *Coriolanus*   196
13. Rethinking Shylock   207
14. *Measure for Measure*'s Hoods and Masks: The Duke, Isabella, and Liberty   221

15	The Transforming of *Henry V*	237
16	Headgear as a Paralinguistic Signifier in *King Lear*	249

The Cause is in My Will: A Bibliography   265
Index   276

Illustrations

1 The four drawings by John Webb from the Inigo Jones
  Cockpit *page* 168
2 Johannes De Witt's sketch of the Swan in 1596   198

Acknowledgements

Since all these essays were written over the course of more than twenty years spent studying Shakespeare, they arrive in print conjoined to a load of debts that I am more than happy to acknowledge here. I hope that my colleagues across the world who have helped with various elements in the book will recognise at least a little of what I owe them in preparing these essays. Above all, the late John Orrell is owed a debt he would probably not wish to acknowledge. Others, such as John H. Astington, Martin Butler, Alan C. Dessen, Richard Dutton, Mac Jackson, Mariko Ichikawa, James Shapiro, Bruce R. Smith, Tiffany Stern and Robin Headlam Wells, deserve all the credit they already have, to which I would like to add my own, having gained so much from numerous conversations with them, both in human exchanges and through letters and emails. In particular I should like to thank my erstwhile colleague, Mark Hutchings, for his careful checking of my text. It is equally necessary to acknowledge and thank the many other authors and scholars listed in the Bibliography, whom I have consulted through their publications.

I have also made extensive use of the pictures supplied here, along with the various analyses to which they have been subjected. Pictures are a massively attractive way of entering a subject, though the lack of photography four hundred years ago is a loss that we all suffer from.

Finally I would like to record my enduring gratitude to Sarah Stanton, at CUP, with whom I have worked on and off for more than forty years. The fertile interaction between authors and their publishers is often noted, but in my view has rarely been so productive as ours.

Note on the Text

Many of the sixteen chapters comprising this volume first appeared as book chapters or journal articles in a variety of sources. It would be difficult to achieve consistency in the footnotes across all sixteen chapters. For this reason, the style and numbering of the footnotes in each chapter have been modified as little as possible.

CHAPTER 1

Introduction

That most truly and subtly political play, *Julius Caesar*, provides the epigraph for this book, in a form that is about as incongruously misapplied as anybody could expect. Caesar's curt answer about his decision comes when his wife and friends argue with him about his going to the Capitol that day. 'The cause is in my will.' He offers this short and defensive sentence in irritated deference when his wife urges him not to go. Asked to explain why he insists on going, all he allows himself to say are these words, that it is his personal and private choice. My own cause is, however punningly contrived, far simpler than Caesar's. The chapters that follow weave round the fringes of Will Shakespeare's plays. They study some of the less direct impacts of that cultural event now usually called the Shakespearean moment. At first they deal with features of their time that can all too often be ignored when attempting close readings of the plays. The later chapters focus more directly on aspects of various plays, in order to draw attention to some of the local and immediate factors that influenced their original staging. These factors range from Shylock's moneylending to the use of headgear in *Measure for Measure* and *King Lear*. They all stem from the desire to know a little more about the life and the times that brought Shakespeare's plays into being.

They share the bald assumption that most of us now make routinely, that the plays from four hundred years in our past are mostly the product of a single and singular mind, one that knew exactly what he was doing, in that routine (and yet highly profitable) new activity of writing to entertain London's first theatre audiences. For the most part they seek to engage with various aspects of their original audiences, trying to identify features of the plays that our customary attention to the word on the page lets us overlook.

They start with the impact of governmental attempts to constrain, if not completely control, the business of playing in London, chiefly through those remarkable years of the 1590s. This was the decade when

Shakespeare's first plays appeared on stage. His personal options, and the choices that he made, as they emerge from the theatre history of the time, are examined here. Of necessity, theatre history ranges fairly widely. It has to include a range of more general and pervasive considerations. These include Henry Carey's contribution to government's control of playing, plus an overview of the work done by the Revels Office, together with the organisation and the enduring competition amongst the various playhouses over the period (roughly 1585–1642). Behind them is my now-chronic quest for whatever small traces can be detected of audience attitudes through those resplendent years. The later chapters consider how these factors in their different ways must have affected five of Shakespeare's best-known plays.

These essays were compiled over the space of about twenty years. First, in the 1990s, I wrote two speculative essays. The first, Chapter 11 here, developed some matters raised in my *Playgoing in Shakespeare's London*. It assessed the people, mostly at the higher social levels, who are known to have attended plays up to 1642. The other, Chapter 4, looked at the probable relations between Shakespeare and his first patrons, the Lord Chamberlain Henry Carey, the Lord Admiral Charles Howard, and Henry Herbert, Earl of Pembroke, short-lived patron of a Pembroke's company from 1592. Disbanded by August 1593, this company was said to have played *Titus Andronicus*, according to the titlepage of its 1594 quarto. Several of Pembroke's leading players joined the new Chamberlain's in May 1594. But between 1593 and 1595 Henry Carey's son George was engaged in a long quarrel with Henry Herbert over a possible marriage between Carey's daughter and Herbert's son William, then only fifteen, much later dedicatee of the First Folio. Despite the Pembroke's company performance of *Titus* and perhaps other early Shakespeares, there is nothing positive to say their author was a member of Pembroke's. All we can be sure of is that up to May 1594 he was working as a poet, writing his two epyllions.

After writing these first two essays, I embarked on a lengthy excursus through the background of early playing. Beginning with what I called a crisis of theatrical overproduction in 1614–18 (Chapter 8), I pursued its origins in the playing crisis of 1594 (Chapter 5), an event I came to call 'the great divide'. A range of other side-effects then loomed. They included questions about the original stage dress for *Measure for Measure* (Chapter 14) and continued in 2000 with *King Lear*'s use of headgear, especially crowns and coronets (Chapter 16). By then, *Playgoing in Shakespeare's London* had prompted so much commentary that I felt obliged to deepen a few of the holes I had dug to excavate its evidence. Concern about the degree of official control then evoked Chapters 3, 5 and 9. The need to streamline the contents of my two books of those years, *The Shakespeare Company 1594–1642* (2004) and *Shakespeare's Opposites: The Admiral's Company 1594–1625* (2009), produced enough digressions into theatre history to warrant the rest of this book. The final five essays here all deal with the impacts of local conditions on specific plays, from *The Merchant of Venice* in 1596 to *Coriolanus* in 1608.

Another preoccupation, looming bigger and bigger as the years went on, was what could be found about the choreography, what kinds of movement were used on the early stages. Were there three doors for players to enter the stage, or only two? What might the first players have done to cope with the Globe's two large structural pillars on the stage, while the Blackfriars had none? This was an issue I first broached early in the new century, in several seminars, and much later in a paper written for a book that raised a key question, whether the ear or the eye had priority in early modern theatre. The fact that the early audiences more or less surrounded the players gives the ear special value, allowing the audience to spread completely round in three dimensions, whereas the eye favours two dimensions and a frontal position for the spectator. The primary word, 'audience', implies priority for hearing, while 'spectator' indicates only seeing. I spent a long time poring through early texts, in a culture where learning demanded consciousness of word origins, to find which of the two words predominated. The outcome was, of course, inconclusive, although the ear does seem in the earlier years to have been favoured over the eye. I am still inclined to believe that the earlier writing for listeners was gradually supplanted, at least on stage, by attractions available to the eye.

As part of this, and given the richness of so many recent contributions to this period in theatre history, I have learned what you might loosely call a lot. The last forty years have been a fertile time for Shakespeare scholars. This latest generation has provided much new work. John Astington, for instance, after writing his admirable book on the plays staged at court, has provided his own overview of acting through the whole period, with features and information that certainly far outdo what I attempted originally in 1970. Other writers, such as Peter Hyland, listed in the bibliography here, have extended the range that in 1970 I thought was sufficient for my own overview. So the essays in this book are diverse studies of some rather less regarded features of the period.

A consistent assumption behind them all is that Shakespeare was a truly great writer, who found himself creating a new product for a new kind of audience. I suspect that he cared rather less about his products than we do now, but he could never forget those omnipresent playgoers, who thought him a great creator, and who, in his own lifetime, made his fortune. The chapters in the second half of this book approach the plays themselves rather more directly than do the contextual concerns of the first section. They too, however, direct attention to features we usually pass over, sometimes without registering how comprehensively they require the plays to be seen as features of, and composed for, their own time.

Behind them all is the confident assumption that Shakespeare's local circumstances profoundly influenced him, whether they entailed the daily business of staging his and other men's plays, or his own acute awareness of the needs of the audiences he helped to set them up for. Since the events he created on his stages were part of a huge complex of attitudes and ideas that have now utterly vanished, we have to believe that we can gain fresh information about how to read the plays if we develop a stronger idea of what the distractions might have been through those twenty years while he was writing for the stage. Even such relatively minor matters as the shadowy presence of the Master of the Revels, censor and critic of all the plays his company performed, or the chronic suspicion, even hatred, of play-acting that prevailed amongst London's many churchgoers, are part of these attempts to decipher what might have been in his mind while he wrote.

This sort of guesswork tantalises scholars for many reasons. Among the most difficult is Shakespeare's own readiness, possibly based on a formal financial contract, to hand over all his completed play manuscripts, roughly two a year, to his fellow-players. Their livelihoods depended on them. That must have been a major feature of his mind-set. The absence at his home in Stratford of any evidence about his past in London has rightly invoked guesswork about his retirement there when he ended his career in London. But we can only speculate about it. We cannot, for instance, be sure whether Shakespeare ever felt that, from 1594 onwards, the option of working for money instead of for Spenserian poetic glory and a higher social standing than that of the common player ever made him dislike the fate that London's higher powers chose for him. Given the number of his sonnets that appear to be self-decrying, it seems likely that he was never single-mindedly devoted to play-writing. If so, he must have concealed any such reaction from his fellows, and therefore from us. Perhaps such private doubts were why he invested so heavily in buying properties not in London but back home in Stratford. Did he feel that London playwriting was a socially inferior activity? This, and other equally odd and unattached possibilities, lurks here under the claims about his mentality that biographers tend to make. Some of those dangling titbits are nibbled at here.

Recent biographers such as Park Honan, Peter Ackroyd, and even Katherine Duncan-Jones have relied heavily on Sam Schoenbaum's scrupulously careful two-volume *William Shakespeare: A Documentary Life*. They all pay more attention to the personal elements and the plays that resulted from the bard's work in London than to the complex factors controlling those labours. Henry Carey for instance, the first Baron Hunsdon, who became Shakespeare's patron for the last three years of his life, having by then employed James Burbage for nearly twenty, was one major influence that we take too little note of. As Lord Chamberlain from 1585, the authority behind the Master of the Revels, Carey made himself patron of the new company he set up in May 1594. He might well have advised his agent, the Master of the Revels, to secure Shakespeare as one of his new group of players. That was a decision made by and with Carey's kind of high authority. In the various narratives of Shakespeare's career, the activities of Burbage and his two sons have attracted more notice than Carey, but he must have been a key influence behind this crucial switch of his activities. Most people now would applaud Carey's influence in 1594, even though there is nothing to say what degree of coercion or compulsion was entailed in the shift from poet to playmaker.

What might have affected Shakespeare's mind and ambitions in the early summer of 1594 is another major background factor. We can be sure that his plans for his future changed quite drastically in May. It was the month when his second great epyllion, *The Rape of Lucrece*, first appeared in a London bookshop. This put him on the way to replacing Spenser as England's supreme poet. But it was also the month when he chose, or more likely had chosen for him, a different career, not as poet but as player and writer in the newly founded Lord Chamberlain's playing company. The other of the pair of new companies formed in that crucial month, the Lord Admiral's Men, had all six of Marlowe's plays gathered together for their use. Shakespeare, an equally well-known playwright, was inserted along with his ten previously written and acted plays into the other new company. It must have been high authority that set Shakespeare on his way with the Chamberlain's Men.

Carey authorised each company to play at one of London's two newly licensed and approved playhouses. The Chamberlain's Men were allocated to the Theatre in Shoreditch, and the Admiral's to the Rose on Bankside. It was hardly by chance that both of the leading players in each new company,

Edward Alleyn and Richard Burbage, had close family links with the owner of their allocated playhouse. In February 1592 Alleyn became the son-in-law of Philip Henslowe, who had built and owned the Rose from 1585. Richard Burbage was son to James Burbage, who had built the Theatre in 1576. Almost all the players in the two teams knew and had worked with each other before. The new deal was ingenious, and thorough. It set up two familiar and family-based teams of the country's best players firmly located in two London playhouses, as a doubled-up replacement for the single and now-decayed royal company set up eleven years before, the Queen's Men.

It is quite certain that somebody in high authority gathered up all Marlowe's and Shakespeare's plays from the various companies that had been staging them, and parcelled them out between the new pair. This was for an obvious reason: to provide each of them with a repertory consisting of the best-known plays of the time. From our remote perspective, this looks as if it must have been the outcome of an edict from on high. The dead Marlowe could not object to it, and the living Shakespeare could not prevent it. Given the range of companies the plays belonged to, only the Lord Chamberlain, through his deputy the Master of the Revels, could have managed it. So, whatever Shakespeare wrote in his sonnets, we can never be sure whether he really objected to such an abrupt shift in his ambitions. It forced him to withdraw from the long process of making his name as London's most promising new poet in place of the dying Spenser. Instead he turned to the hectic day-after-day drudgery of playing and playmaking. Lower in social status than writing poetry, in 1594 playwriting offered money without the high esteem we now award it. What is certain is that few people would now think Carey's re-direction of his career was a bad turn.

The plays themselves raise myriads of interrelated questions about their provenance. Often seemingly trivial, they nonetheless have the capacity to stretch the modern reader's imagination. *The Winter's Tale*, for instance, concludes with that thoroughly improbable 'discovery' scene, in which the statue of Hermione, thought dead for the last sixteen years, is brought back to life. The play usually assumed to be its immediate successor, *The Tempest*, closes with a comparable 'discovery', in which the young lovers, Ferdinand and Miranda, are revealed to be keeping themselves hidden in Prospero's cell, and not making love but playing a game of chess. What was it that made Shakespeare in his last plays adopt such a distinctively anti-realistic set of devices for his closures? Was he by then so far through his career that making games out of his plays became a mark of his impending withdrawal? Many critics have thought so.

Introduction

Modern people usually read their Shakespeares, or watch them on stage, with a multitude of usually automatic and unthinking preoccupations. Reinventing new versions of the plays has become an almost unstoppable urge for stage directors. Some of us prefer to stick with the written texts, flawed in transmission though they pervasively are, creating our own imagined versions of them as what we like to think might once have appeared at the Globe. Given the awful struggle editors of the plays have to go through to achieve a viable version of what was always a variable sequence of words, the still less attainable desire to reconstruct original staging seems not just remote but impossible. Performance on stage is instant and unrepeatable, however repetitious theatre has become since Shakespeare's time. All sorts of factors change daily in the theatre, above all the audiences and the collective mindsets they bring to each performance.

The revelations employed at the conclusions of *The Winter's Tale* and *The Tempest*, that pair of what we usually call the last plays, always invoke new worlds of complex and variable interpretations. They provoke a wide range of emotional/intellectual responses, simple and intricate, from the banal through the baldly comic to the intricately poetic. This book tries to avoid most of this inevitable splurge of speculation, however productive it might be, in favour of a more material concern with a few of the immediate phenomena that impacted on the plays when they were first written. Mostly they are questions largely forgotten until now. I hope these studies might help a little to smooth out some of the endless weave of concerns about the riches inherent in all the plays. They might, of course, merely complicate the struggle to make better sense of the infinitely complex tangle of interests in the plays. At best, they might serve to tidy up some of the rough edges in our knowledge. I can only hope that they offer a few tangible insights into the intricate complex of interests that these days represents the Shakespearean 'moment'.

There is no need to apologise for pursuing these ideas about what those original conditions might have been. What I call here 'the Shakespearean penumbra', that dark space lying between the texts themselves and the patchy items of knowledge we have about how they were designed to be staged, was so integral to Shakespeare's mind when he wrote the plays that it tends nowadays to generate more concern than do the texts themselves. That is not a reason to leave it in the dark.

Some of us, myself especially once I first met Sam Wanamaker in 1980, attempted to make a reconstruction of the Globe, and a version of the Blackfriars, close to the Globe's original location. We built these structures in order to use their products as experiments, to help us see what forms of staging work best in such simulacra of the original playhouses. The two constructions, one based on a best guess about a shape known all too little, and that very vaguely, since its original was demolished, the other based on John Webb's version of Inigo Jones's seventeenth-century plans for an indoor playhouse, both proved revelatory, but in surprisingly opposed ways. Building a new Globe was itself a learning process, chiefly about the constraints imposed by Elizabethan timber construction methods and the practical exigencies enforced by such jerry-built structures. Building to John Webb's plans was a revelation about how complex the original design process must have been. It showed how the original drawings themselves register changes of mind as the concept evolved, and how many smaller problems in Webb's final depiction remain unresolved. Although the same master-carpenter, Peter McCurdy, built most of both structures, what we learned from the indoor playhouse construction of 2013 was work of a quite different order than the Globe's. The least it taught us was how intricate, and carefully studied, both sets of designs were.

I began my own study of Shakespearean theatre long ago, in the 1950s. Quite early on it gave me the conviction that a great deal of wonderful work was being done. It appeared, however, in different holes and corners, academic or practical, in history, in new theatre, and in historical architecture. Too little of it was gathered together in any sort of holistic view. It seemed right to attempt an overview, since it seemed surprisingly easy to put the pieces together and make sense of the picture they seemed to offer. For me, this impetus produced in 1970 the first of what gradually transmuted into four successive editions of *The Shakespearean Stage*. Since that first step, our knowledge of this period in historical theatre has multiplied immensely, growing far beyond the capacity to pack it all into a single book.

It helped my own studies to diversify, first into what we could find about the early audiences (*Playgoing*, eventually in three editions), then into building a version of what seemed a plausible shape for the Globe and its roofed partner. This was done thanks to Sam Wanamaker's intensive backing. So finally we could put both of those products to work. We began to run experiments at the new Globe and the indoor Wanamaker Playhouse, trying out the most likely forms of retrievals of the staging that such simulacra of the early stages seemed to make possible. Now, after some time, it really does seem to be having a beneficial effect on the staging of the plays, giving them a little more of their original three-dimensional character.

Introduction

Nonetheless, of all these lengthy tasks, retrieving the most likely versions of the original staging still seems the least accessible. The evidence is both evanescent in history and the most subject to modern prejudices. You can try to reconstruct a version of the early playhouses, and even try to replicate some aspects of what might have been done with the performances that Shakespeare witnessed. But you cannot even begin to try re-creating the original audiences, their mindsets, their physical conditions, and least of all their expectations. Audiences are inescapably modern.

Theatre then was almost the only regular form of public entertainment on offer. Concerned to do no more than spend an idle afternoon in London's raw weather, through six work-free afternoons every week two or three thousand individuals would have packed themselves in together at the Rose, the Globe or the Red Bull. They would have enjoyed a unique collective experience, both unimaginably intense and utterly unrecordable. One of the most basic points about early staging that has emerged through the last four decades is that performances were always massively complex operations, a convergence of many skills and many minds, all bonding into a uniquely tight and vibrantly vivid occasion. No form of record can recapture the intensity of such an event. We are grasping at cobwebs when what we want to find is bricks.

Bricks are an obvious metaphor. For the most part I have tried to cleave to the more material features of the time, just as all the bard's biographers try to create the illusion that what they are providing are the hard facts of one man's life, spent four hundred years ago producing some of the greatest plays the world knows. Shakespeare biography is very largely an art, or an act, of fiction, bearing about as much relation to the historical realities of the period 1564–1616 as a cobweb has to a brick wall. Far too many products of this scrutiny of the penumbra that surrounds Shakespeare's twenty years of writing in London, before he escaped with his loot back to his home and his wife and children in Stratford, are not much more tangible than what a spider spins from its gut. Its manifold uncertainties probably throw more shadow than light on what was in Shakespeare's mind while he was writing. It gives us few hard answers. But even if in doing so it stimulates a few more questions, we can comfort ourselves by thinking that everything it makes for us is part of the global and needful response to Shakespeare's endless fertility.

CHAPTER 2

Henry Carey's Peculiar Letter

In November 1596 residents of the Liberty of the Blackfriars asked the Privy Council to stop James Burbage and his company at the Theatre from using his new playhouse in their precinct. This well-known petition contains some puzzling statements. The petitioners complained, for instance, that

> all players being banished by the Lord Mayor from playing within the Cittie by reason of the great inconveniences and ill rule that followeth them, they now thincke to plant them selves in liberties.[1]

What seems strange here is not the company's plan to start growing in the liberty of Blackfriars, but the claim that the Lord Mayor had recently banned playing inside the city. No papers survive to say when or even that such a ban was issued. The authority that normally sent out such orders was not London's mayor but the Privy Council, acting for the monarch. Yet the thirty-four petitioners – residents of the afflicted liberty – should have known what they were saying. They were led by Elizabeth Russell, sister-in-law to William Cecil, Lord Burghley, who chaired the Privy Council. The others included Richard Field, the printer from Stratford who had issued Shakespeare's narrative poems in 1593 and 1594. Though the claim that the Lord Mayor had banned playing in the city does echo twenty years of mayoral complaints to the Privy Council, it is distinctly mysterious. Just which Lord Mayor was it who took authority to initiate this unique ban on playing inside the city? Had the Privy Council, which had resisted Guildhall's pleas before, nothing to say about it and no say in it?

Henry Carey, the first Lord Hunsdon, Lord Chamberlain, and the Privy Council member who might have been most concerned, had died in July, some months before the petitioners set down their complaint. Burbage's

---

Original publication: "Henry Carey's Peculiar Letter," *Shakespeare Quarterly* 56 (2005), 51–75.
[1] E.K. Chambers, *The Elizabethan Stage*, 4 vols. (Oxford: Clarendon Press, 1923), 4:319–20.

new indoor playhouse was built for use by the company that Carey himself had set up in May 1594 as the Lord Chamberlain's Men. At the time of the petition, William Brooke, Lord Cobham, Carey's successor as Lord Chamberlain, was less interested in helping Carey's company, now the second Lord Hunsdon's; it may even have been Brooke's objection that, in the same year as the petition, made them change the name of their most celebrated new creation, Sir John Oldcastle, to Sir John Falstaff.² Brooke, himself a resident of the Blackfriars precinct, was unsympathetic to the company's scheme, as was the younger Carey, since his signature appears on the petition immediately below Elizabeth Russell's. Both Brooke and George Carey would surely have known whether or not the Lord Mayor had recently managed to impose a ban on playing inside the city.

Asking why the petitioners should have attributed such a ban to the Lord Mayor rather than to the Privy Council takes us back deep into the story of a power struggle that entangled Shakespeare's company through its first years. I believe the ban may have been laid down in May 1594, when Henry Carey as Lord Chamberlain and Charles Howard, the Lord Admiral, first set up their two new companies. In effect, I think, the Lord Chamberlain's and the Lord Admiral's Men were created by their patrons as a duopoly to replace the monopoly of the former Queen's Men. I have written elsewhere about their scheme to create a pair of new companies and give them fixed playing places in the suburbs.³ It was then, I believe, that they agreed to accept a ban on playing inside the city and to send their two companies off to play only in the suburbs. There the Lord Admiral was in authority, and two playhouses, the Rose (in Surrey) and the Theatre (in Middlesex), were already in regular use. Confining playing to the suburbs of Middlesex and Surrey would keep it out of the Lord Mayor's jurisdiction, and as a result, they no doubt hoped, might halt the stream of mayoral pleas to ban all playing everywhere.

The idea that Carey and Howard, in concert with the Lord Mayor, set up an agreement in 1594 for playing in and around London has significant implications. While in the absence of key documents such an idea is

---

² See, for instance, Gary Taylor, "The Fortunes of Oldcastle," *Shakespeare Survey* 38 (1985): 85–100.
³ See Gurr, "Privy Councillors as Theatre Patrons," in *Shakespeare and Theatrical Patronage in Early Modern England*, Paul Whitfield White and Suzanne R. Westfall, eds. (Cambridge: Cambridge UP, 2002), 221–45. Charles Howard was Lord Chamberlain through 1584 until he became the Lord Admiral, when the chamberlainship passed to Carey, his father-in-law. The term *duopoly* for the two companies is Richard Dutton's, though he cautiously marks it as not affirmed until 1598 in the Privy Council's surviving orders (*Mastering the Revels. The Regulation and Censorship of English Renaissance Drama* [Iowa City: U of Iowa P, 1991], 111). I offer a summary of some of the consequences of establishing a duopoly in 1594 in *The Shakespeare Company 1594–1642* (Cambridge: Cambridge UP, 2004), 1–40.

only a hypothesis, the clearest reading of the evidence suggests that the two authorities of central and city government worked together to settle their differences over which locations the professional playing companies could use then and in the future. That hypothesis, considered along with the surviving documents, also suggests that the agreed solution continued to be an issue after the two companies began playing in 1594. The story of the Privy Council and city government's power struggle over plays colours this reading.

Seen from a long historical perspective, the success of Shakespeare's company in the years following its creation appears an obvious step in the unstoppable growth of professional playing and the production of the great plays they contributed to English (and later global) culture. The political manoeuvres surrounding the duopoly's establishment, however, suggest that their creation was far more risky and their success more doubtful than we would like to think. That the Lord Chamberlain's Men were denied the use of an indoor playhouse in the Blackfriars until 1608 affirms that risk. Extant papers from the 1570s onward show that quite a few mayors had unsuccessfully pleaded with the Privy Council to ban playing in London.[4] They were forced to plead because it was the Council that issued orders about playing, as it did for all theatre closures resulting from increases in the number of plague deaths. Surviving letters show the Council allowing playing, for instance, on 23 December 1578 (a letter also going to the magistrates of Middlesex and Surrey, where the custom-built playhouses stood), 18 November and 3 December 1581, 11 April 1582, and 26 November 1583. Banning or staying orders, mostly because of plague, survive from 7 May 1587, 25 July 1591, 28 January 1593 (for plague, including Middlesex and Surrey), and 3 February 1594. After 1594, orders about playing went only to magistrates in the two counties, bypassing the city itself.[5] I suspect that something happened in that year, in a strange consonance with the Blackfriars petition, which allowed the Privy Council to stop regulating playing inside the city even as it continued to close other public venues in an attempt to limit the spread of the plague.

What may be the key document in the struggle between the pro-playing Privy Councillors and the anti-playing mayoralty is preserved in the *Remembrancia* of the City of London, a patchy but vital transcription of letters written to and from Guildhall. This collection includes a copy of a letter sent on 8 October 1594 by Lord Chamberlain Henry Carey from his Privy Council office at Nonsuch Palace to the Lord Mayor, Sir Richard

---

[4] See Chambers, 4:271–316.   [5] Chambers, 4:319, 325, 332–33.

Martin, at the Guildhall.⁶ The letter implies that Shakespeare's company wanted an indoor playhouse from the outset; it may also explain why Elizabeth Russell and her co-signatories believed that it was the Lord Mayor who had stopped playing inside the city. Composed less than five months after Carey's playing company had been established, while the first chill of the coming winter was in the air, it delivered a blunt request in his characteristically curt and businesslike manner.

> After my hartie comendacions, where my nowe companie of Players have byn accustomed for the better exercise of their qualities, & for the service of her Majestie if need soe require to plaie this winter time within the Citye at the Crosse kayes in Gracious street. These are to require & praye your Lordship the time beinge such as thankes be to god there is nowe no danger of the sicknes) to permitt & suffer them soe to doe; The which I praie you the rather to doe for that they have undertaken to me that where heretofore they began not their Plaies till towards fower a clock, they will now begin at two, & have don between fower and five and will nott use anie Drumes or trumpettes att all for the calling of peopell together, and shalbe contributories to the poore of the parishe where they plaie according to their habilities And soe not dowting of your willingness to yeeld hereunto, upon their reasonable condicions I comitt yow to the Almightie. Noonesuch this viiith of October 1594.
>
>   Your lordships lovinge freind
>   H. hounsdon
>
> To my honorable good freind Sir Richard Martin knight Lord mayor of the Citie of London.⁷

The archivist who transcribed the *Remembrancia* at Guildhall, probably Giles Fletcher, marked the letter with a marginal note that reads 'For players to bee suffred to play within London.' On the face of it, as Chambers and many others have interpreted it, Carey was simply asking that his new company be permitted to perform its plays through the winter at the city's Cross Keys inn, an indoor venue often used for playing in previous years. Six of the players who were drawn into the new Lord Chamberlain's company in 1594 are on record as having played at the Cross Keys with

---

⁶ The letter from Carey to Martin is reprinted in *Malone Society Collections: Part I* (Oxford: The Malone Society, 1907–), 1:1, 73–74, hereafter cited as *MSC*. The *Remembrancia* were the records kept by the City Remembrancer, who from 1586 to 1605 was Giles Fletcher. Of the nine volumes, Volume 1 covers 1579 to 1592, and Volume 2 covers 1593 to 1609.

⁷ *Remembrancia*, quoted here from *MSC*, 2:33; Chambers reprints the letter with some alterations, for instance, adding a mark to open the parenthetical phrase in the third sentence that in the *Remembrancia* version has only the closure (4:316).

Strange's Men on 5 November 1589.[8] Evidently they objected to now being forced to play through the winter at their assigned open-air playhouse in the northern suburbs. In other words, the impetus was their reluctance to use only the Theatre in Middlesex's Shoreditch as their licensed location.

Henslowe's *Diary* shows that the Admiral's had been playing through that summer at the Rose to the south in Surrey. A surviving order of the Council in 1598 specifies the Theatre and Rose as the venues of the Lord Chamberlain's and the Admiral's Men respectively, saying that the two companies could play nowhere else, but in 1594 the Chamberlain's Men thought differently. They had been used to performing indoors through the winters of previous years, but now were required to perform out of doors all the year round. This seems to indicate that someone, either the Lord Mayor or the Privy Council, had recently excluded them from playing within the city limits. If it was not a mayoral order, Carey would not have needed to ask for the Lord Mayor's permission, and the Blackfriars petitioners in 1596 would not have needed to jog the Council's memory. Nothing survives to say that, in all his years as Lord Chamberlain, Carey ever made a similar request. It does seem that, as the new companies' first winter drew on, Carey's players were pestering him because they preferred the indoor location they had used in previous winters to their outdoor amphitheatre.

But the wish to play indoors in winter is only a minor element of the letter's subtext. Its chief impetus, both for the company and for Carey, stems from the probability that playing at the city's inns had recently been banned, as the petition from Blackfriars residents was to claim. The most likely reason for Carey to make such an exceptional request must, I believe, have come from an agreement made between the Lord Mayor and the two Privy Councillors when they took on the patronage of the duopoly companies – an agreement to ban all playing within the city limits. Such an agreement would correspond to their licensing of the two suburban playhouses. Carey's aim was not just to secure wintertime comfort for his players and their customers but also to test the possibility that, despite the ban on playing at the city inns, the issue might still be open to change. Had there been no prior agreement between the Council and the Lord Mayor, there would have been no need for Carey to seek mayoral consent to a breach of the new ban.

It appears, therefore, that Carey was laying down a blatant challenge to the incumbent Lord Mayor. His letter is crucial as evidence largely because

---

[8] Chambers, 4:305–6.

not a single Privy Council document has survived from the period between 27 August 1593 and 1 October 1595. Consequently we can only guess at what orders the Councillors may have issued when the duopoly of the Lord Chamberlain's and the Lord Admiral's Men was first set up, as I propose it was, in May 1594.[9] The documentary evidence that does survive, however circumstantial, suggests that the two Privy Councillors who made themselves patrons of the new companies included in their new deal, first, a concession to the Lord Mayor to ban playing at London's inns and confine it exclusively to the suburbs outside the Lord Mayor's jurisdiction; and, second, an agreement licensing only the two playhouses with which members of the companies had family affiliations. The Lord Chamberlain's company included Richard Burbage, son of the Theatre's owner, and the Admiral's was led by Edward Alleyn, son-in-law of the Rose's owner. Privy Council letters of 19 February 1598 and 22 June 1600, quoted below, specify the Rose and the Theatre as the two licensed playing places in the London suburbs of Surrey and Middlesex. An order of June 1600 and another of 31 December 1601 replaced those theatres with the Globe and the Fortune. All of the later orders were directed to the county magistrates, not to the Lord Mayor.

These later orders provide one strong reason for believing that the issue of earlier licences must have accompanied or closely followed a ban on playing inside the city. The absence of Privy Council papers between 1593 and 1595 argues that the original ban was laid down during that gap. The Council's strict regulation of playing both before and after 1594 makes it almost unthinkable that they should have abnegated their authority in this one instance and left it to the Lord Mayor to issue the ban. Since nothing in the *Remembrancia* speaks of such a ban, the Blackfriars petitioners were most likely echoing the vague recognition that the ban was a matter of agreement between city and government, one maintained (and celebrated)

---

[9] The absence of Privy Council records for 1594 leaves uncertain the date of the duopoly's establishment, and much depends on one's interpretation of the Carey letter. Ancillary evidence about the two patrons, however, is very persuasive. The new companies both appeared at the end of May 1594, and the deal was acknowledged in 1598 to keep the duopoly sharing exclusive rights to perform in London and for the queen. That it was firmly in place before that is evident in the court's records of their sole access to royal performances, as it is in their exclusive use of the Rose and the Theatre. Indeed, considering that the Chamberlain's and Admiral's Men took almost equal shares in performances at court from 1594 till 1600, the choice of plays for the winter of 1596, when, in Brooke's only occasion as Chamberlain, he allocated all six performances to the Shakespeare company, might be seen as an apology for the Falstaff trouble. A separate testimony is that someone with real clout set up the two companies' repertoires of plays in 1594, because all of Marlowe's plays appear to have gone to the Admiral's and all the early Shakespeares to the Chamberlain's, gathering them in from several older companies. See Andrew Gurr, "The Great Divide of 1594" in *Words That Count: Essays on Early Modern Authorship in Honor of MacDonald P. Jackson*, Brian Boyd, ed. (Newark: U of Delaware P, 2004), 29–50. It is reproduced as Chapter 5 in this volume.

by the city. Carey's letter makes it at least likely that the duopoly and the ban on playing inside the city were established as part of a deal made four years before it was reaffirmed and recorded in the Privy Council minutes of February 1598.[10]

By 1595, Carey had been Lord Chamberlain for nearly ten years, taking on the role when his son-in-law Charles Howard moved up to become the Lord Admiral. Both men had been supporters of playing since the early 1580s. Carey had made James Burbage his servant some years before becoming Lord Chamberlain, after Burbage left Leicester's Men to work as the impresario owner of the Theatre. Carey did not set up any company under his own name until 1594, probably a policy decision made because he was responsible for all professional playing. Nor had his ally Howard acted as patron to a playing company while he was Lord Chamberlain, but made Edward Alleyn his servant and started a new company under his name only upon giving up the chamberlainship. Alleyn retained the Lord Admiral's livery in later years when he moved from the Admiral's to perform with Strange's Men, an act that must reflect, if nothing else, Howard's interest in the player. Carey and Howard made a convenience of the 'service' they had from James Burbage and Edward Alleyn. Using them to anchor the new companies made good sense, as did the licensing of the two playhouses with their family connections and their location in counties where Howard had leverage with local magistrates. Carey and Howard held concerted views about what needed to be done to protect the Chamberlain's obligation to entertain the queen. A duopoly with playhouses licensed for them in the suburbs was an exceptionally neat solution to several problems, as we shall see below. This fact, when seen in the wider context of Carey's letter, makes it difficult to believe that the duopoly came into being accidentally or gradually over a period of time.

Carey's letter is most remarkable because it was written at the height of the twenty-year struggle between several Lord Mayors and the Privy Council over professional playing in London. Extant letters offer occasional glimpses into the long-running negotiations between the two authorities. The Lansdowne papers, for instance, contain a strong letter from Lord Burghley to Martin during his brief tenure as Lord Mayor between July and September 1594, criticising 'the small care yt seamed was had emongest yow of the government of the estaite of the Cittye (as in not seking good and godlie meanes, for preventing the contynewaunce and increase

---

[10] The main point of the order of 19 February 1598 (Chambers, 4:325) was to forbid an intrusion on the existing duopoly by a third company.

of the infeccion of the plage and not providing for the poore Souldiers & others that swarmed in multitudes in your streetes.'[11] Archbishop Whitgift, as a Privy Councillor and head of the church, was involved in the matter of playing as early as 1589. On 6 March 1592 the then Lord Mayor, Sir William Webbe, invited him to consult with 'certein of *our* Brethren the Aldermen' on the use of obscenities in plays.[12] On 18 March it was Martin, along with an alderman from the Grocers, who was instructed to open discussions with the Master of the Revels.[13] Sadly, no other record of these discussions has survived.

Carey's subtext hints at some intricate political scheming by the Privy Council in response to the complaints about playing.[14] The letter's origins may lie in recent mayoral attempts to link the midsummer 1592 apprentice riots in Southwark to the Rose on Bankside.[15] Behind that evidence of the conflict over playing stands the other subtext – that the Lord Chamberlain's Men in 1594 objected to the requirement that they use their open-air playhouse through the winter. We shall consider later why the Admiral's company was more ready to accept winter playing at the Rose.

Subtexts are always open to debate, and readings are necessarily hypothetical. Nonetheless, Carey's letter and a few other documents preserved in the *Remembrancia* and elsewhere present patches of evidence enabling us to identify what led to the establishment of a new pair of companies in 1594, what followed from it, and what other circumstances might inform the subtext of Carey's letter. If there was an agreement in that year between the Council and the Lord Mayor to ban playing in the city, it constituted a major step forward in several ways. It had something substantial for both sides in the dispute, offering a cure for more than two decades' worth of problems between them. Freeing the city from playing entirely would have given the mayoralty a victory that would release the Privy Council from the city's chronic complaints. For the other side, the suburbs had enough

---

[11] *MSC*, 1:2, 211.   [12] *MSC*, 1:1, 70.   [13] Chambers, 4:309.

[14] Conflict over plays between the Privy Council and the Court of Aldermen became apparent as early as May 1572, when the Court objected to a Council order 'written', as the minute reported, 'in the favor of certein persones to haue in there howses, yardes, or back sydes, being overt & open places, such playes, enterludes, commedies, & tragedies as maye tende to represse vyce & extoll vertwe, for the recreacion of the people' (Chambers, 4:269). Unlike the 1598 order specifying the suburban playhouses, this was not an attempt at licensing. In November 1583 the Court itself recorded making an allowance for the new Queen's Men to play in the city 'at the sygnes of the Bull in Bushoppesgate streete, and the sygne of the Bell in Gratiousstreete and nowheare els within this Cyttye' (Chambers, 4:296). The Bull, which also staged prizefights, was an outdoor venue, while the Bell may have been an indoor venue like the Cross Keys. Negotiations between the Council and the Court often involved some give-and-take, as I believe they did with the duopoly scheme.

[15] For an engaging if rather fanciful account of the occasion for these riots, see Richard Wilson, *Will Power: Essays on Shakespearean Authority* (Detroit: Wayne State UP, 1993), 22–46.

purpose-built playhouses to give the players somewhere to perform, allowing them to fulfill the one major duty the Lord Chamberlain could not ignore – to supply the queen and court with professional performances each year. Some such agreement was certainly reached at one point or another during this period, because the inns had been closed as places for staging plays seemingly by 1596 and certainly before 1598, when the duopoly was in full swing.

The chief inspiration behind Carey's letter was probably pressure from his new company, reluctant to play outdoors in winter, since nobody else would have specified the use of the Cross Keys. That, plus Carey's irritation at having to voice such a request, may help to explain its terseness. But more likely he was equally irked by doubts about whether the mayoralty would stick to the new agreement that I hypothesise. Perhaps what stimulated him to write was his company's objection to this aspect of the deal between the Councillors and the Lord Mayor. He may also have intended to test how rigidly the mayoralty was going to maintain the agreed terms and to test their solidity, especially once he knew who the next Lord Mayor was going to be.

That knowledge must have given Carey good reason to doubt whether the agreement would endure. A full set of rearrangements between the two sides, if established in May 1594 as I have suggested, could have been nothing like a simple or final concord. Both negotiating parties were members of governing councils, working committees – and committees rarely achieve a complete and lasting consensus. The Lord Mayor changed annually, and there was no guarantee that any mayor would uphold an agreement reached by his predecessor. Both sides were fluid. The Privy Council's impatience with the professional companies emerged in July 1597, when yet another letter of complaint arrived from the Lord Mayor, and the Council issued an order to close all the suburban playhouses and pull them down – an order that the Councillors themselves soon forgot.[16] Guildhall's mix of committee views shows up in the varying degrees of hostility expressed in successive mayoral letters, and still more in the reluctance of individual aldermen in the livery companies to support the mayoral stance against

---

[16] The thinking behind the Privy Council's drastic order of 28 July 1597 has been much debated (by Glynne Wickham and William Ingram, among others), but nothing conclusive has been found to explain what prompted it. See Glynne Wickham, *Early English Stages 1300–1660*, 2d ed., 3 vols. in 4 (London: Routledge and Kegan Paul; New York: Columbia UP, 1959–91), Vol. 2 (1576–1660), Pt. 2, 9–29; William Ingram, "The Closing of the Theaters in 1597: A Dissenting View," *Modern Philology* 69 (1971–72): 105–15; and Andrew Gurr, *The Shakespearian Playing Companies* (Oxford: Clarendon Press, 1996), 106–10. Carey was out of the story by then, but Howard was present and signed the order.

playing. Charles Whitney has produced ample evidence from the records of the Bakers', Plasterers', Clothworkers', and Tallow-chandlers' companies to show that the well-known antagonism of successive mayors toward play-going and their annual letters of complaint to the Privy Council received little backing from the handicraft guilds.[17]

Whitney identifies John Spencer, a wealthy clothworker and alderman, as an especially antitheatrical voice in the Court of Aldermen, and it was Spencer who Carey knew would be the incoming Lord Mayor at Michaelmas 1594. Spencer's letters to the Privy Council show him as utterly opposed to all professional playing and as the most antagonistic of all the mayors to the Privy Council's support for professional companies. In the years preceding 1594, he had already made himself less than a favourite of the Council. An alderman of the Clothworkers' guild from 1587, he served as sheriff in 1583–84, pursuing papists with such ardour that he wrongly incarcerated a group of the queen's musicians, including Antonio Bassano.[18] Carey's own mistress, Aemilia Lanier, was a Bassano, and Carey's knowledge of the incident just might have influenced his attitude toward Spencer. Essentially a merchant trader, Spencer was accused in 1591 of engrossing the entire English trade with Tripoli for himself. In April 1598, while he was still making his presence felt at Guildhall, the Privy Council ordered him to surrender his share of £200 for the cost of goods pirated (as 'spoile') from Italian traders by his ship the *David*.[19] He turned his house, Crosby Place in Bishopsgate Street, into London's most sumptuous mansion, yet his own parsimony and animosity were notorious.[20]

Like all London's mayors, Spencer was knighted during his one-year term of office, an odd fallout from the uniquely short-lived lordship that

---

[17] Charles Whitney, "'Usually in the werking Daies': Playgoing Journeymen, Apprentices, and Servants in Guild Records, 1582–92," *SQ* 50 (1999): 433–58.

[18] *Calendar of State Papers, Domestic Series, of the Reign of . . . Elizabeth, 1581–90*, ed. Robert Lemon and Mary Ann Everett Green, 12 vols. (London: Longman, 1856–72), 2:198–202, hereafter cited as *CSPD, Eliz*. For other information about Spencer and his activities as a businessman (including his nickname, 'Rich Spencer'), see the entry titled "Spencer, Sir John," in the latest edition of the *Oxford Dictionary of National Biography*, ed. H.C.G. Matthew and Brian Harrison, 60 vols. (Oxford and New York: Oxford UP, 2004), 51:861–62.

[19] *Acts of the Privy Council of England, New Series*, ed. John Roche Dasent, 32 vols. (London: His Majesty's Stationery Office, 1890–), 28:397–98, 454, 604. A marginal note to the letter of 23 July 1598 to Spencer is marked 'Sir John Spencer's contumacy' (604). Charles Howard as Lord Admiral must have had a hand in the *David* affair, since his office brought him enormous rewards from a share in the profits of piratical privateering. When Spencer's time in office ended, the Council ordered his successor, Stephen Slany, to inquire into Spencer's sale of offices during his mayoralty.

[20] Crosby Place was a notable enough edifice to be transferred in pieces in the eighteenth century for reconstruction on the riverfront in Chelsea. In 2004 it was restored and reopened as a Tudor show-house.

the mayors enjoyed. He received no other honours from Burghley's government. Whitney identifies Spencer as the chief target of Dekker's *Shoemaker's Holiday*, which captures Spencer's personality in the character of Sir Roger Oatley, the Lord Mayor who appears in the opening scene objecting to his daughter's alliance with the Earl of Lincoln's nephew. Dekker's image of the grim Oatley is set in opposition to the cheerful Simon Eyre, the model of what Eyre's own handicraft apprentices regarded as a good and generous mayor.[21] Spencer made a particularly easy target for Dekker's satiric attack. In March 1599, when Dekker began the play, Spencer was in the public eye because of his only daughter Elizabeth's marriage to William, the second Lord Compton, later the first Earl of Northampton. On the face of it, Spencer's marrying his daughter to Lord Compton was the reverse of Oatley's insistence that his 'girl' was '[t]oo mean' for the Earl of Lincoln's nephew, since 'Poor citizens must not with courtiers wed.'[22] But Spencer's quarrels with Lord Compton were a public joke. In March the lord actually had Spencer put into Fleet Prison for maltreating Compton's betrothed and, more pointedly, for refusing to pay the agreed-upon dowry.[23] In the previous January, John Chamberlain had written to Dudley Carleton that 'Yt is geven out that the Lord Compton shall marry our Sir John Spensers daughter of London on these conditions that he geve him £10000 redy mony with her, and redeeme his land that lieth in morgage [sic] for £18000 more.'[24] The magnitude of such sums shows Spencer's eagerness to marry Elizabeth into the aristocracy and also explains his reluctance to pay the price.

On 15 March, John Chamberlain wrote that 'Our Sir John Spenser of London was the last weeke committed to the Fleet for a contempt, and hiding away his daughter, who they say is contracted to the Lord Compton, but now he is out again and by all meanes seekes to hinder the match, alledging a precontract to Sir Arthur Henninghams sonne: but upon his beating and misusing her, she was sequestred to one Barkers a proctor and from thence to Sir Henry Billingsleyes where she yet remaines till the matter be tried.'[25] Billingsley had succeeded Spencer as Lord Mayor. Later in

---

[21] Charles Whitney, "The Devil His Due: Mayor John Spencer, Elizabethan Civic Antitheatricalism, and *The Shoemaker's Holiday*," *Medieval and Renaissance Drama in England* 14 (2001): 168–84.

[22] Thomas Dekker, *The Shoemaker's Holiday*, ed. R. L. Smallwood and Stanley Wells (Manchester, UK: Manchester UP; Baltimore: Johns Hopkins UP, 1979), 83 (1.1.11–12).

[23] *CSPD, Eliz.* (1598–1600), 5:169. Elizabeth Spencer Compton's first son, born in 1601, was baptised Spencer Compton.

[24] *The Letters of John Chamberlain*, ed. Norman Egbert McClure, 2 vols. (Philadelphia: The American Philosophical Society, 1939), 1:67.

[25] Chamberlain, 1:73.

the year Lord Compton, evidently a keen playgoer, smuggled Elizabeth away from Crosby Place in a baker's basket.[26] In 1601, when Elizabeth's first daughter was born, Chamberlain wrote that 'the hardhead her father relents nere a whit'.[27] The ex-Lord Mayor, a notorious skinflint yet owner of the most sumptuous house in London, was a ripe subject for London gossip. Four months after Spencer's stay in the Fleet, the Admiral's Men paid Dekker £4 for the playscript and then quickly put it on stage.

Whitney suggests that the play's satire of Spencer is 'good nature[d]', but that seems too mild a reading.[28] Dekker has Simon Eyre in his civic generosity build Leadenhall for the city, while Oatley is presented as a miser. When Spencer died in 1610, he confirmed the accuracy of Dekker's portrayal by leaving none of his enormous wealth for city or public uses. His son-in-law Compton spent it instead.[29] Spencer was an object of hatred to Londoners who were less affluent than he was, which meant almost everyone, including some Privy Councillors, not least Carey. Dekker's choice of a play in praise of handicraft apprentices, whom the mayoralty regarded as the city's poorest and most disruptive citizens, a play in which a gang of apprentices armed with cudgels outface a gathering of gentry with swords, suggests that he had an agenda hostile to the London authorities, with more than a hint of approval for the apprentice rabble-rousing near the Rose that upset Guildhall in 1592 and after. Dekker's portrait of Spencer in Oatley, while carefully avoiding any direct allusion, has a distinct air of triumphalism about it.

The varying attitudes to playgoing held by the different mayors has been obscured more than a little by the failure of Chambers and others to record the mayors' names when transcribing their letters.[30] It is clear that other mayors took a much less stringent view than Spencer's on what had to be done about plays and playing. Several meetings between aldermen and Privy Councillors in 1592 and 1593, involving Richard Martin and especially William Webbe, the Lord Mayor from October 1591 to 1592, may have

---

[26] Versions of the baker's basket had already appeared onstage with Falstaff's laundry basket in *Merry Wives* and in a parody of *Romeo and Juliet* at the Rose in Haughton's *Englishmen for my Money* of 1598. Elizabeth Spencer did not, however, suffer either Falstaff's or the Haughton gull's fate.

[27] Chamberlain, 1:124.   [28] Whitney, "The Devil His Due," 180.

[29] The wittily self-interested Sir John Harington wrote to Compton in 1610 when Spencer died, recommending that Compton visit Bath to improve his health and bring his inheritance with him (*The Letters and Epigrams of Sir John Harington*, ed. Norman Egbert McClure [Philadelphia: U of Pennsylvania P, 1930], 141–42). Harington lived at Kelston, three miles from Bath.

[30] The best-known transcription of the papers with a direct bearing on playing in London is in Chambers (Appendix D, 'Documents of Control', 4:287–335), but he does not include the names of the signatories at Guildhall. His own versions of the *Remembrancia*, edited with W. W. Greg for the Malone Society in 1907–11, are more helpful and less modernised in transcription.

helped to generate the Privy Council's duopoly scheme and the ban on the use of London inns. Carey's peculiar letter, written in the knowledge that Spencer was to be the next Lord Mayor, sits like a cherry on top of a fruity mix of political manoeuvres over whether and where the professional companies could play.

If, as I hypothesise, the May 1594 deal between the two Privy Councillors on the one side and Cuthbert Buckle as Lord Mayor on the other included the Council's acceptance of a permanent ban on the use of city inns for plays, then it was a brilliantly elaborate new arrangement with far-reaching implications. The duopoly companies would play only in the suburbs, with Privy Council authorisation for each to use a licensed playhouse. No other companies would be allowed. (The order of 1598 was prompted by the intrusion of a third company.) The mayor and the Court of Aldermen should have been delighted to enforce the accompanying ban on playing inside the city. The authorities in Surrey and Middlesex, now responsible for regulating playing in their jurisdictions, would have to bow to this ruling, since Carey's partner and son-in-law, Charles Howard, the Lord Admiral, had become Lord Lieutenant of Surrey in 1585 and, from 1580, had chaired the commissions for the peace that ruled the magistrates and justices in both Surrey and Middlesex. He thus held direct sway over the two counties where the suburban playhouses stood. Such power was a major convenience, as was the more personal fact that Alleyn had worn Howard's livery for the past dozen years, while Burbage (owner of the Theatre in Middlesex and father of Richard, who led Carey's company) had worn Carey's livery for even longer. From the players' point of view the whole deal was an adjustment made to suit a set of alliances that were already in place.

In such an adjustment the biggest gain for the Privy Councillors, besides limiting the number of companies competing for attention in London and thus perhaps reducing mayoral complaints, would have been that the Lord Chamberlain could fulfill his duty of entertaining the queen with good plays at Christmas more amply than before. Previously, one company – the Queen's Men – had held a near-monopoly on playing in London and for the queen. Set up in 1583 to promote playing quality, that company had been in serious decline since the death of Richard Tarlton, its clown, in 1588. With Alleyn and the Marlowe plays in one new company and Shakespeare and his plays in the other, the two Councillors knew there was now good hope of a high standard of plays at court. Having two companies licensed to play in the London suburbs was a better insurance against failure to deliver plays at Christmas than when the Queen's Men and other companies were competing for London places in the face of Guildhall's attempts to suppress them. The Court of Aldermen had in 1583 reluctantly allowed performances by the Queen's Men at city inns, but that concession was long dead, and new companies had overtaken the Queen's in quality. The break-up of some companies during the plague of 1593, and the more recent deaths of several patrons and consequent disappearance of the companies they had patronised, made the need for a new arrangement urgent in the spring of 1594 if the Lord Chamberlain was to continue fulfilling his royal duties.

Carey's letter was sent to his 'good freind' Martin early in October, probably because by then Carey knew all too well the view of playing held by the next Lord Mayor, who was to take office on 29 October. Martin had become Lord Mayor in July, when the incumbent, Cuthbert Buckle, died unexpectedly. If Carey and Howard drew up an agreement with Buckle, it would have been made in late spring. Martin's views were known to Carey because he had been the Aldermen's representative in negotiations with the Lord Chamberlain's executive officer, Edmund Tilney, since 1592. When, in September, Spencer was elected the next mayor, his hostility toward plays would have seemed to threaten the Privy Councillors' rearrangement. Carey could have guessed that the incoming Lord Mayor was likely to renew the annual complaint to the Council about playing. We can speculate that his letter went to Martin three weeks before Spencer became Lord Mayor in the hope that a positive reply from Martin might forestall whatever Spencer would write when he assumed office.

Sir Richard Martin was a wealthy magnate, one of the queen's two official goldsmiths. He was Warden of the Mint in 1560 and became Master in 1580, a post he held till his death in 1618.[31] In 1593 he sued the executors of the Earl of Leicester's estate for more than £2000 long owed him for his contributions to the earl's grandeur.[32] He was not, however, comparable to Spencer as a wealthy businessman and entrepreneur, and he was removed from his aldermanship in 1602, allegedly for debt. First made alderman in 1578, he served as sheriff in 1581, and Lord Mayor twice, both times completing the term of someone who had died in office – first in May 1589, when Martin Calthorpe died, and again in early July 1594, in place of Cuthbert Buckle. As a member of the Court of Aldermen, he had been involved in several dealings with Whitgift and then with Tilney as they sought to find a way to satisfy Guildhall's desire to have all professional

---

[31] John Chamberlain reported that he was 'very neere an hundred yeares old' at his death (Chamberlain, 2:105); in fact he was 84, two years younger than Charles Howard, who outlived him by seven years.
[32] *CSPD, Eliz.* (1591–1594), 386–87.

playing banned. On 12 April 1593 he was one of two aldermen sent to the Council to negotiate the closing of all places of assembly in order to limit the spread of plague and the danger of more apprentice riots, 'towching the presente suppressinge of bearebaitinge, bowling alleyes, and such like prophane exercises within this Cytie, and the liberties thereof, and other places neare adioyninge'.[33] In both functions he was deeply engaged with the question of what to do with public playing. In 1594 he served on a commission with other aldermen who had been mayors, John Hart and William Webbe, and several Privy Councillors, including Charles Howard. Martin knew the two Privy Councillors most concerned, just as Carey and Howard knew Martin's views about playing in the city. Neither Martin nor his predecessor, Buckle, is on record as issuing letters of complaint against playing.

It is unthinkable that Martin would have failed to respond to Carey's letter, but either he chose not to do so in his official capacity, or else Fletcher did not have Martin's response transcribed, since no reply is noted in the *Remembrancia*. It may be that Martin did not wish to inscribe any formal acceptance or rejection of the request. That he did not consent to Carey's request, though, becomes obvious in the light of James Burbage's actions the following winter, when he set about building a new indoor playhouse in the liberty of the Blackfriars – inside the city but safe from the Lord Mayor.

This sequel to the Cross Keys plea strongly indicates the thinking of Burbage and his tenant company about where they wanted to perform plays at this time. The company's wish that Carey might get them access to the Cross Keys evidently had behind it the weight of their desire to leave their open-air playhouse for the winter and to play indoors. They had been able to do so in previous years until playing at the city's inns was banned, and now they wanted to continue the practice. James Burbage himself, despite the consequent loss of his rents from the Theatre, clearly shared the view that the company ought to have an indoor venue for the winter, since, when Carey's appeal for permission to play at the Cross Keys was rejected, he drew on his own financial resources to build an indoor theatre in the Blackfriars liberty. We know that Carey, who lived in the Blackfriars precinct himself, gave Burbage's revised plan at least his tacit backing from the outset.[34]

---

[33] Chambers, 4:314.
[34] Carey wrote to the seller of the Blackfriars property in January 1596, 'vnderstanding that you have all redie parted with part of your howse to somme that meanes to make a playe howse in yt' (*MSC*, 2:1 [1913], 123). Carey died six months later, on 22 July, and without his support the new playhouse became a lost cause.

For Shakespeare's company, the remarkable significance of constructing the Blackfriars playhouse has emerged only slowly. Burbage's creation of his new indoor playhouse in 1596 has traditionally been seen as fortuitous compared with his building of the Globe in 1599 from the remains of the Theatre. For Burbage to invest all his spare cash in the Blackfriars used to be seen as a sad but insignificant accident in comparison with the amphitheatre that Jonson called 'the *Globe*, the Glory of the Banke'.[35] In fact, when linked with Carey's letter asking for use of the Cross Keys in 1594, the Blackfriars construction that started in the winter of 1595 indicates that both the company and its chief backer expected to operate on the old system, playing outdoors through the summer and indoors in winter, a system that in the event could not be reinstated until 1608. The unique arrangement into which the Shakespeare company, now the King's Men, entered when Richard Burbage retrieved possession of the Blackfriars playhouse in 1608 fulfilled the wish for a roofed winter playing-place voiced fourteen years earlier in Carey's letter to Martin.

The preference of Burbage and the Shakespeare company for switching venues between summer and winter seems a little eccentric, if only because the other half of the duopoly apparently had no similar ambition, and because no indoor playhouse besides the Blackfriars was built until 1617. Yet after 1608 the two-playhouse policy helped the King's Men to dominate London theatre for thirty-four years (or forty-eight years if one counts from 1594), as long a continuous run as any company in English history. Indoor playing during the winter seems to have been adopted as company policy within its first five months. We can only speculate on why Alleyn's company, in contrast, was happy to use the Rose throughout the year. Possibly Alleyn was loyal to his father-in-law, Henslowe, and his profits; possibly he preferred the larger playing space and the larger audience capacity that the open-air playhouse offered compared with the upper rooms of city inns. Conceivably he may even have thought that the journey to the Rose on Bankside, either by ferry or over London Bridge, was less muddy than tramping northward through London's streets to the Theatre in Shoreditch. The Admiral's Men's preference is a subject that invites further investigation.

The idea that the establishment of the duopoly and the ban on city playing happened together in 1594 is necessarily conjectural. There is no hard evidence of a ban by the city or of the Privy Council's original licence for

---

[35] Ben Jonson, "An Execration upon Vulcan," *Works*, ed. C. H. Herford and Percy and Evelyn Simpson, 11 vols. (Oxford: Clarendon Press, 1925–47), 8:208.

the two suburban playhouses in Shoreditch and Bankside to which later orders refer. These should have gone out in May 1594 from the Council to the magistrates of Middlesex and of Surrey, but the papers are lost. The Guildhall *Remembrancia* are equally silent about a mayoral ban on plays inside the city in 1594. In the absence of the Privy Council's own register for the period between August 1593 and October 1595, nothing survives to indicate what orders may have been issued during that crucial time. Nonetheless, the circumstantial evidence is heavy and consistent across a wide range of related features.

First, if the deal set up by the two Councillors in May 1594 had been negotiated with that year's Lord Mayor, Cuthbert Buckle, his death in July would have put the whole agreement at risk, particularly once Spencer was elected the next mayor. That is no doubt why Carey's letter was written early in October, before Spencer's installation, to test Martin's position. Carey may have been hoping to anticipate and override Spencer's known opposition to playing by soliciting a favourable response from the current office-holder. If his appeal was rejected, both parties would know where they stood. Carey may have felt that Martin would not be so bold as to deny his request, and that this small concession over playing inside the city would help to weaken the next mayor's position.

If so, the ploy did not work. Guildhall's *Remembrancia* show that the new Lord Mayor was quick to register his objections, first to the Swan, then under construction in Paris Garden on suburban Bankside, and more broadly to the staging of plays anywhere. Only five days after his inauguration, on 3 November, Spencer wrote to Lord Burghley, head of the Privy Council, asking for the closure of all playing places in the vicinity of London. His letter was the most forthright of any mayor's until then. He began with the obvious cause, in righteous indignation over Francis Langley's construction of the Swan, begging Burghley 'to bee a means for vs rather to suppress all such places built for that kynd of exercise then to erect any more of the same sort'.[36] He confronted the justification 'alleadged by soom for defence of these playes that the people must haue soom kynd of recreation & that policie requireth to divert idle heads & other ill disposed from other woorse practize', arguing that the plays' 'vnchast fables, lascivious divises shifts of cozenage & matters of lyke sort' did nothing of the kind.[37] Above all, he wrote, careful to remind Burghley of the recent riots in Southwark, playhouses had become meeting-places 'for all vagrant

---

[36] *MSC*, 1:1, 75. A complete transcription of Spencer's letter of 3 November 1594 to Lord Burghley appears in *MSC*, 1:1, 74–76.
[37] *MSC*, 1:1, 75.

persons & maisterles men that hang about the Citie, theeues, horsestealers whoremoongers coozeners connycatching persones practizers of treason & such other lyke'.[38]

As an alderman and sheriff in the earlier 1580s, Spencer had been deeply involved in efforts to control apprentice behaviour. This may have been when his opposition to playing hardened into implacable hatred. He included in his letter the standard arguments that irreligious views in the plays corrupted 'our apprentices and servants' and that the crowds of play-goers hindered trade. He concluded,

> I thought it my duetie beeing now called to this publique place to infourm your good *Lordship* whome I know to bee a patrone of religion & lover of virtue & an honourable a friend to the State of this Citie humbly beeseaching you to voutch-safe mee *your* help for the stay & suppressing not only of this which is now intended by directing your lettres to the Iustices of peace of Middlesex & Surrey but of all other places if possibly it may bee whear the sayed playes ar shewed & frequented.[39]

He opened his attack with his objections to the new Swan, possibly to emphasise the Council's evident failure to allow only the two playhouses in the suburbs. Apprentice riots in Southwark strengthened his case for having all playing-places shut down. Although asking that the magistrates of Middlesex and Surrey be ordered to close their playhouses, he made no mention of any previous deal with Buckle or the licensing of the Rose and the Theatre. Possibly he made no mention of an agreed ban because he felt his request should override any such deal.

Some of his letter's vehemence may have come from his anger at the brazenness of Carey's request, but it may also reflect his knowledge that Carey and Howard had already managed to create an arrangement that, while limited and limiting, was also successfully protecting the playing companies. As Whitney describes Spencer's angry letter,

> It can be read in two ways: either at face value as an emphatic call for the suppression of all public stage-plays, or as a strategic effort to oppose the post-plague increase in theatrical activity that was beginning. If the former, Spencer would be refusing to go down the road that most of his colleagues had either already favored or would favor – accepting suburban performances in exchange for a ban in the city. If the latter, the subtext would be a willingness to cooperate if the Privy Council were really to demonstrate that it was serious about limiting the London theater to two companies in the suburbs.[40]

[38] *MSC*, 1:1, 75.   [39] *MSC*, 1:1, 76.   [40] Whitney, "The Devil His Due," 175.

Since there is no record of the Privy Council doing anything in reply to Spencer's letter, it is understandable that, two weeks before his year in office ended, he should write again, on 13 September 1595, confirming the first of Whitney's readings by calling for the 'present stay & finall suppressing' of all playing.[41] Whitney hails that 'finall' as the first such totalising request by any Lord Mayor.[42] Spencer wanted an immediate closure that would become a permanent one. Happily, the Council ignored him.

Another body of evidence about the Privy Council's activities – evidence about the closing of public places in time of plague – throws further light on relations between the two sets of authorities and also supports the likelihood that the duopoly and the ban coincided in 1594. Plague stoppages strained mayoral and Council actions painfully and chronically, and spilled messily into the concern over playing. Spencer's hatred of playing was only the most colourful feature of a long tradition of mayoral complaints to the Privy Council that started before 1576, when the first durable playhouse, the Theatre, came into use, and intensified in the early 1580s, when Spencer first took office as an alderman. The rise of playing by the professional companies in London was a bone of contention, associated with the plague epidemics, and soon joined them in becoming a chronic irritant in the never-well-oiled mechanism of relations between the Council and Guildhall.

The need for an authority with the power to close all places of public assembly when plague threatened was recognised in the London-centred system of reporting plague deaths established in 1553. It required the growing number of parishes in London and its surroundings – 113 parishes in and around the city by 1625 – to declare weekly totals of deaths from the plague so that the grand total could provide a basis for ordering closures. Since most of the new parishes spread well beyond the Lord Mayor's authority, the regulation of plague closures had to come from the Council. A set of Council orders setting out the counting system was printed in 1592 and reissued in 1593, 1594, 1603, and 1625, the worst of the plague years. One set of orders related to the country outside London, another to London and its immediate environs.[43] The London orders were mostly produced by Guildhall, but because the city did not control the suburbs and the liberties it was the Privy Council that had to authorise the execution of

---

[41] *MSC*, 1:1, 76. Whitney, "The Devil His Due," 176–77; Whitney quotes from Chambers, 4:318.
[42] Whitney, "The Devil His Due," 176–77.
[43] Much of the best information about the plague can be found in F. P. Wilson's *The Plague in Shakespeare's London* (Oxford: Clarendon Press, 1927), 14–16. Wilson's appendix deals with the weekly 'bills of mortality' (189–208).

these orders. Not infrequently the Lord Mayor would urge the Council to close all places of assembly, including the suburban playhouses, because the number of plague deaths was climbing. In the early 1590s, closures became an issue not only because of plague but also, equally pressingly, because of apprentice riots. The two issues interlocked once various mayors equated playhouses and the crowds they drew with places where apprentices were thought to hatch their plots to run riot.

The riot that occurred in Southwark on Midsummer's night, 11 June 1592, by apprentices from the Clothworkers, Spencer's own livery company, was immediately reported to the Privy Council by Lord Mayor William Webbe. Writing the morning after the night's affray, he was blunt, declaring that the Knight Marshal's men, acting on a warrant from Carey himself, had mishandled the situation.

> Beeing informed of a great disorder & tumult lyke to grow yesternight abowtt viij of the clock within the Borough of Southwark, I went thither with all speed I could, taking with mee on of the Sherifes, wheare I found great multitudes of people assembled togither, & the principall actours to bee certain servants of the ffeltmakers gathered togither out of Barnsey street & the Black fryers, with a great number of lose & maisterles men apt for such pourposes. Whearupon having made proclamation, & dismissed the multitude, I apprehended the chief doers and authors of the disorder, & have committed them to prison to bee farther punished, as they shall be found to deserve. And having this morning sent for the Deputie & Constable of the Borough with Divers other of best credit, who wear thear present, to examine the cause & manner of the disorder, I found that it began vpon the serving of a warrant from my *Lord* Chamberlain by on of the Knight Mareschalls men vpon a feltmakers servant, who was committed to the Mareschallsea with certein others, that were accused to his *Lord* by the sayed Knight Mareschalls men without cause of offence, as them selves doe affirm. For rescuing of whome the sayed companies assembled themselves by occasion & pretence of their meeting at a play, which bysides the breach of the Sabboth day giveth opportunitie of committing these & such lyke disorders.[44]

Webbe's letter is a cool and clear statement of the affray as he witnessed and heard about it. He does no more than affirm that the playhouse, probably the Rose, was an enabling factor in the riot, and closes with a polite request to say what else, if anything, should be done to punish the offenders. The Privy Council's response, eleven days later, was to place a closure order on all public assemblies, including those at plays. Specifying the troubles in

---

[44] Chambers, 4:310.

the city, it ordered the Master of the Rolls for Middlesex to 'take order that there be noe playes used in anye place neere there-aboutes, as the Theator, Curtayne, or other usuall places where the same are comonly used, nor no other sorte of unlawfull or forbidden pastymes that drawe together the baser sorte of people, from henceforth untill the feast of St. Michaell'.[45] Letters also went to the Lord Mayor and to the magistrates of Surrey, the warning to Surrey specifying the parishes of Newington (for the Newington Butts playhouse), Kentish Street, Bermondsey Street, the Clink, Paris Garden (for the Swan), and the Bankside (for the Rose).

The subsequent riots that Spencer reported during the year he was Lord Mayor must have seemed no less a threat to both governing authorities. The troubles started during the daytime on 13 June 1595, just after Midsummer's night, with apprentices upsetting stalls at Southwark Market in a fracas over the price of butter and at Billingsgate Market over the price of mackerel. They rioted again on 23 June, again over food prices, 1595 being a year of dearth even more severe than 1593 or 1594. Spencer's report on that affray was secondhand but potent. His report took evidence from bystanders, noting

> Examination of Rich. Edery, porter of the Marshalsea, Henry Robinson, girdler, and Garret Saxton, shoemaker, all of Southwark. Edw. Flower, husbandman of Knightsbridge, being at Robinson's shop door, said there was a great stir in London with the apprentices for the good of the Commonwealth; that 1,800 of them had pulled down the pillories in Cheapside and Leadenhall, and set up a gallows against the door of the Lord Mayor, whom they would hang if he dared come out, but he dared not; and that 3,000 were lying in the fields, with bills and clubs, to rescue the apprentices if anything were done to them.[46]

The numbers were probably exaggerated, and those questioned seem to have relished Spencer's timidity in keeping to his house when threatened, probably a mark of the low level of popular support he enjoyed. Though the testimonies made no mention of the playhouses, that did not stop Spencer from including them in his complaint to the Privy Council.

Perhaps inevitably, control over public gatherings at plays and over apprentice riots merged with the question of regulating crowds because of the plague. The danger of spreading the plague made every place where people could congregate in large numbers a chronic worry to the authorities. In his second pamphlet on coneycatching, published in 1592, Robert

---

[45] Chambers, 4:310–11.
[46] Spencer's report on the 1595 Southwark riots is quoted here from *CSPD, Eliz.* (1595–1597), 4:63.

Greene wrote about cutpurses whose 'gaines lies by all places of resort and assemblies therefore their chief walkes is Paules, Westminster, the exchange, Plaies, Bear-garden, running at Tilt, the L. Maiors day, any festiuall meetings, fraies, shootings, or great faires'.[47] Playhouses and baitings could draw people in thousands, and, given that plays were staged during the working day, such assemblies were taken to consist chiefly of idlers and of pickpockets, who had good reason to enjoy large crowds. The mayoralty was quick to start nudging the Privy Council to order closures when plague deaths began to rise, and ostensibly asked for the playhouses to be closed simply because of their capacity to draw crowds. In 1592 and 1595 letters from Lord Mayors Webbe and Spencer used crowds as a reason to argue for playhouse closures on the grounds that apprentices gathered there to plot their riots.

In my reading of this evidence, the terms of this struggle over staging plays in London is explained most clearly by the various locations of which the mayors complained. Up to 1594 the professional companies used the city inns for playing as frequently as, and perhaps even more frequently than, the purpose-built playhouses, the Theatre, the Curtain, the Rose and sometimes Newington Butts. In 1583 the Lord Mayor granted the Queen's Men permission to play at the Bull and the Bell (both city inns), and 'nowheare els within this Cyttye'.[48] Robert Greene wrote that 'A Good fellowe that was newly entered into the nipping craft... In the Christmas holydaies last came to see a play at the Bull within Bishops gate'.[49] Various anecdotes about Tarlton, a Queen's man, locate him at the outdoor Bull and Bel Savage, as well as in the suburbs at the Curtain and the Theatre.[50] According to a complaint by Lord Mayor Hart in a letter of 6 November 1589, Strange's Men had played the previous day at the Cross Keys, as noted above. Carey's peculiar letter tried to renew that traditional practice.

For the next few years after 1594 the Lord Mayors turned to the suburban playhouses as their targets in place of the city inns. Letters written before May 1594 assume that plays were being staged inside the city as frequently as at the purpose-built playhouses. On 12 November 1589 the Privy Council wrote to Archbishop Whitgift about the profanities used in 'comon playes

---

[47] Robert Greene, *The Second part of Conny-catching* (1592), ed. G. B. Harrison (London: The Bodley Head Quartos, 1926), 30.
[48] *MSC*, 2:3, 314.
[49] *The Thirds & Last Part of Conny-catching* (1592), ed. G. B. Harrison (London: The Bodley Head Quartos, 1926), 37.
[50] The anecdotes appear in the second section, 'His sound city iests', of *Tarltons Jests* (London, 1638).

and enterludes in and about the Cyttie of London'.[51] Any performance 'in . . . the Cyttie', apart from those given by the boy company still playing at Paul's, had to take place at one of the city's inns. Within the next year Whitgift stopped the Paul's company from playing, though more because Lyly had been using material about the Marprelate pamphlets than because Whitgift was himself hostile to playing. His main concern was over playing on sermon days and the Sabbath. On 25 July 1591 he was on the Council when it wrote letters to stop plays from being staged on the Sabbath, one to the Lord Mayor about the city inns and others to the 'Justices of Midlesex and Surrey' about the suburban playhouses.[52] On 3 February 1594 the Council wrote a letter, preserved in the *Remembrancia*, to Cuthbert Buckle announcing their ban on all playgoing 'in & about London' because of the plague.[53] That letter is the last surviving document from the Council on the topic of playing within the city limits.

The next known letter to arrive at Guildhall was Carey's to Richard Martin as Lord Mayor. Sent from the Privy Council offices at Nonsuch Palace, the letter was written by Carey in his role as Lord Chamberlain and not on behalf of the full Council. Spencer's subsequent letter of 3 November 1594 asks for the Council to suppress not only Langley's new Swan 'by directing your letters to the Iustices of peace of Middlesex & Surrey but of all other places, if possibly it may bee, whear the sayed playes ar shewed & frequented'.[54] He must have known that an arrangement was in place to allow playing at the Theatre and the Rose. His second letter of 13 September 1595, written not long before his tenure expired, reiterates the complaint about playgoing crowds leading to meetings of 'the refuse sort of evill disposed & vngodly people about this Cytie haue oportunitie hearby to assemble together & to make their matches for all their lewd & vngodly practizes', and concludes with the observation that these people 'ar now rettorned to their old haunt & frequent the Plaies (as their manner is) that ar daily shewed at the Theator & Bankside'.[55] Spencer's targets had narrowed to the Rose and the Theatre. He asked the Council specifically for letters about the playhouses to be sent to the magistrates of Surrey and Middlesex. A marginal note in the *Remembrancia* summarises this letter's contents as 'Toutching the putting doune of the plaies at the Theater & Bankside which is a great cause of disorder in the Citie'.[56]

---

[51] Chambers, 4:306. [52] Chambers, 4:307. [53] Chambers, 4:314.
[54] Chambers, 4:316–17, esp. 317.
[55] Chambers, 4:318. This letter is usually attributed to the new Lord Mayor, Stephen Slany, but Whitney shows it to have been Spencer's ("The Devil His Due," 184n).
[56] Chambers, 4:318.

Playing at city inns was no longer the issue. Similarly the Council's order of 22 July 1596 restraining public playing for fear of plague, written on the day Henry Carey died, was directed only to the magistrates of Middlesex and Surrey, bypassing the city.[57] Carey's letter of 8 October 1594 seems, then, to have been a blatant attempt to ignore what both the Council and the Lord Mayor well knew – that the ban on playing at city inns such as the Cross Keys had already been laid down, no doubt as the Council's explicit concession to the mayoralty.

If the Privy Council did agree to ban all playing at the inns early in 1594, the genesis of its shift of target can, I think, be identified in a letter sent by Lord Mayor William Webbe to Whitgift in February 1592. Probably he wrote to the Archbishop because he knew Carey's and Howard's views and thought Whitgift would be more receptive to another attempt to restrict playing. Webbe's position is identifiable because he never mentions the suburbs and advocates banning plays only from 'this Citie'.[58] In Charles Whitney's reading of this letter, Webbe 'implicitly broaches an arrangement whereby plays would be limited to the suburbs. In forming their new companies in 1594, then, Carey and Howard may have had Webbe's idea in their minds from the beginning, and may have approached the city from that standpoint'.[59] That inference makes good sense. As we have seen, Webbe was Lord Mayor for the year from Michaelmas 1591, and had to deal with the Southwark riot in 1592. His criticism then of the heavy-handed marshals directed by Privy Councillor Carey may have become part of his thinking. Whitgift, as a Privy Councillor himself, may well have passed the idea on to Carey and Howard as a compromise between the positions held by Spencer and his allies on the one hand – to suppress all plays everywhere – and by Carey and Howard on the other – to continue the players' free run of the city and suburbs on the grounds that they served the queen. At a time when London plays and playgoing were becoming more popular than ever, in spite of the long closures during the dreadful plague epidemic of 1593, something had to be done, and much discussion of the problem must have been aired at both committees. The central peculiarity of Carey's letter is that it so crudely ignores Webbe's idea and the consequent agreement, if there was one.

As it happened, Spencer's rule as Lord Mayor had an effect on his successors that he could not have intended. Henry Billingsley wrote a letter as Lord Mayor on 28 July 1597 that took much of its wording from Spencer's.

---

[57] Chambers, 4:319.   [58] Chambers, 4:307–8, esp. 308.   [59] Whitney, "The Devil His Due," 175.

But that turned out to be the last of the long sequence.[60] In Whitney's words, 'Spencer's approach, to which the city remained committed in 1597, helped write the city out of anything resembling a partnership in regulation.'[61] Two subsequent Privy Council orders about playing confirm this observation. An order of 19 February 1598, directed only to the magistrates of Middlesex and Surrey, sought to prevent a third company from setting itself up in London as a rival to the companies already licensed to play in the city. Instigated by Charles Howard, the order affirmed quite emphatically that

> licence hath bin graunted unto two companies of stage players retayned unto us, the Lord Admyral and Lord Chamberlain, to use and practise stage playes, whereby they might be the better enhabled and prepared to shew such plaies before her Majestie as they shalbe required at tymes meete and accustomed, to which ende they have bin cheefelie licensed and tollerated as aforesaid, and whereas there is also a third company who of late (as wee are informed) have by waie of intrusion used likewise to play, having neither prepared any plaie for her Majestie nor are bound to you, the Masters of the Revelles, for performing such orders as have bin prescribed and are enjoyned to be observed by the other two companies before mencioned. Wee have therefore thought good to require you vppon receipt heereof to take order that the aforesaid third company may be suppressed and none suffered heereafter to plaie but those two formerlie named belonging unto us, the Lord Admyrall and Lord Chamberlaine, unles you shall receave other direccion from us.[62]

Henry Carey's son George, who had become Lord Chamberlain at his father's death, was evidently maintaining his father's policy under pressure from Howard. To transfer the official title of Master of the Revels to the magistrates of Middlesex and Surrey in letters that ignored the London mayoralty entirely would have been one of Howard's sardonic jokes, made in recognition of his success in finally securing the plan of 1594 without giving the Lord Mayor grounds to write more complaints. It was Howard who now had control of London playing, as his interventions in 1600 to have his company's playhouse license transferred from the Rose to the Fortune make clear. On 12 January he wrote a warrant marked 'Att the Courte, at Richmond', specifying that 'my Servant Edward Allen' should

---

[60] *MSC*, 1:1, 78.
[61] Whitney, "The Devil His Due," 178. On 28 July 1597 the Lord Mayor and aldermen wrote to the Privy Council, and on the same day the Council wrote to the justices of Middlesex and Surrey to suppress all playhouses (Chambers, 4:321–22). See note 16 above.
[62] Chambers, 4:325. The eight members of the Council who issued this letter included the Lord Chamberlain (George Carey) but oddly not the Lord Admiral himself.

be allowed to build the Fortune. On 8 April Howard, George Carey, and Cecil signed a letter to the magistrates of Middlesex confirming the warrant that authorised the nearly completed Fortune.[63] The Council's major order on 22 June reaffirming the Admiral's licence at the Fortune and the Chamberlain's at the Globe was a bald reassertion of the deal that I am proposing was set up in 1594. In the order of 22 June, the Council took care once again to placate Guildhall by renewing the ban on playing at inns: 'And especiallie yt is forbidden that anie stage plaies shalbe plaied (as sometimes they haue bin) in any Common Inn for publique assemblie in or neare about the Cittie.'[64] That was the flip side of the licences for the Globe and the Fortune. To add emphasis to its authority and its act of appeasement, the order specified that it should be written out a number of times, and that 'seuerall Coppies shall be sent to the *Lord* Mayor of London, and to the Iustices of the Peace of the Counties of Middlesex and Surrey'.[65]

It thus appears that Carey's letter to Martin in 1594 was affirming several things. The most obvious was his company's readiness to alter the times of its performances, ostensibly to appease mayoral hostility to late closing. More likely such readiness reflects the standard accommodation to the earlier arrival of darkness in wintertime, offered now so as to seem like a concession to Guildhall. Large crowds emerging in darkness in a central thoroughfare like Gracechurch Street would be a concern to the authorities. Somewhat less obvious is the way the letter shows Carey's willingness to do what his new company asked of him. Clearly they had expressed their regret at losing access to the city inns for playing in winter. Carey must have acknowledged that, seeing at the same time that the request for access to the Cross Keys gave him an opportunity to test the strength of the agreement with the mayoralty.

His company apparently felt that the much greater capacity of the open-air playhouses in the suburbs did not outweigh the convenience and comfort during the winter of a roofed venue inside the city. Carey took that seriously enough to give his support for James Burbage's plan in the following winter to build in the Blackfriars liberty. In its own way that plan accomplished the goal first proposed in Carey's letter to Martin, but without the obvious effrontery of Carey and his testing of the ban less than

[63] Chambers, 4:326, 328.   [64] Chambers, 4:329–31, esp. 331.
[65] Chambers, 4:331. A footnote to the relations between the Council and the mayoralty over playing is a letter the Council sent to the Lord Mayor on 11 March 1601, ordering him to check that the boy companies were observing the Lenten closure. Since his lack of authority over the two liberties concerned was well known to both parties and Howard was present at the meeting that issued it, the letter seems to have more than just a hint of dismissive arrogance in it.

six months after it was instituted. A new playhouse in the Blackfriars did entail playing inside the city, but it escaped the ban by copying the example of the nearby Paul's playhouse with its location in a liberty free from the Lord Mayor's control. Playing at the Cross Keys in the winter of 1594 would have meant flouting the ban quite flagrantly. Playing at the Blackfriars a year later was an evasive tactic that achieved precisely the same outcome without breaking the agreement between the Privy Council and the mayoralty of the sort I have hypothesised.

In 1594 Burbage's Theatre was eighteen years old, and its lease had only three more years to run. The Rose, eleven years younger, had undergone a substantial enlargement only two years before. That may be another reason why the Lord Admiral's Men made no attempt to imitate the Chamberlain's and forsake the Rose during the winter. Throughout the previous two winters the Rose had been well used, and the idea of changing locations seasonally may not have appealed to the Admiral's as much as it did to the Chamberlain's. Possibly Alleyn did not believe in the Burbages' larger vision, which took another fifteen years to realise, when, as the King's Men, they had much greater clout than in 1596. The final irony of the King's Men setting themselves up to play seasonally at the Globe and the Blackfriars was that in 1608, the same year they agreed on that system, King James sold the whole Blackfriars precinct to the city. This commercial deal gave the city fathers the power to close down playing inside Blackfriars, but it came too late. By then the royal valuation on playing, with every company in London now taking its name from a royal patron, removed the power of intercession both from the Lord Mayor and from the Privy Council.

CHAPTER 3

Venues on the Verges
London's Theatre Government between 1594 and 1614

In November 1594 two of London's venture capitalists set out to build playhouses in different suburbs of London. It was hardly a new kind of investment. Three already existed, in northern Shoreditch and on Bankside south of the river. At the beginning of November one of the new venturers, Francis Langley, set out to build the Swan half a mile west of the Rose. At the same time the other, Oliver Woodliffe, bought the old Boar's Head inn in Stepney with the explicit intention of converting it into a playhouse.[1] We might ask why they should both have thought it worth laying out money on such ventures when two of the existing three playhouses were already in daily use, the Rose with the Admiral's Men to the south, and the Theatre with the Chamberlain's Men to the north. Langley and Woodliffe clearly expected other companies to use their new premises. I suspect that once Henry Carey's famous letter to the Lord Mayor of 8 October 1594 had resulted in either the stand-in Mayor, Richard Martin, or his imminent successor, John Spencer, rejecting his request, Langley and Woodliffe recognised their chance to build more venues on the city's verges for other companies anxious to compete with the chosen two. The effect of their ventures, and the longer-term effect of the London authorities' attempts to restrict the venues for playing, is one line of consequences that needs to be traced. Beyond that are two even bigger issues. First, what was it in the events of 1594 that led James Burbage to build his Blackfriars in 1596, and second, how much can that initial fiasco tell us about what lay behind Shakespeare's decision to join the new Chamberlain's Men in 1594, and his subsequent commitment as their full-time writer?

Original publication: "Venues on the Verges: London's Theatre Government between 1594 and 1614," *Shakespeare Quarterly* 61 (2010), 468–89.

[1] Woodliffe's plan would have been pointless if playing at the city's inns was still permitted. His and Langley's actions do seem to affirm my theory ("Henry Carey's Peculiar Letter," *Shakespeare Quarterly* 56 (2005), 51–75 and chapter 2 in this volume), that in 1594 the Lord Mayor secured an agreement with the Privy Council to ban all plays from being staged at any inn within the bounds of the Mayor's authority in the city and Chapter 2 of this volume.

For Shakespeare's sake, if no other, we might begin by going forward twenty years to trace the thinking behind a much later decision, when the Globe burned down. Quite a few years ago I published a comment that in 1613 the Globe's sharers were expensively sentimental and even more uneconomic when they decided to rebuild their outdoor playhouse after the fire had destroyed it that June.[2] Theodore Leinwand took this up with a last-minute insert to his study of the economics of early modern theatre, arguing that such an interpretation of the decision (reiterated in my 1996 book about the playing companies) is 'plausible' but simplistic. Instead he reckoned that what he called 'a number of other emotional choices' might have been involved.[3] Since then others have commented on the idea, most recently Tom Rutter, who suggested that the decision to rebuild was not so much sentimental as 'an investment in the Jacobean status economy'.[4] The sharers' decision to rebuild the outdoor playhouse in 1614 has provoked plenty of speculation. Most provocatively, Douglas Bruster, pursuing his own line on theatre economics, set up a fresh (if not refreshing) taxonomy for the various approaches to the economic question. Concisely and pungently he separated them out into what he called the 'rash' and the 'reckoned'.[5] In his perspective Leinwand's view of the rebuilding of the Globe represents the former and mine the latter, emotion versus accountancy. The question why the Globe was rebuilt in 1614 is worth revisiting, and not only because few of us like to be thought of as emotionless accountants. Knowing more about what lay behind this choice might influence our ideas about what vision of the future James Burbage had when he bought and transformed the Blackfriars property in 1596. That could affect what we consider Shakespeare and his company thought at the time, and not least, although here offered only as a sidetrack, perhaps track down what led him to write *The Merchant of Venice*, with its resounding account of the effects of usury on those who make use of it, at precisely the time when the aftermath of the Blackfriars crisis on Burbage, the company's

---

[2] In "Money or Audiences: the Choice of Shakespeare's Globe," *Theatre Notebook* 42 (1988), 3–14. I delivered a version of this first part of the present article at the fifth American Shakespeare Center conference, held at the new Blackfriars theatre in Staunton, Virginia, in October 2009.
[3] *Theatre, Finance and Society in Early Modern England*, Cambridge University Press, Cambridge, 1999, pp. 140–43.
[4] Rutter, in his chapter on 'Adult Playing Companies, 1603–1613' in *The Oxford Handbook of Early Modern Theatre*, Oxford University Press, Oxford, 2009, pp. 72–87, p. 78, gives the housekeepers' decision a much more searching analysis than this soundbite suggests.
[5] Douglas Bruster, "On a Certain Tendency in Economic Criticism of Shakespeare," in Linda Woodbridge, ed. *Money and the Age of Shakespeare: essays in new economic criticism*, Palgrave Macmillan, Basingstoke, 2003, pp. 67–79, esp. 75.

financier, was at its worst.[6] By the end of 1596, when Shakespeare wrote his play, the new Blackfriars playhouse looked appallingly like Antonio's shipwrecked argosies.

The issue of the Globe's rebuilding after the 1613 disaster has to begin with the well-documented fact that by that July, when its loss meant that the company had to revert to its indoor playhouse, the Blackfriars was already proving markedly more profitable than the outdoor playhouse. Moreover, since unlike all the other playing companies the King's Men had the unique luxury of owning two playhouses, they had no need to rebuild the Globe. The decision to do so cost the company's housekeeper-sharers an enormous amount of cash that they had no need to spend. Why did they bother? It was not a fully collective decision, because it seems that at least two of the current 'housekeepers' declined to pay up. One of them was John Witter, the inheritor of Augustine Phillips's share in the Globe. He opted out, and sold his share to Henry Condell, who was backing his neighbour and fellow-churchwarden at St Mary's Aldermanbury, John Heminges, along with the two Burbages, in the wish to rebuild. It seems impossible not to accept that the other housekeeper who opted out was Shakespeare. Along with Heminges and Richard Burbage he had just bought rooms in the Blackfriars gatehouse, and must have felt unwilling

---

[6] Shakespeare's characterisation of usurous Shylock must have seemed dreadfully pertinent to members of the company in 1596. Burbage had built the Theatre with borrowed money, much of it from his brother-in-law John Brayne, and the loans he took out from venture capitalists to build the playhouse gave him regular trouble with his creditors. That running sore proved even more of a crisis with the Blackfriars. In the documents known as the 'Sharers' Papers' of 1635 over the housekeeping shares in the Globe and the Blackfriars playhouses, Cuthbert Burbage testified that 'The father of us Cutbert & Richard Burbage was the first builder of Playhowses & was himselfe in his younger yeeres a Player. The Theater hee built with many Hundred poundes taken up at interest.' Over his similar debts for the Blackfriars, Cuthbert declared, 'our father purchased it at extreame rates & made it into a play house with great charge & trouble' (quoted in Gurr, *The Shakespearean Stage*, Cambridge, 2009, Appendix 3, p. 278). In 1591 Richard was reported to have used a broomstick to defend his father's Theatre against its creditors. He must have felt even more defensive over the debts incurred by the Blackfriars, which went into crisis just when Shakespeare wrote *The Merchant of Venice*. M.M. Mahood asserts (New Cambridge edition, p. 1) that the reference to the wrecked *Andrew* in the play's 27th line fixes the date of its composition 'not earlier than the late summer of 1596'. Such a dating coincides exactly with the Blackfriars crisis, since James Burbage's argosy, his new Blackfriars venture, was shipwrecked in November of that year. Shakespeare, whose own father had been accused of usury, and who made similar exactions in Stratford himself, and who had friends like John Combe, a money-lender, characterised the loan sharks of London who old Burbage was indebted to as aliens, the Shylocks of the time. This seems one of those inversions and indirections that energise the game of application in his plays. With Burbage's own son playing the feckless Bassanio, friend to victim Antonio, any play about usury must have seemed appallingly apt in 1596. It certainly explains why two years later the Burbage sons, rather than go as their father did to London's loan sharks, opted to ask for the extra money to pay for the Globe from their fellow-players. One might even wonder if the court order that William Wayte took out in 1596 to protect himself from Langley, Shakespeare and others might not in some way have been related to the Blackfriars crisis.

to double his outlay or worse by paying out his proportion of the second Globe's cost. He may even have chosen this decision time to sell his Blackfriars playhouse share as well as his interest in the Globe to the others. Three years later his will bequeathed his part of the Blackfriars gatehouse to his daughter Susannah, but not a share in either playhouse. So, despite the absence of documents, we must assume that some time between 1613 and 1616 he got rid of his interest in both. Knowing his chronic parsimony, it seems a safe assumption that the extra cost of rebuilding the Globe in 1613 was what made him decide to withdraw. You might call that an accountant's judgement.

So what can we make of the other playhouse sharers' decision that they would rebuild the Globe when they did not need to? It seems that the 'housekeepers' who chose to rebuild the Globe were thinking in distinctly old-fashioned terms, harking back to 1594. The same men asked Carey to challenge the new ruling about playing exclusively at the outdoor playhouses in the suburbs and get them the Cross Keys. Whatever desires prompted Carey's letter of October 1594 had not altered in 1613. They persuaded James Burbage to build the Blackfriars in the heart of the city in 1596 because he thought it was in a precinct safe from the Lord Mayor. Even more to the point, because if access to the Cross Keys really had been refused in 1594, it shows that the company's sharers still wanted to move indoors for the winter.

The balance of power in attitudes to professional playing in London between on the one side the Lord Mayor and Aldermen of Guildhall and on the other the Privy Council is basic to the situation in summer 1594. While the Council had direct royal backing and overall responsibility for the government of the entire country, the annually elected Lord Mayor was responsible for the city and its great variety of inhabitants, with their massive resources in trade and their almost equally massive capacity to cause trouble when they gathered in crowds. We do know that after October 1594, particularly with the need to close public assemblies when there was risk of plague infection, the Privy Council started directing its orders about the crowds assembling at plays not to the Lord Mayor, from whom for the past thirty years they had endured a lengthy and often strident correspondence, but to the magistrates of Middlesex and Surrey. Mayoral complaints continued to arrive, but from then on they were specifically about the suburban playhouses, not about playing inside the city. No precise records survive to say why this change happened. By deconstructing Carey's letter to the Lord Mayor of October 1594 in my previous article, I tried to build, however tentatively, a bridge of fairly enlightened guesswork over the vast hole that exists in the Privy Council's archive of papers, the absence of all its records between 27 August 1593 and 1 October 1595. Such a bridge needs to have even more weight of heavy questioning dropped on it.

The first question about the letter remains: what precisely were the circumstances that led Carey to write it, addressed to the soon-to-retire stand-in Lord Mayor Richard Martin? Equally important, why did his letter ask for his new company to have the Cross Keys and not any other inn? In 1583 the Guildhall Aldermen allocated the Queen's Men to two inns, 'at the Sygnes of the Bull in Busshoppesgatestreete, and the sygne of the Bell in gratiousstreete and nowheare else within this Cyttye'.[7] We know that the Bull, like the Bel Savage, had an open-air courtyard where plays and other athletic shows were given. The Bell on the other hand may have had an indoor upper room for shows. It seems that the Aldermen of 1583 were allocating the company one possible venue of each kind for them to use, depending on the weather. A later Lord Mayor reported that Strange's Men had played at the Cross Keys on 5 November 1589, a distinctly wintry afternoon. From this I would like to think that the Cross Keys possessed an indoor venue.[8] Otherwise, why should the new Chamberlain's Men, composed as it was of several former Strange's players, have asked to use it for the winter instead of the far more capacious but outdoor Theatre that they were currently using?

---

[7] From a license of the Court of Aldermen, 28 November 1583, *Malone Society Collections* II.3 (1931), 314. Burbage himself is known to have been to a play at the Cross Keys in 1579. He said so in his 1588 deposition against Margaret Brayne, his sister-in-law and creditor, PRO.C24/226/10/pt 1.

[8] Assumptions about the Cross Keys and its possible playing spaces have varied over the years between what used to be the routine idea that it had an open yard, to the opposite supposition that it had an indoor and probably upper room big enough to stage plays. David Kathman has begun to investigate the shape and character of the inns inside the city that were used for playing up to 1594, but his study of the Bell and the Cross Keys has not yet appeared. In *The Oxford Handbook of Early Modern Theatre*, p. 163, he gives most credit to the assumption that the playing-place at the Cross Keys must have been indoors. Glynne Wickham argued in 1972 (*Early English Stages, 1300 to 1660*, Routledge, 1972–81, II.2, pp. 99–100) that of the four main city inns used for plays, because the Cross Keys and the Bell were winter quarters, unlike the Bel Savage and the Bull, they must have offered indoor venues. The main evidence supporting this is the fact that Strange's Men were said to be using the Cross Keys in November 1589, and that it was in October 1594 that Carey asked for his own company to have it. This (and the Mayor's refusal to allow it) seems to be confirmed by Burbage's subsequent decision to build the Blackfriars. The only positive evidence that I know suggesting that both the Bell and the Cross Keys had yards is a passage in the Tarlton *Jestbook*, which says that Tarlton played games with the famous horse owned by a servant of Essex's called Banks at the two venues. Banks's horse was unlikely to have done his tricks indoors. Different jests, of course, refer to Tarlton performing at all four inns at one time or another, and the naming of the inns may simply be an attempt by the compiler to give an air of authenticity to the stories. Alternatively, the Bell and the Cross Keys may both have had two spaces suitable for plays, one indoors and the other in a yard. The Bell, located very near the Cross Keys, certainly stood adjacent to an open yard.

That is ground for setting up a marquee full of speculations. Did the new company dislike their allocated Theatre with its outdoor playing? The fact that old Burbage owned the Theatre makes that implausible. More likely, once October and the colder weather loomed, did they seek to do what they and other companies, including the Queen's Men, did previously at the city inns, and play indoors through the winter? That is what James Burbage's subsequent move seems to affirm, when early in 1596 he acquired a property in the liberty of the Blackfriars for a new indoor playhouse. The strongest deduction is that he saw it as an ideal replacement for the indoor room at the Cross Keys, which most likely had been refused to the company in 1594, either by Martin or by his far more militant successor as mayor John Spencer. The Blackfriars offered a much more substantial site for a new playhouse than an indoor room at the Cross Keys inn, since it had far greater audience capacity. Even more to the point, in political terms it had the advantage of being located in the 'liberty' of the Blackfriars, free like St Paul's from the Lord Mayor's control. As it happened it took fifteen years for Burbage's scheme to be fully accomplished, but the concept that it envisaged, creating a new indoor playhouse in central London, was no less potent for the delay.

Burbage's reason for choosing the Blackfriars was very practical. It was in an urban precinct immune from the Lord Mayor's authority, and moreover had already housed two different venues for plays in previous years. The Blackfriars monastery, built magnificently in the thirteenth century with royal finance, was by some way the grandest ex-ecclesiastical site in London. After its closure as a monastery and the expulsion of its Dominicans, Henry VIII's Master of the Revels Thomas Carwarden used a small site there to stage plays. Then in 1576 Richard Farrant, master of the Chapel Children, built a second playhouse on the site for his boys, just to the south of Carwarden's venue. Farrant's space was markedly larger and grander than Carwarden's. Ten years or so after that playhouse was closed Burbage bought an even bigger section of the huge stone-walled complex for his playhouse, the third on the site. This major hall, just south of Farrant's site, was big enough to be used by Richard II for meetings of his parliament. Burbage bought what had been the monks' Upper Frater, accessed by an external stairway of stone. He spent £600 to buy the property along with the seven tenements then occupying it. He demolished them, and spent as much money again building his new playhouse inside the great stone walls with their tall clerestory-style windows.

The new playhouse's seating capacity was at least six hundred bodies, promising a far better income than the Cross Keys or any other inn's interior room. Such a huge investment raises, above all, the question whether he merely expected it to replace the Cross Keys as an indoor winter venue that was free from mayoral interference, or whether he thought it would completely replace his ageing Theatre, and be used for plays all the year round. For some years the Theatre's landlord had been threatening to pull it down when the lease expired in 1597. The first question is whether in 1596 old Burbage had the vision to think that an indoor theatre located inside the city might not merely stand in through the winter for the Cross Keys but replace the Theatre as well, and become the venue of the future for London's play-making. That early, could he have expected the success that the Blackfriars did acquire after 1609?

This has awesome implications. Either he invested so much borrowed money in 1596 simply to provide the company with an alternative to the Cross Keys as their winter venue, or else he really did expect the Blackfriars to become a permanent replacement for the Theatre, bringing his son's company of players permanently indoors, and, in contravention of previous mayoral decisions, keep them inside the city. If the latter was the case, his foresight was even more awesome than his expenditure. On the other hand, it seems evident that in 1594 his son and fellow-players wanted nothing more than to renew their former tradition when they persuaded Carey to ask the stand-in Lord Mayor for the Cross Keys, so that they could play outdoors through the summer and indoors in winter. The old tradition of using seasonal venues was what led them in 1613 to pay a huge amount to reactivate it, instead of performing only at their Blackfriars playhouse all the year round. This, I suspect, shows Burbage's own view, that it would augment the Theatre in winter, not replace it altogether.

At the beginning of 1599 the Burbage sons, chronically short of cash for any investment of their own, and understandably reluctant to follow their father's use of venture capitalists like Shylock, persuaded five members of their fellowship of players (I use Hamlet's term) to give them the cash they needed for the Globe. This was the key option that made the company into a joint-stock operation, and kept it secure for the next forty years. For the past two years they had all been performing *The Merchant of Venice*, with its bloody bond and its heartless money-lender, giving them ample reason to avoid London's usurers with whom their father had entangled himself. It is a safe assumption that they must have been making at least as much money as Henslowe's *Diary* shows the Admiral's doing at this time. Dulwich College, which Edward Alleyn was spending on from before the time the second Globe went up, is said to have eventually cost him ten thousand pounds. When Richard Burbage died in 1619 gossip said he was worth better than three hundred pounds in land, minimal by comparison with Alleyn. The chief reason for that was his distribution of shares in his playhouses to his fellows.

Like his fortune, Richard Burbage's financial thinking was small-scale and conservative compared with Alleyn's. The first Globe itself seems a reversion, based on more than just the material frame that his father had originally erected twenty-three years earlier. The fact that in 1614 he and his brother, plus Heminges and Condell, did commit themselves to the thousand and more pounds that the second Globe is said to have cost, reinforces that conclusion. In April 1619, after Burbage died, Heminges, in his and Condell's response to the Court of Requests suit of John Witter, testified that 'this defendant and his partners in the said playhowse resolved to reedify the same, & this rather because they were by covenante on their parte in the said originall lease conteyned to mainteyne & repair all such buildinges as should be built or erected upon the said gardens or ground during the said terme, as by the originall lease may appeare'.[9] The rebuilding was more than just a financial deal. It was a renewal of what they had first hoped to achieve in October 1594 with Carey's letter.

Nothing survives to identify when or to whom Shakespeare sold his shares in the two playhouses, but if the 1619 lawsuit testimonies have any truth in them they went to Heminges or Condell, most likely in 1613. The decision to rebuild the Globe was made by the core of the old fellowship. Heminges had been a sharer in the company from the outset in 1594. Besides Shakespeare he was the only non-Londoner in the group, born in Droitwich, Worcestershire, a county neighbouring Warwickshire, which meant that he and Shakespeare both came from a country region using a similar accent. Henry Condell, London-born, was in the company from before 1598, and may have been there from the start if he was in the Strange's Men of 1592, that is, if he was the 'Harry' named in the 'plot' of *2 The Seven Deadly Sins*.[10] He became a sharer in the Chamberlain's Men before 1600, buying a housekeeper's share in the Globe with his £100 in 1599 and taking an equal share in the Blackfriars in 1608. Shakespeare left money in his will for memorial rings to all three of his fellows from 1594, Burbage, Heminges and Condell. Those three, with Cuthbert Burbage as his brother's constant backer, were the team-leaders running the company

---

[9] The documents were fully transcribed by Charles W. Wallace, "Shakespeare and his London Associates as Revealed in Recently Discovered Documents," *University Studies of the University of Nebraska* 10 (1910), pp. 47–76.

[10] See Gurr, "The Work of Elizabethan Plotters, and *2 The Seven Deadly Sins*," *Early Theatre* 10 (2006), 67–87.

in 1613, and it must have been those four who bought out the other sharers and had the Globe rebuilt. They were a tight group, having worked together since before 1594. It was Richard's accommodating view of his fellows, plus some practical reasons, that made him allocate them half the Blackfriars shares when he regained his indoor playhouse in 1608. He certainly shared Heminges's and Condell's wish to re-build the Globe in 1613. Such choices were made as a collective decision by this core of fellows.

So Shakespeare was the only survivor from the seven sharing housekeepers of 1599 who opted out of paying to rebuild the Globe. To explain his decision as more than chronic penny-pinching we need to go back to the time when he first joined the Lord Chamberlain's Men. In the years up to 1594 he had taken great care in proof-reading when his fellow-Stratfordian Richard Field printed his two epyllions, but after that he took no trouble seeing any of his plays into print. Lukas Erne claims that he was keen to have the plays read as well as seen on stage.[11] That I doubt, and I would even argue that the plays show little evidence of the concern, common to almost all writers, to have their work immortalised, a point that he claimed was one reason for writing the sonnets. Like Heywood with his claim to have helped write 220 plays, very few of which reached the press, Shakespeare ought to be seen as remarkable for his lack of concern that more than half his plays never got into print in his lifetime. That lack of care was present from 1594 onwards.

The least that re-investing in the new Globe or not in 1613 meant was that it became the moment when he could withdraw from his major London commitments. Perhaps he saw the Blackfriars gatehouse property as an investment worth keeping while shedding the rest. It cost him £140, most of it in cash, on 10 March 1613, and it was as an investment that he bequeathed it to his daughter Susanna. His last visit to London was in November 1614, during the winter season when the company was playing at Blackfriars. It would be good to think that he then visited the new Globe, to see what his colleagues had done with their money, but like so much else about his life that is only a conjecture. Nothing shows that he was ever as committed to his company and the future of the plays he wrote for them as we usually like to think.

Such a contention requires us to look at the little evidence that exists for Shakespeare's commitment to his company from 1594 onwards. The senior members' decision to rebuild the Globe testifies to the tight teamwork that made the company last so long without it ever having any single

---

[11] Lukas Erne, *Shakespeare as Literary Dramatist*, Cambridge University Press, Cambridge, 2003.

obvious leader. Richard Burbage never dominated the company's management as he did its stages, but he spent all of his last twenty-five years in the one fellowship. Heminges and Condell lasted even longer, for more than thirty years, their stints outdone only by John Lowin's forty years up to the closure. Cuthbert Burbage was there even longer than Lowin, working on the managerial side for forty-two years, from 1594 till his death in 1636. The money that this 'fellowship' spent rebuilding the Globe testifies to their continuing amity and their feeling that they worked as a team, on an enduring set of principles.[12] It cannot have only been their success and consequent income which kept them all together. Their continuity affirms them as what John Cocke in 1616 called the 'brotherhood' of players. Taking this into account, it does seem that the desire to run two playhouses, set out in 1594, re-affirmed in 1608 and again affirmed in 1613, was anything but financially determined. After building the Blackfriars' only competitor, the Cockpit, in 1616, their rival Christopher Beeston kept control of the Red Bull but ran different companies, summer and winter, at each. His great profit came from running two companies at his two playhouses throughout the year. He made no attempt to copy the King's Men, a choice strengthening the point that running the one company at the two playhouses cannot have been a financially sensible act. Shakespeare opting out of the rebuild was declaring his new identity elsewhere, in Stratford. How much it may have also been marked by a memory of his own original ambivalence over his decision in 1594 to become a playwright rather than a poet brings us back to James Burbage's expensive option in 1596 to build the Blackfriars.

The company's collective thinking needs to be looked at here. We know the Globe was large and populist, whereas the Blackfriars was exclusive and intimate – these are deductions, not speculation. We know that the Burbages, Heminges and Condell were brought up in a populist tradition which they chose to retain, rather than adopt the option of speaking chiefly to the social elite sitting around them on the Blackfriars stage.

---

[12] A lengthy digression is possible here, about one likely divergence in policy between the two 'duopoly' companies. The Admiral's remained loyal to their outdoor playhouse and citizen repertory throughout, but the Chamberlain's Men seem to have wanted in 1599 and perhaps before that to use an indoor venue to capture the richer end of the audience spectrum, as the boy company using the Blackfriars did from 1600. Richard Wilson, in *Will Power: Essays on Shakespearean Authority*, Harvester Wheatsheaf, Hemel Hempstead, 1993, pp. 46–7, has argued that the company desired to move upmarket in 1599, and Tom Rutter, *Work and Play on the Shakespearean Stage*, Cambridge University Press, Cambridge, 2008, pp. 104–18, has amply supplemented Wilson's case. Burbage building the Blackfriars is the key case in point. Such an upmarket move seems, however, to be contradicted by the four housekeepers' decision in 1613 to invest in a second Globe.

Conceivably, and perhaps more cynically, we might conclude that they liked to be democratic at the Globe in the summer so long as they knew it was more profitable at the Blackfriars in the winter. Such guesswork is seductive today. But was it attractive thinking then? A few other factors bear on what might have influenced their 1613 decision. We should ask, for instance, why the Globe was rebuilt on the same foundations and in largely the same fabric as the first, except for tiles replacing the fatal thatch. Ample evidence survives to say that by 1614 new regulations were pressing developers to build in more durable materials – the Fortune was probably rebuilt after the fire of 1621 in brick, and the Cockpit in 1616 and Salisbury Court in 1629 both had brick frames. The Bear Garden or Hope was commissioned to be built in the same old materials only a month after the Globe fire, but it was the last of its kind, replicating the old Bear Garden in spite of its contract's instructions to copy the Swan. Could it have been at least in part nostalgia for the old Globe's structure that persuaded the core sharers to rebuild it in the same form apart from the roof tiling and the enlarged gabling over the stage? Indeed, could the Alleyn team's prompt decision to rebuild the old Bear Garden as a dual-purpose playing-place have been a factor in the Blackfriars owners' decision not to abandon playing on Bankside? Near neighbours can loom as rivals in quite tangible forms. Unlike the Chamberlain's Men, the Admiral's had stuck loyally to their allocation to the Rose, playing there all the year round, building its replacement the Fortune in 1600 as a square version of the Globe, and never attempting to find an indoor playhouse like the Blackfriars. Their sponsor Henslowe supported the outgrowth from the duopoly by housing Worcester's Men at the Rose after the Admiral's Men moved to the Fortune, but he never bothered with indoor ventures. His son-in-law Alleyn did try, though unsuccessfully.

Some other factors can be invoked to identify the Chamberlain's company thinking besides their finances. In 1594, apart from the comfort of playing indoors in cold weather, we might ask whether such a venue might have brought profit comparable to what the outdoor venues brought in the summer. How did income in winter outdoors compare with the summer takings? We might compare the money Henslowe recorded taking in the summer at the Rose with his winter income through the years when we have his price-lists. In January 1595 a total of 24 playing days brought him £33.18 shillings. That June he received £41.15 from 21 days of playing. In January 1596 he took £31.1 for 26 days, and that June from 24 days he took £36.8 shillings. In total that makes £64.19 in 50 days of winter, and £78.3 from 45 days in the summer months. Over those two years the monthly takings were slightly less than 20% higher in summer than in winter. Could the better income outdoors in summertime have been a factor in the Shakespeare company's preference? In 1594 could the takings from an upper room at an inn like the Cross Keys in winter have matched the expected outdoor playhouse takings? I doubt it. By 1613 they knew that they could make more money playing at the Blackfriars through the summer instead of switching to the Globe and its much larger but cheaper crowds. Odd though it might seem today, profit cannot have been the main reason why the Burbages, Heminges and Condell chose to reconstruct the Globe. It is all too tempting to revert to the simple non-accountant's explanation I used back in 1988, nostalgia.

However, as Leinwand, Rutter and Bruster's doubts make clear, that is not really a big enough word to embrace the truth of such a unique situation and such an exceptional decision. If my reading of Carey's letter of October 1594 is correct, the idea that the company could use one playhouse for summer and another for winter was already strongly in the company's mind. Perhaps a broader term should be 'traditionalism', although like truth itself that word is still an oversimplification. To rebuild the Globe affirmed an old (pre-1594) tradition that twenty years later its four senior beneficiaries thought well worth renewing. Whatever the impact of the 1614 rebuilding has on the idea that in 1596 James Burbage might have envisaged a dominant indoor playhouse inside the city, it certainly does reaffirm at least one of the reasons why in the autumn of 1594 Burbage and company persuaded Carey to ask the Lord Mayor for an indoor venue.

This leaves us with a starkly alternative pair of readings of James Burbage's thinking. We could see him as a visionary recognising that the future of theatre lay indoors, whereas his sons and their fellows two decades later failed to see it as he had, and simple-mindedly renewed the company's preference for playing outdoors through the summer but indoors in winter. Or we could assume that in 1596 he merely sought to create a better venue for winter playing indoors. These alternatives are a version of the pre-revisionist historian's choice, between identifying individual prophets of historical change, or seeing outcomes like the success of the Blackfriars as the effect of theatre economics, the accidents that enforce choices to be made not by individual genius but by force of financial and other circumstance. In 1614 the success of the Blackfriars had already begun to underline the takeover of playgoing by the wealthiest members of London society, a predictably capitalist outcome that has sustained theatre ever since. The Burbage sons were fighting against that takeover by the gentry when they and their colleagues agreed to rebuild the Globe.

Let us revert to the multivalent committee decisions made in 1594, and their impact on Shakespeare. In my view three major policy decisions were made. Two of them relate to the still-unsettled question of the 'duopoly', the establishment of the two new companies in about May 1594. One of these is the choices that accompanied them, how calculated was the allocation to the two suburban playhouses, how thoughtful was the division of players and plays, and why the pair were given exclusive access to performances at Court for the next six years. The other is what changes in the regulation of the playing companies went with the new establishment. Did the Lord Mayor achieve his aim of excluding all playing from inside the city, and did that or the Lord Mayor's reaction to Carey's October letter prompt Langley and Woodliffe to start their new playhouses in Surrey and Middlesex that November? We lapse into more guesswork here.

The third policy decision of that year was Shakespeare's own. He made, or had made for him, the choice of writing plays instead of more poems. He gave up the search for a patron who might finance his verse, exhibited in 1593 and May 1594 by *Venus and Adonis* and *The Rape of Lucrece*, both dedicated to the Earl of Southampton. Instead he accepted a new patron, the Lord Chamberlain. In his own view, as his sonnets testify, this confirmed him for all future time as a lowly player rather than a poet, perpetually stained with playing like the dyer's hand. It was a decision, coerced by authority or not, that he might have made either through foresight, knowing what he might do with plays in the coming years, through his own pessimism over the likelihood of continuing noble patronage, or for the love of money, which presumably he thought more likely to come from playing than from a noble patron.

The effectiveness of the three decisions, the Lord Chamberlain's new policy over licensing only two playing companies, the Lord Mayor's ban on playing inside the city, and Shakespeare's own choice of a career in playwriting rather than as England's new poet, made the summer of 1594 a time of crucial and critical change for the whole nation. Without all three, Shakespeare's fame might be radically different from the one many of us work and live by now. All the thinking behind the three decisions, plus Burbage's later one to build the Blackfriars, has to be inferred. Guesswork can be good or bad, and a set of guessed-at decisions made by committees and the odd individual in 1594 are a precarious base on which to set such large-scale inferences about theatre history.

Until recently, the focus of attention for theatre history has been largely aimed at the two authorities that laid down their orders about playing, the Privy Council and the Lord Mayor. Such top-down impositions mainly evidence themselves in the many attempts to evade their orders. These were extensive, starting with Langley and Woodliffe, and emphasised by the other companies trying to gain footholds in London, particularly at the new Swan and the Boar's Head. Government, of the city on the one hand and of the country on the other, is always heavy-handed, and the mud that is squeezed out from under its heavy feet is often more revealing than the footprints themselves. In summer 1594 the balance of power in attitudes to professional playing in London between the Lord Mayor and Aldermen of Guildhall and on the Privy Council is a basic factor. We do know that from October 1594 onwards, particularly when the need to close public assemblies because of the risk of plague infection came up, the Privy Council for the first time started directing its orders over the crowds assembling at plays to the magistrates of Middlesex in the north and Surrey in the south, not to the Lord Mayor, with whom for the past thirty years they had endured a lengthy and often strident correspondence. Mayoral letters continued to arrive, but from then on they complained specifically about the suburban playhouses, not about playing inside the city. No precise records survive to say why this happened. My article about the Lord Chamberlain's letter of 8 October 1594 to the stand-in Lord Mayor Martin tried, in the process of deconstructing it, to build, however tentatively, a bridge of fairly enlightened guesswork over the vast hole that exists in the Privy Council's archive of papers, the absence of all its records between 27 August 1593 and 1 October 1595. The 'best guess' technique that I used in that article is one that scholars with an interest in what happened to the theatre of this period have long and often painfully put into practice. Such a bridge needs to have even more weight of heavy questioning dropped onto it.

That the playing companies did lose the city inns for playing from 1594 onwards is broadly apparent, not only in the petition of 1596 by the Blackfriars residents which declared that 'all players [are] banished by the Lord Mayor from playing within the Cittie', but by the absence of any evidence for later playing at the Bel Savage or any other inn, and from that summer onwards by the re-direction of the Council's letters about playing to the controllers of Middlesex and Surrey. In their dispute of 1597 with the owner of the Swan, Francis Langley, the ex-Pembroke's players testified that they used that playhouse because of the recent prohibition on playing 'in or neare the Cittye'.[13] The mayoral edict banning plays from the city's inns

---

[13] The various testimonies are reprinted (in modernised spelling) in *English Professional Theatre, 1530–1660*, ed. Glynne Wickham, Herbert Berry, and William Ingram, Cambridge University Press, Cambridge, 2000, pp. 211–15.

must have been issued in 1594. How effective it was remains uncertain.[14] In the power balance, Langley and Woodliffe must have seen the Lord Mayor as a nearer danger than the Privy Council, even though they knew that members of the Council had set up the two new companies. They evidently calculated that its order to keep only the two working in London would not or could not be sustained. We know that the ageing and ailing Earl of Pembroke, who seems to have been ready to give his name to several different groups of players through this decade, had a company under his name at the Swan from 1595 or 1596, until the *Isle of Dogs* crisis in 1597 destroyed them.[15] Similarly the young and pushful Earl of Worcester tried to get his company established alongside the duopoly pair in London, and eventually succeeded, mainly by an alliance with Derby's latest group of players, lodging them at the Boar's Head.[16] In 1600 Lady Derby wrote a pathetic letter to the Lord Treasurer begging him to let her husband enjoy a company of his own, and, whether or not her plea had any effect, the third company was soon accepted, even though a last Privy Council order of 31 December 1601 tried yet again to insist that only two could be allowed. On 31 March 1602 Charles Howard gave in to the pressure and on behalf of the Council notified the Lord Mayor that a third company at the Boar's Head had been approved. The Boar's Head company, then Worcester's Men, having started at the decrepit Rose, went on to play as Queen Anne's Men at the Red Bull. The Swan, whether through the hostility of some Privy Councillors or for other reasons, after 1598 never secured itself as a viable company playhouse. In fact neither Langley nor Woodliffe ever did as well as did the owners of the Theatre and the Rose with their Privy Council-backed companies. Most likely the Council's hostility to Langley and to the efforts of Woodliffe and his successors damaged their ventures. Once King James intervened in 1603, and the third company built the Red Bull, neither the Swan nor the Boar's Head had as much success holding players as even the old Curtain.

Traditionally, most of the historical evidence has been taken from the government's side, edicts like the Privy Council's being seen as the chief

---

[14] Paul Menzer's note about playing in the city after 1594 ("'The Tragedians of the City?' Q1 *Hamlet* and the Settlements of the 1590s," *Shakespeare Quarterly* 57 (2006), 162–82) uses the claim on the Q1 titlepage to ask whether companies continued to play inside the city limits after 1594. The evidence is at best unemphatic. Attempts must have been made to renew playing at the city's inns, but nothing survives to say if they were successful. They were certainly never authorised.

[15] William Ingram has an admirable survey of Langley's activities and the Pembroke's Men playing at the Swan, in *A London Life in the Brazen Age*, Cambridge, Mass., 1978.

[16] Herbert Berry's account of the Boar's Head, its financial dealings and the companies that played there is in *The Boar's Head Playhouse*, Folger Books, Washington DC, 1986.

markers for changes of policy. Such a top-down approach rarely provides much of the ground-level evidence. That end of the political process, where individuals and groups affected by the orders found ways to slide out from under them, is less obvious and rarely put into quotable form. Langley's and Woodford's attempts to set up their new playhouses with new companies are the clearest exemplars of the ground level response to whatever was ordained in 1594. They can be seen as successful, though with none of the obvious brio of the companies the two Privy Councillors set up. Many top-down mandates, such as the notorious orders to destroy all of the playhouses, proved utterly ineffective. But Carey's and Howard's establishment of the two companies in 1594 worked far better than any other known attempt by the authorities to guide the playing companies. However ineffective top-down orders were, their scheme to establish their duopoly of playing companies in opposition to those of other nobles like Pembroke and Worcester invites us to trace their involvement with theatre on the Council more closely.

Their personal concern appears at least ten years before 1594. Carey was on the Privy Council by 1583 when the decision to set up the Queen's Men was made, and may have gained some ideas about how to handle players then. He made James Burbage his servant at this time, conceivably taking him up when he was left out of the new Queen's company. The clearest evidence of the two lords' early concern appears in a letter by William Fleetwood in June 1584. As Recorder of London he reported on a division in the Privy Council's response to a pair of Aldermen, sent as envoys to the Council by the Lord Mayor to ask 'for the suppressing and pulling downe of the Theatre and Curten'.[17] Fleetwood noted the various responses to the order the Council then sent out, including Burbage's irate reply that he 'was my Lord of Hunsdons man', and would do no such thing. Burbage only submitted when shown Carey's signature on the order. Howard, then Lord Chamberlain before taking on the Admiralship, and Carey both objected but eventually signed. No playhouses were torn down as a result of the order, a failure of Privy Council authority reaffirmed several times over the years. Carey and his son-in-law must have found this an early lesson in the tortuous politics and economics of public playing in London, and especially in the complex relations between the Council and Guildhall.

Carey and his son-in-law always worked closely together, each taking a strikingly intimate interest in theatre from 1584 onwards. In that fluid year both of them in succession became Lord Chamberlain, holding that office's

---

[17] Quoted in E. K. Chambers, *The Elizabethan Stage*, 4 vols (Oxford: Clarendon Press), 1923, IV.298.

often-cited duty of fostering professional playing to provide the Queen with her annual entertainments. Such a shared duty helps to explain why Carey gave James Burbage his livery and Howard his to Alleyn. Burbage was one of the few major players of the time not enlisted in the Queen's Men, and as owner of the Theatre a major entrepreneur to boot. Howard seems to have noticed Alleyn while he was one of Worcester's Men. As soon as he gave up the Chamberlainship for the Admiralty he set up a new company under his own patronage and led by his new acquisition Alleyn. Wearing the badge of your master was a powerful acknowledgement of where your allegiance lay, and an explicit assertion of your own authority, at least at second hand. Thomas Walkley, in the Stationer's letter to the Reader prefacing the quarto of *Othello* published in 1622, justified his intrusive letter by citing the old proverb about the deficiency of 'a blew coat without a badge', that is, the loss that came from a servant who wore nothing to show the identity of the eminence he served. Alleyn evidently saw very early that his own best interest lay with Howard.

Both Carey and Howard showed perception in making these two figures their servants. Alleyn's loyalty to Howard shows when he retained his dress and badge with the Lord Admiral's livery while performing as one of Lord Strange's Men, a unique distinction or division of allegiance, and a manifestation of sharp awareness in the wearer of where power and his own interests lay.[18] The Privy Council recorded more concern for Strange's Men while Alleyn was their leader than they ever did for any other company. Strange's sent them a petition in July 1592 asking for a base in the suburbs, accompanying their letter with one from the Thames river boatmen, who needed the work of shipping playgoers. The Council immediately wrote to the justices of Surrey ordering that they must be allowed to play at the Rose on Bankside.[19]

In this analysis, it would be a great help if we knew more about the work of the omnipresent but taciturn executive officer of the Revels, Sir Edmund Tilney. He was the key executive to the two Councillors, more authoritative and more broadly informed than Burbage or Alleyn. Howard's cousin, he probably got his lord's help to secure the post of Master in 1578. He must have been the executive officer manipulating the 1594 deal, as he was with the establishment of the Queen's Men in 1583. It must have been Tilney who alerted the players when the decision to set up the new duopoly was made. It was probably he who chose Marlowe's plays for the Alleyn company,

---

[18] There were family links: Strange's wife was sister to Carey's daughter-in-law.
[19] Chambers, *The Elizabethan Stage* IV.212–13.

and Shakespeare with his plays for the other, despite the fact that several different companies had previously owned them.[20] He was the first person to whom the Council's extant order of 1598 about continuing to run only the two companies was addressed, along with the magistrates of Middlesex and Surrey.

Little is known directly about Burbage's career after 1576 when he created the Theatre, apart from his various building and entrepreneurial enterprises, and the legal disputes they evoked.[21] He seems not to have clashed with the Privy Council again, though he evidently remained Carey's man.[22] Carey and Howard clearly maintained a conjoint policy over plays and playing companies. Neither peer gave their name to any company so long as they held the office of Lord Chamberlain. From 1584 Carey must have seen himself as the leading negotiator between the two fields of authority, chiefly dealing with the Aldermen Richard Martin and Cuthbert Buckle who spoke for Guildhall, while he effectively backed Burbage as sponsor of and profiteer from the leading playing companies. For twenty years both Martin and Buckle, former Lord Mayors by 1594, were regularly sent to the Council to argue for the closure of all playing inside the city.

More pertinent is Carey's and Howard's own high status on the Privy Council over this period. In 1593 its chief personae were, after Lord Treasurer Burghley, the Archbishop of Canterbury, John Whitgift, Sir John Puckering Lord Keeper of the Great Seal, whose authority was stamped on all the Council's orders, followed by virtue of their various official capacities by Henry Carey the Lord Chamberlain, Sir Thomas Heneage the Vice-Chamberlain, Charles Howard the Lord Admiral, Robert Sackville (Lord Buckhurst) the Lord High Butler, Sir John Fortescue Chancellor of the Exchequer, and Sir John Wolley the Latin Secretary, along with Burghley's son, Sir Robert Cecil, who succeeded him as convenor after he died on 4 August 1598. Besides functioning as chief officer of the navy, Howard was Lord Steward of the royal household up to 1585 and from 1597, the

---

[20] An approach to this (very large) question appears in an essay entitled "The Great Divide of 1594," in *Words that Count, Essays on Early Modern Authorship in Honor of MacDonald P. Jackson*, ed. Brian Boyd, Associated University Presses, 2004, pp.29–48, reprinted as Chapter 5 in this volume.

[21] An excellent assessment of the explosion of investment in theatres that started in the 1570s is by William Ingram, "The Economics of Playing," in *A Companion to Shakespeare*, ed. David Scott Kastan, Blackwell, Oxford, 1999, pp. 315–16. He points to the statute against usury of 1571 as the moment when money-lending at a high rate of interest was at last sanctioned officially. That helped to launch the surge of new building in London and its suburbs in 1575–7, and again in 1595–6.

[22] For a broader survey of the Privy Council's interest in plays, and the work of Howard and Carey in particular, see Gurr, "Privy Councilors as Theatre Patrons," in *Shakespeare and Theatrical Patronage in Early Modern England*, ed. Paul Whitfield White and Suzanne R. Westfall, Cambridge University Press, 2002, pp. 221–45.

Earl of Derby serving in between. Various other officials such as Sir Francis Knollys, Treasurer of the Household, also attended the Council, and a select few other nobles such as the Earls of Derby and Essex (appointed in February 1593), and Lord Cobham, Warden of the Cinque Ports and later Lord Chamberlain. It was a gathering of real power, encompassing the highest authorities across the country. Burghley was Lord Lieutenant of Essex, Hertfordshire, Northamptonshire and Leicestershire. Howard was Lord Lieutenant of Surrey and Sussex. Carey was Lord Lieutenant of Norfolk and Suffolk. Buckhurst was Lord Lieutenant of Sussex.

Begun in its Elizabethan form by Thomas Cromwell, by 1593 the Privy Council had become a compact assembly of committee-minded personalities. The six or so core figures met at least twice a week at a variety of venues, in official rooms in London when the Queen was there, and at her various locations in the country through the summer. For our purposes, the records of their deliberations are dreadfully incomplete. Even where they survive, for instance through the first eight months of 1593,[23] they minute only a few outcomes from their deliberations, and fail to note even more. Mostly the extant '*Acts*' simply supply texts of the letters and orders that resulted from their discussions. They are not what we would think of as minutes of their decisions. They cite reports that had come in, often from spies in France and Spain, and orders that were to be sent to various officers of the realm. Some even record letters addressed to the Archbishop, Lord Buckhurst or others when the recipients were themselves present at the meeting. A few special meetings are noted but with no report of what was under consideration. On 8 April, for instance, a Sunday afternoon, a committee of four was convened, but the record of its discussions states only "On Sondaie in the afternoone, viij *Aprilis*, the Lord Treasorer, Earl of Essex, Lord Admyrall and Lord Chamberlaine satt in the Councell Chamber upon a Committee" (*Acts*, 24, p.172). Why that select group, and what did they discuss? It must have been urgent, and yet apparently it had to be kept secret. One wonders how much was discussed then and in other meetings that was never recorded, either because it was confidential or simply because no action by written letters or orders was called for.

Some of the reports hint at divisions within the Council. An enigmatic postscript appears, for instance, after a meeting at Croydon on 6 May, attended by the Archbishop, Essex, Howard, Carey and Wolley. For once Burghley was not there, and we might well wonder why. The *Acts* report

---

[23] *Acts of the Privy Council of England*, ed. John Roche Dasent, Vol. 24 (1593), 1901. These '*Acts*' run from 3 January to 26 August 1593.

that the meeting discussed several minor matters, including a letter to be sent to Wolley and Fortescue of the Council when Wolley was present, and a licence for Strange's Men, who were identified as Alleyn, who wore the Admiral's livery as Howard's man, Kemp, Pope, Heminges, Phillips and Bryan.[24] This was an allowance to tour in the current plague time anywhere beyond seven miles from London and the Court (*Acts*, p. 212). The same meeting also issued some major orders over problems in Ireland. None of the proceedings show anything to justify the postscript, which seems to have been inserted as an acknowledgement of a letter that the Lord Treasurer, himself absent, had delivered to the Council. Otherwise the meeting required no action other than the letter and the licence.

The postscript reflects a difficulty that had arisen between two or more of the people on the Council. It declared 'For the avoiding of anie doubt or difference that may grow for matter of presedence her Majestie's expresse pleasure is that your Lordship shal take present order that everie of them have such place and rank in Counsel and otherwize as their immediat predicessors latelie had, and no otherwize.' This seems to be a response to an order from the Queen to Burghley, the Lordship to whom it was presumably addressed, attempting to quell a dispute amongst the members of the Council then present. Precedence was always a complex and contentious issue. I suspect that the Queen's letter reflected the impact Essex was having, as the latest arrival on the Council. We know how outraged he was a few years later when Howard was promoted Earl of Nottingham, giving him precedence over Essex in processions. Just what provoked the Queen's letter we cannot know, though I would be tempted to associate it with the unreported subject-matter of the previous month's committee meeting, when Essex met with Burghley, Howard and Carey. Four weeks is a likely interim, giving Burghley time to consult the Queen over whatever grievance Essex had brought to that April meeting and get her response to it. His absence from the meeting to which the Queen's letter was delivered may well have been deliberate. Who told the attending members about it is not noted. It may have been Whitgift, addressing the chief culprits, who most likely were Essex and Howard, both of them then present to hear the Queen's opinion.

All the Councillors had a vested interest in keeping her person secure. Through all her last thirty years, ever since the Papal Bull *De Visibili*

---

[24] A week before, at a meeting on 29 April with Howard and Carey both present, the Council had issued a similar open warrant to Sussex's Men, authorising them to play anywhere outside a seven-mile radius of London where there was no plague. This followed a Minute of the Court of Aldermen of the city on 12 April, ordering Richard Martin and Richard Saltonstall, both Aldermen, to go to the Council asking for a ban on bearbaiting and similar activities.

Monarchia of 1571, she had been at risk of assassination by disaffected recusants, and study of the reports sent in by Burghley's spies are a recurrent feature of the *Acts*. The more routine matters concerning the Council, pursuing furtive recusants, assembling military men from various shires, and matters relating to money, especially at sea, included the recurrent problems of plague, which usually affected the players as well as the Lord Mayor quite directly. On 5 April, because the Queen was still in the city, the six Council members then present, Burghley, Puckering, Howard, Carey, Buckhurst and the Earl of Derby, sent a letter to the Lord Mayor, then Sir Cuthbert Buckle, ordering him to take 'some extraordinary care' to avoid any increase in infection by keeping the streets 'sweete and cleane'. As the number of plague victims rose, the Council had to issue the orders about closing playhouses and other places of resort because many of the deaths happened in the suburbs that were outside mayoral control.

The record of attendances at the Council's meetings is revealing. In the first eight months of 1593 where the records survive, up to 26 August, the Council held a total of 99 meetings, at eight different venues according to where the Court was officially in residence. Burghley attended 89 of them. Howard went to the same number, while Puckering attended 80, Buckhurst 76, Carey 73, Robert Cecil 72, Wolley 68, Essex (appointed to the Council on 25 February) 62, Fortescue 48, Whitgift 38, Derby 28, and Heneage 21. Francis Knollys attended 15 meetings, and Cobham two held at Whitehall on Sunday mornings, 22 and 29 April. The number that Howard and Carey attended shows them the most assiduous of all the committee men. The numbers attending varied from three to twelve. The fact that Howard attended the same total of meetings as Burghley, with Carey's attendances not far behind, made them the most informed if not influential figures on the Council apart from the Lord Treasurer himself and Lord Keeper Puckering, whose Great Seal gave official status to all the letters and orders they issued. Carey of course as Lord Chamberlain had the official function of controlling access to the Queen and ordering the state of her household, especially on her travels through the summer, a massively powerful and influential function that made his white rod of office something like a real weapon. He was the Court's central functionary, his protective role requiring his constant presence.

Opposition between the Council allowing plays and Guildhall's objections had been there since the first mayoral complaint in 1564. Two aldermen in particular, Martin and Buckle, were regularly addressed by the Council, not always over playing. In 1593 Martin, on a personal note, begged the Council to help his brother William, Keeper of the Counter, who was being harassed by the city sheriffs over Sir Walter Leveson's escape from his prison and his creditors, who were themselves pursuing the sheriffs because of the escape. Sir Richard had given bonds and sureties for Leveson's debts, and was being pursued for them in law. It was a knotty issue, where the Council had to obey the Queen's injunction that the sheriffs should be protected from the creditors and should not themselves proceed against William Martin, but 'such good order be taken therein by your Lordship as shall stand with equitie and good conscience' (*Acts*, p. 43). Nothing in the records says just how they unravelled this knot of Martin's. Buckle also had dealings with the Council out of his personal interests over the years. They were both on familiar terms with Carey and Howard in particular.

The *Acts* between 26 August 1593 and 1 October 1595, the crucial period for reports of the Council's decisions over playing, are missing, probably as a result of one of Whitehall's fires. A brief summary from the 'Register' for this lost period that survives (B.L.Additional MSS. 11402), says nothing about playing. The only known records of interest in theatre appear in the Guildhall *Remembrancia*, which, besides Carey's letter of 8 October 1594, record one dated 3 February 1594 addressed to Buckle as mayor and signed by the Archbishop, Howard, Robert Cecil, Buckhurst, Puckering and Fortescue. This was a routine ban on performing plays because of the increase in plague deaths. If the theory that Guildhall's ban on playing at the city's inns came later that year is true, this was the last letter addressed directly to the Lord Mayor. Spencer's letter objecting to the Swan also appears in the *Remembrancia* for 3 November 1594, one of his first acts after taking the post at the end of October. Spencer concluded this letter by asking Burghley to order the justices of Middlesex as well as Surrey 'for the stay & suppressing' of all plays. This he repeated six weeks before concluding his term of office, on 13 September 1595. The Council's only recorded action did not come until July of the following year. Addressed to the magistrates of Middlesex and Surrey, not the Lord Mayor, it was simply another routine suppression of plays because of plague.

What the surviving 1593 *Acts* do demonstrate is the power that Howard in particular possessed on the Council. This is evident not just in the frequency of his attendances but in some of his individual actions. The *Acts* for the meeting on 5 June at Nonsuch, for instance, identify him as the person who wrote to the mayor of Windsor on the Queen's behalf asking him to ban all London citizens from the town for fear of plague infection, on the grounds that 'her Majesty's pleasure was by me, the Lord Admirall, signified to you, the Maiour, according whereunto you have (as we are informed) verie dutifully travailed to remove and inhibite such persons as contrarie to her Majesty's said comandement were and sithence have resorted thether' (p. 284). The Court eventually took up residence at Windsor in August. The plague was already dreadfully widespread, and a later letter ordered the cancellation of nine major annual fairs across the country, adding in July one to the Lord Mayor to stop London's own Bartholomew Fair. Howard was an excellent fixer, much better than Carey. The job of making sure that Windsor would remain free of plague for the Queen was really Carey's, as master of the royal Household. But he was absent from the June meeting, so Howard wrote and signed the letter for him. They worked together on such matters, though I suspect it was chiefly Howard who in the next year thought up the idea of establishing the duopoly in imitation of the Queen's Men of ten years before, and who at the same time decided to settle the Lord Mayor's chronic objections with the complete ban on plays inside the city, allocating the companies to the suburban playhouses instead. Only the destruction of Council records for the period leaves this in the realm of hypothesis.

What the papers of the Privy Council and Lord Mayor show are their targets themselves, rather than the thinking behind them. Orders from on high were not obeyed very scrupulously, and much of the more marginal evidence relates to the evasions. The impact of the Council's various orders, such as Burbage's decision to build the Blackfriars, can be discerned only as side-effects. But they do all stem, as does Shakespeare's choice of career, from the changes introduced in 1594. The trickle-down effect of the Council policy that I believe was first set out that summer had its effect on Shakespeare's career as a writer of plays rather than of Ovidian or Spenserian verse, and on the eventual success of the Blackfriars. Opting out of the decision to rebuild the Globe in 1613 suggests that Shakespeare was less committed to the old idea of seasonal playhouses for the company than were the fellows he sent rings to in his will, and may imply that his commitment to playwriting in 1594 was less wholehearted than we normally assume it to be.

CHAPTER 4

Three Reluctant Patrons and Early Shakespeare

In the years up to May 1594 and early 1592 respectively, Henry Carey, the lord chamberlain, and Henry Herbert, the Earl of Pembroke, seem to have spent a lot of their time not becoming patrons of major London playing companies. Their absence from the player-patronising business up till then raises several questions. Some attention has been given, by Herbert Berry, Margot Heinemann, and others, to the possibility that patrons intervened to get specific plays staged[1] but little to how active they were in the practical business of getting companies set up and of keeping them going. Something about this can be learned from three men who for different reasons proved distinctly reluctant to be patrons: Henry Herbert, Henry Carey, and Charles Howard. The policies of different lords chamberlain toward the London companies come into that story. Most to the point, and with strong implications for Shakespeare's early career, is the question of what bearing those policies had on Carey's setting-up of a lord chamberlain's company in May 1594. There is also the question of how much of a joint operation was the establishment of Howard the lord admiral's new company of 1594 alongside Carey's company. The ultimate and most teasing question is what was in Herbert's mind when he set up his new company in 1592.

An early company in the livery of Henry Carey, Lord Hunsdon, is recorded at York on 8 September 1580 and at Exeter and Gloucester in 1582. It appeared at court on 27 December 1582. But after the then lord chamberlain, Sussex, died in the following year and the major companies were decapitated to make the Queen's Men, all the patrons of the remaining companies with a foothold in London seem to have backed away or been

---

Original publication: "Three Reluctant Patrons and Early Shakespeare," *Shakespeare Quarterly* 44 (1993), 159–74.
[1] See for instance Herbert Berry, "The Globe Bewitched and *El Hombre Fiel*" in *Medieval & Renaissance Drama in England*, 1 (1984), 211–30; and Margot Heinemann, "Rebel Lords, Popular Playwrights, and Political Culture: Notes on the Jacobean Patronage of the Earl of Southampton," *Yearbook of English Studies*, 21 (1991), 63–86, esp. pp. 71–72.

fended off. J. Leeds Barroll has noted how the establishment of the royal company served to cut down on competition between great nobles advertising their own glory by getting their companies performances at court.² What should also be noted is how the establishment of the Queen's Men affected the lord chamberlain's subsequent policy toward playing companies. When Sussex died in 1583, the office of chamberlain was transferred first to Charles Howard. This move signalled a substantial innovation in Privy Council policy toward players. Sussex's final illness may have supplied the opportunity to change the policy he had followed through his eleven years in charge of the revels, and the change may be one reason why the office of chamberlain remained vacant after his death in June until the beginning of the following year. Then, on New Year's Day 1584, in the middle of the Christmas festivities, it passed to Lord Effingham, Charles Howard.

Howard's wife, Lord Hunsdon's eldest daughter, Katherine Carey, was the closest blood relative that Elizabeth had, though with no claim to the succession. She became one of the queen's most intimate and reliable friends upon her arrival at court as maid of honour at the beginning of the 1560s. That relationship made her husband a suitable choice for such a quasi-domestic court office as the chamberlainship.³ The fact that he had deputised for Sussex during his illness and was therefore his obvious successor makes the delay in his appointment a mark of how delicate negotiations over the office must have been. Katherine Carey's father also shared the familial closeness to Elizabeth. A man with a distinctively frank personality, he was loyal to his queen, personally unambitious, and a regular ally of his son-in-law on the Privy Council. Sir Robert Naunton described the first baron Hunsdon as

> a fast man to his prince and firm to his friends and servants, and though he might speak big and therein would be borne out, yet was he not the more dreadful but less harmful and far from the practice of my Lord of Leicester's instructions, for he was downright. And I have heard those that both knew him well and had interest in him say merrily of him that his Latin and dissimilation [*sic*] were both alike and that his custom of swearing and obscenity in speaking made him seem a worse Christian than he was.⁴

---

² J. Leeds Barroll, "Drama and the Court" in *The Revels History of Drama in English*, Lois Potter, Clifford Leech, and T. W. Craik, gen. eds., 8 vols. (London and New York: Methuen, 1975–83), Vol. 3, pp. 3–27. For an incisive account of the conditions in 1583, see Scott McMillin, "The Queen's Men and the London Theatre of 1583," *Elizabethan Theatre*, 10 (1988), 1–17, esp. p. 10.

³ For a succinct account of Elizabeth's court, see Simon Adams, "Eliza Enthroned? The Court and its Politics" in *The Reign of Elizabeth I*, ed. Christopher Haigh (Athens: Univ. of Georgia Press, 1985), pp. 55–77.

⁴ See Robert Naunton, *Fragmenta Regalia or Observations on Queen Elizabth, Her Times & Favourites*, ed. John S. Cerovski, The Folger Shakespeare Library Presses, London and Toronto, 1985, p. 53.

Howard and Carey gave Elizabeth good reason to regard them as her closest and most loyal court servants.

After less than two years in the office, though, Howard moved on to become lord admiral, releasing the chamberlainship to his father-in-law, Carey, in July 1585. As chamberlain, Howard had presided over a commission on the navy, and that appointment may have been envisaged as no more than a stepping-stone to the higher office.[5] Conceivably his father-in-law always expected the chamberlainship to revert to himself. Judging from a Privy Council paper of 1584 quoted below, he seems to have been regarded as vice-chamberlain even though he did not actually hold the post while Howard was chamberlain.

However transient Howard's tenure, in two years as chamberlain he fulfilled his duties in the office by reorganising support for the playing companies. In 1584 he fended off the latest city request for the suppression of playing, with backing in the Privy Council from Christopher Hatton. Howard continued the policy he had employed when he deputised for Sussex in the 1570s of supporting players and chiefly the Queen's Men rather than any of the others, including his own. That seems to have been a deliberate choice. His own company was evidently not below standard. After he relinquished the deputy chamberlainship in 1575, his actors played at court twice in the 1576–77 season and again in the following year. As before, they did not perform while he was lord chamberlain in 1584–85, but they returned in the 1586–87 season and regularly thereafter. His father-in-law and successor similarly did not allow his own company to perform at court while he was chamberlain. Carey made one exception to that rule, apart from the joint court performance in 1586: before the chamberlainship passed to him from Howard, he allowed the wearing of his livery by James Burbage, formerly one of Leicester's players, who was then running the Theatre in Shoreditch.

As chamberlains, Howard and Carey seem to have worked closely together on the Privy Council. In June 1584, following a fracas in Shoreditch outside the Theatre and the Curtain, William Fleetwood reported to Lord Burghley on the Privy Councillors' response to the incident. Fleetwood wrote:

> Vpon Sonndaye my Lo. [Mayor] sent ij Aldermen to the Court for the suppressing and pulling downe of the Theatre and Curten. All the LL. agreed therevnto, saving my Lord Chamberlen and mr. Viz-chamberlen, but we

---

[5] See Robert W. Kenny, *Elizabeth's Admiral: The Political Career of Charles Howard, Earl of Nottingham 1536–1624* (Baltimore and London: The Johns Hopkins Press, 1970), pp. 28–29.

obteyned a lettre to suppresse theym all. Vpon the same night I sent for the quenes players and my Lo. of Arundel his players, and they all willinglie obeyed the LL. lettres. The chiefestes of her highnes players advised me to send for the owner of the Theater, who was a stubburne fellow, and to bynd hym. I dyd so; he sent me word that he was my Lo. of Hunsdons man, and that he wold not come at me, but he wold in the mornyng ride to my lord.[6]

Burbage, a bellicose defender of his property and resources, was quick to invoke Carey's support. Fleetwood's account implies that Burbage at first refused to believe that his patron as Privy Councillor would have signed such an order. Only after witnessing Carey's signature and being warned about the consequences of disobedience did he comply. Carey, having joined Howard in openly disagreeing with the decision, may then have worked behind the scenes to preserve Burbage's playhouse, because the order was not carried out.

It was at about this time too that Howard acted to protect the Queen's Men's monopoly on playing in London, granted by royal authority in 1583. The court *Remembrancia* from March 1584 to January 1587 are missing, but the Lansdowne papers have a partial record, including a petition that the Queen's Men sent to the Privy Council appealing for protection from pressure exerted on them by the city fathers, together with the responses from the lord mayor and the chamberlain. Howard's 'remedies' for the city's grievances included setting limitations on the times for playing and, most specifically, declaring 'That the Quenes players only be tolerated, and of them their number and certaine names to be notified in your Lps. lettres to the L. Maior and to the Iustices of Middlesex and Surrey. And those her players not to diuide themselues into seuerall companies.'[7] By keeping such a firmly announced policy in subsequent years, he would have had to disadvantage the company he himself patronised.

For his first nine years as chamberlain, Carey followed the same broad policy as Howard. He protected the companies against the mayor of London, favoured the Queen's Men, and with the one exception did not allow his own company to perform at court. Evidently he worked closely with his son-in-law, whose company became in the late 1580s one of the most frequent performers at court. Their alliance with Carey's own men for the 1586 entertainments may be evidence of collaboration between the two patrons rather than among the players. It is this long history of cooperation between the two men that makes sense of the decision in May 1594

[6] Chambers, Vol. 4, pp. 297–98.   [7] Chambers, Vol. 4, p. 302.

to sponsor two London companies, one Howard's, the Admiral's Men, and the other Carey's, the Chamberlain's Men.

Nonetheless, what happened in 1594 was a distinct shift in policy. The absence of any Chamberlain's company in London and at court through the years up to then is striking. In office Carey, well aware of the principle that led to the establishment of the Queen's Men, was conscientious in supporting that company as the official one and refusing to promote any rival, except perhaps his son-in-law's company. The decline of the Queen's Men in the early 1590s freed him from that inhibition. But something more specific than the hectic rise and fall of the playing companies between 1590 and 1594 must have influenced him as well.

What the two men set up in May 1594 was a duopoly. The model behind the new policy is not far to seek. They had in mind the original establishment of the Queen's Men in 1583. That precedent is evidenced most clearly in subsequent attempts by the Privy Council to maintain the privileges given to these two companies to the exclusion of all others. Orders given in 1598 and 1600 by Carey's son George (who became chamberlain in 1597) to protect the Chamberlain's and Admiral's as the companies with sole rights to play in London parallel the Howard deal of 1584 that gave exclusive rights to the Queen's Men.

This scheme was not laid out, as the earlier one had been, to quell the competitive exhibitionism of the great lords at court. The lord chamberlain needed to create more stability and more durability among the companies that entertained the court than had existed in the previous years. From a Privy Council perspective, the new scheme renewed the rights of the old Queen's Men, with the advantage of securing two strong companies rather than one. The most intriguing aspect of this rearrangement is how extensively the original and radical scheme of 1583, which systematically creamed off the best two or three players from each of the noblemen's companies around London, was incorporated into the 1594 design. Both the Admiral's and the Chamberlain's Men were, in effect, new creations. Who determined their membership?

The innovation certainly gave Henry Carey and his son-in-law a means to limit the competition among the companies. The Rose and the Theatre became the two allowed playhouses, their resident companies the allowed performers. As with Howard's deal in 1584, the lord mayor was appeased by an undertaking to forbid any more playing in the city inns. Carey had to make a special plea later in 1594 to get permission for his company to use one. He wrote to the lord mayor on 8 October asking that his 'nowe companie' should be allowed to use the Cross Keys Inn.⁸ That performance, if allowed, was the last occasion on which the city inns were ever used for playing. Suppression of playing inside the city must have been part of the duopolising deal. Carey so actively upheld the duopoly that Thomas Nashe's comment after Carey's death that his players 'in there old Lords tyme... thought there state setled'⁹ has a true ring to it. In effect, from May 1594 until July 1596 Shakespeare's company knew itself to be based in London as part of a government plan, with accompanying privileges. In the court season of 1594–95, only the Chamberlain's and the Admiral's performed, playing three times each. In 1595–96 the Chamberlain's played four times to the Admiral's three, with one joint performance. In 1596–97, when Cobham was chamberlain, only the Hunsdon company played, six times in all. In the next season, with the new Hunsdon, George Carey, as chamberlain from early 1597, the Chamberlain's played four times and the Admiral's two. No company besides these two performed at court from 1594 until Derby's returned for a performance on 5 February 1600, and the two boy companies arrived in 1601.

That settled state, of course, had strict limits. Henry Carey's priority had been to establish and maintain the new order, not just to support the two new companies of players. His heir's signature in November 1596 on the petition to prevent Burbage's use of his new Blackfriars playhouse may reflect the firmness with which the Careys held to that design, even when the chamberlainship had moved out of the family.¹⁰ Burbage had built the Blackfriars in a liberty to offset the loss of the city inns as winter playing places. Such a renewed intrusion into the city was no part of the deal made between the lord chamberlain and the lord mayor. The inhibition on Langley's Swan in 1597 was part of the same policy.

The deliberate lines of this policy can be seen in the official pronouncements on playing through the following years. A Privy Council order of

⁸ Chambers, Vol. 4, p. 316.
⁹ *The Complete Works of Thomas Nashe*, ed. R. B. McKerrow, 5 vols. (London: A. H. Bullen, 1904–10), Vol. 5, p. 194 (letter to William Cotton, a follower of Carey's).
¹⁰ After Hunsdon's death in July 1596, the post went first to William Brooke, Lord Cobham, with some awkward consequences for Shakespeare's portrayal of Sir John Oldcastle, Cobham's ancestor. But Cobham died in March 1597, and the chamberlainship was promptly transferred to Hunsdon's son George, then aged fifty. There were several court struggles over the post at this time, and George Carey may have been lucky to secure his father's former eminence. He had been in dispute with Pembroke, and Robert Sidney, Pembroke's nephew, was a keen candidate for the office of vice-chamberlain along with many others, including Raleigh and Sir John Stanhope (Millicent V. Hay. *The Life of Robert Sidney, Earl of Leicester (1563–1626)* [Washington, D.C.: The Folger Shakespeare Library; London and Toronto: Associated Univ. Presses, 1984], p. 160).

19 July 1598 stated that 'licence hath bin graunted unto two companies of stage players retayned unto us, the Lord Admyral and Lord Chamberlain, to use and practise stage playes'.[11] The order was to suppress a third company, the new Pembroke's, which had been trying to establish itself in Southwark. Another order of 22 June 1600 tried to check new inroads by specifying not only the two companies but also the two new playhouses, the Fortune and the Globe (which had replaced the Rose and the Theatre), as the only players and places authorised for London performances.[12] The boy companies, both of which appeared at court in the 1600–1601 season, were apparently free of the chamberlain's control at this time.[13]

The purposeful policy evident in these aspects of the management of playing seems clear. The question that remains is how active a part the two patrons took in the formation of their new companies. The companies' emergence involved a lot of regrouping. Though not so wholesale a decapitation of the existing companies as in 1583, this change was yet a broad sweep. The Admiral's was formed around Edward Alleyn, Philip Henslowe, and the Rose. Before its reorganisation in May 1594, the Admiral's Men had split. Alleyn and James Tunstall worked with Strange's from 1591 onward, while the rest toured in the country under the Admiral's name without returning to London. Alleyn and Strange's were noted together as a travelling company in a Privy Council order of May 1593. But from 1594 the different members of this group went their own ways. Strange's, which became Derby's on 25 September 1593, did not appear at court the next Christmas, when the only company to perform was the Queen's; nor did they return to the Rose. Five of Derby's Men went to form the new Chamberlain's. Richard Jones, a former Admiral's man who had been travelling on the Continent in 1592–93, may have returned to rejoin the Admiral's before 1594, but several members of the new Admiral's company were drawn from other groups. Thomas Downton came from Derby's, and John Singer probably from the Queen's, of which he had been a founding member in 1583 and with which he was still associated in 1588. Richard Alleyn, Edward's brother, also in the Admiral's by 1597, was probably a Queen's

---

[11] E. K. Chambers, *The Elizabethan Stage*, 4 vols. (Oxford: Clarendon Press, 1923), Vol. 4, p. 325.
[12] Chambers, Vol. 4, pp. 329–31.
[13] I suspect that when the boy companies insisted on declaring that they played at 'private' playhouses, they were in part protecting themselves from the licensing process that the master of the revels exercised over the 'public' playhouses and players. Paul's Boys had *The Old Joiner of Aldgate* licensed for them by Tilney in 1603 (see Richard Dutton, *Mastering the Revels: The Regulation and Censorship of English Renaissance Drama*, University of Iowa Press, 1991, p. 131), but the Blackfriars Boys, besides being under Daniel's control instead of Tilney's in 1603–04, made less use of the master. Not until after two of their plays had to be censored in 1605 and 1606 did they come under the master's control.

man in 1594.¹⁴ Of the other post-1594 Admiral's Men, Edward Dutton, Edward Juby, Martin Slater, and Thomas Towne, there is no earlier record.

Whether Alleyn had much choice in the composition of the new company is doubtful. Singer's presence suggests strongly that the two Privy Councillors were doing what Walsingham had done with the Queen's, selecting a few men from each of several different groups. Alleyn might have been consulted, but he lacked the authority to select from other companies. Alleyn certainly would not have contributed directly to the equally wide-ranging selection of Carey's company.

The chamberlain's and his son-in-law's initiative in setting up two new companies makes the choice of the players who joined Carey's own company even more of a puzzle. Family connections probably influenced selection of the company's core members. Ferdinando Stanley, Lord Strange, now Earl of Derby, died on 16 April 1594. His widow was sister to George Carey's wife. Derby's widow certainly took an interest in her husband's players because they are recorded at Winchester on 16 May 1594 under her name. From Strange's/Derby's Men, whose credentials included court performances and a longish history of playing alongside Alleyn at Henslowe's Rose, the new company drew five of its sharers, George Bryan, John Heminges, Will Kemp, Augustine Phillips, and Thomas Pope, along with some others. These fellow players did not, however, constitute a full company. Downton and possibly others from Derby's split from their fellows and went with Alleyn into the Admiral's. Carey seems to have deliberately left room in his group for players drawn from other companies. The most notable of these were Richard Burbage and William Shakespeare. Where they came from is a mystery that brings back that other reluctant patron, the Earl of Pembroke.

Near the beginning of the 1590s, players' names in the plots of *2 Seven Deadly Sins* and *The Dead Men's Fortune*, manuscripts prepared for Strange's or the 'amalgamated' Strange's/Admiral's company, probably before 1592,¹⁵ indicate that Strange's Men included 'Mr' George Bryan, Richard Burbage, Richard Cowley, John Duke, Thomas Goodale, John

---

¹⁴ Evidence for the players is taken chiefly from Chambers and from Edwin Nungezer, *A Dictionary of Actors and of Other Persons Associated with the Public Representation of Plays in England before 1642* (New Haven: Yale Univ. Press, 1929), with additions from S. P. Cerasano, "New Renaissance Players' Wills," *Modern Philology*, 82 (1985), 299–304, and from Mark Eccles, "Elizabethan Actors I: A-D" and "Elizabethan Actors II: E-J," *Notes & Queries*, 236 (1991), 38–49 and 454–61.

¹⁵ The most accessible transcription of the evidence from these manuscripts is in *Henslowe's Diary*, ed. R. A. Foakes and R. T. Rickert (Cambridge: Cambridge Univ. Press, 1961), pp. 327–28. An account questioning the standard reading of this evidence is Scott McMillin's "Building Stories: Greg, Fleay, and the Plot of *2 Seven Deadly Sins*," *MRDE*, 3 (1988), 53–6. I find his scepticism overstated.

Holland, Robert Pallant, 'Mr' Augustine Phillips, 'Mr' Thomas Pope, Will Sly, John Sincler, plus a Harry, a Kitt, a Vincent, and several boys.[16] Those with 'Mr' in front of their names are thought to be sharers. 'Harry' may have been Henry Condell, and 'Kitt' may have been Christopher Beeston, both later to appear in the Chamberlain's Men. Some of these players left the company in the changes of 1591–93, probably at Alleyn's break from the Theatre in May 1591. Sincler and Holland seem to have been in Pembroke's. Richard Burbage, too, was not in Strange's in the years when Pembroke's was active. On 6 May 1593 the players named by the Privy Council as Strange's, presumably all sharers, were 'William Kemp, Thomas Pope, John Heminges, Augustine Phillips and Georg Brian'.[17] All of these 1593 Strange's players joined the Chamberlain's in 1594. As previously noted, the mystery is where the other Chamberlain's Men came from.

Several companies had strong players to offer. Sussex's and one section of the Queen's in particular were available, playing first separately and then jointly at the Rose between December 1593 and April 1594. The Queen's Men had broken in two as early as 1590, and by 1594 its players were evidently ripe for reallocation. Apparently Sussex's was well-staffed in 1594 since it played *Titus Andronicus* (inherited from Pembroke's according to the quarto title page), a play demanding at least twenty-six actors for the opening scene.[18] Sussex's had played jointly with Laneham's section of the Queen's in 1590 and 1591. Possibly the same group augmented Sussex's

---

[16] A notably small and skinny player, Sincler has been traced through the plays written later for the Chamberlain's in the parts of Nym, Slender, Aguecheek (a 'manikin'), possibly Thersites (a 'toadstool', 'cob-loaf', and 'fragment'), and probably Robert Faulconbridge, the Bastard's brother, in *King John*, where he is described in terms that fit the other characters. In Jonson's plays for the Chamberlain's Men, a markedly small player took Shift in *Every Man Out*. Nano, the dwarf in *Volpone*, has a larger speaking part than the eunuch and hermaphrodite. Sincler may also have been Asinius Bubo, a 'small timbered gentleman' in *Satiromastix*. Again, there is 'a very little man' in *The London Prodigal*, property of the King's Men in 1605. But who did he play in the Shakespeare plays of the early 1590s, particularly *Titus* itself and *Richard III*? There is no evidence of a part written especially for a thin man in the later *Henry VI* plays (for all that Sincler's name appears in one of them), or in *Richard III*, or in the early comedies. None of the *Henry VI* plays, if originally written for Strange's, features any special part for Sincler. His name in the Pembroke texts may indicate his late arrival in that playing company. *King John*, however, does have a part for him. But the disputed dating of *King John*, which is variously ascribed to 1590 or 1595, makes it no help in fixing the time he joined Shakespeare's company.

[17] Chambers, Vol. 2, p. 123.

[18] *Titus* and its 1594 title page have occasioned a lot of discussion. Paul E. Bennett has suggested that the play dates from 1593, and that its title page simply lists the three companies who shared its performance ("The Word 'Goths' in 'A Knack to Know a Knave'," *N&Q*, 200 [1955], 462–63). The demands of the opening scene might have suggested joint production, but there is no other title page that lists a group of the companies who performed the play in this form, whereas there are several who list a sequence of performing companies. It is also worth noting that several plays of the early 1590s demanded large casts. According to G. E. Bentley, fifteen appears to have been the usual number in a travelling group through the 1590s (*The Profession of Player in Shakespeare's Time*,

numbers in their initial run at the Rose in December and January. Otherwise the fact that Sussex's joined up with the Queen's three months later must indicate a drastic loss of manpower in the interim, for which there is no evidence. Henslowe did not link the two companies by name in December and January as he did in April, but the later identification may merely indicate that he had by then become more familiar with the arrangements of the joint company and the name on its licence. It is also possible that members of Pembroke's, disbanded by August 1593, had joined Sussex's. That might also explain the transfer of *Titus*.

The biggest mystery concerns the players in Pembroke's Men.[19] This company was oddly prominent in its London activities for a company of wholly new players. Besides performing several of Shakespeare's plays and having Marlowe's *Edward II* written for them, they were good enough to match Strange's at court in the season of 1592–93, with two performances to the other's three. They broke up under the pressures of the plague and a difficult tour in August 1593. Henslowe wrote about Pembroke's Men to Alleyn, then traveling with Strange's, on 28 September: 'as for my lorde a penbrockes wch you desier to knowe whear they be they are all at home and hauffe ben this v or six weackes for they cane not save ther carges wth travell as I heare & weare fayne to pane ther parell for ther carge'.[20] Their collapse precipitated the flow of their playbooks into print in 1593 and 1594.

The new Chamberlain's took up several former Pembroke's players, including John Sincler, named in *2 Seven Deadly Sins* as a Strange's man and cited by name at 3.1.1 in *3 Henry VI*, which (as *Richard Duke of Yorke*) was a Pembroke's play by 1593.[21] John Holland, also previously of Strange's, is named there along with him. Sincler is named again in *The Shrew's*

1590–1642 [Princeton, N.J.: Princeton Univ. Press, 1984], p. 213); but several plays demanding large numbers of actors started to appear in the early 1590s – *Tamar Cam* required twenty-nine, and *The Battle of Alcazar* twenty-four.

[19] Chambers thought that Pembroke's was an offshoot of the Strange's–Admiral's amalgamation (Vol. 2, p. 123). David George accepts this and assumes that the amalgamation's other playtexts reverted to Strange's ("Shakespeare and Pembroke's Men," *Shakespeare Quarterly*, 32 [1981], 305–23, esp. p. 307). But that leaves the Admiral's out of account and ignores what happened to *Titus*. There is nothing in Henslowe's letter to Alleyn about Pembroke's to indicate any direct association. Henslowe was reporting business and social gossip to Alleyn, not matters of direct financial interest. G. M. Pinciss is doubtful about Pembroke's being a Strange's offshoot on the grounds that the amalgamated company split into its two component parts for touring during the plague closing of 1593, and that the numbers involved in travelling make it unlikely that three touring companies could have been formed from the original two. He suggests instead that Pembroke's was made up from one of the two Queen's companies ("The Queen's Men, 1583–1592," *Theatre Survey*, 11 [1970], 50–65).

[20] Foakes and Rickert, eds., p. 280.

[21] The naming of players is a vexed question that depends heavily on what sort of manuscript is identified as the source for the printed text and on when the names were inserted in the manuscript.

Induction, most likely from its time as a Pembroke's play. What these two players did after Pembroke's collapsed in 1593 is conjectural, though there is one important clue: the track of Shakespeare's plays recorded on the title page of the 1594 quarto of *Titus Andronicus*, which says it went from Strange's to Pembroke's to Sussex's. Sincler and Holland certainly went from Strange's to Pembroke's and may have gone from there to Sussex's. Sussex's is recorded by Henslowe as performing *Titus* at the Rose early in 1594. When Pembroke's collapsed, Sincler and Holland might have accompanied the play to Sussex's, whence they were taken up for the Chamberlain's.

Conceivably Richard Burbage took the same path. And Shakespeare? When Pembroke's disbanded, Shakespeare was writing his epyllions for Southampton. *The Rape of Lucrece* was entered for printing on 9 May 1594, less than four weeks before the combined performances of the new Chamberlain's and Admiral's Men recorded by Henslowe. Shakespeare must have had some interest in Sussex's since they acquired *Titus*, while the transfer of his entire early corpus of plays to the new Chamberlain's suggests that he had been in the habit of keeping ownership of the plays in his own hands as they shifted from one company to another. Whether or not he actually performed in the companies that had his plays, it seems likely that Sincler, Holland, and probably Burbage, too, stayed with the Shakespeare corpus on its travels until the lord chamberlain descended on them, players and plays, for his new company.

One other factor may have had a bearing on the transfer of players from Pembroke's to Carey's company. After the 1593 break-up, a Pembroke's company does reappear in the records as a travelling group, for instance in the Ipswich records on 7 April 1595 and again the following year. They are also

See Scott McMillin, "Casting for Pembroke's Men: The *Henry VI* Quartos and *The Taming of A Shrew*," *SQ*, 23 (1972), 141–59. The early quartos of *2* and *3 Henry VI* both precede the Chamberlain's company, and the manuscript of *2 Seven Deadly Sins* can never have been in their hands; so both kinds of evidence are sound indications as to where the named players worked before joining the Chamberlain's. The story of the texts of the *Henry VI* plays, and in particular of the relation between the quarto of *The Contention* and the Folio *2 Henry VI*, and between *Richard Duke of Yorke* and *3 Henry VI*, is a complex matter. Some weight has to be attached to the circumstantial evidence for the two quartos being Pembroke's plays and Pembroke's breaking up and selling their playtexts in 1593, shortly before *The Contention* and *Richard Duke of Yorke* were published in 1594 and 1595. That supports the case made by textual scholars who claim that the two quartos are reported texts deriving from a version of the manuscript that eventually was used to print the Folio text. With some help from the evidently memorial character of much of the transcription in the two quartos, not to mention their incorrect versions of the Latin tags, I am inclined to accept that reading of the evidence.

Quotations of *3 Henry VI* and *Richard III* are taken from *The Complete Works of Shakespeare*, ed. David Bevington, 4th ed. (New York: HarperCollins, 1992); quotations from quartos follow Michael J. B. Allen and Kenneth Muir, eds., *Shakespeare's Plays in Quarto* (Berkeley: Univ. of California Press, 1981). Line numbers all refer to Bevington.

in that city's records for 1592–93; so very likely the 1595 company was the residual group following its familiar touring route.²² They had certainly been reduced in status by the losses following their 1593 troubles, whether some of them went to Sussex's in 1593 or directly to the Chamberlain's in 1594. And there may have been another reason why they did not get back to London. Carey's son George was engaged in hostile wrangles with Henry Herbert from the autumn of 1593 until 1595 over a possible marriage of the earl's fifteen-year-old son William (later dedicatee of the First Folio) to George Carey's daughter. The hot-blooded Henry Carey might have seasoned the family animus against Pembroke either by using his office to keep his enemy's playing company out of town or by taking its best players for his new company. That is sheer speculation, but the evidence for Carey's direct intervention in playing matters does give it some credibility.

Very likely it was Carey's original policy of not giving his name to any company while he was chamberlain that had driven James Burbage to Pembroke in late 1591, when he needed a patron for his new company. Burbage wore Carey's livery in 1584; but once Carey became lord chamberlain, his reading of his duties would have precluded his patronage of a new company. So after Burbage quarrelled with the Alleyns in May 1591 and lost Alleyn along with Strange's Men to the Rose, he may well have arranged to form a new company, installing his son Richard as its leader, by applying to Pembroke for sponsorship. What makes that idea plausible is Pembroke's long intimacy with the Earl of Leicester.

Pembroke and Leicester shared many activities through the 1570s and 1580s. Pembroke was married to Leicester's niece, Mary Sidney, in 1577. Leicester visited Wilton early that year, and Pembroke and Leicester took the Buxton spa waters together a few months later. On 20 September 1578, Pembroke was present at Leicester's house in Wanstead when Francis Knollys came to settle the marriage of his daughter, the widow of the Earl of Essex, then pregnant with Leicester's child. Baynard's Castle, Pembroke's London base, was used by Leicester for his discussions with Pembroke and Philip Sidney over Queen Elizabeth's proposed Alençon marriage in 1579. Throughout this time Leicester and his brother Warwick kept companies. Pembroke, however, after his patronage of the apparently short-lived travelling group in 1575–76, did not. Yet, like Leicester, Pembroke was a playgoer. They attended William Gager's play *Meleager* at Oxford together in 1585.²³

---

²² *The Malone Society Collections* (cited in Ch. 2, n. 6), Vol. 2, Pt. 3 (1931), pp. 276–79.
²³ Michael Brennan, *Literary Patronage in the English Renaissance: The Pembroke Family* (London and New York: Routledge, 1988), p. 98.

James Burbage had been a Leicester's man up to the formation of the Queen's Men in 1583. Pembroke may have been present at performances by Leicester's Men for their patron. He was the obvious choice for a former Leicester's player to turn to as a new patron, a senior noble not currently patronising any company. And there are perhaps other reasons for Burbage to have gone that way. After Leicester's death in 1588, the Leicester circle had migrated to the countess of Pembroke, Mary Herbert. She herself was writing plays in 1591–92. An appeal to her husband might well have been the best way to secure the highest level of patronage for the new company. Whether Mary Herbert, Sidney's sister, did intervene to add the new company, playing Marlowe and Shakespeare, to her already long list of creditable literary patronage, it is impossible to say.[24] Pembroke himself was not often in London, in part because of ill health. He was in fact beginning the long decline that led to his death in 1601. A letter from 1595 survives in which he writes that he dreams of death and desires it.[25] Yet late in 1591 or early in 1592, he had chosen to change his long-held practice by giving his name as patron to a new London company. His wife's intervention cannot be discounted. If we judge by the connections of patrons alone, no other great lord would have been more likely as the patron of a new Burbage company in 1592.

Pembroke's name, plus the other circumstantial evidence, strongly supports the view that Richard Burbage, after a start with Strange's in 1590 and 1591, separated from that company at the time of Alleyn's quarrel with Richard's father, James. When Alleyn and Strange's moved to the Rose, Richard helped to set up the new Pembroke's to occupy the Theatre. Only

---

[24] There has been a lot of debate about Mary Sidney's interest in reforming the drama, but none of it has suggested that she prompted her husband's patronage of the new company in 1592. She became the second earl's second wife in 1586, when she was twenty-five. Mary Ellen Lamb tried with some success to demolish the widely held view that Mary Sidney helped a circle of playwrights to introduce French and Senecan drama in an attempt to 'purify' the common English style ("The Myth of the Countess of Pembroke: The Dramatic Circle," *YES*, 11 [1981], 194–202). David Bergeron is a little more positive, noting that thirty books were dedicated to her, the highest number to a woman after Lucy Bedford and Queen Elizabeth ("Women as Patrons of English Renaissance Drama" in *Patronage in the Renaissance*, Guy Fitch Lytle and Stephen Orgel, eds. [Washington, D.C.: The Folger Shakespeare Library; London and Toronto: Associated Univ. Presses, 1981], pp. 274–90). But only one hint links Mary Herbert to her husband's playing company. Pembroke's Men are not mentioned as participants in the 'Astraea' entertainment, probably at Ramsbury, for Elizabeth's visit on 27–29 August 1592, but Simon Jewell, a player in Pembroke's or the Queen's Men, mentions her as a patron in his will. J. A. B. Somerset sees that as evidence for his membership and her sponsorship of Pembroke's ("The Lords President, Their Activities and Companies: Evidence from Shropshire," *Elizabethan Theatre*, 10 [1988], 93–111, esp. p. 109). Margaret P. Hannay also sees her intervening in the patronage of players (*Philip's Phoenix: Mary Sidney, Countess of Pembroke* [New York: Oxford Univ. Press, 1990], pp. 124–26).

[25] Brennan, p. 101.

a year or so younger than Alleyn,[26] in 1591 he lacked Alleyn's stature both literally and figuratively. But he did have similar familial advantages. After Pembroke's collapsed, he may have gone to the Rose with Sussex's for a few months before setting up as the leader of the new Chamberlain's back at his father's Theatre in 1594. Both Alleyn and Burbage used parental property as the London base for their two companies from 1594 onwards.

Shakespeare's place in any of the early companies is uncertain. The case for his belonging to the Queen's has been made as strongly, and on much the same grounds, as for his membership in Pembroke's. He was certainly known to Greene as a player when Greene complained about him in August 1592, with his allusion to the 'tyger's heart' from *3 Henry VI* (1.4.137). That play, not in Henslowe's lists for 1592, must have taken Greene's attention at one of the Shoreditch playhouses (there would be little point in Greene making the allusion if the play was not being performed often enough for the reference to be recognisable). I am almost convinced that Shakespeare was with those plays in Pembroke's company at the Theatre in 1592 and 1593. My reasons are not just the number of his plays showing evidence that some Pembroke's players were in them (*2* and *3 Henry VI* in the versions known as *The Contention* and *The True Tragedie of Richard Duke of Yorke*, *The Taming of the Shrew*, and *Titus*) but the evidence in the early printed versions of *2* and *3 Henry VI* that he was on hand when they were staged. Two details of the early staging, one in *The Contention* and one in *Richard Duke of Yorke*, indicate an influence that most probably came from a reader closely familiar with Holinshed. In the Folio text of *2 Henry VI*, the entry direction at 5.2 reads '*Enter Richard and Somerset to fight*'. In *The Contention* the stage direction reads: '*enter the Duke of Somerset, and Richard fighting, and Richard kils him under the signe of the Castle in saint Albones*'. Richard then explains the point of the 'alehouse paltry signe', reminding the audience of the prophecy that Somerset would die beside a castle. That connection is made in both versions, although in *The Contention* Richard makes it more explicit, saying 'Whats here, the signe of the Castle? / Then the prophesie is come to passe.' The players might have taken the hint about a hanging sign from the text, but it would have helped if the author were on hand to confirm the detail. Another detail in the later play offers quite direct evidence. The Folio entry at 2.6 of *3 Henry VI* simply reports '*Enter Clifford wounded*'. The Pembroke's version has '*Enter Clifford wounded, with an arrow in his necke*'. Holinshed specified

---

[26] Alleyn was born in 1566, Burbage in 1567 (Mark Eccles [cited in n. 14, above], "Elizabethan Actors I: A-D," p. 43).

the type and the location of Clifford's wound, and the Pembroke's text of the play records that the company got it right. This replication of visual details from the play's sources, another instance of which appeared in the staging of *Richard III*,[27] makes it extremely unlikely that Shakespeare was very far from Pembroke's in 1592–93.

The biggest question of all remains. How active a part did Carey and Howard play in the reorganisation of the old companies in 1594? Was it left to the Master of the Revels to allocate the resources? And most to the point, what allowance was made for the resources that each group commanded? The players were collected and redistributed from the resources of several companies. What about the stock of playtexts that each of the decapitated companies had been performing? Was it an accident that Marlowe's plays were all allocated to one company and Shakespeare's to the other? It is not difficult to see how Alleyn's group secured most of their stock, given their chosen playhouse and their financier. But whether the Chamberlain's acquisition of the large run of Shakespeare's plays that eventually found their way into the First Folio had any influence on the composition of Carey's group is a more teasing question. Strange's had played 1 *Henry VI* at the Rose in 1592 if Henslowe's notes about 'harey the vj' relate to it, as recent scholarship indicates.[28] Pembroke's, which had been disbanded for nearly a year when the Chamberlain's were formed in 1594, had played the later parts of the first Henriad in 1592 plus *The Taming of the Shrew* and possibly others from the same pen. More recently Sussex's company had taken on *Titus* from Pembroke's, which had got it from Strange's. Did some of Sussex's players add it to the Chamberlain's stock? If so, who had the later Henriad plays and *The Shrew*?

The best answer may lie in the reason why *Edward II*, another Pembroke's play, did not also join the Chamberlain's. It turns up much later with Queen Anne's at the Red Bull along with other plays from the Henslowe repertory, even though it is not in the records as being played at the Rose up to 1603.[29] That some of the Pembroke's stock of plays went to Henslowe

---

[27] See Andrew Gurr, *The Shakespearean Stage 1574–1642* (Cambridge: Cambridge Univ. Press, 1992), p. 210.

[28] Roslyn L. Knutson has pointed out that Henslowe was scrupulous in recording multi-part plays or plays with sequels, like *Tamburlaine*, Parts 1 and 2 ("Henslowe's Naming of Parts: Entries in the *Diary* for *Tamar Cham*, 1592–3, and *Godfrey of Bulloigne*, 1594–5," *N&Q*, 30 [1983], 157–60). The absence of any such notation for 'harey the vj' indicates that it was a single play, presumably just the first part of the Henry VI sequence, and that Henslowe never had the subsequent plays, two of which went into the Pembroke repertoire. See also Hanspeter Born, "The Date of *2, 3 Henry VI*," *SQ*, 25 (1974), 324–26.

[29] See Roslyn L. Knutson, "Evidence for the Assignment of Plays to the Repertory of Shakespeare's Company," *MRDE*, 4 (1989), 75–89.

while others went to the Chamberlain's suggests that the plays were dispersed when the company disbanded in 1593. But it may equally be that someone took care to set up a parity of sorts between the two components of the 1594 duopoly. What makes the Chamberlain's stock of plays most distinctive, and very likely determined one component in the fellowship of the new company, was the poet who wrote most of it. Somebody, possibly Carey himself, knew enough about the repertory of popular plays in 1594 to see that both companies had a good share. One company got the Henslowe resources, including the Marlowe plays, the other got Shakespeare.

The plays that Henslowe recorded in his diary during the first half of 1594 give some indication of the particular repertoire that the early companies performed and (at the risk of some circular argument) also hint at the composition of the two later companies, the Admiral's and the Chamberlain's.[30] In its run between 27 December 1593 and 6 February 1594, Sussex's performed nine plays that appear only in that run of the diary, including *George a Greene*, printed in 1599 as a Sussex's play, and *Friar Francis*, which Heywood in his *Apology* reported as belonging to Sussex's. *Titus Andronicus* also appeared for the first time, if, as I believe, the earlier 'Titus' that Henslowe records in the entries preceding those for the Sussex company was *Titus and Vespasian*. *The Fair Maid of Italy* also appears for the first time as a Sussex's play. Only *The Jew of Malta*, a regular in the diary since the first Strange's entries at the beginning of 1592, seems not to have been a new introduction by Sussex's. Henslowe appears to have given Marlowe's play to all the companies that performed at the Rose or at Newington Butts.

In the brief period during which Sussex's joined up with the Queen's Men at Easter 1594, the amalgamated company is noted with five titles. Two, *The Jew* and *Friar Bacon and Friar Bungay*, came from Henslowe; one was a Sussex's title, *The Fair Maid*; and one other, *King Leir*, must have come from the other side of the amalgamation since it later appeared in print as a Queen's Men's play. Another new play, *The Ranger's Comedy*, also appeared for the first time. It later reappeared in the Admiral's repertory; so it may have been a new title purchased by Henslowe rather than a play imported by the Queen's Men.

For their three-day run between 14 and 16 May, the Admiral's offered one play definitely Henslowe's, *The Jew*, plus one play that was probably his, *The Ranger's Comedy*, and a new title, *Cutlack*, which Everard Guilpin identified as having belonged to Alleyn in 1598 and which must have come from

---

[30] Henslowe's play-lists for 1594 appear on pages 20–22 of Foakes and Rickert's edition of the diary (cited in n. 22, above).

his personal stock. The most intriguing and possibly most revealing list of plays is one that records joint or alternate performances by the new Admiral's Men and the Chamberlain's for their brief run at the same playhouse.[31] This list is the only extant record of the original play-stock of the Chamberlain's Men. The two companies offered seven plays between 3 and 13 June 1594. The seven of course included Henslowe's *The Jew of Malta*, probably current then because of the Lopez trial.[32] But the others came from elsewhere, almost certainly from the companies where Carey and Howard found the players to staff their new companies. Besides Alleyn's *Cutlack*, *Titus Andronicus* reappeared, presumably with some players from Sussex's. Four new plays appeared, *Hester and Ahasuerus*, *Bellendon*, *Hamlet*, and *The Taming of the Shrew*. The last of these had once been a Pembroke's play, like *Titus*. Where the *Hamlet* came from is uncertain. References to a play of that name had been appearing since 1589, which means that it belonged to one of the older companies then appearing in London, most likely the Queen's.

It is possible to guess more specifically about that from the later history of the seven titles. *Bellendon*, *Cutlack*, and *The Jew of Malta* appear subsequently in the Admiral's lists made by Henslowe. *Titus* and *The Shrew* were part of the Chamberlain's play-stock, to judge from their reappearance in the First Folio. *Hamlet* and *Hester* may also have belonged to the Chamberlain's since these plays never reappear in the Admiral's lists. Possibly the *Hamlet*, like *King Leir*, *The Troublesome Raigne of King John*, and *The Famous Victories of Henry V*, was a Queen's Men's play that passed at this time to the Chamberlain's, to be rewritten sometime later by their resident playwright. The two approved companies did get into the habit of matching their plays, Falstaff with Oldcastle, *Richard III* with *Richard Crookback*, *The Jew of Malta* with *The Merchant of Venice*, and others.[33] Henslowe's addition of a play about Henry V to his list in November 1595 was conceivably to counter the Chamberlain's Men's use of the older play. For Shakespeare's *King John* the favoured date of composition, or even revision, in 1595 would make sense if the company had recently acquired the

---

[31] Carol Chillington Rutter reckons that since *Bellendon* appeared in the Admiral's list shortly after appearing in the list of the joint companies, each play must have been performed separately by each company (*Documents of the Rose Playhouse* [Manchester: Manchester Univ. Press, 1984], p. 83). There seems no reason to doubt this interpretation of the evidence.

[32] Lopez was at risk from February to July 1594, when he was beheaded. Revivals of *The Jew of Malta* coincided with his trials. See Margaret Hotine's "The Politics of Anti-Semitism: *The Jew of Malta* and *The Merchant of Venice*," N&Q, 236 (1991), 35–38.

[33] See Knutson, "Evidence for the Assignment of Plays to the Repertory of Shakespeare's Company," p. 83.

old play and wanted a quick rewrite for its fresh repertoire. Rewriting *The Famous Victories* had to wait until after the first play of the second Henriad, *Richard II*, in 1595; rewriting *Hamlet* and *Lear* took longer still. Apart from the ascriptions to the Queen's on their title pages, there is no evidence that any of these old plays reappeared in their original form on the stage after 1594. But the presence of vestiges from the old Queen's Men in the Chamberlain's does call for some explanation. From the tracking of playtexts, it seems that some players from the Queen's and some from Pembroke's contributed themselves along with their plays in that year to the new Chamberlain's company.

Based with Alleyn's father-in-law, Henslowe, at the Rose, the new Admiral's had a good repertoire. They could add to the Rose's staples, like *The Jew of Malta* and *Friar Bacon*, Alleyn's own stock, which now included *Tamburlaine*, *Doctor Faustus*, and *Cutlack*. They used some plays once performed at the Rose by Strange's and some by the Queen's. Since these plays passed through several companies, they must all have been Henslowe's own property. On the other hand, none of the Sussex's plays in Henslowe's lists for 1594 and none of the Queen's Men's plays brought to their amalgamation with Sussex's in 1594 reappear in the diary. Nor does 'harey the vj'. Most likely these were all taken by the new Chamberlain's. The evidence that Henslowe's lists supply about the short run of the joined companies suggests that to the five-man core of Strange's/Derby's Men, Carey added some of the old Pembroke's (who may later have gone into Sussex's) and a substantial share of the Queen's. Redisposing the Queen's Men in itself helped to endorse his decision to replace the old monopoly with a duopoly. Shakespeare, presumably casting off his allegiance to Southampton in the process, went with his plays to the Lord Chamberlain's Men, which replaced the old Queen's. The plays went with their players. Carey gave his company a rich start.

CHAPTER 5

The Great Divide of 1594

Stepping stones are a help when you need to track your way through muddy waters, and there are not many areas of Shakespeare studies muddier than his relations with Marlowe. Too much of it is lit by the confusing glare of the misleading lights of academic journalism. It needs the careful and measured steps of a Mac Jackson to identify good pathways through the glare and the mud.

Besides the evident reprises of Marlowe's *Jew of Malta* and *Edward II* in *The Merchant of Venice* and *Richard II*, and the allusions in *As You Like It*, theories about interaction between Marlowe and Shakespeare have even extended to finding Marlovian echoes in the *Henry VI* plays, *Titus*, and *Henry V*.[1] There is, however, another association to be made. During his lifetime, Marlowe sold his best-known plays to as many as four different companies of players. In May 1594 they were all put into the hands of a single customer, the Admiral's Men, in a deal that seems to have involved an exchange with some of the existing Shakespeare plays. That was an early testimony to Marlowe's power as a playwright in his own time, and especially his influence with the two great lords, Henry Carey and Charles Howard, who were the government's chief controllers of London's theatre in 1594.[2] Much more remarkably, it appears to show that the organisers of the two officially recognised acting companies set up in 1594, the Lord Chamberlain's and the Lord Admiral's, recognised Marlowe and Shakespeare as the time's two great assets as playwrights. Tracing such an idea demands a positively Jacksonian pathway through the mud.

Original publication: "The Great Divide of 1594," in *Words that Count. Essays on Early Modern Authorship in Honor of MacDonald P. Jackson*, ed. Brian Boyd, University of Delaware Press, Newark, 2004, pp. 29–48

[1] The Marlovian echoes in Shakespeare secured some of Mac's reputation for making the most careful measurements in the arcane practices of language analysis.

[2] For an account of Henry Carey, Lord Hunsdon the Lord Chamberlain, and Charles Howard, his son-in-law the Lord Admiral, and their dealings with the playing companies of the 1580s and 1590s, see Gurr, "Three Reluctant Patrons and Early Shakespeare," *Shakespeare Quarterly* 44 (1993): 159–74. See also the previous chapter in this volume.

Shakespeare's early career as an actor and playwright will be dealt with here only in the context of Marlowe's activities. Marlowe, the more colourful character, whose university degree gave him the ostensible social status of a gentleman, had much more note taken of him in these early years than the countryman Shakespeare. His constant changes of mode in his playwriting – from classical tragedy in *Dido* to heroic tragedy in *Tamburlaine*, religious morality in *Faustus*, satire in *The Jew of Malta*, contemporary political drama in *The Massacre at Paris*, and English history in *Edward II* – seem to have been matched by the frequent changes in his allegiance to the playing companies who bought them. It is as much the story of changing fortunes amongst the playing companies through a turbulent time as of Marlowe's impact on the theatre of his time. Working this story out entails settling, sometimes provisionally, the dates and the sequence of writing for Marlowe's plays, for which the evidence, like so much else about this period, is imperfect, so some of the details offered here are necessarily conjectural. In such mazy marshes tiny details sprout large implications. The plausibility of the story needs to be judged as a whole, in the hope that it will ease the reception of the more speculative parts. The ultimate speculation is just what status Marlowe and Shakespeare had as playwrights a year after Marlowe's hugely sensationalised murder in 1593.

We know that up to his death at the age of twenty-nine Marlowe wrote seven plays and sold them to four different acting companies. On the evidence of its title page and its staging, *Dido Queen of Carthage* was almost certainly the only play that Marlowe wrote for a boy company.[3] A quarto was printed in 1594 as 'Played by the Children of her Majesties Chappell. Written by Christopher Marlowe, and Thomas Nash. Gent.' Given that the title page credits Nashe with a share in its composition, it could date from as late as 1592, when Nashe wrote *Summer's Last Will and Testament* for a boy company. But *Summer's Last Will* was performed for Archbishop Whitgift at Croydon by a boy group who Nashe said had not played for the last year. This must mean that it was a special occasion, and does not suggest that any other play would have been performed then under similar circumstances. The better and more usual assumption is that *Dido* was written much earlier, before the joint Paul's/Chapel boy company was suppressed in 1590, and possibly even before the Chapel Children closed down in 1584. Nashe was at Cambridge from early in 1582 until 1588, when he left

---

[3] In his Revels edition of *Dido Queen of Carthage* and *The Massacre at Paris* (Methuen: London. 1968), H. J. Oliver suggests that the play was written for staging with the actors entering from mansions on each side like the university plays (xxx–xxxi). See also Mary E. Smith, "Staging Marlowe's *Dido Queen of Carthage*," *Studies in English Literature* 17 (1977): 177–90.

for London. In those years he could have collaborated with Marlowe, who graduated BA in 1584 and MA in 1587. Most critics prefer to see *Dido* as a play closely related to Marlowe's university translations of the *Amores*. It has some verbal resemblances to *Faustus*, and may be one of the plays the *Faustus* prologue cites. I am inclined to regard it as Marlowe's first known play, and his only collaboration.

Dido's subsequent history, after its early performance by the Chapel Children, is obscure. It could have joined all the other Marlowe plays in the hands of the Admiral's Men in 1594. The 1594 quarto could have supplied the text for the 'playe of dido & eneus' which the Admiral's Men staged in January 1598, although since no text survives from that performance it is only conjecture that it was Marlowe's. A case might be made for Marlowe's play being on stage in the late 1590s from the faint echoes of it (notably the whiff and wind of Pyrrhus's sword, and the Hyrcanian beast) that occur in Hamlet's recollections of a play of Aeneas's tale to Dido, but no subsequent edition of the play says that it was performed by the Admiral's. Henslowe paid 29 shillings on 3 January 1598 for boys' costumes, and loaned the players another thirty on 8 January 'when they fyrst played dido at nyght'. The inventory of 10 March 1598 mentions a robe for Dido, but also 'i tome of Dido', which would not belong in Marlowe's play as the quarto printed it. At the risk of circular argument (that the post-1594 Admiral's had all of Marlowe's plays including a *Dido* and therefore must have had Marlowe's *Dido*) I would say that the 1598 performance most likely was of Marlowe's play. The performance at night must indicate a special winter showing, possibly at court.

The Admiral's Men were clearly not bothered about having authority to play this *Dido*. Nor did Henslowe pay any money to its author or authors. That may be an important consideration given the strong concern about company ownership of playbooks, and does imply that the Admiral's thought they had the right to play it. A related question is whether they acquired the manuscript from the defunct boy company at some time before 1598 or whether they used the 1594 edition for their script on the grounds that by then they had the right to perform all of Marlowe's plays. The second possibility gains some support from the evidence about the other plays to be considered here.

1 & 2 Tamburlaine were recorded for printing in the Stationers' Register on 14 August 1590. The Register calls them 'twooe commicall discourses', but they were printed in 1590 in octavo as 'Devided into two Tragicall Discourses', and 'sundry times shewed upon Stages in the Citie of London, By the right honorable the Lord Admyrall, his servantes'. Marlowe's name did not appear on either title page. The plays were famous on stage in London from the beginning of 1588. Greene's reference in his preface to *Perimedes the Blacke-Smith* about Tamburlaine 'daring God out of heaven', almost certainly a reference to the end of part 2, indicates that both plays were on stage some time before 29 March of that year, when *Perimedes* was entered in the Stationers' Register. The many references to Tamburlaine in the following years show how famous he became as a stage character. We know that Edward Alleyn, the leading player of the Admiral's Men in the late 1580s, made it his most famous role. And that raises a large question about its early history. Alleyn clearly made the title roles both of the two *Tamburlaine* plays and of *Faustus* his own. But what did he do with them between 1590 and 1594 when he re-formed the Admiral's Men?

On the evidence of the title page for the 1590 printing, the two parts of *Tamburlaine* must have been sold to Alleyn and the Admiral's Men in 1587–88. Marlowe must have written the first part in the years between 1580 and 1587 when he was, however intermittently, at Cambridge. In its way *Tamburlaine* was a Cambridge subject. A number of Cambridge scholars showed interest in the all-conquering Scythian shepherd before Marlowe reached the university. Gabriel Harvey has notes in his copious marginalia which include several indications that Tamburlaine caught his attention. They date from 1566 to about 1590.[4] In 1576 Harvey acquired a copy of a book first printed in 1538, A. P. Gasser's *Historiarum et Chronicorum totius Mundi Epitome*, a synoptic history of the world. Harvey wrote the date 1576 on the title page, 1575 at the end of the dedication, February 1577 on page 277, and 1577 at the end, after the colophon. He annotated the text extensively, most especially against the book's account of Tamburlaine.

Not all of his marginal notes are in the same kind of ink, but they would most likely have been made around 1576 at about the time of his first reading. On page 256, where the text refers to Tamburlaine in the year 1386, 'Tamberlanes Tartarorum Cesar belicossisimus, qui Turcas vicit, & Aegyptum' ('Tamberlane the most belligerent king of the Tartars, who conquered the Turks and Egypt'), Harvey wrote 'Tamerlane oft a Lusty Heard-man, A most valiant & invincible Prynce. His tents ye first day whyte: ye 2 redd: ye 3 black. Bajazctcm Turcarum Imp. in cavea ferrea circumfet, ludibrii causa' ('Bajazeth Emperor of the Turks carried in an iron cage, an object of mockery'). There could hardly be a more succinct summary of the most prominent features of Tamburlaine's story that Marlowe subsequently put on stage, the rise from Scythian shepherd, the three

---

[4] G. C. Moore Smith, *Gabriel Harvey's Marginalia* (Stratford: 1913).

colours of his tents, and the humiliation of Bajazeth. Harvey even seems to have corrected Gasser's spellings into the forms that Marlowe used. On the page before the marginal note on Tamburlaine, by Gasser's 'Paiazites' Harvey noted 'Baiazets, A. Turcarum Imp.', and below the note about Tamburlaine he wrote 'Baiazetes', as a reminder of the account on the previous page. Marlowe followed the Harvey spelling rather than Gasser's. Against 1394 in Gasser Harvey corrected 'Celapinus' to 'Calapinus', the spelling preferred in Marlowe's text. It may of course be coincidence that in the same book Harvey has a marginal note about another of Marlowe's subjects: 'Joannes Faustius ... artem imprimendi libros' ('John Faust, very learned in books'). The book was Harvey's property, and the notes are simply indications of his personal interests. Gasser was not one of Marlowe's sources for *Tamburlaine*. But Harvey's notes do make it clear that both Tamburlaine and Faustus were talking-points in the Cambridge of the 1570s and 1580s.

So the composition of at least the first *Tamburlaine* play came directly out of Marlowe's time at Cambridge. He sold it to the Lord Admiral's Men in 1587 or so, and they performed it in London and around the country for the next few years. The same thing happened to *Faustus*. Where, though, if he was at Cambridge, did Marlowe first meet the plays and the playing companies that set him on the path of writing for the popular players? Cambridge had a long tradition of academic playwriting and performance, including plays about Dido,[5] but Marlowe's were not conceived for the same venue as Legge's *Ricardus Tertius*. The roads Marlowe took between Canterbury and Cambridge and between Cambridge and Paris run through London. It is much more likely that he found his first customers there, and certainly there that he must have seen the plays that stirred him to improve on them. The company that bought his next three plays was there too. It is unlikely that he met the Admiral's Men in Cambridge, though he may have seen them there. Despite the chronic opposition of the university authorities to allowing any performances in the town by professional players, the Town Treasurers' Books show that the Queen's Men played in Cambridge in 1584–85, when they received 24s.8d, but the Admiral's Men are not in the town records till they received 10s in 1588–89.[6]

---

[5] A play about Dido by a Cambridge Fellow, Edward Halliwell, was acted before the Queen there in 1564. William Gager's *Dido* was acted at Oxford in 1583. See Oliver, *Dido*, xxxix.

[6] See Records of Early English Drama (REED) *Cambridge*, ed. Alan Nelson, 2 vols. (Toronto: Univ. of Toronto Press, 1989), 1:313, 323. E. K. Chambers, *The Elizabethan Stage*, 4 vols. (Oxford: Oxford Univ. Press: 1923), 2:135 says that the Admiral's went to Cambridge in 1586–87, information he derived from J. T. Murray, *English Dramatic Companies*, 2 vols. (London: 1910), who notes them as playing there in 1586. But Nelson has no record of any visit before 1588–89.

The Queen's Men received 30s from Trinity College for a midsummer show 'by appoinctment' in 1586, a visit that probably coincided with a town performance, when an unnamed company of players 'yat plaid before Master Maior' got the exceptionally handsome reward of 30s.[7] The surviving evidence indicates that through Marlowe's years the Mayor of Cambridge welcomed the Queen's Men but not the Admiral's. So the first question about Marlowe's customers for his plays is why he sold his *Tamburlaine*s to the Admiral's and not the Queen's.

In 1586 the Queen's Men were the outstanding company of their time, with unique privileges. Formed by royal decree in 1583, the company was set up with the best two or three players from each of the companies of the great lords, Leicester's, Warwick's, Oxford's, and Sussex's. They took Richard Tarlton, the most famous clown, and the most famous tragedians, Knell and Bentley. Their supreme status was unchallenged for most of the decade. Town records consistently show them being paid more than the other companies. In 1584, on the grounds that they had been formed to entertain the Queen, the Lord Chamberlain secured special and unique access from the Lord Mayor for them to play in London, making them the only company officially permitted to act in the city.[8]

It is tempting to speculate why Marlowe chose to sell the two *Tamburlaine*s to the Admiral's rather than the Queen's. The latter might have rejected his offering, though if so it was a commercial misjudgment of some size. On the other hand it is possible that the prologue's loud scorn of the 'jigging veins of rhyming mother-wits' was partly a crack at the Queen's performing practices with its clown Tarlton, famous for his doggerel song-and-dance acts at the end of his company's plays, and partly a signal of approval for the Admiral's practices. Marlowe's friend Nashe reports a brush with Tarlton in the mid-1580s, boasting in *Strange News* that Tarlton had deferred to his 'simple judgement' in 'matters of wit'.[9] Tarlton died in September 1588. Marlowe might have had a firsthand encounter to warrant his objection to jigging moitherers of wit. But that is hardly the best basis for concluding that Marlowe chose to avoid the Queen's Men as his customers. Every adult company had a clown and offered jigs. Since the prologue's distaste is echoed by the printer, who in his address to the reader claimed to have omitted 'some fond and frivolous jestures', the octavo's prologue may have been addressed to the reader rather than to the theatre

[7] Nelson, *Cambridge*, 1.319.
[8] Scott McMillin and Sally-Beth MacLean, *The Queen's Men and their Plays* (Cambridge: Cambridge Univ. Press, 1999).
[9] Nashe, Thomas, *Works*, ed. R. B. McKerrow, 5 vols. (Oxford: Clarendon Press, 1958), 1:319.

audience. Yet it does sound like a Marlovian play-opening. It is similar to the prologue to *Faustus*, which celebrates other stage successes. The Admiral's had no clown so famous as Tarlton. We should acknowledge the possibility that Marlowe opted to sell his plays to the Admiral's Company rather than the Queen's, and that the prologue to *Tamburlaine* indicates the main reason. What negotiations there were before the sale we do not know. A faint whiff of sour grapes rises from the prologue.

Marlowe must have met the Admiral's Men during one of their stays in London. In the 1580s the professional companies were still accustomed to spend most of their time travelling, playing for fairly brief periods in the London playhouses. Not until 1594 did any base themselves permanently there and travel only when they had to. On their travels they rarely spent more than a couple of days in each town or great house before moving on. Since Marlowe could hardly have pursued his first customers around the country, London, the location for their longest runs, was by far the likeliest meeting-place. The better companies tended to work near London through the autumn, visiting the rich East Anglia towns or Kent and Sussex instead of the more remote parts of the country, because it kept them within reach of the Master of the Revels, who had to see their plays before choosing which of them would entertain the Court over the long Christmas season. The Admiral's are recorded at Dover in June 1585 and at Leicester that autumn, but they performed at Court on 27 December 1585 and 6 January 1586. In 1586–87 they visited Coventry, Bath, York, Norwich, Ipswich, Exeter, Southampton, and Leicester. They did not perform at Court that winter, but are nonetheless reported as being in London in a letter of 25 January 1587. The letter, addressed to Walsingham, complains that the playhouses are full and the churches empty because 'the players billes are sett up in sondry places of the cittie, some in the name of her Majesties menne, some the Earl of Leicester, some the Earl of Oxford, the Lord Admyralles, and dyvers others'.[10]

The most likely time for Marlowe to meet the Admiral's Men would have been during their stay in London in and after January 1587. A letter by Philip Gawdy dated 16 November suggests that by then Marlowe had made his bargain with his first customers for both *Tamburlaine* plays. Gawdy describes how a play suspiciously like *2 Tamburlaine* with its execution of the Governor of Babylon caused an accident when staged in London by the Admiral's Men:

> My L. Admyrall his men and players having a devyse in ther playe to tye one of their fellowes to a poste and so to shoote him to deathe, having borrowed

---

[10] *The Elizabethan Stage*, 4:303–4.

their callyvers one of the players handes swerved his peece being charged with bullett missed the fellowe he aymed at and killed a chyld, and a woman great with chyld forthwith, and hurt an other man in the head very soore.[11]

Even if the play was not 2 *Tamburlaine*, the letter shows that the Admiral's were in London that autumn, a likely time for Marlowe to sell them at least the first of his two plays, and possibly *Faustus* soon after.[12] The similarity of its subsequent history to that of the two *Tamburlaine* plays supports the view that it was written at broadly the same time, near the commonly accepted date of 1588.

If Alleyn, as chief player for the Admiral's Men, bought the two *Tamburlaines* and *Faustus* for them to perform in 1587–88, a deep puzzle remains. Why did the three plays never appear thereafter with Alleyn in the repertory of Strange's Men, the so-called amalgamated company of Strange's and the Admiral's, while they played at the Rose in 1592 and 1593? Who performed these notorious plays between their first celebrity with the early company of Admiral's Men and their reappearance in Henslowe's lists for the new Admiral's Men after May 1594? Alleyn himself was certainly with Henslowe at the Rose from early 1592 – he married Henslowe's stepdaughter that October. But he was then a member of Strange's, not the Admiral's, and Henslowe made no record of *Tamburlaine* being performed at the Rose before 30 August 1594, nor of *Faustus* before the end of September 1594. It was not because they were considered old or undesirable stuff: they were and remained for decades the company's favourite plays. *Tamburlaine* appeared fourteen times at the Rose in the fifteen months from mid-1594, and *Faustus* twenty-four times over the next three years. They became the defining features of the Admiral's company repertory. So who had these three plays through the years from before February 1592, when Henslowe's records begin, up to August 1594?

References from the period are distinctly patchy, but the timing of allusions to *Tamburlaine* suggests that there may well have been an interim between 1591 and 1594 when the *Tamburlaines* and *Faustus* were off the London stage. *Tamburlaine* was spoken of with unique frequency, and yet no reference appeared for three years, from 1593 to 1596. After Greene first named it late in 1587, he renewed the allusion in 1587–88, 1589 and 1591. Peele named the play in 1588–89 and 1589, and Nashe named the character in 1592. Three anonymous plays mentioned him in c.1590, 1591, and

---

[11] Ibid., 2:135.
[12] The date of *Faustus* is normally set at 1588, although W. W. Greg made a case for 1592 in his parallel texts edition (Oxford: 1950). The most tangible evidence is in MacD. P. Jackson's "Three Old Ballads and the Date of *Doctor Faustus*," *Journal of the Australasian Universities Language and Literature Association* 36 (1971): 187–200, which argues for a date before 28 February 1589.

c.1592. In 1593 Nashe, Drayton and Harvey named him, Harvey in connection with Marlowe's death, when a libel pinned on a church door on 5 May 1593 was signed '*Per.* Tamburlaine.' Then there is a notable gap up to 1596, when Nashe again referred to him, and four mentions in 1597, by Shakespeare, Donne, Joseph Hall, and 'E.S.', a satirist. Jonson cited him in 1598, Marston in 1599 and c. 1599, Dekker twice in 1599 and twice again, and an anonymous play cited him in 1600. Thereafter there were regular references, especially in plays in 1605 and 1606, and later in other contexts. *Faustus* was almost equally celebrated, but its earliest mention is in 1596.[13] In all that noise the silence from 1593 to 1596 is remarkable.

Both roles were tied to Alleyn.[14] Yet Nashe's praise of Alleyn in *Pierce Penilesse* in 1592 makes no mention of any specific role he played, unless he was the Talbot of *1 Henry VI* that Nashe praises in an adjacent passage. Thomas Heywood's prologue to *The Jew of Malta* as late as 1633 remembered Alleyn as the creator of both Tamburlaine and Barabas, but that was long after, and presumably recalls the years from 1594 when Heywood himself was playing and writing for the Henslowe team. Alleyn was the leading player in the earlier Admiral's Men, in 1588–91, and that was the company that owned the *Tamburlaine* plays when they were printed in 1590. But what happened to them between 1591 and their resurfacing in the new Admiral's Men's repertory in 1594?

The absence of any mention in 1594 and 1595 needs explanation, and one is to hand. Allowing for a little time lag for writing and printing, the gap matches their even stranger absence from Henslowe's *Diary* up to mid-1594. The silence through 1594–95 fits quite closely with the absence of either play from Henslowe's lists between 1592 and 1594. If the lapse into silence was because the plays were not being performed in London, it suggests that they were in the hands of the residual Admiral's company travelling around

---

[13] See Richard Levin, "The Contemporary Perception of Marlowe's *Tamburlaine*," *Medieval and Renaissance Drama in England* 1 (1984): 51–70. The earliest references are: 1587 Robert Greene, *Perimedes*; 1587–88 Greene, *Alphonsus of Aragon* 4.3 (G2v); 1588–89 George Peele, *Battle of Alcazar* (1.2.214–15); 1589 Greene, *Menaphon* (F2r); 1589 Peele, *Farewell to Norris and Drake* (A3r); c. 1590 *George a Greene* (1.1.46–49); 1591 *The Troublesome Raigne of King John* (A2r); 1591 Greene, *Farewell to Folly* (A4r); 1592 Thomas Nashe, *Strange News* (F4r); c. 1592 *Selimus* (2344–46); 5 May 1593 "Dutch Church libel"; 1593 Gabriel Harvey, *A New Letter of Notable Contents* (D3r, D4r); 1593 Nashe, *Christ's Tears over Jerusalem* (A4r); 1593 Michael Drayton, *Idea* (172–73); 1596 Nashe, *Have With You to Saffron Walden* (S4v); 1597 Joseph Hall, *Virgidemiarum;* 1597 Pistol in *2 Henry IV*, 2.4.164–65; 1597 E.S., *The Discovery of the Knights of the Post* (C2v); 1597 Donne, *The Calme* (33); 1598 Jonson, *Every Man In his Humour* (3.2.16–22); c. 1599 Marston, *Histriomastix* (act 5); 1599 Dekker, *Shoemaker's Holiday* (5.4.51–54); 1599 Dekker, *Old Fortunatus* (1.1.187–95); 1599 Marston, *Antonio and Mellida* (Induction); 1600 *The Blind Beggar of Bednal Green* (G2r); 1601 Dekker, *Satiromastix* (4.2.28–89, 4.3.169–71); 1601 Dekker, *Blurt Master Constable* (A3r).

[14] See Samuel Rowlands, *The Knave of Clubs* (London: 1609), 29.

the country while Alleyn was in London with Strange's and Henslowe. The old Admiral's and its plays did not return to the London stage until some of its members joined Alleyn in the new Admiral's Company in May 1594, which reunited Alleyn with his old roles. Such a reading of the evidence is supported by the fact that Marlowe's last three plays went through different hands from the famous three that followed *Dido*.

The Jew of Malta and *The Massacre at Paris* took a quite different path from the *Tamburlaines* and *Faustus*.[15] Machevil's reference in his prologue to the Guise being dead fixes *The Jew of Malta's* writing to a time soon after December 1588, when the notorious French Duke died. *The Massacre* is the story of his death. Both *The Jew* and the play about the Guise must postdate the two *Tamburlaines* and *Faustus*, if only because the history of their ownership was different. What happened to *The Jew* in its first years is unknown, and the date of *The Massacre* is uncertain, though it was certainly written at the beginning of the 1590s. Their difference from the three previous plays is that both were in the hands of Strange's Men at the Rose by 1593. *The Massacre at Paris*, or 'the tragedey of the guyes' as Henslowe more commonly called it, is first recorded with excellent takings as a 'ne' play, performed by Strange's during their brief return to London in January 1593. Its next appearance in Henslowe was as an Admiral's play in June 1594. Henslowe's records position it with *The Jew of Malta*, well apart from the *Tamburlaines* and *Faustus*.

Henslowe records several performances of *The Jew of Malta* at the Rose by Strange's Men between February 1592 and February 1593, when the plague caused a long break. It reappeared in February 1594, now performed by Sussex's Men. It was staged again in the joint or alternate performances by Sussex's and the Queen's Men in April 1594, but the next month it was an Admiral's play. It reappeared in the joint or alternate season of the Admiral's and Chamberlain's Men in May 1594, and thereafter with some frequency

---

[15] *The Jew of Malta* was entered for printing in the Stationers' Register on 17 May 1594, but was not printed. A second Register entry dated 20 November 1632 preceded its publication in 1633. The title page for that printing says it was played 'by her Majesties Servants at the Cock-pit'. *Henslowe's Diary*, eds. R. A. Foakes and R. T. Rickert (Cambridge: Cambridge Univ. Press, 1962), lists Strange's playing it seventeen times between 26 February 1592 and 1 February 1593, Sussex's playing it with the Queen's on 3 and 8 April 1594, the Admiral's on 14 May 1594, with the Chamberlain's on 6 and 15 June 1594, then thirteen times on their own from 25 June 1594 to 23 June 1596. The 1598 inventory lists a 'cauderm' for the final scene. *The Massacre at Paris* was printed in an undated octavo as 'The Massacre at Paris: With the Death of the Duke of Guise. As it was plaide by the right honourable the Lord high Admirall his Servants. Written by Christopher Marlow' (the first time his name was used). Its allocation to the Admiral's Men probably fixes its printing to between 1594 and 1596, when the Lord Admiral became the Earl of Nottingham. The Admiral's Men performed it on 19 June 1594, and nine more times that year.

exclusively as an Admiral's play. The conclusion normally drawn from these records is that the playbook was owned by Henslowe himself, who loaned it out to whichever company was playing at his Rose. That may well be the case. If so, it makes *The Jew* unique among Marlowe's plays as a book sold to an impresario, not to a company. It seems not to have followed quite the same track as *The Massacre at Paris*, since although the later play was, like *The Jew*, performed by Strange's Men, it has links with Pembroke's, who also had Marlowe's last play, *Edward II*.

There is an alternative reading of these hints, though. Alleyn was the player who first made *Tamburlaine* famous. If he lost the early Marlowe plays when he transferred his allegiance to Strange's Men and Henslowe, Strange's acquisition of the next two Marlowe plays may indicate that Marlowe stayed loyal to Alleyn with his new company, and that it was Alleyn who secured *The Jew of Malta* for Henslowe. That embeds it in the muddy issue of the so-called 'amalgamation' of Alleyn with Strange's Men, which needs some careful washing. It relates to the ownership both of *The Jew* and *The Massacre at Paris*. Alleyn may have secured *The Massacre* either for Henslowe the playhouse owner or for Strange's the playing company. That possibility, however, depends on yet another teasing question to which there is no clear answer.

The last purchasers of a Marlowe play were a new company, Pembroke's Men. *Edward II*, written in 1592, was printed in 1594 as Pembroke's. They were a mysterious grouping of players, coming to prominence suddenly at the beginning of 1592, and 'breaking' for lack of money, according to a letter from Henslowe to Alleyn, on their travels in the late summer of 1593. Marlowe's play must have been sold to them while they enjoyed their brief London eminence in 1592–93. Recollections of other Pembroke Men's plays, *2 and 3 Henry VI* and *Edward II* itself, can be found in the only existing text of *The Massacre*.[16] So was *The Massacre* a Pembroke's play before Strange's played it at the Rose in January 1593? Or did it go to them afterwards? There is no sign that, unlike *The Massacre*, *Edward II was* ever a Strange's play. The *Diary*'s records for this time are detailed, and are unlikely to have omitted a mention if *Edward II* had been played by Strange's along with *The Massacre* in January 1593. We must assume either that Strange's for some reason passed *The Massacre* on to Pembroke's after January 1593, or that Pembroke's had it up to 1593 and then passed it to Strange's. It is also possible that one or more of the players who wrote out the text of *The Massacre* for its printing in 1594 had at some point switched allegiance between

---

[16] Oliver, *Massacre*, lv–lvii.

the two companies. The player John Holland was in both, and might have had knowledge of plays from the two repertories.[17]

Any of these explanations would add to the evidence that Marlowe switched his allegiance between 1588 and 1589 from Alleyn and the Admiral's to Strange's with Alleyn, and then moved on to Pembroke's in 1592 or so. That broadly fits the other evidence of Marlowe's writing career at this time. It is certain that he was in London for some part of 1589 when he was writing *The Jew of Malta*, because he was arrested and imprisoned in Shoreditch that September along with Thomas Watson for his part in a street affray and murder. Shoreditch, besides being a suburb noted for its thieves and whorehouses, was the location of the other two playhouses of the time. Marlowe was also in London in January 1592 in the wake of his difficulties at Flushing over counterfeiting, and in Shoreditch that May, when the Constable and Sub-Constable had him bound over to keep the peace.[18] In Shoreditch Marlowe was near the Theatre, not in Southwark near the Rose. That fits his *Edward II* going to Pembroke's Men, who most likely played at the Theatre through 1592. It was also the year when he claimed the familiar acquaintance of two noble enthusiasts of the theatre, Thomas Percy, Earl of Northumberland and Lord Strange. The records of the case in which Marlowe was involved with Richard Baines over counterfeiting at Flushing include a statement that 'The scholar [Marlowe] sais himself to be very wel known to the Earle of Northumberland and my lord Strang.'[19] Lord Strange's Men were at the Rose with *The Jew of Malta* from the beginning of 1592. Some time in that year his loyalty switched from Bankside and Strange's to Shoreditch and Pembroke's.

Kyd's letters to the Privy Council in 1593 about his contacts with Marlowe also mention a noble patron: 'My first acquaintance with this Marlowe, rose upon his bearing name to serve my Lord although his Lordship never knewe his service, but in writing for his plaiers, ffor never cold my Lord endure his name, or sight, when he had heard of his conditions.' Kyd's lord may have been either Strange or Pembroke. Later Kyd claims 'I have served [my Lord] almost theis vi yeres nowe,'[20] i.e., 1587–1593, which

---

[17] John Holland is named as a player in *John of Bordeaux*, a Strange's play, and also in the Folio version of *2 Henry VI*, a Pembroke's play.

[18] Mark Eccles, *Christopher Marlowe in London* (Cambridge, Mass.: Harvard Univ. Press, 1934), 179.

[19] R. B. Wernham, "Christopher Marlowe at Flushing in 1592," *ELR* 6 (1976): 344–45.

[20] Millar McLure, *Marlowe. The Critical Heritage* (Routledge: London, 1979), 34. Kyd's patronage for the six years 1587–93 is thought to have come from the Pembroke circle and especially Mary Herbert, who in 1591–92 was translating a closet play by Garnier, and commissioned Daniel to write its sequel. What that suggests about Marlowe's relations with the Earl of Pembroke and his company of players is unclear. Kyd seems never to have written a play for either Pembroke's or Strange's Men.

would make Pembroke more likely than Strange. A switch of Marlowe's allegiance in the course of 1592 from Strange and Strange's Men to Pembroke and Pembroke's Men fits these testimonies. Marlowe certainly had connections with three different companies, the Admiral's, Strange's, and Pembroke's, up to 1593, and with one or more of their patrons. Which company had which plays, and what transfers there may have been subsequently, are questions that need to be disentangled by looking at the history of these companies, and particularly at what is still commonly called the 'amalgamated company' of the Admiral's and Strange's, that played at the Rose from 1591 to 1594.[21]

That the Admiral's and Strange's Men were separate companies at the end of 1589 is testified by a letter from the Lord Mayor of London, Sir John Harte, to Burghley, written on 6 November of that year. In it he reports his latest attempt to close the playhouses the day before. He 'sent for suche players as I could here of', who turned out to be 'the L. Admeralles and the L. Straunges players'. They responded in radically different ways to his order to stop playing. 'The L. Admeralles players very dutifullie obeyed, but the others in very Contemptuous manner departing from me, went to the Crosse keys and played that afternoon.'[22] That variation in the behaviour of the two companies provides a date when they were clearly not yet merged or amalgamated. The chief evidence for a subsequent 'amalgamation' is based on two pieces of evidence: the record of Court performances, and the theatre 'plot' of *2 The Seven Deadly Sins*. The latter is a tiring-house paper outlining the scenes of the play, and containing the names of most of the players in the cast. It provides some very specific evidence for the membership of the company performing the play. But what company, and when the play was performed, are not as clear as we might wish.

Sorting out the evidence about playing companies and their membership in these changeable years is a tortuous exercise in the kaleidoscope principle. Shake the fragments of evidence and you make one pattern, then shake them up again and you see a different pattern. The old pattern found in *2 Seven Deadly Sins* indicated a company membership amalgamated from two former companies, the Admiral's and Strange's. This and the inclusion of Richard Burbage's name led to the conclusion that it was written in the period up to May 1591, when Alleyn had a sharp quarrel with Burbage's father. Scott McMillin more recently shook the kaleidoscope to dislodge that pattern, suggesting that a better date might be either 1593 or June

---

[21] Andrew Gurr, "The Chimera of Amalgamation," *Theatre Research International* 18 (1993): 85–93.
[22] *The Elizabethan Stage*, 4:305.

1594.²³ Shaken again, the fragments make a different and prettier pattern. There are some items of evidence that seem misplaced in both patterns.

The company's name came from its patron, Lord Strange, but with one player who insisted on wearing a different livery. Having two liveries in one group is what made commentators label them a joint company. When performing in London they were invariably Lord Strange's Men to their contemporaries. Henslowe called the group with Alleyn in it that played at the Rose in 1592–93 'my lord Stranges mene' on and after 19 February 1592. At Court, where the patron's name was most likely to be known, they were also called Strange's: 'George Ottewell and his Companye the Lorde Straunge his players', on 27 December 1590 and 16 February 1591.²⁴ In the 1591–92 season for their six performances they were again Strange's ('ye Servauntes of ye Lo. Strange'), and again for their three in 1592–93. A Privy Council licence dated 6 May 1593 permitting the group to play in spite of the plague in places not less than seven miles from London, names 'Edward Allen, servaunt to the right honorable the Lord Highe Admiral, William Kemp, Thomas Pope, John Heminges, Augustine Phillipes and George Brian, being al one companie, servauntes to our verie good the lord Strainge'. The note specifically says that Alleyn is the Lord Admiral's servant, but that he is part of 'al one companie', the company known as Strange's.²⁵

The plot of *2 The Seven Deadly Sins* contains an exceptionally large number of players' names. Some of the major players like George Attewell, named in Court records as leader of Strange's in 1591, and the clown Will Kemp are not specified. Nor is Alleyn. This may be because the main speaking parts were self-evident, so that only the lesser players needed naming. Pope, Bryan, and Phillips, all on the Privy Council licence of 6 May 1593 as Strange's, are there, as is Richard Cowley, who is mentioned in a letter of Alleyn's in 1593. Other names are Richard Burbage, Will Sly, John Duke,

---

²³ Scott McMillin, "Building Stories: Greg, Fleay, and the Plot of *2 Seven Deadly Sins*," *MRDE* 4 (1989): 53–56.
²⁴ *Malone Society Collections* 6 (1961): 27.
²⁵ Other references confirm the company's patent. *Henslowe's Diary* has (276) a letter from Alleyn to his wife dated 1 August, almost certainly in 1593, from Bristol. It mentions Richard Cowley as deliverer of a letter from his wife, and Thomas Pope's kinsman as bearer of his letter. Both Cowley and Pope are named in the *2 Seven Deadly Sins* plot. Alleyn asks for further letters to be sent 'by the cariers of shrowsbery or to west chester or to york to be keptt till my lord Stranges players com'. Joan Alleyn and Henslowe wrote to him as 'one of my lorde Stranges Players' probably in the same month of 1593, and again to the same address on 14 August, having heard that he had been too sick to play at Bath. On 28 September Joan and her stepfather wrote again, chiefly about the plague and household matters, and with news of the impoverished return of Pembroke's Men to London. This too was addressed 'unto my welbeloved husband mr edward allen one of my lord Stranges players'.

Thomas Goodall, John Holland, Robert Pallant, John Sincler, a 'Kitt' and a 'Harry' who may have been Christopher Beeston and Henry Condell, and a 'Vincent'. Eight of these, Burbage, Sly, Duke, Goodall, Holland, Sincler, Beeston, and Condell, later became members of the Chamberlain's Men with Shakespeare, along with the Strange's men of 1593, Pope, Bryan, and Phillips. Several of them, including Holland and Sincler, seem to have belonged to Pembroke's in 1592–93. Judging from their absence from the names specified as Strange's Men in the 1593 Privy Council licence, Burbage, Sly and others may have been in Pembroke's too.

The chief uncertainty is whether Alleyn was one of the leading players omitted from the plot list. Other senior Admiral's men such as James Tunstall and Richard Jones are not listed either. I think this makes it unlikely that Alleyn was with the group when the plot was made up. If so, the presence of men later associated with Pembroke's fits it too before May 1591 when Alleyn split from Burbage's father James and his Theatre. Pembroke's Company first appeared some time after that date, most likely as a new company set up to occupy the vacated Theatre. Alleyn could therefore have been absent from the *Seven Deadly Sins* list because he had not yet joined Strange's at the Rose, suggesting that the manuscript must have been made for performance in 1590–91. Its presence in the Henslowe papers would thus be a consequence of Strange's long stay at the Rose, and of the new Admiral's Men's inheritance of the demised Strange's property in 1594.

The records of Court performances set out the bones of this history. The Admiral's, strong with Alleyn and his Marlowe plays, played once at Court at the end of the winter revels, on 3 March 1590. In the next Christmas season their only appearances were joint ones with Strange's, on 27 December 1590 and 16 February 1591, whereas the Queen's Men played five times. After that came Alleyn's quarrel with Burbage and his transfer to Strange's. The residual Admiral's then disappeared into the country until 1594. Alleyn's presence strengthened Strange's considerably, because in the 1591–92 season at Court they were clearly the top company. They appeared six times to one by the Queen's, one by Sussex's and one by Hertford's. In 1592–93 they appeared three times to Pembroke's twice and the Queen's once. There is no doubt that through the two seasons from late 1591 the Master of the Revels considered Strange's Men to be the strongest of all the companies, largely thanks to the presence of Alleyn with his Admiral's livery. The earlier Marlowe plays were off with the residual Admiral's in the country, but by then the Court could have seen them already.

The following winter, 1593–94, saw only one Court performance, by the Queen's Men. Pembroke's had broken up, Strange's did not appear, and Sussex's, then occupying the Rose, were not used either. The residual

Admiral's was nothing without Alleyn, and did not appear in London or at Court until it was reconstituted in May 1594 with Alleyn once again as its leader. It was that season's paucity of Christmas shows, the Lord Chamberlain's chief duty to his ruler, that prompted him with his son-in-law the Lord Admiral to set up the new companies in May 1594.

Evidence from the provincial records of the companies supports this reading of the runes.[26] It is possible that on tour the 'amalgamation' at the Rose could have split into its component parts, with Alleyn taking his patent along with some of Strange's to travel as the Admiral's Men while the others toured as Strange's. Unfortunately no names of players are supplied in guildhall records to help this supposition. I think that it is in any case a misconception. An Admiral's company is recorded as touring consistently throughout 1591–93. The Admiral's who visited New Romney on 26 June 1590, Faversham in the same year (*MSC* VII. 140, 62), and Gloucester in 1590–91 (*REED* 312), must have been the group including Alleyn before he left to join Strange's. After that the remnant Admiral's company touring from 1591 to early 1594 generally received far less in payment than Lord Strange's. It is recorded at Bath (*ES* II. 120n) and Folkestone (*MSC* VII.71) in 1591–92, Norwich (*REED*, Norwich, 103), Faversham and Folkestone in 1592–93, and Lydd in 1593–94 (*MSC* VII.63, 71, 110). Whereas Strange's at Faversham in 1592–93 received twenty shillings, the Admiral's received only ten. As the remnant company it was evidently less highly regarded. But without Alleyn did the old Admiral's keep the early Marlowe playbooks? The two companies were not entirely separated, possibly because of their plays. The merger at Court in the 1591–92 season seems to have continued occasionally in the country too. Two records exist indicating that both companies did play at the same town, possibly in a shared performance, at Shrewsbury after Michaelmas 1591 (*ES* II.120n) and at Ipswich on 7 August 1592 (*MSC* II.3 277). It is a great pity that the guildhall accountants were more concerned with the name of the company's patron than those of the players or the plays performed.

In the absence of an 'amalgamation' between the Admiral's with their *Tamburlaine* plays and Strange's with *The Jew of Malta*, I would argue that Alleyn lost his right to play Tamburlaine and Faustus when he left

---

[26] The evidence about the companies touring is far from complete. Nearly half of the planned volumes of the Records of Early English Drama (*REED*) are now out, but many venues, towns and great houses are still unrecorded. *Malone Society Collections (MSC)* have some records, and J. T. Murray's two-volume work published in 1910 still gives some usefully broad coverage. Chambers, *The Elizabethan Stage*, has some summary notes. The notes supplied in the text here refer to the *REED* volumes for particular towns and counties, *MSC* covering Ipswich and Kent. It might be added that where Chambers states that 'therlle of Darbys players and . . . the Lorde Admirals players, the ij amongste' were together at Ipswich 7 March 1594 (*Elizabethan Stage* 2:120n), this entry is not in *MSC*.

the Admiral's to join Strange's, and that in consequence Marlowe's earlier plays were not seen on the London stages between late 1591 and 1594. Why though did Alleyn keep his livery as an Admiral's man while he worked consistently for three years with Strange's? In the 1580s and 1590s, as government regulation tightened, town authorities insisted on seeing the players' patents before giving them leave to play. The names inscribed for each company in guildhall records confirm that. So the possession of the right to wear a great lord's livery was a prerequisite for travelling. That may explain why Alleyn kept his Admiral's livery while playing in Strange's company. It gave him an insurance, a licence to work separately if need be. And need there eventually was. In the event it gave him the right to renew his service for the Lord Admiral by forming a new company under his name in May 1594. And that is where we finally meet the great divide and the lumping together of all Marlowe's and all Shakespeare's plays written up to 1594 in spite of the different companies that owned them.

There is no evidence about who played in the remnant Admiral's group in the travelling years. The membership of the Admiral's up to May 1591 amounted in identifiable names only to Alleyn, Richard Jones, and James Tunstall. Tunstall reappeared in the new Admiral's after May 1594, and probably led the remnant company through the intervening years. Richard Jones travelled on the continent in 1592–93, returning to rejoin the new Admiral's in 1594. The others in the new company were drawn from a variety of groups. Thomas Downton came from Derby's, John Singer probably from the Queen's, of which he had been a founder member in 1583 and which he was still with in 1588. Richard Alleyn, Edward's brother, who was also in the Admiral's by 1597, was probably a Queen's man in 1594 (*ES* II.115). Of the other new Admiral's Men, Edward Dutton, Edward Juby, Martin Slater, and Thomas Towne, there is no earlier record. They could have been members of the touring group through 1591–94.

All this has a strong bearing on the ownership of Marlowe's plays. The Admiral's Men's plays that were in Alleyn's hands up to 1591 ought to have gone with him into the re-ordered Strange's had it really been an amalgamation, but they did not. The appearance of playbooks for the two *Tamburlaine*s and *Faustus* in the resources of the 1594 Admiral's indicates that they came into the new group with the leading tourers and their playbooks. The only other explanation is that Alleyn himself kept his most valuable playbooks for nearly three years unused while he played in the other company. That is unlikely. At the Rose Strange's company had its own resources, including two new Marlowe plays. *The Jew of Malta* and *The Massacre at Paris*, along with Talbot in *1 Henry VI* and *Titus Andronicus*, might have given Strange's enough resources to warrant Alleyn withholding his most famous plays from them, but I suspect that they remained with the touring Admiral's Men. We conclude that Alleyn took advantage of the reshuffle of May 1594 to draw the residual Admiral's company into the new Admiral's group, partly at least so that he could renew his famous roles in the early Marlowe plays.

Marlowe's change of allegiance between the companies is worthy of note for two reasons. The exceptional range of subjects and genres Marlowe chose for his plays does suggest some variety in the companies he wrote for. That point has been submerged by the fact that the whole Marlowe corpus of plays ended up in the hands of the Rose company and its successors. Their later ownership by the one company has been projected backwards to iron out the discrepancies in their earlier history. Clarifying Marlowe's career is one reason for carefully tracking the customers for the plays. The other is to explain how they could all have ended up in the hands of the new Admiral's.

The Lord Chamberlain's action in setting up a new company in May 1594 with Shakespeare in it is well known, but his motives are not. The recent deaths of some major patrons (Sussex on 14 December 1593 and more significantly Carey's relative Ferdinando Strange, now Earl of Derby, on 16 April), and the trouble he had setting up the Queen's Christmas entertainment through the previous season, led Lord Chamberlain Carey to set up what Richard Dutton has called a duopoly,[27] modelled on the Queen's Men's monopoly of eleven years before. With his son-in-law the Lord Admiral he set up a pair of new companies,[28] with players drawn from all the major groups: Strange's, the Admiral's, Pembroke's, Sussex's, the Queen's Men, and possibly others. Carey used as his precedent the establishment of the Queen's Men eleven years before, when the best players were taken from each of the leading companies of the time. He set his own company at the Theatre, whose owner had worn his own livery since the 1580s, with the owner's son as its chief player. His son-in-law Charles Howard set up the other company led by the player who still wore his livery, Alleyn, at Alleyn's father-in-law's playhouse the Rose.[29]

The performances and play titles noted in Henslowe's *Diary* for the first half of 1594 give some indication of the companies drawn on for

---

[27] Dutton, *Mastering the Revels: The Regulation and Censorship of English Renaissance Drama* (Basingstoke: Macmillan, 1991), 111.

[28] See Gurr, *The Shakespearian Playing Companies* (Oxford: Clarendon Press, 1996), 65–73.

[29] This story is told in more detail in Gurr, "Patrons." James Burbage was wearing Carey's livery in 1584, when the Privy Council tried to have his Theatre pulled down.

the new set-up. In those months four companies used the Rose. Between 27 December 1593 and 6 February 1594 Sussex's performed nine plays that appear in the *Diary* only for that run, including *George a Greene*, printed in 1599 as a Sussex's play, and *Friar Francis*, which Heywood in his *Apology* reported as belonging to Sussex's. *Titus Andronicus* also appeared for the first time, if the earlier '*Titus*' that Henslowe records for Strange's was *Titus and Vespasian*. *The Fair Maid of Italy* also appears for the first time as a Sussex's play. Only *The Jew of Malta*, a regular in the *Diary* since the first Strange's entries at the beginning of 1592, seems not to have been a play of Sussex's own. Then in the brief run when Sussex's joined up with the Queen's Men at Easter 1594, they performed five plays. Two of these, *The Jew* and *Friar Bacon and Friar Bungay*, had been at the Rose before, one was a Sussex's title, *The Fair Maid*, and one other, *King Leir*, later appeared in print as a Queen's Men's play. A further play, *The Ranger's Comedy*, also appeared for the first time. It reappeared after May in the Admiral's repertory.[30]

From then on the new Admiral's ran everything theatrical in London. For their first three-day run between 14 and 16 May 1594 they offered one play that was definitely Henslowe's, *The Jew of Malta*, plus *The Ranger's Comedy*, and a new title, *Cutlack*, which Everard Guilpin later identified as an Alleyn role. The most intriguing and possibly most revealing list of plays is the subsequent one, where Henslowe recorded a brief run of joint or alternate performances by the new Admiral's and the new Chamberlain's at Newington Butts. It is the only evidence there is for the original playstock of the Chamberlain's Men before Shakespeare started adding to it. The two companies offered seven plays between 3 and 13 June 1594. They included *The Jew of Malta*, which they may have thought worth a special staging in that month because of the Lopez trial.[31] The others almost certainly came from the companies of the new players. Besides Alleyn's Cutlack, *Titus Andronicus* reappeared, most likely thanks to some players from Sussex's, who were the last of its three owners listed on its 1594 title page. Four new plays appear, *Hester and Ahasuerus*, *Bellendon*, *Hamlet*, and *The Taming of A Shrew*. The last of these had been a Pembroke's play, like *Titus*. Where

---

[30] There is an intriguing question of why some plays, especially *The Jew of Malta* and *Friar Bacon and Friar Bungay*, appear in Henslowe's records at the Rose with different companies. Conceivably they were left behind when the companies went on tour because of the heavy demands they made on staging. A company did not need to take more than four or five plays on tour.

[31] For the theory that Henslowe staged *The Jew* in 1594 to coincide with the two trials of the Jewish Lopez, see Margaret Hotine, "The Politics of Anti-Semitism: *The Jew of Malta* and *The Merchant of Venice*," *Notes and Queries* 236 (1991): 35–38.

the *Hamlet* came from is uncertain. It may have been a Queen's Men's play like *King Leir* and *The Troublesome Reign of King John*, both of which Shakespeare was later to rewrite.

The subsequent history of the seven titles indicates that in May 1594 three of the seven belonged to the new Admiral's and four to the Chamberlain's, a reasonable divide if they played them on alternate days. *Bellendon, Cutlack* and *The Jew of Malta* appear subsequently in the Admiral's lists, while *Titus* and *The Shrew* became part of the Chamberlain's playstock since they reappear in the First Folio. *Hamlet* and *Hester* may have been theirs too, since they never reappear in the Admiral's lists. By tracking the previous ownership of these playbooks we can deduce that besides the five men from Strange's some players came to the Chamberlain's Men from the Queen's and some from Pembroke's, the latter arriving via Sussex's if the title page of the 1594 *Titus* is to be believed. None of the Sussex's plays in Henslowe's lists for early 1594 and none of the Queen's Men's plays brought to their sojourn with Sussex's at the Rose ever reappear in the *Diary*. Nor, of course, does 'harey the vj'.

This alliance of Sussex's, Pembroke's and the Queen's Men along with Strange's may help to explain how all of Shakespeare's early plays were taken into the one company in 1594, but it does not tell the whole story. The sequence of *Titus* owners described on the title page of the 1594 quarto, Strange's, Pembroke's and Sussex's, might explain its arrival in the new Chamberlain's along with some of Sussex's Men.[32] The Strange's Men's inclusion in the Chamberlain's new company might explain the arrival of *1 Henry VI*, just as the Pembroke's membership explains *2* and *3 Henry VI* and *The Shrew*. But it does not say why the other Strange's plays, including the Marlowe plays and especially *The Massacre at Paris*, went to the other new company.

All of Shakespeare's earlier plays, formerly performed by Strange's, Sussex's, and Pembroke's, went into the new Chamberlain's. I used to think that such retentiveness on the part of one humble writer indicated a remarkably, indeed uniquely, strong possessiveness over his products for their financial value, and that he used his plays to buy his place in the new Chamberlain's.

---

[32] The 1594 quarto of *Titus* lists Strange's, Pembroke's and Sussex's as its performers. In his Arden 2 edition (London: Routledge, 1995) Jonathan Bate suggested that the three companies may have combined for a first performance in 1594, the one recorded by Henslowe. I doubt this, since Henslowe was usually quite specific about his performers, naming both of the companies involved in any run of joint performances. The *Titus* title page must rather indicate the sequence of Shakespeare's own company membership: first Strange's, then Pembroke's, then Sussex's, before he joined the Chamberlain's, which the 1600 title page added to the first three.

But no playwright other than Ben Jonson ever retained ownership of his plays once he had sold them to the players. The track through the mud traced to here makes me wonder if there was not some higher agency that gathered the playbooks together for the new companies and enlisted the players who had been acting them to form the duopoly.

The Admiral's, so far as we know, took all the available Marlowe corpus. To the staples used by pretty well every Rose company, such as *The Jew of Malta* and *Friar Bacon*, they added the old Admiral's stock, notably *Tamburlaine* and *Faustus*. They had some plays formerly performed at the Rose by Strange's and some by the Queen's. That gave them five of Marlowe's plays. To these they probably added *Dido*, and possibly also *Edward II* from Pembroke's. This last Marlowe play does not reappear in Henslowe's records after May 1594, but its 1622 reprinting gave it to a later Henslowe company, Queen Anne's Men.[33] If it did not go with the others it was the only play not gathered up in the two otherwise clean sweeps. If it did go to the Rose, then the Chamberlain's got all of the Shakespeare corpus and the Admiral's secured all Marlowe. One wonders how precisely in May 1594 the Lord Chamberlain and his son-in-law and their advisers knew what they were doing when they divided these spoils. If they did, as I believe, settle all of Marlowe's plays on one company and all of the early Shakespeares on the other, it suggests that someone held a strikingly equal esteem for the two writers. Neither had yet got their name into print on their title pages, but somebody reckoned that bundling together Marlowe's plays for the one and Shakespeare's for the other would be the best guarantee of the duopoly's future. In that calculation, it was a convenient bonus that one of the two was still working and was himself a player. History has not devalued the judgment made in 1594.

---

[33] Roslyn L. Knutson offers as a possible though unsubstantiatable explanation for the absence of *Edward II* from the Henslowe records the possibility that it went from Pembroke's to the Chamberlain's. She suggests, though without any supporting evidence, that it could have been taken from them later by Christopher Beeston when he left the Chamberlain's in 1600 for Worcester's, which in 1603 became Queen Anne's Men, who performed it subsequently. See *The Repertory of Shakespeare's Company, 1594–1613* (Fayetteville: Univ. of Arkansas Press, 1991), 230. If *Edward II* really was a Chamberlain's play in 1594 it would have stirred the writing of *Richard II* in 1595.

CHAPTER 6

The Choice between Plays and Poems

A recent article by Bart van Es challenges the general consensus that Shakespeare started his theatre life as a player. It argues that Shakespeare was much more likely to have begun as a writer, not an actor, and that this preference he sustained up to 1594. The minimal evidence for his early years, says van Es, saw him writing plays, and only taking on the business of playing as a part of his work later.[1] While we can recognise that evidence of his writing might survive more readily than would acting with a travelling company, it does seem likely that he started as a poet, if only on the ground that one of his first poems, Sonnet 145, must have been written at the age of 18. If that octosyllabic oddity is correctly identified as a love poem to Anne Hathaway, the fact that a copy remained in the poet's possession, from 1582 in Stratford through to when the sonnets appeared in print in 1609, does support the view that at least he began in his youth thinking of himself as a poet, not a player.[2]

Even through the obscure first years when he probably toured with playing companies Shakespeare was remarkably productive as a writer. Few plays by any author written in the five years up to 1594 have survived in print or manuscript. It is therefore remarkable that through the years before 1594 he seems to have produced nearly ten plays that have survived in print. The current dating for the early plays concludes that this number, partly or wholly authored by Shakespeare, were already on the stage by 1594. Yet for all the jibe in Greene's *Groatsworth of Wit* of 1592 about the Shake-scene having a tiger's heart wrapped in a player's hide, Bart van Es maintains that nothing exists showing he was best known at first as an actor. Greene's

---

Original publication: "The Choice between Plays and Poems," in *Memoria di Shakespeare* 8 (Nova serie, 2012), pp. 169–83.

[1] "'*Johannes fac Totum*'? Shakespeare's First Contact with the Acting Companies," *Shakespeare Quarterly* 60 (2010), 551–77.

[2] See for instance Stephen Booth, *Shakespeare's Sonnets*, Yale University Press, 1977, p. 501; Helen Vendler, *The Art of Shakespeare's Sonnets*, Harvard University Press, 1997, p. 609; and with more detail Gurr, "Shakespeare's First Poem," *Essays in Criticism* 21 (1971), 222–26.

attack was over the presumption he showed in competing with and borrowing in his writing from university-trained writers such as himself. That was the action of a writer. Whether his career started with work as a player is one of the many unknowns of this period. All we know for sure is that in March 1595 he, along with Richard Burbage and Will Kemp, was one of the three signatories who acknowledged receipt of a payment for three plays performed at court by the Lord Chamberlain's Men the previous Christmas. Up to this time his writing is far more obvious than his performing on stage.

Whatever the mysteries of his early career, up to 1594 he must have pushed himself as a poet, however highly reputed he became as a playwright. While young, perhaps he always preferred to think of himself as a poet rather than a player. The sonnets mourning the public means that public manners breed and the indelible stain of the dyer's hand were inserted as marked components in a deliberately self-lacerating argument making the poet's low social status part of what divorced him from his beloved young lord. How truly personal that pose was has to be guesswork. We need to study the context of what happened in 1594 to see if it was of his own free will that he gave up writing long poems like his two great epyllions, spurred as he was, according to the prefatory letters he published with them, by the hope that they would make the Earl of Southampton his patron as a poet. One of the great unanswered questions about Shakespeare is what made him join a new acting company in the same month that his second epyllion appeared in print.[3] Why, instead of following poetry for his career, did he then accept a different patron, the Lord Chamberlain, as an actor?

Venus and Adonis was licensed for printing in April 1593, and *The Rape of Lucrece* in May 1594. Published by his fellow-Stratfordian Richard Field, both had dedicatory letters addressed to the Earl of Southampton, and signed with Shakespeare's name. The letter of May 1594, notably more intimate than the first, declares that his love for Southampton is 'without end',

---

[3] Recently Patrick Cheney has claimed that Shakespeare always thought his poems and plays were 'ongoing interpenetrations' (*Shakespeare, National Poet-Playwright*, Cambridge University Press, Cambridge, 2004, p. 38). Cheney's two books, *Shakespeare, National Poet-Playwright*, and *Shakespeare's Literary Authorship*, Cambridge, 2008, are both designed on the premise that 'Shakespeare ... labors between a literary career in printed poetry and a professional career in staged theatre' and that 'he himself represents a struggle over authorship throughout his career' (*National*, p. 8). The initial volume focuses on the evidence in poems, the second on the plays. Cheney provides an ample amount of extra evidence for the case argued in this article, but neither of his books pays much attention to the crucial decision made in 1594.

and that not only what he has but also 'what I have to do' belonged to his patron.

The first epyllion of 1593 was openly a virtuoso piece, carefully proof-read and full of the sort of erotic images that would and did attract many of the young gentry of the time. It does, however, contain some hidden reservations, one of which seems to parody the tumescence its first part was openly designed to stimulate. The first half, full of Venus's lust, climaxes with hot expectation:

> Now is she in the very lists of love,
> Her champion mounted for the hot encounter.
> (593–594)[4]

But then, against that expectation, built up all through the first half of the poem, the second half, which begins with the following stanza, asserts baldly and immediately,

> All is imaginary she doth prove:
> He will not manage her, although he mount her.
> (595–598)

Adonis's withdrawal and the story of the boar slicing into his groin follow, with Venus's lament. If we count the total number of lines in the poem, 1194, we find that they divide the poem precisely into half at the verses quoted. The halfway moment, the middle of these four lines, introduces Venus's frustration. Quiet mockery of a reader's erotic expectation is built into the poem's structure with silent but mathematical precision.

The second poem, about Tarquin ravishing the virtuous Lucrece, is remarkable in a quite different way, partly because it deals only with the occasion of the rape, and makes absolutely no mention of its massive political consequences until the very final line of its 1855, where there is a bare mention of 'TARQUINS' everlasting banishment'.[5] According to Roman historians Tarquin's gross act was what caused the early monarchy to be expelled from Rome, bringing about the growth of the republic that eventually made Rome great. We know this was a matter Shakespeare studied closely, since after five years with the company writing plays about

---

[4] I quote from the Arden 3 edition, *Shakespeare's Poems*, ed. Katherine Duncan-Jones and H. R. Woudhuysen, London, 2007.
[5] The Arden 3 text adds the apostrophe, which is not in the original. It emphasises the political point that Tarquin's rape led to the expulsion of all the monarchy, not just the doer himself.

England's history he started a new series of Roman history plays about the end of the republic and its return to monarchy, with *Julius Caesar* and later *Antony and Cleopatra*. His most political play of all, *Coriolanus*, written close to the time of this last play in the series, is set in the first days of the new republic immediately following Lucrece's rape. So why in his later years did he apply such close interest in Rome's history to plays and not to more poems? Was *Coriolanus* written as a last word, when he knew that he would never return to the subject with more poetry?

We know that he did become a player as well as a writer for the Lord Chamberlain's Men in 1594. The appearance of his name along with Burbage and Kemp in March 1595 testifies to that. Later Jonson registered his name as one of the players in the 1598 *Every Man in his Humour*. By then we can tell that he knew this was to be his future. His commitment to the company became evident when in February 1599 he joined four fellow players, Kemp, John Heminges, Augustine Phillips and Thomas Pope, in putting up the then gigantic sum of £100 each to help finance the Burbage brothers' construction of the Globe. His reputation as an actor was never very prominent, the highest accolade coming from John Davies of Hereford, who praised his acting of kingly parts in a poem that may have reflected, however obliquely, the view set out in some of Shakespeare's own sonnets about his lowly status as a player.[6] He never achieved stardom as a player, for all that his financial commitment in 1599 testifies to the overt support he was giving to the company he now belonged with.

Then we need to register the evidence, augmented in recent years, that many of his plays were rewrites of older plays, mostly texts from the Queen's Men, or in some cases Pembroke's, which Shakespeare chose to improve over the years between 1595 and 1605. His own *King John*, the two *Henry IV* plays and *Henry V*, *The Taming of the Shrew*, *Hamlet*, and *King Lear*, all have precedents in the known repertory of those two companies.[7] He rewrote at least seven older plays while he belonged to the new company through that first decade, well over half of the dozen or so published from that period in the Folio. We might even add *Merry Wives of Windsor* to the *Henry IV* plays as another development from the old Queen's Men's play, since it exploits the invention of Falstaff in the history series. Some of what we now regard as Shakespeare's greatest works were merely rewrites of plays

---

[6] Davies may well have been one of the 'private' readers of the sonnets noted by Meres and others.
[7] Few scholars dispute the likely influence of *King Leir*, *The Famous Victories of Henry V*, *The Taming of a Shrew*, *The Troublesome Reign of King John*, and the ur-*Hamlet* as sources for the versions in the Folio texts of 1623.

already in the company's repertory. As such, our assumption that he rated the plays he wrote very highly has to shrink quite markedly.[8]

In 1594 Henry Carey, Lord Hunsdon, the Queen's cousin and loyal servant, had massive power. His deputy at court, the man who gave his authority to the chief playing companies, and before whom they rehearsed the plays they hoped would be chosen for the annual performances at court, was Sir Edmund Tilney, Master of the Revels. Did either he or Carey, or both, insist that Shakespeare become a member of the new company?[9] How ready was he in May 1594 to abandon his hopes of getting enough money from patrons like Southampton or another lord to help him write great narrative verse, as Samuel Daniel was doing?

Daniel's choice of career seems to have followed a drastically different path to Shakespeare's. Throughout his life Daniel relied on great patrons for income.[10] His origins are even more obscure than Shakespeare's, though his family was evidently affluent enough to get him entry to Oxford in 1581, although he left before taking a degree (at around that time Shakespeare chose marriage instead of the necessary bachelorhood of study at one of the universities). At Oxford Daniel made good friends, notably John Florio, who helped him to learn French and Italian. In 1585 he translated an Italian book of *imprese* or emblems into English, and later worked at the English embassy in Paris. Subsequently he lived with the Queen's Champion, Sir Edward Dymoke, accompanying him to Italy in 1590. By that time his *Delia* sonnets had started circulating in manuscript, securing their first printing in 1591, tacked on to an unauthorised edition of Sidney's *Astrophel and Stella*. In 1592 he issued a better and larger version, dedicated to Sidney's sister Mary, Countess of Pembroke. This he accompanied with a narrative poem, *The Complaint of Rosamond*, an account told by a ghost about how she was seduced by Henry II and murdered by his queen. This proved so popular that Daniel produced a further, enlarged edition in the following

---

[8] I have in mind the argument that, despite half of his plays never appearing in print during his lifetime, he did wish to see them published, as Lukas Erne maintains in *Shakespeare as Literary Dramatist*, Cambridge University Press, Cambridge, 2003. On the new career that started in 1594, Richard Wilson argues that the major new play of 1595, *Richard II*, represents Richard as the old system of courtly patronage and lies, while Bullingbrook is the 'modern tyranny of consumer demand'. See "'A Stringless Instrument': *Richard II* and the Defeat of Poetry," in *Shakespeare's Book. Essays in reading, writing and reception*, ed. Richard Meek, Jane Rickard and Richard Wilson, Manchester University Press, Manchester, 2008, pp. 103–19, p. 116.

[9] Several essays in recent issues of *Shakespeare Quarterly* debate this question. See particularly those in Vol 60, noted above.

[10] The hugely complex question of patronage for poets throughout the early modern period at large, the need for it and the psychology behind it, are handsomely studied in Robert C. Evans, *Ben Jonson and the Poetics of Patronage*, Lewisburg, PA, Bucknell University Press, 1989.

year. Subsequently he lived at Wilton with the Earls of Pembroke, writing a companion play about Cleopatra to accompany the Countess's own translation of Robert Garnier's French *Tragedy of Anthony*. Possibly thanks to the platform of his place at Oxford, Daniel's career began far more handsomely, if rather less productively, than Shakespeare's.

By 1594 Daniel's reputation had risen to a height. Spenser praised him in his *Colin Clout* of 1595, and Shakespeare echoed his work in his sonnets and the epyllions of 1593 and 1594, as well as in 1595 when he began his new series of history plays with *Richard II* by copying the story told in the first books of Daniel's great epic. The first four verse books of *The Civil Wars* were printed in 1595, beginning with Richard's deposition. The opening stanzas of Daniel's poem indicate that it was a new project under a new patron, Lord Mountjoy, an associate of the Earl of Essex. In spite of or possibly because of shifts from one patron to another and the long labour of his new project, Daniel found himself with a severe shortage of income through the next few years, in marked contrast to the profit Shakespeare was making from the Lord Chamberlain's Men.

Daniel dedicated his next poem, *Octavia*, to Margaret Clifford, Countess of Cumberland, a descendant of the Rosamund he had previously written about. John Pitcher has suggested that, knowing Daniel's *Rosamund*, it was she who might have commissioned him to write his play about Cleopatra.[11] Clifford's husband was making her an all too obvious model for the forlorn wife of Antony while he dallied with Cleopatra in Egypt. In this period such commissions appear to have been one of the few ways to secure patrons who would pay for poets' work. Through the countess Daniel became tutor to her daughter, Lady Anne Clifford. Lady Anne's portrait in triptych, painted in 1646 and now in the Abbot Hall Art Gallery in Kendal, includes a picture of her at fifteen, in 1605, with her two early mentors, her governess Anne Taylor and Daniel, shown backed by an array of books and a lute. She became fond of Daniel, and after his death set up a monument to him in the town where he was buried.

During these years he worked chiefly on *Musophilus*, a long dialogue poem dedicated to Fulke Greville, a patron who Florio may have introduced him to. The poem makes heavy use of Montaigne, whose essays Florio had recently translated into English. It was published in 1599, along with reprints of *Octavia* and his other works, under the general title *The Poetical Essays*. In 1601 his helpful publisher printed his entire opus in a handsome folio as *The Works of Samuel Daniel*. John Pitcher asserts

---

[11] See Pitcher's entry on Daniel in *The Oxford Dictionary of National Biography*.

that this set out his claim, after Spenser's death, to be England's leading poet.

It soon brought him elevation, and a reliable income. From 1603 he came to depend on James's queen, Anne of Denmark. This new role, however, brought him an eminence he did not enjoy. Drawn to her notice by the Countesses of Bedford and Hertford, Anne soon started using him to write her formal entertainments, starting with a masque mockingly derided by Jonson and others. She also got him to work as licenser for the company of boys she patronised, the Blackfriars Children. The masque, staged at Hampton Court on 8 January 1604, brought him to the Court's attention. This public role soon brought down attacks, first over the masque and then as a result of getting the boys to stage his own play, *Philotas*. This irked several major courtiers, notably Lord Treasurer Cecil and Lord Mountjoy, for its close resemblance to features of the Essex trial of 1601. By 1607 he had retreated to a house in the west country, on the Earl of Hertford's estates, near where he had been born. There he remained quietly for the rest of his life. Although in 1610 he wrote the masque *Tethys' Festival* in honour of Prince Henry, and in 1614 a play celebrating Queen Anne's restoration of Somerset House, his last years away from London were dogged increasingly by poor health and slow productivity. Mostly he confined himself to writing a history of England through the medieval period, in prose. This, privately printed in 1612 and immediately reprinted by the Stationers' Company, was extended in 1618. The Queen paid for the second version. He died in 1619, three years after Shakespeare.

Another writer, whose career has far more evident parallels to Shakespeare, is Thomas Heywood.[12] Unlike Daniel, he began as a writer who soon had to support himself by acting. A vicar's son, born probably in about 1573 in Lincolnshire, he studied at Cambridge from 1591, where he saw many plays. After his father died in 1593 he moved to London. In October 1596 he was enrolled in the Henslowe enterprises for the Admiral's Men, when he received thirty shillings from the company for one of his playbooks.[13] Then on 25 March 1598, in an odd echo of Shakespeare's enrollment, Henslowe engaged him as a player for two years. Subsequently he joined Henslowe's second company at the Rose, then the Earl of Worcester's players, who later became Queen Anne's Men. Like Shakespeare, he worked for them as both playing sharer and playwright. As a sharer he several times authorised Henslowe to pay other writers for their playbooks,

---

[12] A striking summary of these two men's parallel careers is by Clare Smout, "Actor, Poet, Playwright, Sharer... Rival? Shakespeare and Heywood, 1603–4," *Early Theatre* 13 (2010), 175–89.
[13] *Henslowe's Diary*, ed. R. A. Foakes and R. T. Rickert, Cambridge University Press, 1961, p. 50.

presumably having the company job of making the decisions whether to buy them for staging. He was a prolific writer, augmenting existing plays and writing many new ones. In 1633, in the Epistle to his *English Traveller*, he asserted that by then the total of his plays amounted to around 'two hundred and twenty, in which I have had either an entire hand, or at the least a maine finger'. His near fifty years as a writer ended at his death in 1641.

Heywood began as a poet, like the others, publishing *Oenone and Paris* in 1594. Obviously an imitation of *Venus and Adonis*, he copied Shakespeare's second epyllion with his play *The Rape of Lucrece* some years later. As a playwright, in *Palladis Tamia* (1598), Francis Meres hailed him among the English writers as 'best for Comedy'. While working for the Admiral's at the Rose he married, and settled in the local parish of St Saviour's, Southwark. From the time he began working for the playing companies he wrote constantly, mostly plays, many in collaboration, and only a few of them published, between 1602 and 1615. Like Shakespeare's, his plays came into print over the next thirty years, often long after their appearance on stage.

In 1608 he moved away from playwriting. His prose translation of Sallust's books about Catiline and Jugurtha appeared in that year, dedicated to the son of the Earl of Worcester, his patron when he acted and wrote for Worcester's Men. The next year saw *Troia Britannica*, his contribution to the concept of a unified Britain, this time dedicated to the Earl himself. Some of the historical material from this he subsequently re-used in his four spectacular *Ages* plays. Probably during the long closure for plague of 1608–9 he wrote in prose his famous defence of playing, *An Apology for Actors*, published in 1612, also dedicated to Worcester. In 1614 he seems to have travelled to Venice and Germany in company with the Earl of Southampton.

This decade of publication and work for various patrons was followed by a ten-year silence, from 1615 to 1624. He remained a playing company sharer, given black cloth to wear at Queen Anne's funeral in 1619, and he may have written plays for Christopher Beeston, his former colleague in Queen Anne's Men, who now owned the second indoor playhouse of the time, the Drury Lane Cockpit. Beeston, who had written verses for his *Apology*, remained his friend through all these years. In 1624 he issued *Gunaikeion, or, Nine Books of Various History Concerning Women*. A folio edition, again dedicated to Worcester, it describes great women down to Queen Elizabeth and his own patron Queen Anne. The dedication declares baldly that he has been short of money.

From here on he made increasing use of his previous publications, recycling many of their stories. In 1631, possibly aware that his powers were declining, he arranged to publish several of his earlier plays, and wrote prefatory material for others, including Marlowe's *Jew of Malta* in 1633. He became more prolific than ever, but from here on most of it was occasional or openly trivial. Like Antony Munday he started writing Lord Mayor's pageants, producing seven between 1631 and 1639. In 1635 he issued his last long poem, *The Hierarchy of the Blessed Angels*, giving it the most elevated dedication he ever essayed, to Queen Henrietta Maria, who was a noted Catholic. The poem carefully by-passes theological issues, instead simply describing the Christian hierarchy of archangels and angels. A digression warmly praises the playwrights Marlowe, Shakespeare and Jonson, while ignoring poets such as Spenser and Daniel. Through his last years he issued several prose works, a book of poems and translations in 1637, and many prefaces and occasional pieces. He went on publishing plays until his death in 1641.

After 1594 Shakespeare took a path somewhere between Daniel the poet and Heywood the playwright. All three came from fairly modest origins, sons of poor country gentry. Daniel's path, relying on patrons, meant that his work declined (it can be seen that way) from the epic verse of the 1590s to the final prose history. Heywood shows how the market for playwriting could sustain a modest life, perhaps inevitably declining into repetition and a long succession of minor works. Neither Daniel nor Heywood's careers say much for relying solely for income on the generosity of great lords as patrons. Shakespeare ended richer than either. The search for parallels must go further.

One celebrated writing career, utterly distinct in the routes it took, was Ben Jonson's. Eight years or so younger than Shakespeare, the stepson of a London bricklayer, his origins were even less significant, and indeed he was regularly derided by gentry for having started working with bricks. In 1597 he entered the Henslowe operations for the Admiral's Men, writing new sections of old plays, and apparently acting Hieronimo in Kyd's classic play, before showing his independence by selling his two *Humours* plays to the Lord Chamberlain's. Asserting his independence in 1600, on the titlepage of the printed text of *Every Man Out* Jonson chose to ignore the company that had staged it, boasting instead that it contained '*more than hath been Publickely Spoken or Acted*'. Its contents mock the company's repertory, including *Romeo and Juliet*, and he also parodied the armorial motto Shakespeare had recently bought for his father, the Law French '*Non sans droict*' (Not without right) by inventing the phrase 'Not without Mustard' and attaching it to the emblem of a boar's head, roast pork. He flaunted his objections to the company's control and cutting of his text, issuing it for the sapient reader, not the ignorant playgoer. It could be said that he was the first writer to uphold explicitly the importance of writing plays as well as poems. From the Chamberlain's Men he moved on to write for the new boy company at the Blackfriars, with *Cynthia's Revels* and other plays, and its more select audiences. By then he was making strenuous efforts to secure patrons for his verse, associating himself openly with lords, gentry and scholars rather than with common players.

None of his patrons gave him a reliable income, so he kept on writing plays. In 1603 or so he sold *Sejanus* to the Chamberlain's as a major Roman tragedy, although the first audiences voiced their dislike. In the first of its printed texts he acknowledged that he had been helped by another writer, a claim that has perhaps too readily led to guesses that Shakespeare had a hand in getting the Chamberlain's to accept it. A couple of years later he sold them *Volpone*, before turning again to write for the boys until they closed down in 1608. He then gave the King's Men *The Alchemist*, celebrating their acquisition of the Blackfriars playhouse from the boys by setting it in a house in the same precinct. In 1612 he followed up *Sejanus*, now better regarded, with a second Roman tragedy, *Catiline*, which he published in imitation of the classical form. By then he was the country's leading poet, and his plays brought him equal esteem.

Jonson remained close to Shakespeare, and seems to have copied his desire for social elevation. In 1603 he imitated the older man by acquiring the armorial arms of an ancestor in Annandale. But he was fixated on noble patronage, and like Daniel was taken up by the Court, writing several of its masques. Jonson differed from Shakespeare above all in the explicitly high valuation he set on his plays, and was consistently determined to get them into print in the forms he personally preferred. But writing plays never became his primary activity. Obsessed with the classical image of the poet as moralist and satirist, he constantly sought the company of the great intellects of his day. The chief difference in Jonson's nature and ambitions from Shakespeare as a writer of plays appears in the restless frequency with which he shifted attention from one company to another.[14]

---

[14] Besides these four, the period had several other would-be poets who tried their hands at verse funded by patronage. Perhaps the best of these, partly because he was a fellow-countryman of Shakespeare's, was Michael Drayton. A playwright as well as a poet, his career was less distinguished than Daniel's, and he continued for much longer than him in essaying to write long poems. His patrons brought him even less success and income than Daniel's.

Shakespeare's own career was settled, either by himself or by authorities whom he could not gainsay, in 1594. Joining the Lord Chamberlain's Men should have cost him some initial price of entry, the payment of which is itself one of the mysteries in this aspect of his story. Commitment to the company as a sharer required him to have contributed, at least by Christmas 1594, a substantial payment to cover the value of his share. Their price varied according to the state of the market. In 1597 and 1602 the Chamberlain's Men's equivalent body, the Admiral's Men, appear to have levied a charge of at least £50 for a full share, one-tenth of the company's total valuation, while by 1612 Queen Anne's Men valued theirs at £80 each.[15] If Shakespeare had retained the ownership of his plays, they might have counted as a financial contribution to his share, although judging by Henslowe's records old plays were sold at only £2 each, which would have meant that all the older plays Shakespeare must have brought them could have been valued by the Chamberlain's Men together at only £20.[16]

One of the many legends about Shakespeare recorded by the first eighteenth-century editor, Nicholas Rowe, was that Davenant had said Southampton 'at one time, gave him a thousand pounds, to enable him to go through with a purchase which he heard he had a mind to'.[17] That seems unlikely as a memory from his enrollment in the new company, since it funded attachment to a different patron, though it is (just) possible that Southampton paid for Shakespeare's entry to the Chamberlain's in the hope of denying him any likelyhood of him becoming permanently dependent on his own generosity.[18] Too many legends and fictions befuddle his relations in the vicinity of 1594 over the 'lord of my love' in the sonnets and the so-called dark lady.

We know nothing distinct about Shakespeare's attitude to his post-1594 employers until 1599, when he contributed cash to help cover the cost of building the Globe. Before that he invested large sums of money back

---

[15] For a summary of the price of shares, see Gurr, *The Shakespeare Company, 1594–1642*, Cambridge, 2004, pp. 94–5.

[16] There is also the question of what authority the Lord Chamberlain's Men in 1594 had to acquire the use of the ten or more of Shakespeare's plays already performed by earlier companies. Either Shakespeare himself had kept them as his personal property while the various companies performed them, as the 1594 titlepage of *Titus Andronicus* most clearly indicates, or conceivably (though there is no known precedent for this), the Master of the Revels took them from the dead companies and handed them over to the live one. For a broad canvass of this complex question, see Gurr, "Did Shakespeare Own his Own Playbooks?," *Review of English Studies* 60 (2009), 206–29.

[17] See E. K. Chambers, *William Shakespeare*, 2 vols, Oxford, The Clarendon Press, 1930, I.62.

[18] Chambers, op. cit., points out that Shakespeare's own lifelong expenditure did not quite reach that sum.

home, buying New Place in Stratford, and funding his father's troublesome esquireship in 1597, which made him a gentleman himself. However long it took him to reconcile himself to acting, writing nothing but a couple of new plays each year, that seems to have become his life from 1594 onwards. He wrote no more major poems. He must have consented to having his name appear on the plays when they began to be printed from 1597 onwards, especially since the company joked about his name on their first titlepages. The hyphen in 'Shake-speare' incorporated a mild joke that had been current at least since Peele's *Edward I* in 1590 (line 761). A line in *1 Henry IV*, written in 1596, may actually show the poet using another joke about his name to entertain his fellow-players.[19]

A few references to the company's experiences do crop up in the plays of these years. The most familiar one is Ford's rueful statement in *The Merry Wives of Windsor* when, speaking in disguise to Falstaff, he uses a simile to describe the loss of his wife: 'Like a fair house, built on another mans ground, so that I have lost my edifice, by mistaking the place, where I erected it' (Folio TLN 975–7). The owner of the land on which the company's playhouse, the Theatre, stood had recently repossessed it after the lease expired, and banned any more playing there, so the company lost its edifice because they had planted it on leasehold land. At much the same time in *The Merchant of Venice* he seems to have offered Richard Burbage a play sympathising over the crisis when the residents of Blackfriars blocked the use of the Burbages' newly-built playhouse. Shylock's bond represented what put Richard under pressure when the London moneylenders, who hounded his father James to repay their loans for building the new playhouse, started badgering his son and heir after James died in February 1597. Amongst so much else, Portia's actions were an on-stage consolation to Burbage for the pressures he was under from his father's theatre and its debts.[20] These two allusions, plus perhaps the later joke when Hamlet questions Rosencrantz and Guildenstern about the players and is told that the boy companies have driven them out of town, are the only direct references Shakespeare makes to the company's activities. The actor playing Hamlet who grieves over this sad story was actually the boy company's own landlord, Richard Burbage, who stood to profit from the boy company's success. Nothing else in the plays matches these oblique references. Shakespeare must have been gratified when in 1603 he was made a courtier, a Groom of the Chamber, along with the other sharers in the

---

[19] See Gurr, "In-jokes about Spear-shakers," *Notes and Queries* 257 (2011), 237–41.
[20] See Gurr, "Rethinking Shylock," *Shakespeare International Yearbook* 12 (2012) Chapter 13 in this volume.

King's Men, but nothing exists to describe his feelings about this new rank.

Little else can be adduced about his attitude to his work from his plays. Whatever he thought of them, others regarded them highly from early on, as we know from the reports by Francis Meres and others, and by the early appearance of his name on their titlepages. Marston, in his *Scourge of Villainy* (1597), instanced *Romeo and Juliet* as obsessively quoted by student playgoers. The writer himself, however, seems not to have taken any care to see his plays into print. None of the quartos received the careful proofing that his two epyllions received. Even *Richard II*, his only play written entirely in verse, in its first versions contained a major cut from the deposition scene, most likely made by the Master of the Revels before he approved the play for performance. A rough transcription of the missing section appeared in the fourth quarto of 1608, but a full version not until the Folio. Interference with his texts by outsiders seems to have been a recurrent feature of the quartos, and Shakespeare made no attempt to circumvent them. In quality, both in the early quartos and the later Folio, lies a huge gap between the immaculate texts of the poems and the shoddy texts of the plays. This gap can only be explained by lack of their author's care for their reproduction.

A large proportion of the texts of many plays published through these years are messy in character and poor in the care with which they were transcribed. Quite unlike Jonson and several others of his play-writing contemporaries, Shakespeare took no personal role getting his plays into print. Jonson insisted on publishing his plays himself, ignoring the playing company's cuts and issuing his own fuller versions.[21] The titlepage of the 1600 *Every Man Out of his Humour* declares boldly that it is a version '*Containing more than hath been Publickely Spoken or Acted*'. Later Barnabe Barnes and John Webster added similar declarations to the titlepages of *The Devil's Charter* and *The Duchess of Malfi*. In contrast to such exhibitions of authorial pride not one of Shakespeare's plays has any such assertion.

Several of the early quartos seem to have gone through some process of playhouse revision before they reached the stage and the press. Mostly the copy seem to have been playbooks cut for performance. Contrasting the total number of their lines with those of the much longer Folio versions shows how ready the players were to shorten their playtexts. In *2 Henry VI* the Folio's full text, apparently close to the author's own copy, published

---

[21] See Joseph Loewenstein, *Ben Jonson and Possessive Authorship*, Cambridge University Press, Cambridge, 2002.

by the King's Men in 1623, has 3355 lines whereas the early quarto, the Pembroke's company's *The Contention*, has only 2234. Its successor, the Folio *3 Henry VI*, has 3217 lines whereas the 1595 *True Tragedy* has 2387. Both of the early printings are close to the length of a normal performance text. The Folio *Taming of the Shrew* also has a nearly normal 2750 lines, whereas the early quarto known as *A Shrew* has only 1594. The quarto text of *The Merry Wives*, printed in 1602, has 1634 lines against the Folio's 2731. Most revealingly, the quarto text of *Henry V*, printed a year after it was first staged, has 1818 lines, little more than half of the Folio's authorial 3381.

The three texts of Hamlet present complex questions about their difference provenances. The first of the three versions in print, the 1603 First Quarto, runs to 2155 lines whereas the Second Quarto of 1604–5, probably printed from the author's manuscript, has nearly twice that number, 4154 lines. It may have sections that were later cut by the author. The rather trimmer and later Folio version is a little shorter, though it still runs to 3906 lines.[22] In this one case, we might conjecture that Shakespeare himself prompted his company to print a better version of his play, the second quarto, but that idea has even less evidence to support it than other details in this account. Not a scintilla of evidence exists to suggest that Shakespeare was ever inspired to copy Jonson and have his plays made available to the reader, in forms and at lengths close to what he originally gave the company to perform.

All the texts that bibliographers think were derived from an authorial manuscript appear at best to be taken from what the company held as spare copies, usually the original manuscripts they received before they got scribes to rewrite both the approved playbook and the individual 'parts' copied from them. The approved or 'allowed book' the censor read and approved for performance was normally created following the company's corrections and adaptations, including the cuts to streamline the play and trim it down to an actable length, although simply cutting the text could be done to the 'allowed book' without any further recourse to the censor.[23] The many shorter versions of the plays in quarto, especially the comedies, testify to Shakespeare's lack of interest in getting the longer authorial versions of his plays into print.

---

[22] My line-counts differ slightly from those of other counters, such as Lukas Erne, *Shakespeare as Literary Dramatist*, p. 141. For the Folio texts I have calculated play-lengths by using the TLN line-counts employed throughout the Norton Facsimile. The Quarto counts are my own, and include stage directions.

[23] For a scrupulous analysis of a company's customary activities backstage in preparing their playbooks, see Tiffany Stern, *Documents of Performance in Early Modern England*, Cambridge, 2009, particularly Chapters 2 and 8.

It has been suggested that the survival of the longer texts in the Folio edition, for the *Henry VI* plays and *Richard III*, as well as for *Hamlet*, indicate his preoccupation with his creations, and lack of care to write what the company needed. That may be so. It might equally be alleged that he was generous in giving the book-keeper and scribes a range of choice when they made their acting versions out of his manuscripts, although if so we should ask why the comedies are so much shorter than the 'serious' plays. Either way, his lack of interest in having them printed suggests he was not concerned with their immortality.

Such lack of concern does suggest that he cared far less for his playscripts than we would like to think. Perhaps the clearest marker of his outlook lies in the two versions of *Henry V*, the only play whose quarto can be identified as made up by players out of the Folio text. That text, printed at only one or so removes from the original manuscript, at twice the length of the quarto, was copied by dictation by two of the company's sharers within less than a year of its first staging in 1599. In the quarto of 1600, Shakespeare must have accepted the resultant half-length version as the only one that would ever appear in print. That might imply that his longer plays, *Richard III*, *Henry V* and *Hamlet*, came to the length they have chiefly to satisfy his own priorities in composition. He must have known the company would trim them to a more manageable length, but he completed the longer version of *Henry V* knowing full well that the multitude of ambivalent presentations of Henry himself, most blatant in what the Chorus declares and what each following Act contradicts, would force the players to simplify it down to a version that made Henry more routinely heroic. The absence of care in getting his own compositions into print may show his sense of privacy, knowing he was writing for himself. More likely, though, such obliviousness shows how little he expected his fellows to do what he claimed his sonnets did, and make their author immortal.

Sidney Lee laid down in his classic biography of Shakespeare that he wrote for money, not for fame. This became the chief feature of what we used to think was his basic outlook on life. In his celebrated 'documentary life' of Shakespeare published in 1986, Samuel Schoenbaum followed Lee in twice highlighting Alexander Pope's famous verse about Shakespeare writing for gain, not glory.[24] Schoenbaum's assessment of the surviving documents confirms this inglorious view of the poet's outlook, at least so far as the plays, and not the poems, are concerned. On the other hand, against

---

[24] Samuel Schoenbaum, *William Shakespeare. A Compact Documentary Life*, Clarendon Press, Oxford, 1977, p. 220.

Lee and Schoenbaum, we might invoke Patrick Cheney's view, which was chiefly based on his reading of Shakespeare's extraordinary poem of 1600, 'The Phoenix and the Turtle'. An intricate analysis left Cheney to conclude that 'The historical context for viewing the literary dynamic in "The Phoenix and the Turtle" lies in the Elizabethan authorial conjunction of printed poetry and staged theatre, together with the fact, uncannily predicted in the poem itself, that an authorized Spenserian (and Jonsonian) culture of printed poetry may be outstripped by an upstart (Shakespearean) culture of performed theatre.'[25] Whatever its initial cause, Shakespeare's enduring fidelity to his acting company from 1594 onwards, and not to the plays he wrote for them, is a small and yet fearsomely intense feature of his writing.

[25] Cheney, *National Poet*, p. 183.

CHAPTER 7

Accommodating the Revels Office

The Master of the Revels usually comes to our attention through the Shakespearean period, roughly from the end of the 1570s. The first Master required to pay attention to play-making was Edmund Tilney. Appointed in 1579, he worked for over thirty years as Master, until his death in 1610. We know about him chiefly that his duty was to read and authorise every play written to be staged in public. He marked on the manuscripts given him by the professional companies for approval everything that he wanted cut or altered, before signing his name on the last page. That, however, was only one of the Revels Office's two distinctly separate duties over plays. The two duties involved quite different activities, and they need to be distinguished from one another.

We know too little about what went on at Tilney's office in St John's, Clerkenwell. His appointment in December 1578 as the government's official censor gave him an onerous new duty. What the local mayors had previously done with visiting players was now centralised, and became Tilney's principal new duty. His patent empowered him to order alterations in every play put before him. He could refuse permission to perform whatever the playing companies delivered to him. Yet we know very little about what he did when authorising a play. Did he read through the scripts on his own privately, or did he, as his new orders explicitly said he must, view every play in performance before licensing it for public showing? In *A Midsummer Night's Dream*, playing the Tilney role, Philostrate tells Theseus that he has seen a rehearsal of the mechanicals' play about Pyramus and Thisbe (5.1.68).[1] In the 1590s did the players offer full rehearsals before the Master for him to censor?

Tilney's original patent, dated belatedly 24 December 1581, was quite specific. Besides the then standard expectation that he would maintain the

---

[1] I have used the Arden 3 Shakespeare for this reference.

Revels stock of garments and properties used for Court shows, it added to this a massive extension of his duties.

> furthermore also we have and doe by these presentes aucthorize and commaunde our said Servant Edmunde Tilney Master of our said Revells by himselfe or his sufficient deputie or deputies to warne commaunde and appointe in all places within this our Realme of England, aswell within francheses and liberties as without, all and every plaier or plaiers with their playmakers, either belonging to any noble man or otherwise, bearinge the name or names of usinge the facultie of playmakers or plaiers of Comedies, Trageies, Enterludes or what other showes soever, from tyme to tyme and at all tymes to appeare before him with all such plaies, Tragedies, Comedies or showes as they shall have in readines or meane to sett forth, and them to present and recite before our said Servant or his sufficient deputie, whom wee ordeyne appointe and aucthorise by these presentes of all suche showes, plaies, plaiers and playmakers, together with their playing places, to order and reforme, auctorise and put downe, as shalbe thought meete or unmeete unto himselfe or his said Deputie in that behalfe.[2]

This augmentation and centralisation of his duties meant that henceforth Tilney would have to amplify enormously what the Revels Office had been accustomed to doing. Formerly, the duties merely entailed organising the royal entertainments over Christmas, and keeping the properties used for them in good condition. Now he was required to control all playing, and to censor the plays that were to be shown to the public. Professional players were to 'presente and recite' their plays before him. That was costly, both for the acting companies and the Revels Office, and for the latter it required new space. In addition to the rooms for storage and preservation of costumes, it demanded a large chamber where the plays could be shown in rehearsal.

The first question to ask about this is how long, if ever, did Tilney maintain this drastic requirement? Most of what we know about his practices derives from the handwritten notes he and his successors wrote on a few surviving play manuscripts dating from 1600 or later. None of these show him doing more than read the manuscripts. If actually viewing all plays was his usual procedure at first, in obedience to the 1581 order, how quickly did he give up insisting that the players 'should appeare before him'? How soon did he retreat to the much easier process of reading the playbooks on his own? And if that was all he bothered to do with them, why should he, as we know he did, acquire a 'Great Chamber' for the Office at Clerkenwell?

---

[2] Quoted by E. K. Chambers, *The Elizabethan Stage*, 4 vols, Oxford: Clarendon Press, 1923, IV.286. This patent is discussed carefully by Richard Dutton, *Mastering the Revels. The Regulation and Censorship of English Renaissance Drama*, Basingstoke: Macmillan, 1991, pp. 47–9.

Simply reading the playbooks that the companies brought him does seem to have become his standard practice sometime in the next twenty years. The trouble is that none of his own 'allowed book' manuscripts has survived. Because they were such a major company asset, only a few 'allowed' plays, all post-1610, survive with his successors' handwriting in them. By then economies of effort had certainly become routine. But the thirty years up to 1610 was a long time, a period when the playing industry grew enormously. There is absolutely no evidence for what the Master did through those years in office.

We do not know if he ever did insist that the entire company planning to perform a new play should attend to read all of it before him. The sole piece of seemingly hard evidence comes from *A Midsummer Night's Dream*, and even that is not secure. In Shakespeare's play Philostrate has been checking what might entertain royalty at court. That was one of Tilney's priorities, separate from his other job of censorship. Simply reading a play in manuscript before signing its last page seems much easier than demanding that the whole company attend to read it through in front of him. Were the play manuscripts delivered to him to read in private from the outset? Both of Tilney's duties need closer scrutiny.

There is good reason to doubt whether the players, with their properties and their individual 'parts', ever took the new plays they needed to get licensed to the Revels Office. *Henslowe's Diary*[3] of the 1590s tells us that Tilney was paid between five and ten shillings to affix his signature on the last page. But we know nothing about how that crucial decision, with all its implications both financial and practical, was made. Nothing in Henslowe's records shows that his companies ever made the trip from Bankside to the Revels Office and back to get their playbooks approved. He does record payments made to Tilney's men at different times, but that suggests they called at the Rose rather than the other way round, and most of the payments were for playhouse licences rather than the allowance of playbooks.

One surviving manuscript of about 1600 shows Tilney giving it close attention as he read it, since he marked it up with comments as well as excisions. Yet his original job specification demanded far more than private reading. Was the company ever expected to book an appearance before him for themselves every time they needed a new play approved? It would have been far simpler just to give him a copy prepared by the book-keeper before

---

[3] See *Henslowe's Diary*, ed. R. A. Foakes and R. T. Rickert. Cambridge: Cambridge University Press, 1961.

the 'parts' for each of the players were transcribed from the approved copy. A later Master, Henry Herbert, did insist that his alterations to the script were to be passed on into the individual 'parts' held by the players, so he presumably received the book to be 'allowed' only in the last days before the first performance, after the 'parts' had been transcribed. A similar abrupt process seems to be indicated by the *Henslowe Diary*.

We do not know what the censoring routine developed into. Perhaps in 1580 the process did start with the players having to enact the whole play in front of Tilney, either in plain dress or full costume, as the Lord Chamberlain's original order demanded. That would have been costly to both the Revels Office and the companies. And if they did 'recite' the whole play in front of him, did they then leave the playbook with him so he could make his annotations and deletions to it before making his decision to 'allow' it for public staging, and only then return it to the players? The later manuscripts indicate that did not happen.

A pair of 'allowed books' with the Master's notes in them survives from the King's Men's repertory. They show both George Buc and his successor Henry Herbert reading them quite carefully. Neither contains anything to suggest they did so while listening to the whole company rehearsing the play in front of them. One, now known as *The Lady's Tragedy* of 1611, used to be identified by the name the Revels Master who followed Tilney, George Buc, gave it, *The Second Maiden's Tragedy*. Buc applied that name because, as he stated in his final note, 'This second Maydens tragedy (for it hath no name inscribed) may with the reformations bee acted publikely. 31 october 1611. G. Buc'.[4] We infer from this that Buc had the manuscript when he gave it his approval, but none of the company were present to supply him with the play's title.

The other surviving King's Men's allowed book is Massinger's *Believe As You List*, of 1630. The Malone Society General Editor, W. W. Greg, stated confidently in 1928 that it 'bears the autograph licence of the Master of the Revels, it is corrected and prepared for acting by a stage-adapter, and shows all the processes through which the copy passed on its way from the author to the prompter'.[5] This falls some way short of the truth. The then Master, Henry Herbert, had insisted that Massinger must rewrite his entire text, changing its setting from modern Portugal to ancient Carthage. None of the preliminary drafts survive, only the 'allowed' copy. Herbert's own notes tell us that on 11 January 1631 he refused to allow the version he had read,

---

[4] I quote from the Malone Society edition, ed. W. W. Greg, Oxford, 1910, p. 78.
[5] Malone Society edition, ed. Charles. J. Sisson, Oxford, 1928, p. v.

'because itt did contain dangerous matter, as the deposing of Sebastian king of Portugal, by Phillip the (Second,) and ther being a peace sworen twixte the kings of England and Spayne'.[6] Not till five months later did he inscribe his permission on the revised copy. The Master's intercessions could occupy quite a time. Massinger rewrote his whole play, changing its setting from modern Portugal to ancient Carthage. If the whole company had to attend more than the once to get its eventual allowance, it would have cost them a lot in both time and money.

The only manuscript with Tilney's notes on it is the confusion of papers that constitute the play of *Sir Thomas More*. They most probably date from 1600.[7] The script shows several different kinds of intercession over the basic text. It affirms quite drastically Tiffany Stern's view that most early playbooks were a scrambled assemblage of independent pages.[8] She describes how complex the business of preparing a playbook was, with inserted pages, cuts, revisions, and other changes. Several individuals normally took part in this process. The More manuscript shows as many as seven different hands affecting it. Apart from Tilney's own comments and cuts, it was heavily revised and rewritten by at least five different people. Many of the changes seem to indicate an attempt, possibly more than one, to alter it so that Tilney would eventually approve it for staging. They did not succeed. There is no sign that it ever appeared on stage. Tilney certainly did not sign the version that has survived in manuscript. This affirms the chief area of contestation as the playbook itself, the written text, not any performance in the great chamber at St John's. The few surviving playbooks with Tilney's or his successors' hands in them show where the Master recorded his views.

So it does seem evident that well before 1600 the playbook Tilney was invited to 'allow' became the sole authority for staging. It was Tilney's only direct form of access to what would be staged. From Henslowe and other accounts we know that it brought in a good proportion of his Office's income. Yet we cannot be confident about just when Tilney came to expect that he need only read through the written text himself, and indeed whether he ever started by listening to readings 'rezited' by some or all of the company's players. All we can be sure of is the far fewer occasions when he

---

[6] N. W. Bawcutt, *The Control and Censorship of Caroline Drama. The Records of Sir Henry Herbert, Master of the Revels 1623–73*, Oxford: Clarendon Press, 1996, pp. 171–2.

[7] Much has been written about the complex assemblage of notes for this play. Level-headed collections of thoughts about it include Scott McMillin's *The Elizabethan Theatre and 'The Book of Sir Thomas More'*, Ithaca: Cornell University Press, 1987, and the edition of the play by John Jowett (Arden Shakespeare, 2011).

[8] *Documents of Performance in Early Modern England*, Cambridge: Cambridge University Press, 2009, Chapter 8: "The approved 'book' and actors' parts," pp. 232–52.

demanded a full 'rehearshall', as Heywood later termed it. These events were necessary, not for his primary duty but only when he had to judge the fitness of a play for performance at Court. Those were the rehearsals that Philostrate had to suffer.

The two distinct activities, censoring ordinary plays and scrutinising the plays chosen for staging before royalty, have not been distinguished as clearly as they should be. The manuscript with the Master's signature of approval on it was basic to every company's activities. Whether in London or on tour they had to keep their allowed playbooks to hand. On tour, they had to be shown to local mayors to prove the Master's signature was on them. At Leicester in 1583, the then novel need for Tilney to license the plays instead of the local mayor was affirmed when two companies, both claiming to be authorised by the Earl of Worcester, arrived only three days apart. The clerk duly echoed his recent instructions from Tilney, reporting 'No play is to bee played, but such as is allowed by the said Edmund, & his hand at the latter end of the saide booke they doe play'.[9] Whether on tour or at a London playhouse, the 'allowed book' was an essential accompaniment to every performance, the company's security. It was portable. With such a form of approval, the close scrutiny that a play which the Master had previously read and then chosen for royal performance required was unnecessary. Only the plays chosen for the Court required special 'rehearsals'. That was when the Chamber at St John's was needed.

We know that the Office had to work full-time between October and January each year, the months of preparation for the Court's Christmas revels. As W. R. Streitberger puts it, 'The Revels season began on 31 October; entertainments had to be selected for the season, the texts of the plays altered to suit the court, productions planned, furniture co-ordinated, scenery designed and built, rehearsals held, stages contracted for and built in whatever hall was to be used for the production, and finally the lighting designed and last-minute fittings installed all before the first performance – no later than St. Stephen's Day (26 December)'.[10] So we must ask: how much empty space did Tilney and his successors have at their Clerkenwell office for full rehearsals? If we assume, as the evidence seems to affirm, that normally to approve plays he merely read them in private, what did he do about Court performances? How much time and space would a full rehearsal of a play chosen for the Court need? Did he review all of them in rehearsal before making his choice? Allowing a play to be seen and heard in

---

[9] Gurr, *The Shakespearian Playing Companies*, Oxford: Clarendon Press, 1996, p. 42.
[10] W. R. Streitberger, ed. Malone Society Collections XIII, p. xx.

public was one thing. Performances at Court were quite a different matter, and not a small one. All the chosen plays had to be made ready for first performance by 26 December at the latest.[11] We need to look further into the timing of such choices, the venue for rehearsals, and their impact on the companies.

To identify what Tilney over his thirty years might have set up as a routine for checking on plays for the Court, we need first to know what were the physical resources allocated to him at St John's. In 1581 Clerkenwell was a new centre for the Revels Office. It moved there from the Blackfriars, which had a small venue for staging plays. In all, over the years the substantial Blackfriars site had three indoor playhouses. The first was close to the then Revels Office. It came into being through the activities, originally to pleasure Henry VIII, of Sir Thomas Cawarden. Effectively the first Master of the Revels, running plays and other entertainments for the royal court, in the 1550s he took over five large rooms in the old Blackfriars, one of which he occasionally put to use as a small playhouse. That was situated north of the more celebrated second playhouse, where in 1576 Richard Farrant built what is now known as the 'first' Blackfriars for his boy choristers. Both were north of the Upper Frater, which James Burbage was to use for the second, far more famous playhouse on the site, built for the Shakespeare company twenty years after Farrant's.

Cawarden used his five rooms in the Blackfriars mainly to store and maintain the large stock of costumes and properties needed for shows at Court. In his time, of course, censoring plays was not a Revels duty. The work then was almost entirely a matter of storing materials for reuse in subsequent Court performances. A memorandum of 1573 specified that the 'cheife busines of the office' consisted in 'makinge of garmentes, In making of hedpeces, and in payntiinge'.[12] It went on to declare, verbosely, that the 'connynge of the office resteth in skill of devyse, in understandinge of historyes, in judgement of comedies tragedyes and showes, in sight of perspective and architecture, some smacke of geometrye and other thynges; wherefore the best helpe for thofficers is to make good choyce of cunynge artificers severally accordinge to their best qualities'. This involved 'laying abrode, turninge, soinge, mending, tackinge, making clene, spunginge, wipinge, brushinge, foldinge and laying upp the king's bardes, bases, caparisons, hanging garments and other stuff and store of the

---

[11] Ibid.
[12] E. K. Chambers, *Notes on the History of the Revels Office under the Tudors*, London: A. H. Bullen, 1907, p. 37.

office'. Individual items might be rented out. The function of the Revels was to maintain materials for the shows at Court.[13]

Cawarden supervised the festivities for Elizabeth's coronation in 1559, but died shortly after. He was followed in office by Sir Thomas Benger, a more casual Master, who ran extravagant shows but left the properties and costumes in a mess. He died in March 1577 heavily in debt, the state of his finances a possible mark of his ineptitude.[14] Some evidence for the troubles his regime got into is cited below. The need for the office to be reorganised, the disorders that led to Tilney's appointment in 1578, was obvious.

Through the 1560s and 1570s the Revels Office consistently endured in chaos. Under Benger it moved away from the Blackfriars to the 'late Hospital of St. John of Jerusalem' in Clerkenwell. That was where Tilney, the longest-lasting and clearly a far more efficient Master, began his long period of control. As part of his duties, he was allocated a house next door to the Revels. He increased its capacity for storage of its rich materials, and seems to have taken over other rooms for use, including a 'great chamber'. This must have been the work-free space where the rehearsals for Court performances, and perhaps initially the 'rehearsals' of plays the players wanted licensed, could be staged.

Tilney was, though remotely, a cousin of sorts to Charles Howard, the Lord Admiral. As Lord Chamberlain in 1583 Howard became officially responsible for the management of the Revels Office. Tilney, probably through Howard's influence, had been officially appointed Master of the Revels in a patent of 24 July 1579, backdated to the previous Christmas.[15] This patent was the first document to specify his extra duties, in the form of the 'furthermore' requirement quoted above. As plays proliferated through the 1580s, growing rapidly in quality and number, this must have added a huge additional burden to the traditional Revels work of keeping the Court entertained.

Lansdowne MSS 86, Article 60, is a survey of the Revels Office accommodation at St John's.[16] It specifies that in 1578 the Office had thirteen rooms in all, one of them a double space. In the entry for the 'Chappell or Churche in the use of Henry Sackforde', it lists a store for use by the officers of the 'Hales and Tentes', the old office to which the Revels was then connected. More pertinently, Sackford also had 'Certeyne Roomes & Lodginges lienege nexte, on the North syde of the saied Chappell... Of

---

[13] Cawarden's records are in the Loseley archives. See Chambers, *Notes*, p. 17.
[14] *Notes*, p. 26.   [15] *Notes*, p. 57.
[16] See *Documents relating to the Office of the Revels in the Time of Queen Elizabeth. Edited, with Notes and Indexes*, by Albert Feuillerat, Louvain: A. Uystpruyst, 1908, pp. 47–49.

which xiij Chambers one ys devided into ije Roome which serveth for A hall and great Chamber Or Dynyng Chamber'. Edward Kirkham, it added, 'yoman of the Revelles maskes and disguysinges, holdeth . . . The great hall. iijre woorking housez. belowe. One Cutting house and one Greate Chambre used as Roomes for the Revelles'. The double room in Kirkham's hands was the one listed as a 'hall and great Chamber Or Dynyng Chamber'. Presumably it was this double space that was used to stage the plays chosen for performance at Court. A later document, a legal affidavit dated 1607, notes about the property 'late in the tenure of Mr. Tylney Esquire' that on the upper floor was 'the great Chamber commonly called The Revels Chamber'.[17] Tilney's own property was additional to these workrooms. He lived next to his offices, and his staff all lived nearby.

It would be nice to know if the rehearsal space was ever also used for the plays the companies wished to have licensed. Clearly it was used for the select few already chosen for performance at Court, and perhaps too any still being considered. Evidence given below suggests that Tilney chose the plays, but on what advice, whether he attended any in question himself, or whether he just made his selection from his memory of the books he had allowed, we do not know. There is no evidence that he ever visited the playhouses, so perhaps the players made their own suggestions, or at least gave him advice about which of their plays they thought good enough for the Court. The sometimes hurried timetable for this process is noted below.

Over the sixty-four years from 1578 till 1642, the offices of the Revels moved around quite a lot. Starting in the rooms alongside Tilney's house at St John's Priory, over its years there the Clerkenwell location drew several of the northern playhouses to its vicinity, notably the Fortune and the Red Bull. Both of these were built quite close to St John's, in 1600 and 1604. We should ask why they chose that area, if they were not required to journey there quite frequently to rehearse their plays in the great chamber. In 1608, however, when both the Fortune and the Red Bull were in full operation nearby, King James granted the entire St John's property to his Stuart cousin, the eighth Lord Aubigny. The Revels offices were shifted to Whitefriars, next door to where the Whitefriars indoor playhouse had recently opened, and not far from where the Salisbury Court playhouse arrived much later, in 1629. The Revels Office was long gone by then. In 1612 it moved just south of St. Paul's, to a rather more reputable site near the

---

[17] Deed 1, Sir Tho. Fowler v. John and Sara Scott, 31 July 1607, The Lang Collection, Library of the Order of St. John, St. John's Gate.

College of Arms, and stayed there till 1630, when it shifted to Cheapside, by St. Mary-le-Bow Church. It remained there until playing was stopped in 1642. Too little is known about these locations for us to tell if they all included a 'great chamber', like the one provided in Clerkenwell.[18]

Recent archaeology on the St John's site seems to indicate that Tilney secured a quite substantial extra space for his Revels work.[19] He was the first Master to need room for plays to be performed there, but even at St John's evidence for the large hall is not very precise. A letter in the records of Sir Julius Caesar, Master of Requests in the 1590s, says something about the 1608 move from Clerkenwell to Whitefriars, which took place while Tilney was still in charge. Endorsed as 'Mr. Tilney's writing touching his office', it reported that the 'Office of the Revells Consistethe of a wardropp and other severall Roomes for Artifficers to worke in (viz Taylors, Imbrotherers, Properti makers, Paynters, wyerdrawers and Carpenters), togeather with a Convenient place for the Rehearshalls and setting forthe of Playes and other Shewes for those Services'.[20] These rooms, together with Tilney's own house and the apartments for his staff, were all part of the St John's estate. Caesar's paper, probably dating from about 1596, covers Tilney's accommodation too: 'In which Office the Master of the Office hath ever hadd a dwellinge Howsse for him self and his Famelie, and the other Officers ar to have eyther dwelling Howsses Assigned unto them by the Master (for so goeth the wordes of ther Patentes) or else a Rente for the same as thei had before they Came unto St. Johnes'.[21] This shows that Tilney secured a chamber where plays could be 'rehearsed', as an integral part of his duties as Master. It is less clear precisely what he used the chamber for.

Caesar did not describe the 'Convenient place' for 'Rehearshalls and settinge forthe of Playes and other Shewes', so we have to study what archaeologists Sloane and Malcolm have identified in their map of St John's after the Reformation. We know the Revels occupied two floors, the upper one extending over the postern gate access towards Tilney's house. The 'chamber' on the upper floor appears to have been a little over twenty feet in interior width, and of uncertain length, although, since it was definitely a 'double' room, it may have been twice the width, forty feet long.

As we have seen, through the 1570s the Revels Office resources were chiefly notable for the decay and neglect of their stores. Properties and costumes used in Court events and then stored for re-design and re-use were

---

[18] A not entirely helpful footnote to the Fortune and Red Bull's siting in Clerkenwell is that after about 1616 neither playhouse supplied any Court performances. By then, though, both playhouses were becoming known as 'citizen' venues.
[19] See Barney Sloane and Gordon Malcolm, *Excavations at the Priory of the Order of the Hospital of St. John of Jerusalem*, Clerkenwell, London. MoLAS Monograph 20, London, 2004.
[20] Quoted in Chambers, *Elizabethan Stage*, I.102.   [21] *Notes*, pp. 70–71.

in serious disarray. The need specified later for a 'greate chambere where the workes were doone and the playes rezited' was put in hazard by decay in the other rooms where the old costumes and properties lay in store. 'A note of sarten thinges which are nedefull to be Redressed in the offyce of the Revelles', written by the Yeoman in 1574, complained about the shortage of finance that was causing the decay. Of the specific problems, the chief defects he listed were

1. Fyrste the Romes or Lodginges, where the garments and other thinges, as hedpeces and suche lyke, dother lye. Is in such decaye for want of reparacions, that it hath by that meanes perished A very greate longe wall, which parte thereof is falne doune and hath broke undoune A great presse, which stoode all Alongest the same, by which meanes I am fayne to laye the garmentes uppon the grounde, to the greate hurt of the same, so as if youre honoure ded se the same it woolde petye you to see suche stoffe so yll bestowed.
2. Next there is no convenient Romes for the Artifycers to wourke in, but that Tayloures, Paynters, Properative makers, and Carpenters are all fayne to wourke in one rome, which is A very greate hinderaunce one to Another, which thinge nedes not for theye are slacke anowe of them selves.
3. More, there ys two whole yeares charges be hinde un payde, to the great hinderaunce of the poore Artyfycers that wourke there. In so much that there be A greate parte of them that have byn dryven to sell there bylles or debentars for halfe that is dewe unto them by the same.[22]

The massive clothes presses were all broken, and could not be repaired. A later note says that new ones had been ordered, but works with them 'are not begon'.[23] This was the business of preserving the huge stock of fabric and other properties. Play-control came later. It was some time after this 1574 'Complaint' that the Revels under Tilney secured the additional 'great Hall' with its 'great chamber' along with a new cutting house and three 'woorking housez' below the hall.[24]

If Caesar was right the 'Convenient place' where Tilney chose his plays for the Court was the 'great chamber'. From 1580 the Court plays became the Office's most noteworthy activity. In his *Apology for Actors* (1612), Heywood reported a story about it from a century before.[25] He wrote that 'one of our best English Chroniclers records, that when Edward the fourth

---

[22] *Elizabethan Stage*, I.83–4.   [23] *Notes*, p. 27.   [24] *Elizabethan Stage*, I.95.
[25] My edition of the Apology (a facsimile reprint of the 1841 Shakespeare Society ed.) has 'Stowe' as the source for the story.

would shew himselfe in publicke state to the view of the people, he repaired to his Palace at S. Johnes, where he was accustomed to see the City Actors. And since then, that house by the Princes free gift, hath belonged to the office of the Reveles, where our Court playes have been in late daies yearely rehersed, perfected, and corrected before they came to the publike view of the Prince and the Nobility.'[26] Wrong though he was about Edward IV putting the Revels there, Heywood himself was thoroughly familiar with the practice. His fanciful summary describes the process undertaken once Tilney had chosen the plays from the companies' current repertoires. That was certainly the routine by 1608, when Heywood most likely wrote his *Apology*. Heywood was writing about Philostrate's Master-like claim to have seen Pyramus and Thisbe in rehearsal, part of his official preparation for presenting shows at Court.

Heywood was writing only of the chosen Court plays. His account says nothing about how plays were first licensed. In spite of the specification laid down in the original patent, once Tilney started simply reading each playscript before signing his 'allowance' at the end, he may never have obeyed the demand that every play had to be 'rehersed' in full before him. That would have more than doubled his workload through the year. The companies would never have taken two copies of their scripts to the Revels, one to prompt their performance, and one for the Master to read while they did so. Therefore the only uncertainty is when, in the first decades before he marked-up *Sir Thomas More* in 1600, did he retreat to merely reading the playbooks?

There are some issues over timing here. In the rapid and hectic three-week process of buying a new play and making it ready for the stage, how soon did the acting companies acquire the good copy of the playbook they then sent to Tilney for his signature? It had to be in a sufficiently complete and perfected form by then. In the Caroline period Henry Herbert made a fuss about the changes he required being incorporated into the players' parts, which suggests he knew they would already have been copied out before the playbook was handed in for his approval.[27] That reflects the pressure of time companies were under while preparing new productions. The Master was under less pressure, though by the 1620s, with four or

---

[26] *Apology for Actors*, 1612, E1v. This book is accessible on EEBO. Heywood's acknowledgement of the Revels being at St John's, incidentally, confirms the assumption that he wrote his book several years before it was published. He must have composed it before the Office moved to the Whitefriars in 1608.

[27] See for instance N. W. Bawcutt, *The Control and Censorship of Caroline Drama. The Records of Sir Henry Herbert, Master of the Revels 1623–73*. Oxford: Clarendon Press, 1996, pp. 42–3, 183. Bawcutt, pp. 42–76, has by far the most exact analysis of what censorship entailed under Herbert.

five companies all regularly offering their latest playbooks for him to allow, Herbert cannot have afforded to be too casual about it.

The Henslowe records tell us how frequently in the 1590s the Admiral's Men sent in their new plays to be licensed. The *Diary* lists two kinds of payment to the Revels. One was weekly, initially five shillings, later ten, and even more by 1600. That was for licensing the Rose as a playhouse. The other was for licensing the plays.[28] These second payments appear far less regularly, though not necessarily because there were fewer of them. On 26 January 1598, for instance, Henslowe records giving Thomas Downton, a leading player, money to pay the Master of the Revels 'for lysensynge of ij boockes xiiij s', that is, two playbooks at seven shillings each. Henslowe noted this as a loan to the company, implying that until then they had not used Henslowe's funds for their licences, but paid the Revels directly. Three more payments are noted in March, and two further on 28 March. Another 21 shillings for three more playbooks was noted on 24 July, and others for the following year in June and December. Before that, it seems, the company had paid without taking any of Henslowe's cash. So for this one company the Revels Office was licensing at least one or two new plays every month in 1598. Through the previous years new plays averaged at least two a month. We can only guess how many more came from the other companies in the same period.

Not untypically, the Revels specification of 1581 was heavy in its demand to punish defaulters. They were to be imprisoned 'without bayle or mayneprise'. It would be nice to know how conscientiously Tilney wielded that order. A later Master, Henry Herbert, signed the official copy of *A Game at Chesse* on 11 August 1624, while probably ignorant of how perilous it was. He can hardly have watched a rehearsal. Had he seen the play staged, he could never have misjudged the political bias inherent in its costuming. After the public staging and subsequent uproar, he had to appear before the Lord Chamberlain of the time, the Earl of Pembroke, to protest his innocence, or ignorance. He got away with it, most likely because Pembroke and everyone else sitting in judgment were complicit, tacitly applauding the play's audacity. Such an excuse would hardly have worked if Herbert was known to have actually viewed the play in rehearsal.

Did Tilney and his successors ever insist that plays must be fully enacted before him or his deputy? *Henslowe's Diary* shows that they were usually licensed quite quickly. Dekker and Chettle received full payment for their

---

[28] Gurr, *Shakespeare's Opposites. The Admiral's Company 1594–1625*, Cambridge: Cambridge University Press, 2009, pp. 89–90.

tragedy called *Agamemnon* on 30 May 1599, and the note of payment to the Master for its licence followed only four days later: 'pd unto the m^r of the Revelles man for lycensynge of A Boocke called the tragedie of agamemnon the 3 of June 1599 . . . vij s' (*Diary*, p. 121). Munday's two Robin Hood plays moved from page to stage equally quickly. That left little time for the whole company to visit St John's.

It seems obvious that the Revels ran two wholly different kinds of test for new plays. One was censoring the playbooks, which the Master read in his own time. The other, for the performances at Court, entailed what were usually called 'rehearsals'. It seems that only these, plays already given the Master's licence, were what had to be staged in the great chamber at St John's and the later Revels sites. This economy by the Revels went along with others. Streitberger believes that 'gradually over the course of Tyllney's early Mastership companies seem to have been expected to supply their own [costumes for plays at Court]'.[29] He thinks this happened 'by the mid-1580s, at the latest by the early 1590s'.

We know a little more about the preparation of plays for the Court than we do about Tilney's more routine censorious readings. Once the plays were chosen, companies had to put in some hurried preparations. Entries in *Henslowe's Diary* for Dekker's play 'cald the hole hystory of Fortunatus' begin on 9 November 1599.[30] The first is an 'earnest' to Dekker of two pounds for writing the play. Following this is another of three pounds on 24 November, and on 30th another pound 'in full payment of his booke of fortunatues'. The next day Henslowe noted a further loan of another pound for 'the altrenge of the boocke of the wholl history of fortewnatus'. Early in December Downton received ten pounds from Henslowe 'to by thinges for Fortunatus', indicating that it was being prepared for its first staging at the Rose. Then on 12 December Dekker received another two pounds, 'for the eande of fortewnatus for the corte'. Evidently selected for royal performance very soon after, or perhaps even before, its first staging in December, it needed altering for the royal occasion. Probably the company urged it on the Master because they wanted to use it to advertise the name of their imminent new playhouse, the Fortune in Clerkenwell. John Astington thinks the Court performance was held at Richmond Palace on 27 December.[31] It appeared in quarto in 1600, complete with its Prologue and Epilogue for the Court, along with another prologue for the Rose ('this small Circumference must stand, / For the imagined Sur-face

---

[29] Streitberger, *Collections* XIII, p. xix. [30] See *Diary*, pp. 126–8.
[31] *English Court Theatre 1558–1642*, Cambridge: Cambridge University Press, 1999, p. 236.

of much land,' it said, apologetically). The Court prologue was a dialogue between two old men, who address the Queen. The 1600 titlepage specified 'As it was plaied before the Queenes Majestie this Christmas'.

These arrangements had to move forward very quickly. The company's other contribution to the Court revels at Richmond that Christmas was *The Shoemaker's Holiday*. It was staged four evenings later, on the first of January. This play was rather less fresh in the company's repertory. It first appears in the *Diary* as a payment made to Dekker on 15 July 1599, well before his *Fortunatus*. Tilney had plenty of time to make this other choice from the company's repertory. But he must have 'allowed' *Fortunatus* shortly after the final payments were made to Dekker at the end of November, deciding almost immediately to add it to Dekker's other play for the Court. His decision to add *Fortunatus* to the list for Christmas must have been made some time in the week following 1 December, when Dekker got extra pay for making changes to his script, and well before the 12th, when Downton got the cash to buy properties for presenting it at Court. That leaves less than a week for Tilney to have viewed a performance in the Revels 'great chamber'. Dekker's prologue and epilogue, and the alteration of its ending, must have been ready before then, because the Master had to approve the revised version. All this was done while it was playing at the Rose.

Given that through these years the companies introduced new plays to their repertories at least every third week,[32] taking an entire performance to the Revels Office in winter would have been a major burden both in time and cost. The idea that, for his routine duty of censoring plays, the Master ignored his initial patent, simply reading and correcting the playbooks, seems irrefutable. When he chose them for performance at Court, however, it seems that all the selected plays had to be viewed in costume and rehearsed in full, in versions that included all the changes to the allowed text that the company introduced once Tilney made his choice. They had then to be 'rehearsed' in his 'great chamber' so that he could approve the modified versions. Economy of effort except when great dignitaries are involved is an entirely natural tendency.

---

[32] Carol Chillington Rutter, *Documents of the Rose Playhouse*, Manchester: Manchester University Press, 1984, p. 28, writes that the machine 'devoured a new play a fortnight'.

CHAPTER 8

The War of 1614–1618
Jacobean Absolutism, Local Authority and a Crisis of Overproduction

In April 1624 the Norwich authorities, having received a letter from somebody on the Privy Council that expressed sympathy for their bans on public playing, used it as their ground to forbid the next company that arrived with a royal warrant from playing in the city. They had enough courage, allied to their conviction that playing corrupted the poor, to argue that the Privy Council's letter supporting their position overruled the King's signet on his licence to the company. The Stuart kings were gradually downrating the Privy Council to a function far below the position in government that it held under Elizabeth. If this incident came to his notice, James might have felt that he had another reason among the many he had already cited to take more and more of a direct hand in the country's government.

Predictably, the outcome of this conflict between central authority and local government was stormy, although it stayed entirely local to Norwich, where it blew up and died down. The Lord Chamberlain did try to take a hand in it from London, but it remained essentially a local matter. And yet it had wide implications, not just for the players, and it reflected a struggle that had been going on for a decade already. The Norwich authority's records state that

> This day Francis Wambus brought into this Court A Bill signed with his Majesties hand... whereupon there was shewed forth unto him the Letters directed from the Lords of his majesties most honorable privie Counsell Dated the 27th of May 1623... whereupon the said wambus peremtorily affirmed that he would play in this City & would lay in prison here this Twelvemoneth but he would try whether the kinges Command or the Counselles be the greater... the said wambus was accordinge to the Counselles order Comanded to forbeare to play within the liberties of this City And he

Original publication: "The War of 1614–1618: Jacobean Absolutism, Local Authority, and a Crisis of Overproduction," *ELR* 26 (1996), 138–54.

nevertheles answered that he would make tryall what he might doe by the kinges authority for he said he would play.¹

Norwich chose to use the Privy Council's authority against the King's signature on his written licence that the players carried. The issue at stake was a nice question, roughly handled. The players, wearing the King's daughter's livery as royal servants, Francis Wambus and his Lady Elizabeth's company, made an attempt to test which authority was the stronger on that same day, April 24, by setting up a playbill saying that a play called *The Spanish Contract*² would be played at the White Horse inn. Norwich promptly imprisoned Wambus, who admitted to the court that he had written the playbill himself. The Mayor eventually released him on a bond paid by Wambus' co-leader John Townsend. In September Wambus returned to Norwich with Townsend carrying a letter from the Master of the Revels Henry Herbert which said that he had been freed from his imprisonment on the Lord Chamberlain's authority. This letter Wambus used to demand the repayment of Townsend's bond. The Norwich court stood its ground and refused to give the money back.³ Playing on their home ground, they won easily against the touring company.

The Norwich affair was a belated instance of a fight between royal authority and local councils that rumbled most loudly over four years, from 1614 to 1618. It erupted periodically through the following decades, and finally blew its top with the Parliamentary decree of September 1642 closing down all playhouses. That had been the fervent wish of most of the mayors in the country for seventy or more years. The closure became inevitable as playing became more and more closely identified with its royal protector, and the protector's authority weakened. The context for the conflict of 1614–1618 is a measure of how deep were the animosities that surfaced in 1642, and how long they had been rumbling. The full story, which might more tactfully be called (using Hayden White's term for the self-conscious re-ordering of historical⁴ details into a coherently suggestive account) the "emplotment," has to be based on the struggles that took place

---

¹ Transcribed in Records of Early English Drama, *Norwich 1540–1642*, ed. David Galloway (Toronto, 1984), p. 180.
² The play has been lost. Its title suggests that it was written to ride on the same wave of anti-Spanish feeling that produced *A Game at Chess* a few months later.
³ See REED *Norwich*, pp. 180–83. Six years went by before the Lady Elizabeth's returned to play at Norwich.
⁴ Dasent, *Acts of the Privy Council of England, 1615–1616* (1925), p. 86.

in James's second decade to fix the professional companies in London, and the spillover consequences for the companies that travelled.

Hostility to playing on the part of local authorities was widespread and rarely wavered, even though few seem to have gone to the length that (for instance) Chester did of refusing the players who visited the town any gratuity at all. To judge by the municipal records across the country, the strength of the hostility to professional playing in most local authorities, including London, was quite specific. It was notably greater than it was to bear- or bull-baiting or to solo or team entertainers like tumblers and acrobats. What prompted it was not just a matter of religious hostility to the kind of public leisure pursuits that did the devil's work. Nor was it just a matter of the riots and affrays which the authorities expected to take place when large crowds gathered. Something more basic, a prejudice that was in complex ways rooted in the idea that audiences should not pay money to witness the counterfeits and con-tricks which happened when men and boys pretended to be what they were not, was at work somewhere under this broadly-felt animus. What really inspired it is about as extricable as taking the religious motives out of the political in 1642. It certainly reflects the beginnings of a basic animus against Jacobean absolutism, which Norwich and many other town corporations saw as the protector of playgoing.

In some respects the animus did have a religious basis, since the towns which made the most intense efforts in the 1570s either to preserve or to suppress the local Corpus Christi plays were often the same towns which showed most hostility to the professional players. It is equally possible that the growth of hostility to playing under the Stuarts can be related to the growth of political hostility to the Crown. But there is no clear way to identify such broad and collective motivation. What can be done is to give this broad pro- and anti-animus over plays a more local and particular role in the period 1614 to 1618 in government, as a test for what it shows about the differences within those monolithic fictions, the government and the people.

This case exemplifies the difficulty of making any judgment based on fixed prejudices, and more directly on the convenient but dangerous assumption that the monarchic government ever had a consistent policy toward playing and the playing companies. To put it mildly, there is little sign of uniformity or even consistency in royal and in Privy Council policy over playing in London in these years. As his younger children grew, James extended the patronage system that he had initiated in 1603–1604 by making them patrons the major companies. By 1611 his younger son Charles and his daughter Elizabeth had their own companies, bringing the total of royally patronised groups in London to five. With the Queen's Revels Children, now practically an adult group, that made six companies struggling to perform in London. The trouble with this was that by then there were only four playhouses available to them, and the Privy Council consistently blocked attempts to open new ones. In the years from 1611 to 1618 the companies played a kind of musical chairs with their theatres. The King's Men had their Globe and Blackfriars, one of which was always idle because they refused to rent it out while they used the other one. The Queen's had the Red Bull. The Prince's had the Fortune. The ex-boy company used the Whitefriars until its lease expired in 1612, then merged with the Lady Elizabeth's, using the Swan and later the Hope. Prince Charles's played at the Curtain.

Revels Office and Privy Council policy was fairly constant. They licensed six royally patronised companies, but only tolerated four in London. On March 29, 1615 the Privy Council summoned the leading representatives of the London companies to present themselves before it. It named two players from each of four groups that it wanted to speak to. From the King's Men it asked for John Heminges and Richard Burbage; from Queen Anne's, Christopher Beeston and Robert Lee; from the Palsgrave's (formerly the Prince's), William Rowley and John Newton; from Prince Charles's (I) Company, Thomas Downton and Humphrey Jeffes. This shows that with the disappearance of the last of the boy companies and the recent merger of the two companies that were patronised by James's younger children into one, the six companies of 1611 had shrunk to four, which became the set number of approved playing companies by 1615.

London could not accommodate easily more than five companies, even at the height of their social standing under Charles. The six of 1611 could not maintain a presence in London on equal terms, whether because of the surplus in trade they created or because of the shortage of playhouses. So by 1615 the former boy company had merged with the Lady Elizabeth's and that merged group had in turn joined up with the Duke of York's to take the Duke's new title as Prince Charles's company. That left the four groups whose leaders the Privy Council summoned in 1615. Apart from a few rather short-lived incursions by outside groups, four became the normal number of London companies through the next twelve years and even after. Not until 1629, when Richard Gunnell built the third hall playhouse, Salisbury Court, did five companies play regularly in London again. Although no record exists of any formal declaration being made about the allowed total, the Revels Office through 1614–1618 accepted four as the maximum for London. On January 29, 1618, for instance, the Master of the Revels summoned Heminges from the King's to see him 'in the name of the four companyes'.[5]

The shrinkage was due to more factors than the economic pressure of the increase in supply to the same-sized market of playgoers. By 1614 the most obvious limitation was the serious shortage of playhouses. The Hope stank of bears and dogs. The Curtain, built in 1577, was not much better, because it was now by a long way the oldest amphitheatre in London.[6] It was also the one with distinctly the lowest reputation.[7] So long as the King's kept their two playhouses for their own exclusive use, the other three companies of 1614 had not enough good playhouses available to them.

A new playhouse was urgently needed, but besides the predictable opposition of the city, the Privy Council was actively unhelpful. On September 26, 1615 it issued instructions to block a venture by Philip Rosseter, musician and former manager of a boy company, who allied himself with Edward Alleyn and others to build a new playhouse at Porter's Hall designed to match the Blackfriars.[8] In the event the Porter's Hall playhouse enjoyed only a single performance, if that, before the Privy Council closed it down.[9] By this time, with the success of the King's Men at Blackfriars as their model, the impresarios and financiers, and very likely the players too, did not want another amphitheatre. The Hope was undesirable according to the players, and the Curtain was too old. What the companies and their financiers all wanted was a new hall playhouse. That was what the short-lived Porter's Hall was designed for. A subsequent and more successful enterprise, Christopher Beeston's adaptation of a cockpit outside the city in Drury Lane into a playhouse, was directed by the same inspiration. By 1614 the familiar presence of one leading company of adult players performing daily in a hall playhouse was crying out for imitation. So the Hope

---

[5] *The Dramatic Records of Sir Henry Herbert, 1622–1673*, ed. J. Q. Adams (New Haven, 1917), p. 48. Besides the number he specified in 1618, Herbert makes two later references to four companies as the authorised number, in 1623 and 1636 (*Herbert Record Book*, pp. 25, 65). Four continued to be Herbert's preferred number of London companies, despite the rise to five in Caroline times, since he still named only four in 1636. But that was at the outset of a long closure. Five companies got restarted in 1638.

[6] Still in use in 1622, it had the longest life of any unreconstructed playhouse in London, more than the forty-three years of the two Globes together, or the forty-two of the two Fortunes.

[7] See John Orrell, "The London Stage in the Florentine Correspondence, 1604–1618," *TRI* 3 (1977–78), 155–81, p. 171.

[8] The order is quoted in *ES* IV, 343. Another Privy Council minute of January 27, 1617 instructed the lord mayor that 'certaine persons that goe about to sett up a Play howse in the Black Fryaers neere unto his Majesties wardrobe, and for that purpose have lately erected and made fitt a Building, which is almost if not fully finished', were doing so contrary to several prohibitions, and that the King that day had given instructions to pull the building down. *MSC* I, 4 & 5, p. 374.

[9] S. P. Cerasano, "Competition for the King's Men? Alleyn's Blackfriars Venture," *MRDE* 4 (1989), 173–86.

stands in history as the last and shortest-lived amphitheatre playhouse in London. Thanks in large part to the evident value the Blackfriars had for the King's Men, probably endorsed by the widely known fact that a hall playhouse could bring in larger revenues than an amphitheatre, from this time on the only new playhouses were halls.

There are widespread implications in this upward transfer of company ambitions. It suggests that all the London companies now saw what James Burbage had envisaged first in 1596, that the future lay in enclosed and roofed theatres. After several decades of the professional companies travelling under Elizabeth and playing in guildhalls, where the doors were strong enough to give the gatherers absolute control over who saw the performance, that is hardly surprising. It may also indicate that for all the divisions apparent inside the Privy Council itself the companies still felt more secure with the social elite than with the groundlings. Behind that thought is the certainty that the Court and the great patrons were the best protection the companies now had against the repressiveness of urban officialdom, both in the city of London and in towns like Norwich.

It leaves unclear the least tangible of these considerations, the question of the companies' continuing loyalty to their basic clientele, the traditional London populace. The events of 1614–1618 included a gradual dividing of audiences according to the kind of playhouse they could afford. How comprehensively and how early the Fortune and Red Bull became the "citizen" playhouses while the Blackfriars and Cockpit became gentrified is the most complex question of this period. In one sense the change must have been immediate, because the halls cost so much more for admission than the amphitheatres. On the other hand, changes in repertory plays and practices came much more slowly.

How the attitudes and the practices of the companies changed is part of the argument about the separation of the great (or canonical) cultural tradition from the "little" tradition of populist culture.[10] The most likely of all these possible motives in the players themselves is of course the commercial one. The shifts in company placements at the different kinds of playhouse indicate that they were most strongly motivated by the financial advantage given them by the wealthier clientele who went to the hall playhouses. Against that is the fact that the companies themselves, and their plays, found it quite easy to switch in both directions between halls and amphitheatres even in the 1630s. There is no ready way to identify whether

---

[10] Alexander Leggatt's section on 'Popular culture' has some cogent points to make about this in terms of the traditions, in *Jacobean Public Theatre* (London, 1992), pp. 32–39.

the initiative lay with the playgoers at particular playhouses or with the companies who served them.

There are two ways of marshalling the evidence about all this. One, the usual route, is to look at London and the government's exercise of control over the companies through the Lord Chamberlain and the Privy Council. The other and less frequented route is in the civic records around the country. What happened to the membership of the two companies squeezed out of London by 1614 is one part of the larger emplotment. The story of what companies did on their travels under the early Stuarts is the second. It is also a remarkable indication of communal and authoritative attitudes to playgoing.

The Privy Council's policy was always about London. Court entertainments came from the London companies, and increasingly from the hall companies. What they did elsewhere was their own concern, and that of their hosts in the provincial towns. Some towns such as York and Bristol had inns converted for playing as London had up to 1594. Only London had the freedom to build playhouses in the suburbs of Middlesex and Surrey that Charles Howard, the Lord Admiral, gave to the early impresarios (he was Lord Lieutenant of Surrey, and headed the commission for the magistrates in Middlesex). From 1594 fixing playhouses in the suburbs became an element of the Privy Council's policy. That, under Elizabeth, was mercifully consistent. It appeased the Lord Mayor and exploited the suburbs for London playing. But elsewhere, as the Privy Council's role faded under James and his policies came under attack from a variety of quarters, the players increasingly had to rely on the King himself and his patents authorising their right to play to underwrite their travels outside London. That was what produced the initial conflicts in 1614–1618 between the royal licence and country hostility.

In London the companies had more trouble from the shortage of playhouses than from the authorities, who controlled them largely by restricting their venues. The embargo that the Privy Council laid on Porter's Hall in 1615 made it clear that, despite the privilege given the King's to play at Blackfriars, the Council remembered its old undertaking of 1594 to the Lord Mayor to keep playhouses out of the city. The city's own opposition to playing inside the city walls had certainly not diminished. Christopher Beeston, the only one to succeed in opening a hall playhouse in this decade, was a good deal more tactful than the Rosseter-Alleyn consortium at Porter's Hall when he made the second attempt to imitate the success of the King's Men at the Blackfriars with his Cockpit, but even he ran into major troubles over it. He avoided the Privy Council's and the city's disapproval by finding a site that stood outside the city in the West End near the Blackfriars. An old circular hall used for public displays of cockfighting, the original Cockpit was located in Drury Lane. That put it close to the rapidly growing wealthy suburbs of Westminster and to the Inns of Court which provided a large proportion of the more affluent audiences, but left it free like the suburban amphitheatres from the threat of city restraint that now hung over even the Blackfriars. For all the ostensible protection against the city's hostility that the Privy Council gave to playing, the two administrations seem to have worked together in restricting entrepreneurs from speculating with new hall playhouses.[11] And James himself, while he did regularly put his great seal on the annual licences for the professional companies, took no interest in the problem of the shortage of playhouses.

Built shortly after the Porter's Hall theatre opened and was promptly closed, towards the end of 1616, Beeston's Cockpit was even smaller than Burbage's Blackfriars. Its design may have been hampered by constraints on new buildings in the West End, which allowed new constructions only in the form of enlargements to existing structures, and that by not more than one-third. If the plans that Inigo Jones, the royal surveyor, drew up for an unnamed hall playhouse in about 1616 were commissioned by Beeston, they met this restraint very neatly. Jones as the King's surveyor would have had first-hand knowledge of the constraints on new building.[12] The plans made use of the existing circular auditorium of the old cockpit, cutting into the circle with a square stage and a rectangular tiring house behind it. Auditorium capacity was augmented with boxes flanking the stage, and ranks of benches or "degrees" on either side of the music room above the stage. Its total audience capacity was probably less than five hundred, but the much higher prices that could be charged at this superior kind of venue evidently still made it a good investment in Beeston's eyes.

Indirectly it was the high prices for admission rather than the Privy Council that gave Beeston his main trouble. The basic story behind the

---

[11] The city took over control of the Liberties in 1608 as a royal concession in return for raising a large grant of money for Crown expenses, which were well out of control. In later years the city seems, however reluctantly, to have accepted the status quo, allowing the King's Servants to continue playing in the Blackfriars, but that remained a unique privilege. There is no indication that they supported the local residents in their petitions of 1619 and 1635 about the crowds that went to plays there. Neither the Privy Council nor the city allowed any other playhouse to open in London before 1660.

[12] For an account of Jones's plans for Beeston's Cockpit, see John Orrell, *The Theatres of Inigo Jones and John Webb* (Cambridge, 1985), ch. 3.

attack by a gang of apprentices on the new playhouse on the Shrove Tuesday holiday in March 1617 has been told before.¹³ It gives the first clear indication that playgoing was highly prized by London audiences, and it reveals a problem over the use of hall playhouses that Beeston, for all his cautious manoeuvres to circumvent the various obstacles that officialdom might have put in his way, evidently never anticipated.

The boy companies who had always played in halls and the King's Men who followed them at Blackfriars did not suffer any of the difficulties that Beeston found with his Cockpit. The boy companies were a small-scale alternative to the predominant adult companies at the amphitheatres. The King's Men took themselves off to the Blackfriars for only half the year, and used the Globe for the other half. Only when Beeston took his company from its usual playhouse, the Red Bull, to the new Cockpit did the problem of financially segregated audiences come into the open. Beeston took the Red Bull players and their plays away from the amphitheatre, where the apprentices could see them for a penny, to the Cockpit where they would have to pay six times as much. Their objection to paying that price cost Beeston dearly.

Queen Anne's Men at the Red Bull had a solid repertory based on Heywood and Rowley's plays, a resource not dissimilar to the fare on offer with Dekker's plays at the nearby Fortune. Taking it to Drury Lane and out of the reach of their pockets enraged the city's apprentices. On their traditional holiday at the beginning of Lent a gang of more than a thousand marched to the Cockpit and broke in on the players. There was a fierce fight, one of the players killing an apprentice with a pistol shot in the head. The attackers were too many for the players, and smashed or burned everything they could get their hands on. An official report says that they "wounded divers of the players, broke open their trunckes, & whatt appareil, bookes, or other things they found, they burnt & cutt in peeces; & not content herewith, gott on the top of the house, & untiled it, & had not the Justices of the Peace & Sherife levied an aide, & hindred their purpose, they would have laid that house likewise even with the grownd."¹⁴ It was an invasion. Drury Lane was a long way from apprentice territory. Their grievance was precisely with the players who had left their old Red Bull home and its audiences and gone off into the alien West End.

Some time before the Cockpit's troubles the Lady Elizabeth's Men left the Hope and merged with Prince Charles's. Faced with using the old

---

[13] See Gurr, "Money or Audiences: The Impact of Shakespeare's Globe," *Theatre Notebook* 42 (1988), 10–12.
[14] Quoted in *JCS* VI, 238.

Curtain, the merged group asked Alleyn to help them find a new venue. That did not get them far. Alleyn, having lost his investment in the new hall playhouse at Porter's Hall and now beginning to turn his attention and his finances to the foundation of Dulwich College which was to immortalise him, could not have been keen in 1616 to invest large sums in yet another new playhouse. Indeed, he appears to have tried in 1617–1618 to set up a co-ownership deal with some of the sharers from the company who were using his Fortune that was comparable to the King's Men's at the Globe and Blackfriars. That was a sign of his reluctance to invest much in playing or of the beginnings of his withdrawal from what was still regarded as a less than respectable kind of business. He was still the businessman and the respected entrepreneur of playing and bear-baiting, as is evident from the number of times the companies approached him for help of one sort or another. But he was setting up the College of God's Gift and was shortly to take as his third wife a daughter of the Dean of St Paul's. As such, he was no longer a venturesome impresario.

What these London struggles show most obviously is the pressure that the London companies were under from the shortage of playhouses. This led them into an illegal practice of forgery that became one of the chief weapons in the war of 1614–1618 in the country. From 1614 the Master of the Revels began issuing annual licences to the London companies. What some of the companies did with them gives us evidence both about the London pressures and about life for the players in the rest of England.

The second body of evidence, the provincial travels and the practices of the travelling companies in 1614–1618, tells a graphic story that sets Francis Wambus on high as culprit and victim. The provincial records are where the war's effects appear. It was a long war, one fought by the players against the local mayors, using as their chief weapon the papers issued by the Revels Office, which took the King's name and great seal to give the players their license to perform, as their main form of coercion to the local authorities to give the companies leave to play. Wambus' imprisonment in Norwich in 1624 was a belated consequence of that struggle. It was a war that exploded out of a new practice that the companies developed in 1614 when they were suffering from the shortage of London playhouses.

Out of this situation the practice started of using 'exemplifications or duplicates' of company licences in order to multiply the number of travelling companies. Warned by the Lord Chamberlain, Norwich first seized on this practice in 1616. It was in fact stamped on at least twice, under rather peculiar circumstances. In 1616 William Herbert, the Lord Chamberlain, sent the player Joseph Moore around the country with an official letter naming various players who were travelling on fake patents. Moore was a leader of the Lady Elizabeth's which had recently left London because of the shortage of playhouses and started travelling itself. The letter Moore carried for the Chamberlain, presumably based on good information, identified the chief culprits and the companies they claimed to run. It reads, in the copy which Norwich took for its municipal records,

> whereas Thomas Swynaerton and Martin Slaughter beinge two of the Queens Majestes Company of players havinge separated themselves from their said Company, have each of them taken forth a severall exemplification or duplicate of his Majestes Letters patentes graunted to the whole Company and by vertue therof they severally in two Companies with vagabondes and such like idle persons, have and doe use and exercise the quallitie of playinge in diverse places of this Realme to the great abuse and wronge of his Majestes Subjectes in generall and contrary to the true intent and meaninge of his Majestie to the said Company And whereas William Perrie havinge likewise gotten a warrant whereby he and a Certaine Company of idle persons with him doe travaill and play under the name and title of the Children of hir Majestes Revels . . . And wheras also Gilberte Reason one of the prince his highnes Players having likewise separated himself from his Company hath also taken forth another exemplification or duplicate of the patent granted . . . And likewise one Charles Marshall, Humfry Jeffes and William Parr: thereof Prince Palatynes Company of Players havinge also taken forthe an exemplification . . . These are therfore to pray, and neverthelesse in his Majestes name to will and require you upon notice given of anie of the said persons by the bearer herof Joseph More whome I have speciallye directed for that purpose that you Call the said parties offendors before you and thereupon take ther said severall exemplifications or duplicates or other ther warrantes by which they use ther saide quallitie from them, And forthwith to send the same to me.[15]

The named players were to give bonds that they would go immediately to Whitehall and answer to the Lord Chamberlain for their offences. Moore was the thief set to catch the thieves. He was also, perhaps less than voluntarily, working to protect the monopolistic status of the authorised London companies against any rivals.

The Chamberlain repeated this circular seven years later, in 1624. This time, instead of using Moore from the Lady Elizabeth's, which had just resumed playing in London, he used Gilbert Reason, one of the "vagabondes" named in the 1616 letter. On January 29, 1625 Reason showed the Norwich authorities a printed warrant from the Lord Chamberlain to "all

---

[15] The Norwich authorities, who had originally caught Swinnerton out in March 1616, made a transcript of the Chamberlain's letter on June 4, 1617. It is printed in REED *Norwich*, pp. 151–52.

Maiors Sheiriffes Justices of peace Baliff's Constables & other his Majesties officers", noting how many "grantes Comissions & lycences which they have by secret meanes procured both from the kinges Majestie & also from diverse noblemen by vertue whereof they doe abusively Clayme unto themselves a kinde of licentious fredome to travell aswell to shew play & exercise in eminent Cities & Corporacions within this kingdome as also from place to place without the knowledge & approbacion of his Majesties office of the Reveles & by that meanes doe take upon them at their own pleasure to act & sett forth in many places of this kingdome diverse & sundry playes & shewes which for the most part are full of scandall & offence both against the Church & State".[16] The state felt the need to reassert its control through censorship. This time the letter named no names, but insisted that no company could travel without authorisation from the Master of the Revels. From then on the Master appears to have followed the practice that George Buc initiated during the 1614–1618 war, of issuing the patented companies with annual licences to travel. Companies travelling with a forged licence were using one authority to soften another. The discovery of their deception cannot have done much to warm mayors toward the travellers.

Another body of evidence from the provincial records reflects the struggle in a different way. Possibly as a means of licensing new companies without actually increasing the number fixed for London, the Master of the Revels started licensing other royal companies ostensibly based in provincial towns. John Daniell was licensed to run a company of boys for Queen Anne following her 1613 visit to Bristol, who became known as the King's Children of Bristol. Another company of King's Players based in York started soon after. This only added to the pressure from central government on the local authorities to tolerate visiting troupes. Bristol in April 1618 copied out a formidably emphatic circular letter from on high about the

> grant unto John Daniel gent Aucthoritie to bring upp a Companie of Chilldren and youths in the quallitie of playing Enterludes & Stageplaies. And wee are informed yat not withstanding his Majesties pleasure therein, that there are some who uppugne and resist the said aucthority in contempt of his Majesties Lettres Patentes. In consideracion whereof and for the further effecting & performance of his Majesties pleasure therein Wee have thought good to grant unto the said John Daniell these our Lettres of Assistance Thereby requiring you and in his Majesties name straightly chardging &

[16] REED *Norwich*, p. 188.

commaunding you and every of you not only quiedy to permitt and suffer Martin Slatier John Edmonds & Nathaniell Clay... to play as aforesaid.

This militant order was directed to all towns.

The essential context for this fight is covered in a document that sits in the Kent records, at Hythe, set down in 1615. Hythe was worried about visiting companies, and the town council made a thorough note about its view of the new situation that had been developing since James became king, and its own conclusions about what the procedure should now be. Elizabeth had issued a Proclamation in May of 1559 laying it down that the civic authorities had to censor and approve all plays before they could be shown to the populace. This was really the first of a series of attempts to suppress the Corpus Christi plays, the 'Mystery' tradition of local play-acting, but it drew the travelling companies into its compass from very early days. The printed Proclamation was made the basis for all Elizabethan civic records of payments to the playing companies for their initial performance in front of the mayor, payments that the Leicester authorities recorded for each visit as a sum 'more then was gaythered' at the guildhall door. Such enforced charity to quasi-vagrants rankled with the local authorities.

That form of local censorship was officially superseded by the appointment of the Master of the Revels as early as 1578, but the local authorities continued to follow the prescription of the 1559 Proclamation until Elizabeth died and for some years after. James did not need to renew this Proclamation, because the Revels Office was now in full control as censor and controller of the companies and their plays. So by about 1610 the civic records of grants to travelling companies begin to disappear. Mayoral approval of the first performance was no longer necessary. The players had royal licences, and were under the central control of the Revels Office which issued them. This meant that the practice of mayoral performances stopped, and the question of what remaining right the local mayor now had to control and restrict the playing companies in his precinct came to the surface. Players used local inns, usually without the initial courtesy visit to the mayor. Most civic records of payments to visiting companies in the later years of the Stuarts were to send them away without performing. How often they came and performed without any payment and a consequent note in the civic records we do not know. At Canterbury in 1635 the only note there is of any company performing there is from a letter the mayor wrote to his Archbishop to justify his sending away of a royally licensed company after they had already played for eight days at a local inn. He was trying to preempt the complaint about his ban that the company had said

The War of 1614–1618

they would make against him to the Privy Council.[17] In the event all the Council did was reprove the company for playing in time of Lent. Such conflicts of authority were the root cause of the war of 1614–1618.

On 24 April 1615 Hythe's records contain a long note which must by then have become fairly representative of civic attitudes to playing. I quote it in full.

> Whereas divers Comon Players of Enterluds as well of the kings Majestie as of the Queene Prince & nobles of this Realme have used to come to this Towne & shewinge theire Comissions unto Master mayor or his deputie & the Jurats have beene permitted to play within this Towne and lymitted to play but a certayne number of playes & those at convenyent tymes one the working dayes or holydayes & forbydden to meddle with any theire playinge or pastyme one the Saboth daye wherewith the said Players have seemed to be satisfied and promised to performe such lymitacion & to observe the tymes as they were required and yet have practized the contrary wherein they haveinge beene by the Mayor of this Towne & other the Officers forbydden & resisted have bearded & opposed them selves against the said mayor and Officers standinge uppon the validitye of theire Comissions & proceeded in their playinge contrary to ye majestrates expresse commandement in that behalfe For remedye whereof it is at this assembly thought fytt & theruppon ordered & decreed that the Players of Enterluds of the kings majestie, the Queene or Prince of this Realme comeinge to this Towne & shewinge their Comissions unto Master Mayor or his deputy & the Jurates of this Towne for the tyme beinge be allowed to play two or three playes within this libertie at the most (and no more) to be played on the workeinge dayes & holydayes in the daye tyme or Eveninge (the same playes beinge fully ended before eight of the Clock at nyght in ye winter & in the Sumer before nyne of the Clock at night,) And no play in any wise to be played on ye Sabbath day, And if ye said Players of ye kinges majestie ye Queene or Prince shall at any tyme heer after come unto this Towne & doe not play any play at all heere then this assembly are content that ye Chamberlyns of this towne by the appointment of Master Mayor or his Deputy for ye tyme beinge doe once in one yeare give to any one Company of them x s. as a gratuety or benevolence in that they forbeare to playe heere, And that the players of Noble men of this Realme comeinge to this Towne & shewinge theire Comission as aforesaid be allowed to playe one or two playes within ye libertie of this Towne & noe more at the most, to be played only on such dayes and at such tymes as is last before mencioned & lymitted, And if it happen that any players doe at any tyme hereafter indevor to play within this libertie contrary to the trewe meaning of this decree Then this assembly doe order and decree that ye mayor of this Towne for ye tyme beinge or his Deputy & the

---

[17] See Gurr, "The Loss of Records for the Travelling Companies in Stuart Times," REED *Newsletter*, 19.2 (1994), 2–19.

> Jurats & other the Officers of this Towne shall altogether denye & forbyd ye said players to play, and alsoe comaund all & every the inhabitants of this Towne to forbeare goeinge to theire playes, And that if any the Inhabitants of this Towne shall refuse to obaye such comaundement herein or doe take parte with ye said Players or goe to theire playes contrary to the Comandement of any ye said Officers or if ye Master or ownor of any house within this Towne shall suffer any players to play in their houses or backsides contrary to this decree or contrary to the expresse comandment of any ye said Officers then every person soe offendinge shalbe bound to the good behavior & further shall for theire offence theirein forfaite & pay to this Township the somme of xx s. to be levyed by distresse & sale of the goodes of ye person Offendinge & for want of goods by imprisonment of ye boddy of ye person offendinge without bayle or mayneprize until ye said forfaiture by payed, And it is further ordered & decreed that if any suit or trouble doe aryse or be brought against any officer or other person of this Towne for the denyinge of any Players according to the Tenor of this decree then ye same shalbe defended at the Chardges of this Township.

This, besides being a valiant attempt to impose order on the chaos that civic procedures had evidently fallen into, seems principally to be an attempt to renew the local control over visiting companies that the Proclamation of 1559 had originally given to town authorities under Elizabeth, and which Hythe at least felt was now being eroded by the superior powers vested in the carriers of the royal warrants that licensed the professional companies. In the context of the time Hythe's declaration made a forthright contribution to this war between central and local government. There are no records in the Hythe archives that show any sign of the kind of confrontation that occurred in 1624 between Francis Wambus, carrier of a legal royal licence, and that year's mayor of Norwich.

Basically the war of 1614–1618 was diplomacy by other means, an attempt by central government to force local authorities to accept visits by the approved playing companies. It was a reimposition of the general terms of the 1559 Proclamation, trying to give the travelling companies access to the towns, although it avoided laying the direct costs and the responsibilities entailed by the Elizabethan system onto the local authorities. Inevitably it reflected the fact that royalty now favoured playing, despite all the local opposition of the country's mayors. When you calculate the strength of the hatred of playing so consistently manifested by so many of the local mayors, it is little wonder that Parliament banned all playing when royalty lost control in 1642.

CHAPTER 9

Metatheatre and the Fear of Playing

Acting at the new Globe in broad daylight shows what an anachronism the modern tradition of stage realism is on such a stage. The inherent and manifest artifice of playing in such a venue makes attempts at psychologically plausible acting ineffective, and certainly misconceived. The original staging at the Globe was more openly unrealistic than modern conditioning can admit. Shakespearean expectations in staging and viewing plays differed from ours more widely and deeply than we now recognise. One of the fitter words for the early concept of acting might be anti-realism. It is evidenced in all the Shakespearean plays wherever you look for it. We talk now about the danger on stage of breaking the illusion. Setting up any kind of illusion was a concept the Elizabethans were extremely wary of.

Anti-realism in Shakespeare's time was not just a matter of the acting traditions inherent in such standard features as soliloquies, where someone talks out loud to himself so that the visibly present audience can hear his thoughts. That was an obvious enough anti-realist convention. Writers who set down stage directions such as 'Blanch speaketh this secretly at one end of the stage' (*Fair Em*, 235), or the direction for Kate in her first scene in the alternative version of *The Taming of the Shrew*, 'She turnes aside and speakes' (*The Taming of a Shrew*, 274), were using a tradition generated by a period concerned to make its illusions self-evidently illusory. Dialogue set in verse was another. These anti-realist traditions were employed quite deliberately and knowingly. They had pervasive effects in all areas of playwriting. Their origins were a part of what might be identified as a persistent fear of playing.

Fear of 'play', the opposite to work, was not the only consequence of Weber's Protestant work-ethic that developed with the Reformation. The

Original publication: "Metatheatre and the Fear of Playing," in *Neo-Historicism. Studies in Renaissance Literature, History, and Politics*, ed. Robin Headlam Wells, Glenn Burgess and Rowland Wymer, Boydell and Brewer, Woodbridge, 2000, pp. 91–110.

hatred of plays and playgoing that boiled out of the English churches from the 1570s onwards was far more positive and much more considered than we usually think it now. It was certainly more than a knee-jerk reaction by Puritans to the idea of ordinary people enjoying themselves. Behind the churchmen's diatribes sat a real fear of illusion, and a revulsion against the deliberate dishonesty it was based on. When we use the term that Stephen Poliakoff gave to his play, 'breaking the illusion', we give voice to the high value now credited to the higher arts of illusion. Such a valuation angered and even terrified many Elizabethans. William Perkins, the sharpest of all the reasoners in the late Elizabethan church, put the case against all forms of deception succinctly and comprehensively. 'An illusion,' he declared, 'is the work of Satan, whereby he deludeth or deceiveth man. And it is twofold: either of the outward senses, or of the minde.'[1] The sermon in which he made this point was aimed at witchcraft, the most overtly Satanic of the various professions that used the arts of illusion. Perkins did not bother to make stage-playing one of his examples of Satanic deception, but plenty of other pulpit-thumpers did. Play-acting was comprehended along with witchcraft as deliberately deceptive illusions which were the Devil's work.[2] He actually used the standard term of praise for good acting as lifelike when he spoke of the Devil impersonating Samuel to deceive Saul. He 'did it so lively and cunningly, as well in forme of bodie, as in attire and voice, that Saul thought verily it was the prophet'.[3]

For the Tudors the lies of illusionism were visible on stage just in the actors' clothing. Dress bespoke the person, and therefore stood out as the most accessible form of deception. The Tudor sumptuary laws grew out of the view that clothes ought to depict the wearer's social status, if not character. Care that outward appearance should accurately reflect the inner person became a weapon in the case that playing was a devilish deception. There were nearly as many attacks on stage-players for their misuse of attire as for their bawdry. Sir John Harington was alert enough to the danger to

---

[1] *A Discourse of the Damned Art of Witchcraft* (Cambridge, 1608), quoted by Tetzeli von Rosador, 'The Sacralizing Sign: Religion and Magic in Bale, Greene, and the Early Shakespeare', *Yearbook of English Studies* xxiii (1993), p. 32. Stephen Greenblatt's essay 'Shakespeare and the Exorcists', in *Shakespeare and the Question of Theory*, ed. Patricia Parker and G. Hartman (London, 1985), pp. 163–87, takes a rather more metaphysical view of the relations between witchcraft and theatre.

[2] A succinct account of the connections that were recognised across different countries and different religions between witchcraft, conjuring tricks, and devilry is in Henk Gras, *Studies in Elizabethan Audience Response to the Theatre, Part 1: How Easy is a Bush Suppos'd a Bear? Actor and Character in the Elizabethan Viewer's Mind. Part 2: As I Am a Man. Aspects of the Presentation and Audience Perception of the Elizabethan Female Page* (New York, 1993), I.189–96.

[3] William Perkins, *The Works of that famous and worthie minister of Christ, in the universitie of Cambridge, M. W. Perkins* (Cambridge, 1603), p. 120.

offer an ironic defence of 'dissimulation' through dress in his defensive *Treatise on Play* composed in 1597, in the decade when professional acting got its first official recognition as a recreation for Londoners. To Harington 'Play' entailed all forms of recreation, from dice-playing to theatre, and he took care to include a comprehensive summary of the range of the games of outward deceit that Tudor 'players' used in everyday life:

> Wee goe brave in apparell that wee may be taken for better men then wee bee; we use much bumbastings and quiltings to seeme better formed, better showlderd, smaller wasted, and fuller thyght, then wee are; wee barbe and shave ofte, to seeme yownger than wee are; we use perfumes both inward and outward to seeme sweeter then wee be; corkt shooes to seeme taller then wee bee; wee use cowrtuows salutations to seem kinder then wee be; lowly obaysances to seeme humbler then we bee; and somtyme grave and godly communication to seem wyser or devowter then wee bee.[4]

To which, being the exhibitionistic charmer he was, he added that the gain from such deceits was that the users might with luck actually turn into what they pretended to be: '*Labour to bee as you would bee thought*', he concluded, an immaculately puritan-like precept which neatly defused the charge that any such pretence was inherently devilish.

But he was rare for his time in taking such a generous attitude to pretence and illusion. Shakespeare was by no means the only playwright to admit the close analogy between the deceptions of playing and, if not witchcraft, then definitely its equally criminal companion, counterfeiting, the coinage of false icons. The tricky Warwick in *3 Henry VI* speaks derisively of 'tragedy...played in jest by counterfeiting actors'.[5] John Cocke, an Inns of Court student writing a 'Character' of a 'Common Player' in 1615, called him '*a daily Counterfeit*'.[6] Marlowe, who defended the counterfeiting of coins in his 'Atheist' lecture, and was caught doing it in the Netherlands in 1592,[7] was much less defensive about such deceptions than most of his contemporaries, but his older Canterbury neighbour, Stephen Gosson, laid great stress on their immorality in his most trenchant diatribe, *Playes Confuted in Five Actions*.

---

[4] See Norman Egbert McClure, ed., *The Letters and Epigrams of Sir John Harington* (Philadelphia, 1930), pp. 41–2.
[5] II.iii.27–8. Quotations from Shakespeare are from *The Complete Works*, ed. Stanley Wells and Gary Taylor (Oxford, 1986).
[6] In J. Stephens, *Satyrical Essayes* (London, 1615), p. 292.
[7] See R. B. Wernham, 'Christopher Marlowe at Flushing in 1592', *English Literary Renaissance* vi (1976), pp. 344–5.

> In Stage Playes for a boy to put one the attyre, the gesture, the passions of a woman; for a meane person to take upon him the title of a Prince with counterfeit porte, and traine, is by outwarde signes to shewe them selves otherwise then they are, and so within the compasse of a lye.[8]

To pretend to be someone else was to deny one's own God-given identity. Any form of disguise for role-playing, whether by witchcraft, to get money from the performance of plays, or for such openly deceitful profits as cony-catching or coining fake money, was ungodly behaviour.

For Elizabethans, playgoers or not, the hazards of deception were a constant concern. Their fascination with trickery of any kind is evident in the popularity of the cony-catching tracts from the later Tudor period, and in only slightly different ways in Jacobean pamphlets like John Gee's diatribe of 1624, *New Shreds of the Old Snare, including the apparitions of two new female ghosts*. Gee wrote two pamphlets which drew heavily on the old attacks on playing from the 1570s, but he deployed them for a rather different purpose. The title of his first pamphlet explains his objective: *The Foot out of the Snare: with a detection of sundry late practices . . . of the Priests and Jesuites of England*. The snare was the Catholic entrapment of gullible young ladies by the use of magic and illusion. Gee recounts the devices he claimed were used for the snares in gleeful and improbable detail. They were chiefly hallucinatory shows, involving dressing women as ghosts who spoke to their victims about hellfire. Gee himself, writing only a few years after the notorious pamphlets about cross-dressing, *Hic Mulier* and *Haec Vir*, was a regular playgoer, and made no attempt to suggest that plays could be as dangerous as were the Jesuits with their seductive tricks. His pamphlets rode on the swell of anti-Spanish and anti-Catholic feeling that generated *A Game at Chesse*, rather than on any more plainly Christian concern. To some degree he reflects a gradual easing of the concerns about the dangers of playgoing and witchcraft that had begun to develop by the end of James' reign, and as part of it some relaxation of anti-realism in the theatre. He was redirecting to a more specifically religious end the same general fear of the dangers of setting up deceitful illusions.

Professional players were condemned for staging illusions because they pretended to be people other than themselves, which was a basic dishonesty. They hid the true villainy or virtue of their characters behind the roles they played for money. They broke the laws of social rank by dressing in the robes of kings and gentry, when their own social rank was vastly inferior.

---

[8] *Playes Confuted in Five Actions* (London, 1582), sig., E5r; reprinted in *Markets of Bawdrie*, ed. Arthur F. Kinney (Salzburg, 1974), p. 177.

They showed boys dressed as women. Deception in any form was a lie, and therefore playing was an exemplar of deceit. 'Every man', said Gosson, 'must show him selfe outwardly to be such as in deed he is.'[9] Dress was the mark of status, and every time a player wore velvet the deception was manifest. Sumptuary laws made velvet a mark of the gentry, and no player could be a gentleman. Worst of all, wearing a crown on stage was manifestly to burlesque greatness. Stubbes' *Anatomy of Abuses* upheld the sumptuary laws, complaining of common citizens that 'it is not at any hand lawful that they should wear silks, velvets, satens, damasks, gould, silver, and what they list', with the sad result that 'it is verie hard to knowe who is noble, who is worshipfull, who is a gentleman, who is not' (sigs. C7v, C2v). Players sinned in the same way. For a player to wear pretentious clothing was to partake in the satanic exercise of illusion.

There are ample signs that the players knew the dangers inherent in these practices, particularly in the earlier plays of the 1590s. It is also possible to identify some of the steps they took to acknowledge what they were doing, whether they did so defensively or aggressively. Through the first two-thirds of *Richard III*, Richard confides in his audience not just that he is an actor but how he will use his roles to deceive the world's characters on the stage. Telling the audience about his planned deceits, Richard offers himself in the familiar image of the actor entertaining an audience by openly playing his devilish part. As he explicitly says, he will 'seem a saint, when most I play the devil'.[10] He is a player both in the character of Richard and as a devilish trickster. His 'I' declares that, for the knowing and the naive alike, both playgoers who have suspended their disbelief consciously and those who are sunk in the stage illusion, he is the actor playing Richard who is playing a devil playing a saint.

The design of the early stages gave him help in this. To confide in the audience he sets himself at the edge of the stage, next to the throng in the yard, on what was known classically as the *platea* or street area. There he could speak his soliloquies and his asides directly to the audience. He positions himself close to them, allying himself with them against the other players on stage, his victims. That intimate proximity, along with the success of his devilry, seduces the audience into a more or less involuntary alliance with him. They see his tricks, feeling superior as they stand literally behind him, knowingly watching him deceive everyone from the innocent Lady Anne and his brother Clarence to the would-be devilish actor Buckingham. Since he identifies his tricks to them as acting he never deceives

---

[9] Ibid., p. 177.   [10] I.iii.338.

the real audience. They even find themselves on his side when he seduces Lady Anne. Indeed, the outrageous effrontery of her seduction might be seen as a teasing version of what Richard had already done to his theatre audience.

In the second half of the play, however, once he has made himself king, he has to assume the authority position at the *locus*, in the centre of the stage next to the *frons*. This transforms his relations with the audience. Many modern actors, including Ian Richardson and Edward Woodward, have said how Richard's behaviour changes once he takes the crown.[11] Now he is on the throne he has to play a kingly part, and necessarily takes up a position more remote from his former intimates in the yard. He now occupies the place where before his victims stood. The audience's sympathy for the man who has confided in them and made them his allies while making fools of the other characters then ebbs away. He is changed from attacker to defender, becoming a beleaguered victim making the mistakes which he prompted in others during his earlier manifestation. Iago works similarly in a later play, putting the audience on his devilish side while he gulls Othello, who is later to ask if he has Satan's cloven hoof.

The close relations that everyone knew existed between acting and evil operated in all the plays of this period in complex and pervasive ways that we ignore at our peril. The association of playing and deception with evil is basic to Elizabethan thinking. We can see it in *Hamlet*, where the hero's initial revulsion against his society changes into a game of acting that sucks him into performing the same evils as his enemy. Elizabethans were conditioned to be sensitive to the complexities entailed in the exercise of minding true things by what their mockeries be. They well knew that the actor had what Robert Weimann has chosen to call 'bifold authority', the double power of the player and of his role.[12] They rarely lost sight of that duality, as we so willingly do now.

Fear of playing was not really an innovation in Shakespeare's time, although the religious schisms of Protestant England gave it fresh intensity. The concept of 'playing' as metatheatre, a form of pantomime, had a long

---

[11] See for instance Edward Woodward: 'The play for me is very much split into two phases. When Richard realises that the crown is within his grasp, he changes very rapidly and dramatically.' *Shakespeare in Perspective II*, ed. Roger Sales (Harmondsworth, 1985), p. 110.

[12] Robert Weimann, 'Bifold Authority in Shakespeare's Theatre', *Shakespeare Quarterly* xxxix (1988), pp. 401–17. The phrase is from *Troilus and Cressida*, V.ii.144–5, where Troilus rails against Cressida's infidelity: 'Bifold authority, where reason can revolt / Without perdition'. A rewarding study of the varying degrees of credulity over illusion, in such matters as the Martin Guerre case and the wolf boy, as well as Bishop Corbett's joking verse about the innkeeper whose memory of the play made him think of Richard III as Richard Burbage, is in Henk Gras' comprehensive survey, *Studies in Elizabethan Audience Response to the Theatre, Part 1*, pp. 211–48.

life before the 1590s, when we might see realism beginning to enter the concept of theatre seriously for the first time. A fourteenth-century manuscript gives four definitions for '*ludo*', I play, the Latin term which remained the basis for the language of play-acting until the sixteenth century. All four definitions have some relation to theatre. They are

> Principio id est narrare; secundo id est decipere; tertio sit voluntatem propriam habere seu operare in opere; quarto sit adorare ydola.[13]

The first is about story-telling, the second about deception or symbolism, the third means playing or toying with something, while the fourth identifies idolatry. None of these four head-meanings deals directly with play-acting, but they were all invoked in one form or another by the critics of playing in the sixteenth century. In a more theatrical context, Medwall's *Fulgens and Lucrece* opens with one character telling another that he thought from his dress he must be a player, and is told that the current misuse of clothing makes it impossible to distinguish a player from a real person.[14] Robes and furred gowns hide all, as Lear was to say much later. That is a concept familiar in any age. What made it so potent in Shakespeare's age was the freshly explicit association with satanic malevolence given it from the pulpits.

A complication to this fear of playing is the difference between the views of one level of society and another amongst the early audiences. Jonson, the most socially sensitive and most learned of the time's writers for the stage, was overtly suspicious about the business of deception for reasons that were not specifically religious. As Jonas Barish says of his writings, 'Wherever you look... within the plays or outside them, in structure or in moralising comment, we find a distrust of theatricality, particularly as it manifests itself in acting, miming, or changing, and a corresponding bias in favour of the "real" – the undisguised, unacted, and unchanging.'[15] Jonson preferred plain truth to the alchemy of art, and yet he was torn by the subversive possibilities that lay in the comedy of metatheatricality. Hence he both condemned false play-writing poets in *Poetaster* and insisted on playgoers as judges of what they saw. Barish adds, 'it is precisely the uneasy synthesis between a formal anti-theatricalism, which condemns the arts of show and illusion on the one hand, and a subversive hankering after them on the other, that lends to Jonson's comic masterpieces much

---

[13] Stephen James Killings published this discovery from a manuscript in the Biblioteka Uniwersytecka, Poland (IQ 158), on the REED Internet Bulletin Board on 21 January 1997.
[14] *Fulgens and Lucrece* 43–56, in *The Plays of Henry Medwall*, ed. Alan H. Nelson (Cambridge, 1980).
[15] Jonas Barish, *The Antitheatrical Prejudice* (Berkeley, 1981), pp. 151–2.

of their unique high tension and precarious equilibrium'.[16] Other writers showed similarly ambivalent sensitivities. The aristocratic Sidney showed the stretch of social difference by his mockery of the players' attempts at realism with monsters made of brown paper. Some writers of plays deplored the conspiracy between players and their audiences when they combined to prefer the illusions of spectacle over the poets' eloquent words.[17] The learned always condemned the ignorant for their willingness to suspend their disbelief in fictions. That can be seen in Sidney's day when the professional adult companies first started to entertain the court with stronger stuff than the low realism of companies of boys pretending to be men, offering school plays and shows of youthful eloquence. But fear of illusion ran through all social levels. The never-changing preference of the authorities in the towns and regions outside London for music and acrobatics rather than plays manifests the same suspicion of the dangers of realism.

Isolating the more fundamental reasons why so many people feared and anathematised playing so strongly at this time is not easy. Some of it certainly relates to the development of distinctly English versions of Protestant theology. In the pulpits, theatres and their practices were often associated with popery and the idolatry that later evoked the doctrine of iconoclasm. Some critics explicitly related the falsity of clothing and players' rituals to Catholic practices. John Rainolds saw a feature of these popish practices in the Passion plays, which he called 'profane and wicked toyes'.[18] But for all the evident favour which plays found among Catholics as against the surge of Protestant disapproval, the suspicion of illusion cannot be so easily divided across the religious schism. Catholics may have valued the symbolic truths inherent in their icons more than the Church of England could, but on both sides of this divide there was equal fear of the dangers of deceit and illusion.

Most of the fears about the power of illusion found their natural target in the theatre.[19] The anxieties that recent critics have identified in the plays and games when boys cross-dressed as women, and the citations of the religious perils of transvestism condemned in Deuteronomy 22:5, may have been overstated or at least misconceived in recent years.[20] If the

---

[16] Ibid., p. 154.
[17] See Andrew Gurr, *Playgoing in Shakespeare's London*, 2nd edn (Cambridge, 1996), pp. 86–98.
[18] John Rainolds, *Th'Overthrow of Stage Playes* (London, 1599), sig. X3.
[19] Stephen Orgel writes succinctly about the widespread anxiety marked by concern over crossing genders, in *Impersonations: The Performance of Gender in Shakespeare's England* (Cambridge, 1996), pp. 28–30.
[20] Orgel, however adroitly, takes a fairly extreme position over the 'anxieties' directed at the homoeroticism of boys cross-dressing. Peter Hyland, on the other hand, sees cross-dressing as a familiar

theatre was expected to be anti-realist and metatheatrical, there was no danger in the illusion of boys playing women, any more than there was in boys playing men in school plays. The basic implication behind the attitude that so many upper-class Tudor commentators took to men play-acting as compared with boys is that adults imitating adults were too close to reality for comfort. Boys mimicking adults, on the other hand, could not easily be confused with their models. This may have had something to do with that other and more general preference of the time, to have boys playing women's parts in the adult companies. The patriarchal view of women could not admit that real women might counterfeit real behaviour, whether virtuous or vicious. Suspicion of deceit was general, and it went far beyond that one feature of the early staging.

The now-famous debate between Gager and Rainolds in 1592 about acting, in which the great Italian Protestant exile Alberico Gentili intervened, did concern itself with the prohibition in Deuteronomy over men or boys wearing women's clothes. Because it was an academic debate, on an issue where the question of students performing plays had always been a fraught matter, it can be read as a well-publicised contention whose importance as a statement of beliefs at the time might easily be overstated. It was really not much more than another consequence of the general fear and distrust of illusion. Rainolds claimed that boys dressing as women on stage provoked lust in men, a claim that it might be thought could apply equally well to women on stage: 'a womans garment beeing put on a man doeth vehemently touch and move him with the remembrance & imagination of a woman; and the imagination of a thing desirable doth stir up the desire'.[21] This condemns any kind of depiction of women on stage, so it is understandable that those who favoured plays found against Rainolds. Gager's counter-argument in this regard amounted to little more than that the Holy Bible did allow cross-dressing. Gentili, intervening over which kind of law was being invoked, moral or ceremonial, found in his favour. The question never loomed very large in London, and certainly not among the regular playgoers there. At no time was it more than an academic debate, since the discussion was confined only to plays staged by students at universities.[22] It takes its own slant on the general concern over realism in play-acting.

---

convention, as it was in Japanese Kabuki theatre. See Hyland, '"A Kind of Woman": The Elizabethan Boy-Actor and the Kabuki Onnagata', *Theatre Research International* xii (1987), pp. 1–8.

[21] *Th'Overthrow of Stage-Playes* (London, 1599), p. 97.

[22] See Paul Whitfield White, 'Theater and Religious Culture', in *A New History of Early English Drama*, ed. John D. Cox and David Scott Kastan (New York, 1997), esp. pp. 138–42.

Staging plays at universities had its defenders even among those who condemned public playing in London. The chief grounds for the defence were that it helped students to improve their oratorical skills as students of rhetoric. Oratory claimed to be superior to acting, since orators built up the real emotion their words expressed inside themselves, while actors did not. They were not, therefore, imposing any illusion on their audiences. By contrast, tragedy was a game, the deceitful sport of academic pastimes. All that players could offer were the trappings and the suits of woe. That within was different from what was on show. Such ambiguous disclaimers were of a piece with Heywood's disavowal about boys playing women, when, in his *Apology for Actors* (1612) he asserted confidently that audiences had no difficulty identifying the boys who played women (sig. C3v). The deceit was openly metatheatrical, and so could not be subjected to the charge either of satanism or lechery.

A more distinct resemblance to the debate over the role of playing in universities appears in some of the earlier plays which insisted that depicting history on stage had a special value. Sidney's preference for poetry over history was converted by some of the earlier writers for the stage into the claim that whereas tragic poets were liars, history was the truth. The opening scene of the Queen's Men's *The True Tragedie of Richard the Third*, printed in 1594, has Truth confront and displace Poetrie. Truth asks 'What makes thou upon a stage?', to which Poetrie replies fairly enough, 'Shadowes', the standard image of the player as a dark and two-dimensional version of reality. Truth answers 'Then will I adde bodies to the shadowes', promising to replace poetry's fictions with history's reality. When Poetry mocks such pretension, asking 'will Truth be a Player?', Truth's response is 'No, but Tragedia-like for to present / A Tragedie in England done but late'. The play makes the claim to offer 'Truthes pageant', a version of Shakespeare's story of twisted King Richard. Such a claim, made by the Queen's own Men, that they offered something more substantial than the fictions of player-shadows, suggests a more weighty concern than the old discomfort over Plato's charge that all poets are liars. It does admit that their history plays are propaganda, perhaps, but counters it with the self-justifying assertion that their story has the strength of truth. And truth denies illusion. There is a similar affirmation in the sub-title of *Henry VIII*, 'All is True', with its apparent (and unjustifiable) claim for history's ability to avoid the falsities of the stage's fictions.[23]

---

[23] This view is largely based on the analysis of the Queen's Men's plays by Scott McMillin and Sally-Beth McLean, *The Queen's Men and their Plays* (Cambridge, 1999), pp. 166–7.

Such early concern to deny illusion might almost have ranked the Queen's Men with Shakespeare's rude mechanicals, concerned as they are for the realism of their presentation. The mechanicals' prologue in Act 5 of *A Midsummer Night's Dream* has to tell the ladies that

> we will do no harm with our swords, and that Pyramus is not killed indeed; and for the more better assurance, tell them that I, Pyramus, am not Pyramus, but Bottom the weaver. This will put them out of fear.[24]

The exact character of the illusionism game that the Chamberlain's Men were able to stage at their theatre by 1596 with this play needs this context of the different levels of concern about illusionism. Undoubtedly, the fear of illusion receded as playgoing became a more established and respected social exercise under King James. Tracing that history, though, is work for another study than this.[25] What would be more immediately useful is to track a few instances where fears of illusionism might have manifested themselves in the plays, which our own acceptance of stage realism has obscured.

Many of the metatheatrical games in the plays of Shakespeare and Jonson are familiar enough, from Jonson's stage keeper setting out his contract with the audience in the Induction to *Bartholomew Fair* to Polonius claiming to have played Caesar when he was killed by Brutus/Hamlet, anticipating what happens to him as Polonius in the very next scene of the play. Beaumont went even further with such reminders than his master Jonson. *The Knight of the Burning Pestle* (1607), the most extreme of all the mockers of realism, outdid its metatheatrical peers by offering from the first lines not just a play within a play but a play within a play within a third play. It used Rafe the apprentice to burlesque the mechanics of stage representation by, in the third of the interlocked plays, sending him to fantasy 'desarts' where errant knights' steeds are elephants, and apprentice Rafe rejects the idea of love at first sight with remote princesses in high towers in favour of his London lass. Each of the three plays uses a more subversive level of anti-realism than its predecessors. Tricks with metatheatricality were an essential outcome of the discomfort writers and their audiences shared, as

---

[24] *A Midsummer Night's Dream* III.i. 16–20.
[25] A major extension to this study of the fear of illusion would be what changes took place as stage-playing became a more secure feature of London's everyday life. We might probe the development of the term 'personation' at the turn of the century, for instance, as a mark of the gradual acceptance of the idea that one man could respectably pretend to be another. Stephen Greenblatt quotes its summation as the art of impersonation in *Leviathan*, when Hobbes cites the Latin 'Persona' as meaning 'the *disguise*, or *outward appearance* of a man, counterfeited on the stage'. Patricia Parker and David Quint, ed., *Literary Theory / Renaissance Texts* (Baltimore, 1986), p. 221.

staging techniques grew more sophisticated, over the dangers that lay in the deceptions of realism.

As a last stir of the evidence before looking at what the need to proclaim illusion as a game might have done to the early performances, the role of the boy companies offers some insights. The reasons why the more educated in Shakespeare's time chose to favour boy companies over adult players are of course complex and inaccessible. Playgoers were more overt in expressing their concerns over the spectacle than in acknowledging why they tended to choose one type of performer over the other. The more openly voiced prejudices were hostile to any sort of playing. Most of the others were too inconsistent and too variable to convince the modern reader. An intriguing variety of alternative motives, some distinctly hair-raising, have been adduced as the real explanation. Digging into the more covert reasons for the Tudors to think of boy players as more respectable than adult players turns up a lot that could rather loosely be called dirt. Some of it, though, might help to scour and clarify the standard assumptions about the early attitudes to playing.

The social range of boy acting was quite wide, and the practical range, in the different uses and venues, even wider. Schoolmasters staged plays to teach their pupils how to speak in public. Choirmasters used their songsters to entertain their patrons and the court. In the later sixteenth century some of them offered their productions to a wider market, and at the end of the century two companies of boys, both set up for plainly commercial profit, became a major feature of London playing for seven or eight years. This kind of playing, socially more respectable in its origins than the companies of travelling adult players, contrasted with the boys employed by the adult companies to play women's and juvenile parts. Glynne Wickham has suggested that boy players were caught between two concepts, the emblematic and the imagistic, between the old practice of parody, descending from the medieval boy bishop tradition, and a new one of pseudo-realistic and even naturalistic presentation, culminating in the boys who played women in adult companies.[26] The companies of boys stand at the emblematic end, the boys playing women in the adult companies at the naturalistic. This may be too streamlined a view. How much of their earlier emblematic role survived through the apparent triumph of a more realistic mode with the rise of the adult companies is a large question where simple polarising can mislead.

---

[26] Glynne Wickham, *Early English Stages 1300 to 1660* (London, 1959–), II.10.

The educational cachet that derived from the use of playing in schools to train children in public speaking was one which the professional adult players could never claim. By contrast with such a manifestly respectable motive for playing, the adults could claim only a commercial motive. But inside this different motivation there may have been a further division between Catholics and anti-Catholics. The few famous schoolteachers who upheld playing in the 1570s and 1580s when the adult companies began to displace the boy companies at court included the acknowledged master of the art of school-playing, Richard Mulcaster, and also the defiantly recusant Almoner of St Paul's choir school, Sebastian Westcott. Westcott's Catholicism has been linked with the favouring of plays by other Catholics in the argument that public playing served as a substitute for the loss of Catholic church ceremony and its communal rituals. That does not apply very closely, however, to the division between boy and adult players, nor to the opinion of the many who approved the performance of school plays while deploring public playing. All we can say with confidence is that the motives were complex, often muddled, and wholly prejudiced. One of the major motives generating the long-running preference for boy company plays, I would argue, was their physique, not as sex objects but because their imitation of adult behaviour was manifestly only an imitation.

Elizabethan credulity, a willingness to engage with the fiction as fact, through realism, is not an easy concept to pin down in the flow of historical events. Throughout the 1590s and early in the new century there is evidence that love of the illusive art of spectacle prevailed alongside what has been called the 'theatre of estrangement'[27] which the revived boy companies learned to promote in the early seventeenth century. Played by adult companies, *Faustus* was exciting to the more ignorant in its audiences chiefly because it put on show the terrifyingly real prospect of being dragged down to hell. The famous anecdote about a group of actors finding too many devils on stage and spending the night in prayer, and Middleton's glancing reference to how an audience took fright during a performance when the theatre's timbers let out a cracking noise,[28] indicate the tension that such subjects could generate in their audiences. A noise from the timbers of the courtroom at the trial of Ann Turner, whom Frances Howard had consulted as a witch, gave even the educated audience there a similar fright.[29]

---

[27] Neil Carson, 'John Webster: the Apprentice Years', *Elizabethan Theatre* vi (1978), pp. 76–87.
[28] T. M., *The Black Book* (1604): 'Hee had a head of hayre like one of my Divells in Dr. Faustus when the old Theater crackt and frighted the audience', in A. H. Bullen, ed., *The Works of Thomas Middleton* (London, 1875), VIII.13.
[29] See David Lindley, *The Trials of Frances Howard: Fact and Fiction at the Court of King James* (Basingstoke, 1993), p. 148.

Edward Alleyn showed the same edginess by wearing a cross round his neck while playing Faustus.[30] An insurance policy so displayed in public admitted the fear that playing could become serious, and that God might punish the deceptions of the stage. By 1616 Jonson could mock such simple-minded fears of Satan's arrival onstage with *The Devil is an Ass*, but however hidden or derided it was in the later years, the fear remained a constant pressure on writers, players and audiences. It put a heavy emphasis on the need for overt metatheatricality in performance. It certainly made the 'theatre of estrangement' that the boy company at Blackfriars launched through the years 1600 to 1608 an activity that was reassuring as well as entertainingly satirical for its audiences of gallants and students.

Much of the drama of this period can be seen as fluctuating nervously between the extremes of realism and estrangement. Like the alienation of audience from the emotions of the actors in Brecht's *Verfremdungseffekt*, the obviousness of the pretence could save the participants from the fear of being really deceived. That fear was part of the motivation behind making Richard III so blatantly persuasive in his overt 'acting' of his deceits, behind Hamlet's moral anger at all the 'seeming', the spying and lying at Denmark's court, and even behind the widely reiterated preference for the playing of boy companies over adults.[31] As Stephen Orgel notes, Moll Frith became notorious for her appearance on stage in the form of a transvestite, not because she deceived the spectators.[32]

So what were the positive effects of this fear of illusion on early playing? The list of effects has of course to start with the absence of scenery and the mobility of playing on bare stages. But the 'bare stage' was far from being the only aid to anti-realist staging. The transparency of disguise in the plays was almost always a given, privileging the audience over the characters on stage. It might range from the uncrowned and therefore unkingly King Henry V wrapped in Erpingham's cloak or the boy-player's triple covering of Rosalind / Ganymede / Rosalind, down to Bottom in his ass's head. Its transparency was always recognisable to the audience, with only the other characters left in ignorance. Such a privileging helped to reduce the seriousness of the counterfeit. That Richard could seduce and successfully

---

[30] Samuel Rowlands, *The Knave of Clubs* (1609), p. 29. William Prynne noted gleefully in *Histriomastix*, 1633, fol. 556 'the visible apparition of the Devill on the Stage at the Belsavage Playhouse, in Queen Elizabeth's dayes (to the great amazement both of the actors and spectators) while they were there prophanely playing the History of Faustus (the truth of which I have heard from many now alive who well remember it) there being some distracted with that fearful sight'.

[31] Orgel, *Impersonations*, p. 41, notes that the attacks on cross-dressing were the effect, not the cause, of the Puritan charge against players as users of cross-dressing.

[32] Ibid., p. 107.

propose marriage to the distraught Anne over her murdered husband's body was an extreme that the early playgoers felt reassured they themselves could resist.

Along with non-realist staging, another consequence of anti-realist concern might be found in the use of verse. Rhyming verse, the 'jigging veins of rhyming moither-wits', as Marlowe dismissively put it, shifted in the plays of the 1580s into blank verse, more naturalistic yet still controlled by rhythm. Verse in any form, though, is an anti-realistic form of human expression. When Laurence Olivier started his career as a film director with his *Henry V* in 1944, he found the verse a major impediment to cinematic realism. Spoken soliloquies and asides are of a piece with the overt pretence that speaking in verse entails. Prologues and choruses that compare the staging of the story, and commentating characters like Richard III, Iago and Edmund who keep the audience informed of their acts of deception, are all elements in the apparatus of non-realistic staging.

Remembering the predominance of verse – elevated and unnatural speech – we should ask why the plays written for the boy companies consistently used prose. One of the less plausible conjectures about that is that it acknowledged the fact that boys could not deliver Marlowe's mighty line as eloquently as men could. Since the more than ostensible object of every boy's schooling was studying to the point where they learned to deliver 'speeches well pronouste, with action lively framed', as the teacher, choirmaster and playwright Richard Edwardes put it,[33] that seems unlikely. It would be more rewarding to reverse the argument, taking prose to be the normal form of human speech, available to the boy players because they ran no risk of being taken seriously, while the adult players used verse precisely to differentiate their speech from the ordinary. Boys playing adults speaking prose had a physical reason for not generating the illusion of reality as adults would. Adults speaking prose, unless they were relegated to the lower and comic status of citizens and rustics, ran too much risk of seeming realistic to be used on the public stages. Characters like Iago speak prose chiefly when they are pursuing their devilish villainies.

The implications of early acting being positively anti-realistic reach a long way into our assumptions about early staging. As an exemplar of what a renewed consciousness about metatheatrical staging might offer, consider the problem of getting corpses offstage at the end of a play. Michael Neill has argued that funeral processions were employed as stage spectacles, in

---

[33] *Damon and Pithias* (London, 1565), Prologue, 23. His object, based on the Horace taught in schools, was 'in all such kinde of exercise decorum to observe'.

particular as a way of ending tragedies, chiefly because they allowed the bodies to be taken off without making any overt breach in the finale's illusionism.[34] Unfortunately, this was by no means the invariable practice. Most of the plays did provide means for bodies to be removed if they died on stage in the middle of the play, but too many of them for our modern comfort end with a sprawl of untransported bodies. In *Hamlet*, for instance, Fortinbras singles out Hamlet alone for the funeral procession, leaving Claudius lying there by his throne, still wearing his regal crown, Gertrude the Queen, and bleeding Laertes, all of them in full view with no means of quietly or, better for stage realism, invisibly vanishing.

For most tragedies some means was usually found to remove the principal bodies at the end. Taking only a few examples from Shakespeare, in *Titus Andronicus* Lucius gives instructions for the removal of all the bodies, each in a distinct way. Coriolanus is given a soldier's funeral procession (V.vi.148–9: 'Take him up./Help three o'th' chiefest soldiers; I'll be one'). *Julius Caesar*, to which we shall return shortly, closes with a similar military procession, when Octavius says (V.v.77–8) 'Within my tent his bones tonight shall lie,/Most like a soldier, ordered honourably.' *Macbeth's* last scene, V.xi, poses only the question of taking away the hero's easily portable head, if we assume that in the earlier scene Macbeth drags the body of Young Siward off after killing him in his last act of child-slaughter (V.vii.14). In some of the other plays, however, lesser beings appear to have been left on the stage. In *Othello*, the two principals lie on the bed, the bed's curtains are closed (V.ii.375: 'Let it be hid'), and the whole apparatus was pushed off through the central opening. But that left Emilia's corpse. We might assume that she was carried off as part of the evidence against her husband, when Lodovico instructs Cassio to escort Iago to prison. Otherwise, the question how they removed the extra bodies recurs here.

Clearing them away is a careful provision in other tragedies. In *Antony and Cleopatra*, faced with the heroine's magnificent corpse sitting there in her regal finery, Caesar orders (V.ii.346–7) 'Take up her bed,/And bear her women from the monument'. That would have removed the stage property and the other corpses in a similar fashion to *Othello*'s. *King Lear* has a relatively orthodox closure of a like kind. Certainly it is hard to see it damaging emotional realism with the problem of ridding the stage of its clutter of bodies in the finale. There are, none the less, several bodies to be removed. At V.iii.228 the Folio Albany orders the gentleman to 'produce

---

[34] Michael Neill, '"Exeunt with a Dead March": Funeral Pageantry on the Shakespearean Stage', in David M. Bergeron, ed., *Pageantry in the Shakespearean Theater* (Athens, Ga., 1985).

the (their, Q) bodies' of Lear's two elder daughters. They are laid out on stage when Lear enters with the dead Cordelia. So Lear and all three of his daughters lie dead and visible as the signal mark of the first family's disintegration. Edmund has died offstage, which helps to strengthen the family grouping here. Then, nine lines from the end Albany says 'Bear them from hence'. He does not specify whether the two elder daughters were to be included in this withdrawal, but it would have made a tidier closure, and the parade of the dead would re-unite the family that was divided in the first scene. This closure, like the others, is in stark contrast to the disjuncture that happens at the end of *Hamlet*.

Hamlet's closure raises all sorts of questions, not least because of a small change between the Second Quarto and Folio versions which may reflect the difference between the author's first idea about it, represented in Q2, and the staged version that the Folio text records. Horatio first says 'give order that these bodies/High on a stage be placed to the view' (V.ii.321–2), a not inappropriate phrase and location after such a metatheatrical drama. But Fortinbras supersedes this order with a further one, singling out Hamlet and awarding him a military funeral: 'Bear Hamlet like a soldier to the stage' (340). The arrival of Fortinbras, still in the general's armour of his previous appearance in IV.iv, gives him a military aspect that was meant, amongst other things, to remind us of all the other plays which ended with their dead military heroes carried off by four captains. That Fortinbras himself appears dressed as a general makes sense of his order that the funeral procession for Hamlet should be a soldierly one. It explains why, however uncomprehending he is of what has gone on, he gives the order that Hamlet should be borne 'like a soldier' to the 'stage' for his funeral.

None the less, it is an odd pronouncement for Fortinbras to make, even with such an outsider's ignorance. Giving this order he makes a major and unjustified deduction. Horatio, the insider, has proposed that all of 'these bodies' should be placed high on a stage 'to the view'. The Second Quarto text reaffirms this by making Fortinbras then say 'Take up the bodies' (345). But the Folio, the text supposed to be derived from a playhouse manuscript, makes that a singular: 'Take up the body'. Without having heard any details about how Claudius the Danish king, Gertrude his queen, Hamlet and Laertes were killed, in this version Fortinbras declares that only Hamlet should be honoured with a military ceremony. He knows nothing about the 'wounded name' which worried Hamlet and made him insist that Horatio must tell the world. The patronising declaration that Hamlet was likely to have proved most royal 'had he been put on' is a soldier's tribute to someone whom Fortinbras sees as having great promise but no achievement. How little this outsider knows of what has just happened on the stage. Yet he, rightly we might think, picks out Hamlet alone from the four corpses on stage for this honour, and not the dead king of Denmark.

What are the consequences of Fortinbras giving the order to award only Hamlet a dead soldier's rites? He is wearing exactly the same accoutrements as the ghost on its first appearance, in armour, beavered, with a marshal's truncheon. The ghost would have been pleased to see his son honoured in such a way. But when the original Hamlet was carried off by four soldiers, we must ask what the rest of the cast did with the corpses of Claudius, Gertrude, and Laertes. There were only two choices: either stage hands mutely carried them off, without ceremony, or the three dead characters stood up to take their final bow once the military procession was offstage. All editors and commentators assume that the players invariably took the first of these choices. I wonder whether the higher levels of metatheatrical expectation that I have tried to show existed in the early theatres might not have allowed them to take the second. There is a little evidence for this, some of which takes us back to *Julius Caesar*.

Contemporary comments do not tell us much, apart from references to 'plaudities', to say what normally happened at the end of a play. Was it standard practice for the cast to take a bow? Curtain-calls only came in with proscenium-arch stages and their front curtains, but it is at least possible that the whole company customarily returned to the stage to close the performance. Applause was certainly solicited, as various epilogues indicate. Puck ends *A Midsummer Night's Dream* asking the audience to 'Give me your hands', the King at the end of *All's Well that Ends Well* invites 'gentle hands' in return for 'our hearts', and Prospero asks for 'the help of your good hands' in his epilogue to *The Tempest*. *Henry VIII*'s Epilogue speaks of the ladies bidding their menfolk to clap. These, however, are all single figures, alone on stage. Moreover, while applause in the form of the 'shouts and claps' that greeted Henry V's return to England after Agincourt (*Henry V*, V. Chorus.11), was in the form we still use, it was keyed differently from the practice in modern theatres. Michael Drayton wrote of sitting at a play he had written and hearing the 'Showts and Claps at ev'ry little pawse,/When the proud Round on ev'ry side hath rung'.[35] Applause was not held back till the end, although the audience's way of congratulating the players was certainly to clap. No play-endings suggest that any other players joined the final speaker on stage, and something more than

---

[35] *Idea*, Sonnet 47, *Works*, ed. J. William Hebel (Oxford, 1931–41), II.334.

the recurrent clapping should have marked the acknowledgement that the day's performance had concluded.

Marston confirmed that applause was given to specific lines in his 1598 satire *The Scourge of Villainy*, when he noted the enthusiasm that law students showed at the plays the Chamberlain's were then staging at the Curtain. His Luscus, who speaks 'Naught but pure *Juliat* and *Romio*', recites the verse from his copy of the playbook, and 'speakes in print, at least what ere he sayes / Is warranted by Curtaine *plaudeties*'.[36] The question such observations about recurrent applause raises is whether any more special or heightened form of ceremonial was the norm at the conclusion of the performance. Audiences used to shouting and clapping throughout the play had none of the silent attentiveness which goes with a truly realistic performance. Their sense of an ending needed some other feature than a bit more applause to acknowledge that the two hours traffic had come to a final halt. Nothing in any of the plays or commentaries suggests that a final bow by the whole company, an early version of the curtain-call, was ever practised. But some form that modulated between the emotions of the finale, whether comic or tragic, and the return to the reality of the theatre there certainly was. It destroyed what vestiges of illusion the ending might have drawn the audience into, and helped to give explicit emphasis to the metatheatrical game that audience and players had shared.

A majority of all the plays, especially the histories and tragedies, ended with a formal procession leaving the stage. Love comedies closed with an exit in pairs hand in hand through the central opening, symbolic of achieved harmony. Very few surviving play-texts offer any suggestion that the performance did not reach its final close with these massed exits. But there are enough special cases to suggest that the players did not stop with the last of the in-character speeches. Epilogues were a fashion that came and went. At the end of *2 Henry IV*, for instance, the original Epilogue's speech finished with a dance and, on his knees, a claim that he would pray for the Queen. This derisive claim, with its elaborate acknowledgement of Falstaff's popularity, may have been a mocking reminder of the traditional way the old plays featuring Vice figures like Falstaff ended, with a dance and a prayer for the monarch. There is a little evidence for the idea that it was customary to close every play with a public prayer for the monarch, but if so, it was a custom that largely died out by the 1590s. Chambers[37] noted the *2 Henry IV* Epilogue along with three other endings from plays

---

[36] *The Scourge of Villainy* (London, 1598), sig. G7v.
[37] E. K. Chambers, *The Elizabethan Stage* (Oxford, 1923), III.550 n.3.

dated before 1593, including the verses that conclude *A Knack to Know a Knave*:

> And Honestie will pray upon his knee,
> God cut then [sic] off that wrong the Prince of Communaltie.
> And may her dayes of bless never have end,
> Upon whose lyfe so many lyves depend.

He added to these instances the end of the epilogue to a 1619 text, *Two Wise Men and All the Rest Fools*, where the speaker says 'It resteth that we render you very humble and hearty thanks, and that all our hearts pray for the king and his family's enduring happiness, and our country's perpetual welfare. *Si placet, plaudite.*' This was the conclusion to a set of published dialogues, not a play, most likely written for an Inns of Court staging. It was most likely a hangover from the earlier tradition that the public stages had abandoned by the mid-1590s.

This old tradition may well have been replaced or usurped by a more durable one, following the play with a song-and-dance afterpiece, a jig. Such a standalone *bonne-bouche* would certainly have been an explicit indication that the afternoon's entertainment was finally over. Unlike the solemn prayer, it would have ended the play in a festive spirit. No jigs that can clearly be identified as play-endings have survived, although two rhyming texts, one by Will Kemp of Leicester's and the Chamberlain's Men and one by George Attewell of the Queen's and the Admiral's, may be scripts for such performances.[38] Feste's song at the end of *Twelfth Night* may originally have been a specially written form of jig, akin to the dance with which the Epilogue's speaker concluded *2 Henry IV*. The 'bergomask' which Theseus demands at the end of the mechanicals' play in *A Midsummer Night's Dream* was meant to function as a signal for the closure of the revels. An outside witness to the custom of ending performances with a jig is Thomas Platter's report that when he went to the Globe on 21 September 1599 and saw *Julius Caesar*: 'at the end of the play they danced together admirably and exceedingly gracefully, according to their custom, two in each group dressed in men's and two in women's apparel'.[39] If the dance was a jig, as most commentators take it to be, it must have imposed on the audience a strong disjunction, a major shift of mood from the solemnity of the funeral march that carried Brutus offstage, and Antony's final praise for him.

---

[38] See Charles Read Baskervill, *The Elizabethan Jig* (Chicago, 1928), 21 and 22, pp. 444–64.
[39] Ernest Schanzer, 'Thomas Platter's Observations on the Elizabethan Stage', *Notes and Queries* cci (1956), pp. 465–7.

Jigs, usually bawdy knockabout pieces sung to rhymed ballad metres, were eventually abolished at the Globe, but we cannot tell precisely when. It was possibly at about the time when *Julius Caesar* and *Hamlet* were first staged, since Will Kemp, the company's most eminent jig-maker, left them late in 1599 to dance his way from London to Norwich.[40] The company certainly gave up jigs after 1609, once they had the Blackfriars consort of musicians instead to entertain the audience. The musicians, a famous group, played during the preliminaries and the interacts to their plays, and could easily have sent customers away with more music. Hamlet's contempt for Polonius with his taste for jigs and bawdry may have echoed sentiments already being expressed by members of the company. The move to Blackfriars with its superior forms of entertainment and more gentrified tastes must have been in their minds from 1596. But jigs there were on the Globe's stage. One ended the story of the death of the noblest Roman, Brutus. The real doubt is about what might have happened between the closing funeral procession and the arrival of the jigging songsters. Did the company first reassemble to take the plaudities, and did the remaining corpses then stand up to join in? Did none of them troop back on stage to take their bows, and if so, whatever did the corpses left on stage do? I wish we knew.

A metatheatrical and anti-realist frame of mind might lead us to expect a lower level of emotional realism at the end of a tragedy, perhaps even a reversal or peripeteia of the collective sympathy. Whatever we think might have happened to the last corpses, there is something very attractive in the idea of a jig concluding *Hamlet*, as it seems to have concluded the original performances of *Julius Caesar*, but with a distinctly better relevance to the play. In *Hamlet* a jig following the play would have made a nice comment on the persistence in the audience of the Polonian taste that Hamlet had derided. Such a closing irony would have put a final gloss on the play's insistence that the whole performance was anti-realist, metatheatre, a play within a play. It became visibly only a 'play' when the dead got up and slowly walked away. Reverting to the dead Polonius' taste then became a logical sequel.

Snug the joiner and Bottom did voice their concern about how the realism of the mechanicals' lion or the death of Pyramus might frighten the Athenian ladies. That splendid parody of their fears about the dangers that lay in excessive realism was set in a play whose metatheatricality emphasised how fully its audience was consciously indulging in its own dangerous dreamworld of illusionism. It seems that in 1596 fear of playing was

---

[40] See Gurr, *The Shakespearian Playing Companies* (Oxford, 1996), p. 291.

intimidating enough and pervasive enough to early modern audiences to make a whole play out of it. The mechanicals, in expressing the need to reassure their courtly audience that 'I, Pyramus, am not Pyramus, but Bottom the weaver' (III.i.18–19), acknowledged the dangerous illusions of stage realism far beyond their own basic level. However rudimentary and banal their idea of staging was, their concern over excessive realism was no less real than their lord's, and in a rather different context ours. We need to heighten our consciousness about the places where the early players' sharp use of metatheatricality impacted on their performances, and how deeply they might have affected the original staging practices and therefore our reading of the plays.

CHAPTER 10

Why was the Globe Round?

Before audio amplification arrived, the essence of listening was proximity to the speaker. Hence the design of the early playhouses: spaces in which the listeners could all get as close as possible to where the speaker was delivering his speech. That is the obvious reason why so many of the early playhouses had circular or polygonal shapes, in types from the Cornish 'rounds' to the Globe.[1] As part of his argument for rebuilding St Paul's Cathedral with that huge baroque dome that stands in the heart of London, Christopher Wren pleaded that it would serve a 'vast auditory', not for people to see, but to hear. Like the Globe, St Paul's was designed for listeners, not viewers. Until technology invented loudspeakers and audio amplification and created surround-sound, the closer you could get to a speaker the better you could hear. Proximity to the source of the sound used to be the highest priority in the design of a theatre. Even standing or sitting directly behind a speaker you lose less than ten per cent of the volume. All English playhouses built before 1660 were constructed so that the audience could position itself all round the stage.

The Worcester College drawings, made by John Webb in 1660–61

This design is the one set of drawings surviving from the early modern period which has a good claim to represent an ideal playhouse of its period. For all the current debate over the precise origin of the drawings, it conforms perfectly to what I think must have been the Jacobean concept of a good indoor playhouse, precisely because the design was made for audiences to hear, not to see. As drawn by John Webb in 1660 or so, these

---

Original publication: "Why was the Globe Round?" in *Who Hears in Shakespeare? Auditory Worlds on Stage and Screen*, ed. Laury Magnus and Walter W. Cannon, Fairleigh Dickinson University Press, Madison, 2012, pp. 3–16.

[1] An obvious example of the earliest such sites in England is the Cornish 'rounds', the 'plain an gwary' places used for plays and some kinds of sport. Borlase's drawings published in 1754 of two such sites are reproduced in the *REED* volume for Dorset and Cornwall, Toronto, 1999, pp. 404–5.

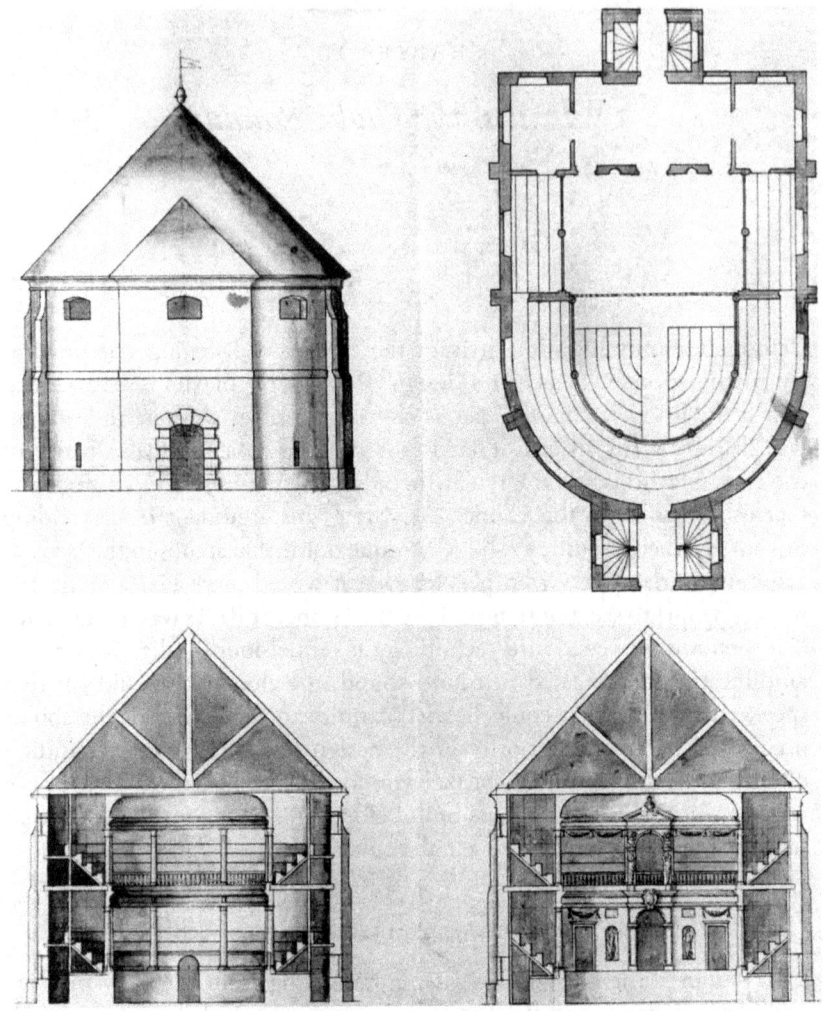

1. The four drawings by John Webb from the Inigo Jones Cockpit.

drawings, now carefully preserved at Worcester College, Oxford, are a pearl of great price.[2] The two beautifully composed sheets offer an example of

---

[2] They are kept in the library of Worcester College. John Webb, Inigo Jones's assistant and successor, left many of his and Jones's books and papers to his son. His widow sold them to Dr George Clarke of Oxford, who gave them to the College.

what early English architects could create in setting out a full image, in plan, sections and exterior, of the playhouse design they thought would best suit their age. They are a model plan for a playhouse of a highly specific type, if only because they are so clearly designed for the hearer rather than for the viewer.

As such, it is impossible to believe that John Webb could not have conceived them long before the Restoration's need for scenic staging and a proscenium arch made itself felt. He must have been copying a much older set of papers, presumably prepared by his recently deceased master, Inigo Jones, that were intended to be for an ideal indoor playhouse of the Jacobean or early Caroline period. It is truly regrettable that the possibility of Webb basing these drawings on an existing set from an earlier time is at present an unverifiable hypothesis. It is unthinkable that, even though amongst the uniquely fresh opportunities for new playhouses open when Webb drew them, the Cockpit in Drury Lane, once thought to be the product of these drawings, had just returned to use as one of the very few playhouses still in use after the long closure, Webb could have thought they would suit the innovative kind of theatre design that Davenant and his rivals expected to become possible under the new regime.

The fact that the identity of the drawings is still not firmly verified should not prevent us from analysing them to find just what Jones or Webb thought appropriate for a new playhouse at any time. Analysis of its many meticulously calculated details indicates quite unequivocally that its origin and concept must have long preceded the Restoration's introduction of perspective staging. It is a brilliant design for a theatre in the round, intended for hearers rather than viewers, the kind of venue that was standard in all the Elizabethan and Jacobean playhouses for which we have some record. If nothing else, the sheer quantity of seating it provides at what nowadays we think of as the exclusively 'backstage' area signifies that.

To judge by what we can make of the scale and dimensions used for the drawings, the playhouse's interior width measures forty feet, and the length fifty-five feet. This is not very much smaller than the measurements of the Blackfriars, which we know was built inside a rectangle with dimensions of forty-six feet by sixty-six feet, although it is not quite certain whether these were the interior or exterior dimensions. John Orrell, in his examination of the Worcester College design, thought it was constructed to a five-foot module, although this raises some anomalies which he felt must explain its being made for an adaptation of a pre-existing cock-fighting pit of 1607, which he thought Jones's design was intended to enlarge with its squared end.³ Whatever the background factors that may lie behind the drawings, they do appear to mark out Jones's concept for a new indoor playhouse of perhaps the second decade of the seventeenth century, the period when the Blackfriars was leading the way so strongly towards the idea of London theatre moving indoors. Above all, the Worcester College drawings reveal a quite distinctive allocation of the dispersal of seating for the different social ranks (and prices paid) in the early audiences, and distinct means of access to them.

The floor plan, with its different points for audience access, shows the most superior customers in rank and privilege entering from the smaller staircase at the rear. In that route they were accompanied by the would-be stool-sitters, the gallants who came to hire a stool and sit on the stage by entering through the stage doors, as Dekker so derisively described them in *The Gull's Hornbook*. This necessary rear point of access is what allows us to calculate the remarkable difference in the distribution of places for the richer and poorer customers. If we allow the standard eighteen inches of body space that Jones allocated for the scaffolding erected to accommodate spectators at the shows for King James at Christ Church Oxford in 1605, the benches positioned behind the stage front in the Worcester College drawings could provide room for approximately 30 people in each of the four boxes flanking the stage, which were accessed either at the front through a door from the stage or, for the rearmost seats, from the main entrance via the rear corridor of the galleries. Another 60 or more also got access from the rear stairway to the four sets of degrees shown on the stage balcony at the same level as the upper box seating at either side of the music room. The chief form of access for all of these upper-level sitters was from the stairway behind the stage.

The likelihood that up to fifteen additional gallants would sit on stools on the stage itself raises the total sitting capacity in the backstage area for the people paying most to almost two hundred, almost all of whom would have progressed to their seats through the rear stairway and the tiring house, in the same way that the lords who at the Globe chose to sit in their exclusive rooms on the stage balcony came to their seats through the tiring house.

---

³ See John Orrell, *The Theatres of Inigo Jones and John Webb*, Cambridge: Cambridge University Press, 1985, Ch. 3, esp. p. 50. Orrell followed Iain Macintosh in identifying the design as originally made for Christopher Beeston's Cockpit playhouse of 1616. This theory has been largely discredited by Gordon Higgott, who re-dates the drawings as done by John Webb in 1660 or 1661. It is entirely possible that Webb took his designs from an original set of drawings by Jones, especially since the Cockpit was still available and in use as a playhouse at the Restoration. Orrell's account includes a precise description of the interior decoration, including the most likely forms of colouring and plastering.

The price of half a crown for a seat in a box and probably little less than that for the balcony's degrees, not to mention the extra sixpence for a gallant to hire a stool so he could sit on the stage itself, made the takings from those using the rear staircase for their access distinctly more profitable to the playhouse owners than the takings through the main entrance stairway facing the stage.

This two hundred-seat capacity makes a strikingly large number of people who, for all their proximity to the speakers, would have lost the best positions for viewing the stage action. And they were the costliest seats in the house. If to that obvious clash with modern thinking you add the extraordinary feature of the pit's seating, with its sharply curved benches that follow the line of the galleries above them, accessed from the central aisle and almost facing across to each other rather than to the stage, you have an auditorium disposition that is totally at odds with the usual cinematic arrangement facing the screen designed for modern theatres. Moreover the audience capacity for this area, the part we think of as in front of the stage, with its two levels of gallery and pit, provides rather less than a hundred spaces at each level of the galleries, plus another sixty in the curved section of the pit in front of them. That gives the capacity in the 'front' of the stage roughly two hundred and fifty seats in all. Altogether, a full audience capacity of about four hundred and fifty is not much less than the standard calculation for the usual capacity at the Blackfriars.

These figures have awesome implications. The social mix of an audience totalling four hundred and fifty, the cheaper half of them positioned facing the stage and the richest two hundred, all the most celebrated and highest in social rank, sitting beside and behind it, is completely alien to most modern auditorium designs. We know that a seat in a box flanking the Blackfriars stage cost half a crown, two shillings and sixpence or one-eighth of a pound in the old currency. That was five times the price of a seat in an upper gallery facing the stage, while a seat in the pit was usually double that, an odd reversal of the outdoor playhouse system, where standing in the yard was the cheapest place to be, and the galleries cost twice as much. Here the galleries offered the cheapest seats, where, as Jonson described them, a shop's foreman could join the other listening judges for his sixpence. It is evident that the Worcester College designs distribute their audience utterly differently from any modern theatre, where the more you pay the better you expect your view of the stage to be. This discredits many of our usual assumptions, such as that the seating in the lords' rooms at the Globe was only located on the stage balcony because its sitters wanted to be seen by the *hoi polloi* in the galleries and yard rather than to see the players. The

Globe's lords' rooms were privileged for hearers, not for viewers. The same was true for the whole concept behind the Worcester College drawings. So the evidence, here and elsewhere, tells us quite unequivocally that in all the pre-Restoration playhouses proximity to the stage was designed for hearing, not for seeing. This was the single most essential feature of the Jones/Webb drawings, and strongly affirms the likelihood that they were originally created several decades before the date of 1660–61 when John Webb re-drew them.

This primacy of hearing over seeing in early theatre design gives us grounds for rethinking several features of the choreography employed for Elizabethan staging. It also, however, raises the question about one particular and quite distinctive feature of the design of the Elizabethan stages which may have to modify my case. Architects always declare that a given structured space dictates the sort of behaviour that will go on inside it. That is largely valid, at least at the subconscious level. But practical features can themselves gradually affect the pressures physical shapes impose by habitual use, and, even without humanity's natural tendency to allow the instantaneity of vision to prevail over the thought-impacts on the ear, one distinctive feature of the early London playhouses and the Worcester College drawings that must have imposed itself heavily in time on the players and the audience responses. This was, specifically, the stage front or *frons scenae*. I believe that eventually this feature altered the forms of use that the players made of their stages when performing their plays.

The tradition out of which the original playhouses were built was certainly based on hearers, but I believe that the creation in the first custom-built playhouses of different versions of the three-entry *frons scenae* with flanking doors for the opposition and a central opening for major entries eventually came to modify the effect of playhouses in the round meant for hearers. It was a structure most explicitly and clearly identifiable at the Rose in Southwark as much as in Webb's design (or copy) with its ornate central archway. Very slowly this design began to create a more two-dimensional way of thinking about staging. Above (or behind) all the acts on stage I believe that the *frons* as a feature of early playhouse stage design began to insinuate the priority of visual over aural effects. Throughout his writing career Shakespeare exploited the auditory shape of his playhouses, but it has to be said that near the end, in some of his last plays, he seems to have made use of a form of staging, one peculiar to the all new playhouses constructed in London from 1576 onwards, that offered a strong acknowledgement, however involuntarily, to the priority his audiences may always have been inclined to give to the visual over the verbal.[4]

Nowadays two-dimensional or proscenium-arch staging loses a play like *Richard III* much of its originally designed choreography. The precisely patterned features of that play's movement on the first stages created a model exemplifying Shakespeare's and his contemporaries' emphatically three-dimensional, all-round concept of their staging. The Theatre, the most likely venue for which *Richard* was written and probably first staged, was a circular space, like the Swan and the Rose. The audience literally surrounded Richard on the stage. The lords on the stage balcony, so carefully separated from the crowd in the yard yet part of the same audience, made an obvious circuit of listeners to the stage action. Knowing how this was expected to work helps to generate a distinct sense of what Shakespeare must have planned would happen to his hero/villain a little over halfway through the play. As we should all know, when the stage is at the centre of an encircling audience, three-dimensional blocking makes the movement and status of the actors equally concentric. The king stood or sat in centre-stage, the courtiers surrounding him, always facing inwards towards him, while any alienated and hostile commentators would prowl around the flanks at the stage's limits, muttering their asides to the audience standing or sitting in the outer circuit. Being closest to such marginal commentators, the yard's audience heard from them the anti-authority versions of the truth, the contrarious assertions that audiences always want to hear. *Richard III* opens (or begins: 'opens' is a proscenium-arch term) with Richard prowling round the edge of the stage confiding to the audience his hatreds and his plan of action. His direct address seduces the crowd at his feet and over his head. He makes them his intimates, sympathetic to the outsider's position at the court. With bold frankness he confides his feelings to them, and invites them to mind his words in collaborative secrecy with him alone, bonding them to him. In the scenes that follow the remote king, Richard's elder brother, sits on his throne in the centre while the courtiers group themselves round him, speaking at centre-stage as Richard prowls behind them keeping his bond with the understanders in the yard. The audience is positioned both metaphorically and literally behind Richard while they watch him through the first half of the play as he fools the authority figures in stage centre. From this marginal location he sets up all the

---

[4] This section of the paper uses material that I offered originally in Germany in 2003, published as "Shakespeare in Three Dimensions," in *In the Footsteps of William Shakespeare*, ed. Christa Jansohn, Studien zur englischen Literatur Bd. 20, Munster, 2005, pp. 73–85.

murders, of his brother Clarence and the young princes, and displays his theatrical wooing of the Lady Anne, who stands in the centre alongside the coffin containing her husband murdered by Richard, as he acts his trickster part with obvious and easily shared relish.

But then in Act 3 this concentric choreographic pattern is reversed. Once the king his brother has died, and having had everyone else who stands between him and the throne murdered, it is Richard who, now crowned, has to occupy the king's position at centre stage. Shakespeare programmed this transformation into the stage postures, and coerced the audience's thinking accordingly. Richard's own prowling role on the margins is now reversed. At last he occupies his chair of 'state' at the centre of the stage, but in that new role he becomes just as isolated an authority figure as those we have seen him murder. Now, distanced from his former intimate contact with the audience at the stage's edge, he loses the close familiarity that he formerly exploited. Remote from us, we witness him facing the three messengers bringing their bad news and striking the fourth, before he learns that the last set of news is good. Deprived of his usual control, and removed from the position where he can speak directly to the audience, he loses its sympathy. We become happy to hear and to watch him go down.

It is not difficult to find a similar concentric choreography in the other plays, perhaps most notably in those where central authority is a major issue, like *Henry V*, *Othello*, and *King Lear*. Such choreography, assuming a circle of audience watching the plots going into place round a central authority figure, was the widespread, standard practice on these stages. In Middleton's *The Revenger's Tragedy* Vindice moves just like Richard, confiding in the audience while fooling all the authority figures standing in the centre. When we first meet Hamlet in the play's second scene, the initial court scene, he too stands alone, not where from the discussion by Horatio and the sentries we might expect to find him but on the margins of the stage, apart from the authority figures perched on their central thrones, and confiding his savage asides to the groundlings. There his place is that of the comedians, who always spoke intimately from the margins next to the audience rather than from the central *locus*.

Robert Weimann has argued, I think rightly, that all early English staging was based on the interaction between what he calls the *locus* and the *platea*, the place of central authority as against the stage margins.[5] The authority position he locates at the centre of the stage, the geometrical heart of the

---

[5] Weimann's book setting out this concept is *Author's Pen and Actor's Voice. Playing and Writing in Shakespeare's Theatre*, Cambridge: Cambridge University Press, 2000.

whole theatre, accessed through the central opening in the *frons scenae*. That was where the stage throne was positioned, the chair of state or 'state' that Claudius as king in the second scene of *Hamlet* is sitting in when he taps its arm and derisively declares that poor Fortinbras thinks it is 'disjoint and out of frame' (it obviously did not look askew, from whatever position you observed it, although Marcellus later declares that something in it is 'rotten'). For this scene the throne would be brought onstage through the central opening in the *frons*, whence Claudius and his court would also enter. That was the stage's point of access for authority. When the stage hands drew back the 'cloth of arras' that later Polonius hides behind and is stabbed through, they would normally be opening the way for a colourful procession of dignitaries to enter the stage. The stage centre, several paces forward of the central opening, was the focal point, its authority massively enhanced by the fact that all the celebrity figures in the audience themselves stood clustered most closely around it. The three stage entrances in the *frons scenae*, so decoratively and emphatically set out in John Webb's drawing, demanded visual recognition and acknowledgement from the audience. If you entered through the centre, you had authority. If you entered by a flanking door, you were in contest with those who entered through the centre. I believe it was because of this emphatic positioning, in the physical design of the stage as well as in the mental predisposition of the auditors, that the priority we now give to the eye over the ear as spectators started to develop its power.

A generally circular and criss-crossing pattern of movement, evident in so many plays, does not fit precisely with the Jones/Webb design, which for audio purposes had its centre at what we would call the very front edge of the stage. There was everything to be said for that focus when good hearing was the essential need. Two speakers facing one another at the centre-front of the stage, where later stages had the footlights, could easily be heard interacting from all sides, their dialogue highlighted by their body language. In a theatre of the Webb design nobody would have been much more distant from them than twenty feet. Whenever the play called for a chair of state in the centre, all the speakers would have stood facing towards it, with those in what we consider to be the audience's standard viewing positions having to contemplate their backs. Such a disposition of the various stances, the inevitable consequence of playing in the round, intensifies the audience's feeling as they watch from behind the stage's watchers that they are eavesdroppers, and makes the clown's or outsider's occasional direct address to them an engaging exception. So long as it was in the round, with all stage entrances and exits routinely through the flanking stage doors, that worked well. The only complications that could have arisen were with 'discoveries' concealed behind the hangings covering the central opening.

On the whole these were rare events. On three occasions in *The Merchant of Venice* Nerissa 'discovers' the three caskets for Portia's suitors by drawing back the hangings, and *Volpone* begins with its Barabbas-like hero hauling them aside to reveal his collection of treasure. The central opening was not used very frequently, either for discoveries or for the great to enter by, but it was all the more potent for such minimal use. Most of the characters in any play would normally use as their entry-point one of the doors (or separate sets of hangings) on either side of the central opening. As marginal figures in what you might call dramatic opposition to one another these offset entry-points were natural to them. The Rose in particular, with its three bays each containing one doorway, the flanking ones angled at 28 degrees or so against the central bay, made the oppositionality of the non-central doors a feature whenever any antagonists made their separate entrances.[6] Such opposition is obvious in *A Midsummer Night's Dream* when Oberon as King of the fairies enters not through the central opening, which he should use as an authority figure, but by one of the flanking doors, just as Titania, his Queen, enters by the other. 'Ill met by moonlight, proud Titania,' says Oberon. They greet each other with the hostility we have already been warned about, so coolly signalled by their differentiated points of entry. Only at the end of the play do they show their repaired harmony by exiting together through the central opening. Such harmonious departures side by side and probably hand in hand were the routine means for closing a love comedy.[7] When the lovers are at last united they always expected to depart together in pairs through the central opening. Only in *Love's Labours Lost* does the play supply reasons for them to exit separately, the men by one flanking door, the boys playing the women by the other, because "Jack hath not Jill".

On stage, oppositionality was the norm. This form of staging is made most obvious by the opening of *Romeo and Juliet*, when the Montague

---

[6] That is the angle of the bays as measured by the archaeologists. See Julian Bowsher and Pat Miller, *The Rose and the Globe – Playhouses of Shakespeare's Bankside, Southwark. Excavations 1988–90*, Museum of London Archaeology Monograph 48, London, 2009, p. 43. A more normal measurement, calculating the angles from the inside of the polygon as the deviation from a straight line of 180 degrees, would make it 152 degrees.

[7] Following a closely similar line of enquiry, we ought to ask ourselves whether, at the ending of *Measure for Measure*, the Duke's two hamfisted proposals of marriage to the silent Isabella would not have been answered in the original performances by her mutely taking his hand before they both go offstage together as the first of the four pairs of marriage partners through the central opening.

servants enter by one of the flanking doors and meet the Capulets entering by the other, before starting their fight at mid-stage. The Montagu and Capulet parents follow their servants onstage through the same opposed doors. Subsequently it is for the Duke of Verona, appearing through the central opening, from where, stepping forward into centre stage to part the contestants, all of whom have to turn and face him in his central position, to enforce peace. He quiets the contestants from the centre of the stage, the *locus* of authority. Through the rest of the play all the entrances and exits take place through the opposing doors, with only Juliet's bed occupying the central space, and perhaps her tomb at the finale. The tragic conclusion has all the surviving Montagues and Capulets united in grief, so they must exit side by side through the central opening.[8]

In such of the choreography as we can deduce from these plays, the flanking doors gave most immediate access to the *platea*, the common ground of the street round the stage edge, while the central opening admitted authority. The early audiences routinely expected to accord the doors and their users those distinct significations. In an equally familiar pattern of contrast some clowns could mock the potency of the *locus* by also emerging through the central hangings. Several jokes refer to popular clowns like Richard Tarlton or later Timothy Read sticking their head out through the central hangings to pull faces before making their entrance onto the stage. From there they would always head straight for the front edge of the stage, the peripheral *platea* where the lower-ranked people belonged. There they spoke intimately to the audience, literally face to face with the groundlings. The actors whose territory was the edge of the stage, the marginal *platea*, were expected to be clowns or outsiders and deceptive villains like Hamlet and Iago, or Richard III before he made himself king.

This pattern can be seen renewing itself in plays across the whole range of the Shakespeare canon. Not until the late plays are there any signs of a divergence from the three-dimensional patterning. *The Winter's Tale* and *The Tempest* in particular were new in demanding that their audiences focus on what was inside the central opening of the *frons scenae*, invisible to any viewers sitting on the stage balcony above them. This appears to have applied to both the outdoor Globe and the indoor Blackfriars, which I have argued elsewhere made *The Tempest* the one play clearly identifiable as written specifically for the indoor Blackfriars.

---

[8] There are difficulties in their doing this easily if the Capulet monument occupied the central opening, of course. For discussion of the varying possibilities, see Leslie Thomson, "'With patient ears attend': *Romeo and Juliet* on the Elizabethan Stage," *Studies in Philology* 92 (1995), 230–47, and Andrew Gurr, "The Date and the Expected Venue of Romeo and Juliet," *Shakespeare Survey* 49 (1996), 15–25.

Hermione's motionless statue in the finale of *Winter's Tale* is the most obvious such case for making special use of the alcove in the centre of the *frons scenae*. From the superiority of the lords' rooms at the Globe, the lords would not have been able to view the caskets in *Merchant*, or Volpone's treasures in Jonson's play, but they did have a wonderfully intimate view of the actions of Morocco, Arragon and Bassanio as they made their choice of casket, and as they watched Volpone gloating over his riches. Hermione as a statue, however, even before she comes to life, demanded an especially close scrutiny, and has to remain motionless, while to those above her she was invisible. Her pose as a statue is unique in Shakespeare. It was the first and only time he kept his audience in the dark, in order to shock them with Paulina's eventual revelation of her improbably long concealment.

The shock of the living statue was not just a matter, like Agatha Christie, of concealing the crux of the story for a banal revelation at the end. On stage it was not Leontes and his admiring description, followed by his amazement when she moves, that demanded the focus of everyone's gaze, but the sight of the motionless figure standing in the alcove, and then, when so potently urged by Paulina, beginning to move. Hermione had to stand hidden behind the hangings that Paulina draws back to reveal her, and there she remains until she is called on to move, slowly stepping forward into full view. Her first movement was the second revelation, and anyone sitting on the stage balcony above the alcove would be deprived first of the statue and then of her moving. If it were ever staged in the playhouse that I believe Jones designed, everyone in the expensive boxes flanking the stage and the gallants on their stools in front of them would have seen Hermione, but none of the sixty people positioned on the balcony surrounding the music room, one-eighth of the entire audience, could have seen what everyone else was gaping at. The end of *The Winter's Tale* should be seen as a breakthrough, inartistic term though that is, for the stage prioritising the visual over the aural.

The Tempest was written to partner *The Winter's Tale* along with Jonson's *Alchemist*, chiefly for the Blackfriars, which resembles Jones's design in so many features.[9] While its use of the central opening lacks the vital need to view the vision that the revelation of Hermione demands, it gives exceptional priority to Prospero's 'cell', which can only have been the curtained central opening in the *frons*. Prospero must emerge from there with

---

[9] We know that, like the Jones design, it had boxes flanking its stage, three entry spaces in its *frons scenae*, and a curved circuit of galleries. For the likelihood that *The Tempest* and *The Alchemist* were written specifically for performance at the Blackfriars, see Gurr, "*The Tempest*'s Tempest at Blackfriars," *Shakespeare Survey* 41 (1988), 91–102.

Miranda to begin his long explanation of the storm and shipwreck we have just witnessed. That location asserts for him the authority and control he then announces he has over the chaotic events of the storm. Soon Caliban too emerges from it when Prospero calls him, parodic like the old clowns exploiting the traditional location of authority. Its identity in the play as the source of Prospero's power, where his book of magic rests, returns potently in the finale, when first Prospero opens it to show Alonso and the courtiers the sight of Ferdinand and Miranda playing chess there. They do promptly emerge from the opening to join the crowd on stage, but the sight itself, with all the symbolism that a game of chess possessed as opposed to amorous clinches, makes the event affirm Prospero's injunctions about the properly respectful distance between the lovers. And then some time after that, Prospero orders Caliban along with Alonso's servants Stephano and Trinculo to go back into the cell to prepare the feast he promises all the dignitaries, restoring the clowns to their traditional roles as servants to the great, before he finally directs all the courtiers (plus the ship's master and boatswain) through the same central opening to close the play. As in all the late romances, the ending is marked by this restoration of harmony, and signalled by everyone's departure through the central opening. Prospero's own departure follows his epilogue, and takes him off through the same opening.

As we know, in about 1600 Shakespeare altered the terminology he used for audiences from 'auditor' to Jonson's contemptuous and dismissive 'spectator.' The last plays show signs of a not dissimilar modification that also seems to mark a shift in his priorities. While any of his plays or those of his contemporaries could have been staged at either the Globe or the Blackfriars, the vision of Hermione, curtained off beneath the stage balcony until Paulina reveals her, seems to be the first and almost the only explicit acknowledgement that Shakespeare ever put on stage, through a single climactic moment, for the necessity of giving priority to sight over hearing. In quite a substantial degree I believe that *The Winter's Tale*'s chief in-joke, for all that it was aimed principally (though fairly quietly at Ben Jonson), and that led Shakespeare to make his explicit ascription of the art of Hermione's statue to the ingenuity of Giulio Romano, and have Leontes call it 'her natural posture',[10] was also what marks the beginning of the gradual process that finally brought three-dimensional staging to its end.

---

[10] See Gurr, "Shakespeare's Many-headed Audience," *Essays in Theatre* 1 (1982), 52–62. My theory that Shakespeare used Giulio Romano as an oblique allusion to Aretino's *Postures* has been endorsed, quite independently, by the art historian Bette Talvacchia, in *Taking Positions. On the Erotic in Renaissance Culture*. Princeton NJ: Princeton University Press, 1999.

Can we ever get Shakespeare now in the three-dimensional form that he used and expected? I think not. Our playhouses and our thinking about theatres are nowadays inextricably bound into two dimensions, not three. Physical shapes and mental constructs work together in our time to give absolute priority to the eye over the ear. Today, too, we can use spotlights to make the eye focus on what our directors think are the important moments, and audio aids to allow audiences to sit all too far away from the stage and its immediacies. Beginning with the gradual acknowledgement that three entry doors at the back of the stage would come to dominate movement at the Globe, today the thoroughly two-dimensional flat screens of cinema and television tell us to witness with our eyes not our ears, watching the staged events far more passively than the Elizabethans in their eavesdroppers' positions. Such passivity also dominates our thinking about stage action. Our modern sense of ourselves, and the long-growing individualisation of audiences, has been imposed on us gradually over the last three hundred years, new theatre designs turning us into private spectators sitting in the comfortable dark as invisible, hidden and mute eavesdroppers. Such distancing inhibits us from behaving like the crowd with its collective passions that shared the plays at the early playhouses. Michael Boyd, Director of the Royal Shakespeare Company at Stratford, declared in 2010, prior to the new theatre opening there, that 'we have 3D in our bones'.[11] In our skeletons, perhaps, but not in our heads, nor in the well-practised expectations of modern audiences. I do not believe that it is possible to re-train spectators now so that once again they might start thinking and behaving in the ways that an Elizabethan crowd was habituated to do. All we can do, I hope, is at least to register a little of what that massive alteration has lost us.

---

[11] In press reports, e.g. *The Guardian*, 2 September 2010, p. 9.

CHAPTER 11

The General and the Caviar
Learned Audiences in the Early Theatre

In Renaissance drama the art of what Jonson called 'application' (*Works* 5.18–19) has and is a sad history. The fragments of evidence that we have about the readings that Elizabethans 'applied' to and from their plays denote a striking disregard for what modern sensibilities like to make of the semiotics of theatre events in the Renaissance. That they did apply the stories from past times to their present time there is no doubt. Walter Raleigh's cautionary note in the Preface to his *History of the World* says it all:

> I know that it will be said by many, That I might have beene more pleasing to the Reader, if I had written the story of mine owne times having been permitted to draw water as neare the Well-head as another. To this I answer, that who-so-ever in writing a moderne Historie, shall follow truth too neare the heeles, it may happily strike out his teeth. (61)

'Water' Raleigh of course wrote this toothlessly in the Tower where his proximity to the well-head had confined him since 1603. The question his comment raises is whether those writers who recognised the need to keep their distance from the truth kept it so remote that modern attempts to identify it have to founder in a different kind of water.

We can and do read and rifle those writers' texts for clues as to where the writers may have meant to apply them. Intentionality has an intricate relationship with the semiotics of all exchanges between writer and reader, whether the expected reader is a noble patron or a lowly understander in the yard at the Globe. Some current critical theories discount contemporary or even authorial readings on the grounds that reading, like living, should take place in the present. One of the activities of the present, however, is delving into the readings of the past. And that puts to the test the whole issue

---

Original publication: "The General and the Caviar: Learned Audiences in the Early Theatre," *Studies in the Literary Imagination* 26 (1993), 7–20.

of New Historicism, the hermeneutics of censorship, and the conceivable authority of readings that may or may not be found in these texts.

The wish to replicate the semiotics of the original exchange, whether it was designed for the solitary patron, the solitary reader, or the collective theatre audience, itself needs to be contextualised.[1] The textual principles of the New Oxford edition of Shakespeare are determined by the target of the original 'performance text' of Shakespeare's plays, however that may be identified. This target they justify first by the view that Shakespeare's compositions were originally conceived as work for the stage. It argues that the texts themselves served only as scripts for the players, reminders of the words to be spoken, part of a much more fully conceived original performance the details of which have been lost because the only form of record was the written word. Secondly, it supposes that the full production process of any play entails team-work, and that the author's original script is only one of many contributions to the end-product. Therefore, the essential product, for players and editors alike, is the first staged performances by the playing company and in the theatre for which it was originally written. And since the first audiences would have been as familiar as was the theatre, the semiotics of the early performances must be the chief target for any reconstruction of the concept that generated the play. That motivating principle works as much for editors as it works for the scholars who tried to build a reconstruction of the Globe in Southwark.

Inevitably, reconstructing the semiotic exchanges of the original performances raises the question of what "application" playgoers might have made, or might have been expected to make. That is equally a requirement whether the target is the whole theatre experience or the author's private expectations. For New Historicists, performance critics, theatre historians and semioticians, the audience's expectations and mindsets in Shakespeare's theatre are a vital area for study. It is not an easy task. Until recently, most projections about audiences were based on the expectations that could be identified from the writers' texts. That process works only up to a point, and leads into arguments that become suspiciously circular. Evidence about the mindsets of Shakespearean audiences is appallingly meagre. Probing that evidence delicately and very tentatively is an obligation for modern scholarship.

---

[1] The probably different relations of playwrights to their different kinds of patron, on the one hand those who gave companies their names, and on the other hand those who paid at the playhouses, have not been studied, chiefly because of the paucity of evidence for any noble patron's influencing the plays written for his company. The Earl of Leicester's patronage may possibly have prompted Leicester's Men to perform Protestant polemic in the 1570s and 1580s. See Paul Whitfield White, 'Patronage, Protestantism, and Stage Propaganda in Early Elizabethan England,' *Yearbook of English Studies* 21 (1991), 39–52.

There is, to start with, the question whether collective audience reactions can be expected to work in the same way as those of an individual, solitary reader. The kind of 'application' invited by the composers of emblem books, with their ponderous and elaborate visual metaphors, may have been similar to emblematic spectacles in pageants and masques, or the hellmouth in *Faustus* and the cauldron in *The Jew of Malta*. But there is no evidence to confirm that hypothesis. On the other hand there is ample evidence to confirm the expectation of 'application' in written texts. That can be found for instance by contrasting manuscript 'libels' that use real names with the tactful evasiveness of printed references to real events and people.[2] But the kind of attention given to written texts is not the same as to spoken and performed texts, whatever the authors may hope. Could a large, diffuse and socially mixed theatre audience be expected to respond in the same way as a learned reader?

One exemplar for the application of contemporary politics in a reading is the manuscript notes that the fourth Earl of Pembroke made in his 1625 edition of Chapman's *Conspiracy and Tragedy of Byron*. Looking through the play in the 1630s, Pembroke recorded the analogies he found in the 1608 play with his own time. This was the reading of history to be found in Raleigh and educated gentry like Fulke Greville, identifying applications to the present in the past. It is, I think, inherently different from the kind of application that plays invite in performance. Satire or covert allusion of any kind needs a different reaction in public from what the private reader may find. The *frisson* of recognition that goes with an intended and therefore pointed allusion or application has to be fairly general, to be felt and shared in the crowd. What evidence there might be for that kind of application needs seeking out. It depends very largely on the question of how divided audiences were thought to be.

One of the easier first suppositions to make is that audiences were deeply divided socially, and therefore in the level of education that set their minds. Some of the playhouses used a higher admission charge to limit access to the higher levels of society. Others were more wide-ranging. Shakespeare's own company from 1609 onwards used the same plays to cater to the richer end of the market at the Blackfriars in the winter and the poorer end at the Globe in the summer, though the Globe, which was their only playhouse for the ten years from 1599, did cater to both extremes of the playgoing

---

[2] "Where Medway greetes old Thamesis silver streames," an anonymous poem defending Essex against Cecil and others, is a case in point. The evidence can be found in Arthur Marotti's collections of early seventeenth-century manuscript collections of poetry and Pauline Croft's study of manuscript 'libels'. See Pauline Croft, 'The Reputation of Robert Cecil', *History Today* 43 (1993), and Arthur Marotti, *Manuscript, Print, and the English Renaissance Lyric*, Cornell University Press, 1995.

population. The social and educational range creates an initial difficulty because almost all the evidence for audience reactions comes only from the literate and usually from the most educated. The evidence itself is predisposed to favour the learned. In theatres, where the spoken word and spectacle gave stage performances a special value for the illiterate, that is a limitation. The hints and fragments of evidence from the literate are all we have about the whole social spectrum.

Jonson is the prime candidate for study, if only because he displayed his own learning so aggressively and condemned the audiences of his time so consistently. His games of allusion and application in his plays provide some of the more reassuring evidence for the sophistication of playgoers in his time. Even in his work, though, the type and level of possible applications ought to engender caution. In 1619 his lengthy escape northwards from London's pressures gave us the record of his talks with Drummond of Hawthornden. They show, so far as the breathless Drummond could be taken to have recorded Jonson's outpourings accurately, some distinctly ponderous reading habits. He evidently read the *Faerie Queen* in the light of Spenser's letter to Raleigh, citing "that in yt paper S. W Raughly had of ye Allegories of his Fayrie Queen by ye Blating beast the puritans were understood by ye false Duessa the Q. of Scots." His application of his own play *The Devil is an Ass* summarises it in similarly curt terms (*Conversations* 9, 17).

It is of course difficult to place Jonson neatly as either learned reader or alert playgoer. He does appear to have been fooled by Shakespeare on at least one occasion.[3] In his own tongue-in-cheek dismissal of 'application', he made a social and educational distinction between the art of writing and reading on the one hand, and the trade of application on the other. In 'The Epistle' to *Volpone*, dated February 1607, he wrote that

> Application, is now, growne a Trade with manie and there are, that professe to have a *Key* for the deciphering of everything, but let wise and noble persons take heed how they bee too credulous, or give leave to these invading Interpreters to be over-familiar with their fames, who cunningly, and often, utter their owne virulent malice, under other mens simplest meanings.

The wise and the noble would presumably refuse to admit the tongue in Jonson's own cheek when he wrote that.

---

[3] A debatable question. Jonson's irritable comment to Drummond of Hawthornden about Shakespeare's giving Bohemia a sea coast when everybody knows 'yr is no sea neer by some 100 miles', makes even the mightily learned Jonson seem gullible, in the light of Shakespeare's deliberate switch of the two countries, Sicily and Bohemia, from his source.

A rather similar differentiation to Jonson's between learned and simple readings can be found in Joel Altman's elegant and learned account of 'rhetorical enquiry' in the sixteenth century as the story of how drama in the schools and inns of court developed as a testing of legal and political hypotheses. It bases its analysis on a fairly high level of expectation about audiences' participation in the mental exercise of giving a play its proper 'application'. The learned at the Inns of Court in London were deeply practised at games of allegorising, and courtiers were expected to do the same with court masques. Was that also a feature of the popular theatre? A lot of modern interpretation is based on the assumption that it was. Is there much evidence that might justify this optimism?

We might expect the most learned writers in the world of London's theatre to appeal chiefly to the more learned in the audiences. That implies a separation of literacy and learning from the surface story. The concept of levels of understanding is basic to this. It lies behind most modern readings of the Shakespearean drama. Regrettably, the evidence for multi-level audience reactions has never been studied closely.[4]

There is little point in trying to identify a typical audience in a time so subject to constant change, when each playhouse appealed to a slightly different taste and companies and their repertories altered so rapidly. What may have been typical in 1590 when *Tamburlaine* was all the rage was old stuff in 1615, when a playgoer might bring the book of a play with him and read it while the play was performed in the theatre.[5] It was different again after 1625 when plays became respectable literature, and even the king read and made notes on them. The development historically in the audience through this period seems to have been as radical as the development of plays, though the evidence is not so well documented.

Such evidence as there is for audience mindsets clusters chiefly in the middle period, when Shakespeare was writing. Even there, it is hard to pin down much that is clearly symptomatic of audience thinking and reaction. Rough guides to popular interest such as the blurbs on play titlepages do little besides confirm the existence of the lower end of the market the

---

[4] Some years ago I proposed that Webster set up a binary reaction to his Duchess, with the final couplet of the play. The popular response was expected to be simple pity for her virtue, whereas the response of those who knew their Horace ought to have been more ambivalent (*Playgoing* 83–84). Responses to the idea have been mixed.

[5] In 1615, Henry Peacham published a book of epigrams and satires, *The Mastiv.* It includes a satire, '*Trahit sua quemque, Voluptas*,' about the visitors to a bookshop. The verses include these lines: 'Last comes my scoffing Friend of scowring wit,/Who thinks his judgement bove all Arts doth fit./He buyes the *Booke*, and hastes him to the *Play*,/Where, when he comes, and reads, Heer's stuffe doth say' (I.iv).

playwrights were catering to. Pursuing the signs of the trade of application, what needs to be sought out is evidence that the playwrights themselves, and even better their audiences, did have an interest in and capacity to seize on the applications we now find in the plays. The accounts by playgoers of the plays they saw give few hints of any wide variance in response, though their authors range in social status from Simon Forman the astrologer and quack to John Manningham at the Middle Temple.

There is plenty of evidence to suggest that a popular and simple reaction to the plays was the prevalent one. Anti-semitism, for instance, has long been a problem for modern students of *The Merchant of Venice*. Its precursor, *The Jew of Malta*, has attracted less concern mainly because it has been staged less often, and because its function as a black comedy, indifferently cynical about all religions, the Children of the Promise, Christians and Turks alike, has exempted Barabbas from the opprobrium that has attached to Shylock. But recently Margaret Hotine has suggested that Henslowe revived *The Jew of Malta* at the Rose in 1594 precisely in order to make it coincide with the judicial hearings against Dr Lopez, the Portuguese Jew who was executed a few months later (Hotine 35–38). This, if true, indicates that at least one impresario expected his theatre audiences in 1594 to read Marlowe's play as prejudicially and simple-mindedly anti-semitic.

A similarly prejudicial reading of Shakespeare's *Richard II* in February of 1601 is indicated by the fact that the Essex conspirators paid for it to be performed the day before their attempted coup. A play that upheld the wrongfulness of Bullingbrook's taking the crown from Richard would hardly have suited their suggestive purpose. They must have intended the performance to be seen as a reminder of one significant historical precedent for Elizabeth to be displaced by her unhappy general. These days we read *Richard II* as an account of the deposition more intricately balanced and less clearly favourable to Bullingbrook than that.[6]

Some of the blurbs on the title pages of the middle-period play quartos read like advertisements. Their accounts of their contents often appear to be sensationalist and uncomprehending. The 1590 octavo of *Tamburlaine* advertises the following on its title page: 'Tamburlaine the Great. Who, from a Scythian Shephearde by his rare and wonderful Conquests became a most puissant and mightye Monarque. And (for his tyranny, and terrour

---

[6] For a sceptical and reductive account of this incident, see Barroll 441–64. Other indications of scepticism over the 'application' of texts can be found in studies of the censors, notably Finkelpearl and Dutton.

in Warre) was tearmed, The Scourge of God.'[7] More temptingly, Munday's second Robin Hood rewrite when published in 1601 was called 'The Death of Robert, Earle of Huntington. Otherwise called Robin Hood of merrie Sherwodde: with the lamentable Tragedie of chaste Matilda, his faire maid Marian, poysoned at Dunmowe by King John.' The 1600 quarto of *The Merchant of Venice* tells us about 'the extreame crueltie of *Shylock* the Jewe towards the sayd Merchant, in cutting a just pound of his flesh: and the obtayning of Portia by the choyse of three chests'. Curiously, the 1600 quarto of *Edward IV* says that it contains 'His mery pastime with the Tanner of Tamworth, as also his love to faire mistrisse Shoare, her great promotion, fall and miserie and lastly the lamentable death of both her and her husband. Likewise the besieging of London, by the Bastard Falconbridge, and the valiant defence of the same by the Lord Maior and the citizens.' Sentimentality and spectacle. The more graphic events in the stories, thought of in highlighted plot summary, and their tear-jerking effects were the plays' most noteworthy features. Did the original audiences misread the range of applications in their plays so comprehensively?

In the earlier period, the Tudor years up to the 1590s, there are some hints that the more learned or academic members of the audiences held themselves aloof from the populist devotion to the spectacles shown on stage. It is worth tracking that aloofness through the years up to Hamlet's caviar for the general. The early evidence suggests that the popular theatres had not yet established the domination over the Court and the boy companies that they secured after 1590. In the prologue 'at the Black fryers' for *Sapho and Phao* (published in 1584), Lyly proclaimed that 'our intent was at this time to move inward delight, not outward *lightnesse* and to breed (if it might bee) soft smiling not loude laughing'. That was addressed to an audience of gentles in an expensive hall auditorium, not the crowds who enjoyed the clowns in the amphitheatres. Lyly's declaration of intent relates in ways worth probing to the *locus classicus* of early anti-popular theatre, Sidney's *Defence of Poesie*, and to some other early manifestations of social divisiveness among playgoers.

The evidence for this story begins with the publication of George Whetstone's *Promos and Cassandra*. The play was dedicated to his 'friende, and Kinsemann, *William Fleetewood Esquier, Recorder of* London', and dated 29 July 1578. The dedication is an odd piece but is important if only because it clearly lodged in both Lyly's and Sidney's minds, and gave them a precedent for their own differentiations between the popular and the proper kind

---

[7] An assessment of the contemporary reactions to *Tamburlaine* is given in Levin.

of stage performance as they imagined it. Whetstone's account is odd for the way it is composed. He offers a distinction in the plays written across Europe between two extremes, the Italian and the German:

> [A]t this daye, the *Italian* is so lascivious in his commedies, that honest hearers are greeved at his actions: the *Frenchman* and *Spaniarde* folowes the *Italians* humor: the *Germaine* is too holye: for he presentes on everye common Stage, what Preachers should pronounce in Pulpets.

Citing the extremes suggests that praise of a middle course is to follow. The English stage was the obvious candidate as Whetstone's model for moderation. But that does not happen, for reasons that may have been high-principled, but were certainly also local and practical.

As Recorder of London, William Fleetwood had plenty of reason to be concerned professionally with London's fast-developing popular theatre. In June, 1584, he wrote to Lord Burghley reporting a split in the Privy Council when the Lord Mayor of London had ordered the two playhouses in Shoreditch, the Theatre and Curtain, to be pulled down, and his own confrontation about it with the Theatre's owner, James Burbage. In his letter of dedication Whetstone shows that he knew Fleetwood's position in his alliance with the Lord Mayor against the players. So instead of holding up English plays as a model for the Italians and Germans, he attacks them too.

> The *Englishman* in this quallitie, is most vaine, indiscreete, and out of order: he fyrst groundes his worke, on impossibilities: then in three howers ronnes he throwe the worlde; marryes, gets Children, makes Children men, men to conquer kingdomes, murder Monsters, and bringeth Gods from Heaven, and fetcheth Divels from Hel. And (that which is worst) their ground is not so imperfect, as their workinge indiscreete: not waying, so the people laugh, though they laugh them (for theyr follyes) to scorne: Manye tymes (to make mirthe) they make a Clowne companion with a Kinge: in theyr grave Counsels, they allow the advise of fooles: yea they use one order of speach for all persons: a gross Indecorum, for a Crowe, wyll ill counterfet the Nightingales sweete voice: even so, affected speeche doth misbecome a Clowne. For to worke a Commedie kindly, grave olde men, should instruct: yonge men, should showe the imperfections of youth: Strumpets should be lascivious: Boyes unhappy: and Clownes, should speak disorderlye: entermingling all these actions, in such sorte, as the grave matter, may instruct: and the pleasant, delight: for without this chaunge, the attention, would be small, and the likinge, less.

Something between a paradox and a contradiction sits in the middle of this. Whetstone specifies the 'indiscreete' nature of English plays in terms of three neoclassical precepts. To Castelvetro's unities of time and place (invoked in English here for the first time), he adds the decorum of character stereotypes that Richard Edwards had outlined for his boy players of the 1560s in his prologue to *Damon and Pithias*. Whetstone then applies to this English theatrical mix of tragic and comic the basic Horatian precept about the 'pleasure and instruction' principle. The grave old men instruct, the clowns delight, and the mix makes both principles digestible. In that lies his paradox or contradiction.

Grave matters, the affairs of kings, should not be mixed with 'pleasant' matters, the affairs of clowns, even though both are accepted as necessary for a good play. The English players are wrong because they 'use one order of speach for all persons'. Clowns 'should speake disorderlye' to distinguish themselves from the grave and noble. This hardly goes along smoothly with his previous objection that their aim is only to incite laughter, 'not waying, so the people laugh'. Anything for a laugh is bad policy in the theatre, even though pleasure (Italian or not) must mingle with German instruction. And yet laughter is acknowledged as a needful component in the 'mingling' kind of drama.

Sidney evidently remembered Whetstone's dedicatory letter when, a couple of years later, he composed his *Defence of Poesie*. It repeats the charge about the unities of time and place, and clarifies what Whetstone left confused by focusing on the question of 'mingling'.

> But besides these grosse absurdities, how all their Playes bee neither right Tragedies, nor right Comedies, mingling Kings and Clownes, not because the matter so carrieth it, but thrust in the Clowne by head and shoulders to play a part in majesticall matters, with neither decencie nor discretion: so as neither the admiration and Commiseration, nor the right sportfulnesse is by their mongrell Tragicomedie obtained. (III.39)

Like Whetstone, he accepts the need to mingle the grave ('admiration and Commiseration') with the comic ('right sportfulnesse'). Both are needed, but should not appear in the same play: 'the whole tract of a Comedie should be full of delight, as the Tragidie should bee still maintained, in a well raised admiration' (III.40). Sidney of course was a potent influence on learned and academic audiences. His point was renewed soon after the publication of the *Defence* in 1595, in Joseph Hall's 1597 poem of Juvenalian railing, *Virgidemiarum*. Scorning the stage 'huf-cap termes and thundring threats' and more specifically Edward Alleyn's playing of Tamburlaine and the 'stalking steps of his great personage', Hall also objected to how

> mids the silent rout
> Comes leaping in a self-misformed lout

> And laughes, and grins, and frames his Mimick face,
> And justles straight into the Princes place.

In his essay, Sidney next sharpens Whetstone by what he chooses as the focus of his attack, 'loude laughter'. English plays suffer, he says, in 'having indeed no right Comedie in that Comicall part of our Tragidie, wee have nothing but scurrillitie unwoorthie of anie chaste eares, or some extreame shewe of doltishnesse, indeede fit to lift up a loude laughter and nothing else'. He wants no mingled or mongrel forms of drama, but his real target is audience laughter, which is the product of 'onely a scornfull tickling'. It lacks 'decency and discretion' (III.40). Evidently Sidney had suffered from the coarseness of his fellow-playgoers' responses in English auditoriums as much as from the plays themselves. Hall, reading Sidney after the *Defence* was posthumously printed, felt enough of the same kind of aloofness to repeat the charge against the new theatregoers of the 1590s.

Sidney's argument uses Whetstone fairly directly, though whether in deliberate allusion or from a good memory it is hard to be sure. His reuse of 'indiscretion' and 'scorn' suggest an unconscious memory. Lyly's voicing of his preference for 'soft smiling' over 'loude laughing' a year or two later is an even less direct reference. He shared the two earlier writers' concern for 'inward delight, not outward lightnesse', but he evidently expected to get it from his gathering of gentles in a hall auditorium. By the same testimony, the loud laughing that Whetstone and Sidney deplored must have been a feature of the popular plays at the amphitheatres they attended.[8]

The main cause of the change that came about in the 1580s and 1590s is most likely the arrival of Kyd's and Marlowe's plays in 1587. Marlowe's own attitude to his popular audiences was, of course, challengingly dismissive. The Prologue to *1 Tamburlaine* invites the audience to 'View but his picture in this tragic glass, and then applaud his fortunes as you please.' He, along with his publisher in the epistle to the reader of the 1590 octavo, implicitly maintained the Sidneian divide, this time between theatre audiences and the more affluent and therefore presumably discriminating reader, dismissing the conceits that clownage kept in play from the printed text. Marlowe's other prologues were equally challenging to the stage audience. Machevill as prologue to *The Jew of Malta* declares of its protagonist, 'I crave but this – grace him as he deserves.' The play is a trial, an exhibition of human

---

[8] Sidney was introduced to Gabriel Harvey during the month of July, 1578, when Whetstone wrote his letter. Gosson's *School of Abuse*, financed by the Lord Mayor but dedicated to Sidney, came out in 1579. Spenser wrote to Harvey in October of that year that Sidney had scorned Gosson's pamphlet. The *Defence* certainly suggests that Sidney knew Gosson's work. Harvey and Spenser were both keen playgoers who presumably shared the Whetstone/Sidney resistance to loud laughing.

activities. Judgement is what the audience is asked to do with this testimony. In succeeding years Jonson was to take the concept of 'judging spectators' even further (Gurr, *Playgoing* 86–91).

Shakespeare picks up loud laughter over the paradox of Pyramus and Thisbe's lamentable comedy, which, says Egeus, 'when I saw rehearsed, I must confess, Made mine eyes water, but more merry tears / The passion of loud laughter never shed'.[9] Puck has a gentler audience in his master, of whom he says, 'I jest to Oberon, and make him smile' (2.1.44). He also knows the loud response to pratfalls, though. In the same speech he tells how when he pretends to be a stool that a gossip tries to sit on and she falls over, 'the whole choir hold their hips, and laugh / And waxen in their mirth, and sneeze, and swear / A merrier hour was never wasted there' (2.1.55–7). The nobility in Shakespeare, however, are not always so restrained as Oberon. In *As You Like It*, Duke Frederick is told by his courtier that along with his daughter and Rosalind 'the roynish clown at whom so oft / Your grace was wont to laugh', Touchstone, has fled (2.2.8–9).

The key and perhaps final text here, as in so many other matters theatrical, is *Hamlet*. However easily the morose Duke Frederick could be made to react with more than a smile, Prince Hamlet was a challenge of a higher order. Hamlet's complaint against the visiting players' clown is distinctly Sidneian. Along with the 'inexplicable dumbshows and noise' of the tragedians, he reckons that the groundlings are all too subject to the clowns 'that will themselves laugh to set on some quantity of barren spectators to laugh too, though in the mean time some necessary question of the play be then to be considered' (3.2.40–43). But Hamlet is not much for comedy beyond his own clownish disposition. His preference, at least in the pressurised environs of Denmark's prison, is for a revenge play rather like Marlowe's *Dido*, which was decidedly caviar to the general. In a state which leads him to note in his own tablet-book that the monarch of Denmark himself 'may smile and smile and be a villain' (1.5.109), neither loud laughing or soft smiling are likely to match his favour.

From Sidney to *Hamlet* is not a really long stretch, especially if we allow that audience preferences might have altered rather more slowly than those of the playwrights. Nonetheless, if there was a substantial change in Tudor and Stuart playgoing, it came between those two times. It is Sidney who provides the basis for Stephen Greenblatt's differentiation between the kind of Rabelaisian laughter that 'affirms the oneness of the body with the earth

[9] *A Midsummer Night's Dream*, 5.1.68–70.

and celebrates the crossing or destruction of boundaries', Bakhtin's carnival, as against the Sidneian laughter which draws sharp distinctions by its patronising emphasis on social differentiation. 'It is important', says Greenblatt, 'to distinguish between a laughter that levels – that draws lord and clown together in the shared condition of the flesh – and a laughter that attempts to inscribe ineradicable differences' (116). Whetstone, Sidney, and Hall wrote in the dominant mode of social divisiveness. The absence subsequently of any further expression of the preference for soft smiling over loud laughter may signify the disappearance of that selfconscious social division from the playhouses and indicate the triumph at least for a time of the Rabelaisian togetherness. Falstaff's universal popularity not only with the groundlings but also with educated playgoers as various as Leonard Digges and Sir Edward Dering must have helped dissolve some barriers.[10] In 1598 as high a grandee as the Earl of Essex could joke about another grandee being a Falstaff (Dutton 103). At this time the reporters of plays, Manningham in 1602 and Forman in 1611, show no consciousness of possible divisions within the audience. The disappearance of the distinction possibly marks a new kind of dominance in playhouse audiences, a faith in their shared and collective opinion about what they were witnessing. Jonson's sour claims that playgoers went for what pleased the eye more than the ear were the only identifiable attempt through the early Stuart period to maintain that there was still an important distinction to be observed, a differentiation of learning and mind within theatre audiences worth identifying and appealing to. The divisions that came later are evident in the differences between the playhouse types (hall and amphitheatre?) and their admission prices, and to a lesser extent in their repertory.

What such middle-period collectivity does not indicate, however, is what it might have done to the new trade of application. On that issue much use has been made of the most tangible evidence for applied readings, the work of the stage censors. Debate has been stirred about tacit self-censorship in the writers, a thought that can readily promote the assumption that they expected radical and extensive application. Yet the evidence from the censors is hardly more encouraging than that from play title pages. Tilney, Buc, and Herbert in the few texts where evidence of their censoring

---

[10] Digges wrote verses about Shakespeare's plays, probably for the First Folio in 1622, including praise of Falstaff. Citing a variety of King's Men's plays, he writes: 'Yet these sometimes, even at a friend's desire / Acted, have scarce defraied the Seacoale fire / And doore-keepers: when let but Falstaffe come / All is so pester'd.' Dering in the 1620s adapted the two *Henry IV* plays into one, concentrating on the Falstaff scenes.

hand surviving show more concern for specific verbal offensiveness than applicability. More attention was given to references that might offend foreign ambassadors or living Londoners than to large political issues.

Moreover, the things subject to censorship show a disconcertingly random concern for the things we might expect to be subject to 'application'. Some subjects that we would think obvious targets were censored, others were ignored. Part of the deposition scene in *Richard II* was cut while Elizabeth was alive, but Richard's onstage murder was not, any more than the far more sensational murder of Edward II in Marlowe's play. I suspect that it would be oversophisticated to argue, as might be done, that the kind of selective censorship which chose to delete the deposition scene of *Richard II* and its politically loaded display of a reigning monarch abdicating, and yet leave the actual murder untouched, is a mark of an extremely subtle censorial mind. The 'application' of Richard's deposition to Elizabeth would presumably have been much sharper for the Essex supporters than the regicide. But there is little else that gives support to such a reading.

Such evidence about applications of plays as there is after 1600 does suggest that there was some readiness to read some plays in terms of contemporary events, acting exclusively at the level of courtiers and gentry. Of Annabel Patterson's two most famous cases of failure to censor an application (17), the staging of *Richard II* on the afternoon before the Essex revolt can be seen as suggesting that the Essex conspirators applied it much more earnestly than the players or indeed most of the audience at the time. It served them as a pre-judged exercise, a familiar reminder of the application they had long made of Richard's case to Elizabeth. This application was widely recognised and acknowledged, though it worked much more sharply on the courtiers and lawyers who tried the conspirators than the general populace. The more extraordinary and self-evident case, *A Game At Chess*, is an indication that nobody, from the censor himself to the poorest Londoners in town in the vacation month of August, could miss its admittedly broad and blatant application. The Master of the Revels, Henry Herbert, gave his licence to the play as early as June, 1624, well before the sensational performances started in August. He must have shared in the calculations and the planning that went into staging the play at a time when the Court was on a progress in the country and therefore slow to react.

But to return to *Hamlet*. The play contains exemplifications not only of the grandee's scorn for loud laughter but also an acknowledgement of the bias of censors, and two exemplars of the art of application itself as authors might use it. Being a protégé of royalty and master of the play's court revels, Hamlet himself was expected by the king to serve as censor to the players and their Mousetrap: 'Have you heard the argument? Is there no offence in't?' asks Claudius (3.2.232). Like Herbert in 1624, Hamlet had his own reasons for misleadingly reassuring his king. 'Poison in jest' could be applied two ways, like any play about a royal murder. But the semiotics of the 'Mousetrap' scene are distinctively ambivalent. Hamlet's application of the murderous tale of Gonzago, writ in most choice Italian, to his own and Claudius's secret, was private to Claudius, himself, and the watching Horatio. Hamlet was applying information that he knew only he shared with his target audience Claudius. It was a secret between them, an intimate piece of insider trading that the general such as Ophelia could only be ignorant of.

Earlier in the play Hamlet himself, model for his time, makes the most pointed application of all. The 'rugged Pyrrhus' speech which was so to his caviar taste could be applied to his own situation with a precision that speaks very highly for the new trade. The Player recites to black Hamlet a speech in which King Priam/Claudius is murdered by a Pyrrhus black as his purpose, delaying only while the collapse of Troy made him pause so that he 'like a neutral to his will and matter / Did nothing' (2.2.480–1). Pyrrhus/Hamlet then strikes, and sets Hecuba/Gertrude to weeping. This self-exemplar of a precedent story which has a precise application to Hamlet's own case is private to the hearer; the Player is as innocent of its applicability as was Augustine Phillips over playing *Richard II* for the Essex conspirators in 1601. But it so precisely evokes its hearer's situation that it could serve as a model for all modern applicators.

That initial self-application is matched by others later. Hamlet's reference to Nero as he prepares to visit his mother explains why Shakespeare changed the king's name from the Fengon of his sources to Claudius, admitting the allusion to Nero's murder of his mother, wife to the Emperor Claudius. And there is the even more ingenious twist in the Mousetrap story when Hamlet tells Claudius that the poisoned king is killed not by his rival brother but by his nephew. This, prophesying Hamlet's future killing of the uncle-king at the same time as it explains his knowledge of the past killing of the brother-king, gives a fresh dimension to the Mousetrap's application, future as well as past.

All of these applications germinate in the mind of the one character, the best-educated grandee in the play, the student Hamlet. Whether that should be taken as a deliberate sign that interest in the trade was narrowly confined in the mind of its best author to the few Hamlets in Shakespearean audiences is open to question.[11] The work of identifying applications must be seen as unrewarding if the only prime candidate as practitioner of the art is the rarest individual created by the time's most demanding author. As it happens, *Hamlet* has one further application that spreads the scope more widely. In the process it may indicate something of the author's expectations from his audience. When Polonius says that he once acted Julius Caesar and was killed in the Capitol, Hamlet comments that it was 'a brute part of him to kill so capital a calf there' (3.2.105–6). For playgoers who had seen Polonius recently taking the role of Caesar in the Globe's *Julius Caesar*, and Hamlet playing Brutus in the same production, it was a nice insider's application. But when in the very next scene Hamlet kills Polonius, the application turns into a prophecy that neither character could have anticipated. That moment was common to the author and his audience. The general got their caviar in this play.

[11] It is necessary to be rather more sceptical about large-scale applications than small local allusions, which can normally be tied in more tightly through linguistic echoes. Shakespeare did make small local allusions to similar events occasionally. The most unquestionable is probably the conflation of Marlowe's line from *The Jew of Malta* with the stories about his death in the "great reckoning in a little room" (*As You Like It* 3.3.15). I have a personal suspicion that the reference to Giulio Romano in *The Winter's Tale* was also part of an interior game, an exchange as secret as Hamlet's with Claudius, between Shakespeare and Jonson (see Gurr, "Many-headed Audience" 57–60).

CHAPTER 12

Headless Coriolanus

By the time he wrote *Coriolanus*, Shakespeare had twenty years of experience writing plays for the Globe and its predecessor stages. We can be sure that he knew precisely what staging resources he could afford to build into his plays, whatever actual venue his company was using at the time. He must have been utterly familiar with the standard practices and requirements for their staging. Just what they were is a tease, given that we have lost so much information, and have so little hard evidence to rely on. But they are a vital feature of his plays. The printed play-texts sit there surrounded by dark penumbra, all the largely unspoken assumptions about the stage that Shakespeare shared with his fellows and their audiences.

The 'late' Roman play *Coriolanus* puts to the test one of the most basic features of the staging that he shared with his audiences of the time. Robert Weimann's enticingly plausible version of early staging sets up what he calls the opposition between *locus*, the central position where authority made its pronouncements to the world at large, and *platea*, the marginal site round the stage's edge, where the villains and clowns could speak their asides directly to the audience.[1] This dualism fits *Coriolanus*'s most likely choreography almost to perfection. It therefore makes a reasonable test of one of the currently dominant assumptions about what lay in the Shakespearean penumbra.

We can be sure that some form of archetypal stage design must have existed in most early writers' minds while they were composing their plays, however extravagant their demands appear to have been on occasions. As an employee of the professionals, Shakespeare must have been cautious and careful in what he asked them to stage. The Weimann concept usefully tests this, although generalising of this kind is never a straightforward process. In 2006, for instance, Erika Lin raised some relevant doubts over just where

---

[1] See Robert Weimann, *Author's Pen and Actor's Voice. Playing and Writing in Shakespeare's Theatre*, Cambridge University Press, 2000, especially Chapter 7.

Weimann identified the sites for the central *locus* and the marginal *platea* on the early stages.[2] Noting the recurrent need for major characters to move away from the *locus* in the course of a play, she questions Weimann's apparent claim that authority had always to be positioned on a fixed site in front of the central opening. Consequently she felt some difficulty conceiving how an authoritative *locus* character might operate when he or she had to speak to the audience from the *platea*. In its turn, this passes too easily by three other basic features of characterisation in early theatre. First, the large open space of the stage demanded movement, so a fixed location for any character seems unduly restrictive. Second, the stage posts both constrained and dictated the possible varieties of movement. And third, from the early 1590s so many of the major characterisations called the morality of any action into question that any fixed location itself must call the connotations of its locus into question.

Many plays make quite obvious use of the status of the different *loci*. Othello the simple soldier, for instance, at first speaks from centre stage, the authority position, but once he is seduced by the flirtatious Iago into taking over his own marginal role, and starts ranting about his faithless wife he does it prowling round the edges of the stage. That is an obvious feature with such a spacious stage. Movement always had to be fluid across these broad spaces, so the two denotative locations, and their use in relation to the three stage doors, cannot have been invariable.

The question of how fluid the use of the stage was in fact raises a much larger question. Even before the last decade of Elizabethan times, plays were appearing where the authority of the central character is open to doubt. What did that sort of play do when re-appropriating the standard patterns established by Weimann's distinction between centre stage and stage edge? This study takes a tentative dip into the complex choreography that might have been used in one such case.

Consider first the classic anomaly between the two chief configurations of the early playhouses, Johannes de Witt's sketch of the Swan, and the far more sophisticated set of drawings by John Webb, based most likely on an earlier design of an indoor playhouse by Inigo Jones.[3] One has a pair of arched double doors, whereas the other has two single doors with flat lintels, flanking a broader arched central opening.

---

[2] Erica T. Lin, "Performance Practice and Theatrical Privilege: Rethinking Weimann's Concepts of *Locus* and *Platea*", *New Theatre Quarterly* 22 (2006), 283–98.

[3] See Chapter 10 for the Webb drawings. While the drawings have been much debated, I am inclined to accept the conclusions of Hosley and Orrell. See Richard Hosley, "Three Renaissance English Indoor Playhouses", *English Literary Renaissance* 3 (1973), 166–82; and John Orrell, *The Theatres of Inigo Jones and John Webb*, Cambridge University Press, 1985.

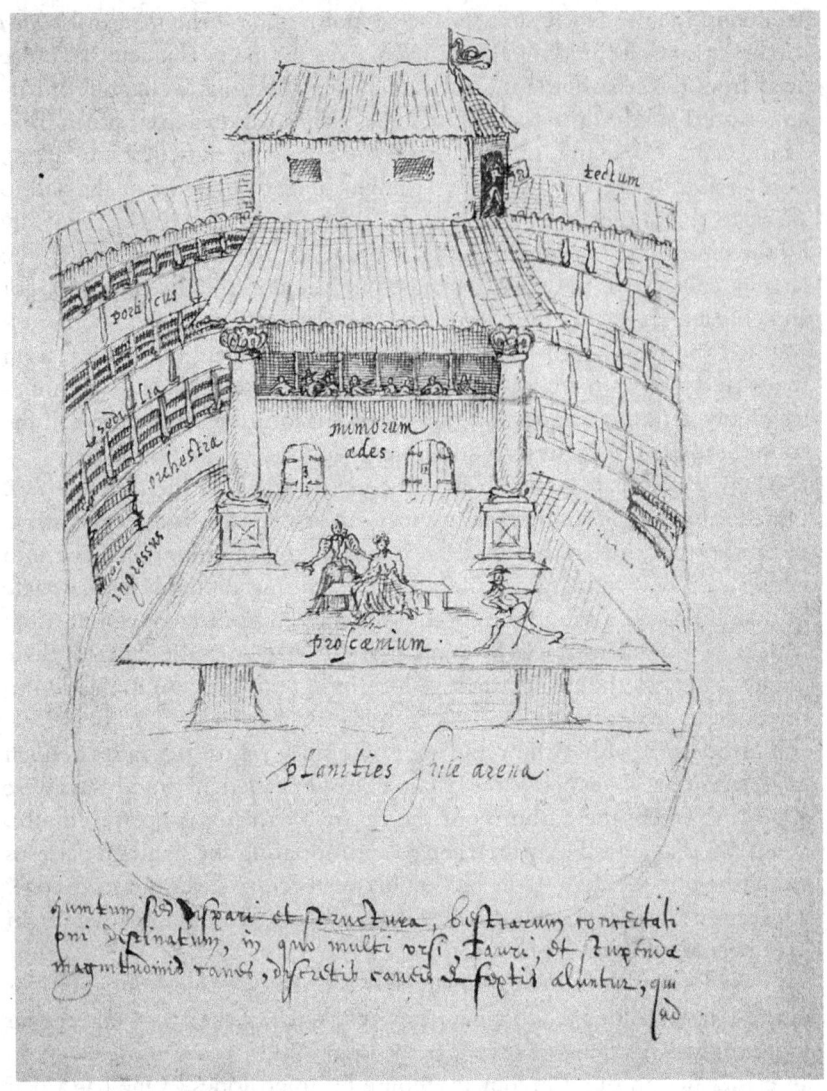

2. Johannes De Witt's sketch of the Swan in 1596.

The Swan's two heavy double doors stand in sharp contrast to the single and singular three-entrance stage *frons*, with no doors hung in any of its openings, that appear in the only other picture of an early stage, the Worcester College designs. Its auditorium clearly shows that it was made for a playhouse intended for hearing rather than for seeing. Evidently an indoor venue, it is drawn with typical Jonesian finesse as a highly decorated (and no doubt meant to be brilliantly coloured) early version of a truly intimate theatre.

These designs have been analysed quite thoroughly. Johannes De Witt's representation of the Swan's stage in particular has provoked much discussion, and a lot of debate about early staging has been based on it, since it was first discovered in 1888. The second set of drawings has had similar scrutiny, as noted above. They have even been directly re-employed, forming the basis for a version of the Blackfriars, the Sam Wanamaker Playhouse, now in use at the new Globe. The first spectators attending that new venue found that its auditorium had been all too obviously designed for people to listen to what was said, rather than to view what was being acted physically on the stage.

In spite of the Swan's two doors in its *frons*, the second set of designs certainly upholds the strong case, based on stage directions and related evidence, which appears to confirm the view that three openings in the *frons* soon became the standard provision. Despite De Witt, most surviving plays seem to demand, besides a stage with a broad central opening or 'discovery space', as we now call it, usually concealed behind a set of hangings, one doorway on each flank, each of them fronted either by hangings or a real single door. This disposition of three openings, two of them opposed or at least in parallel, does seem to have been needed, if not by the Elizabethans then certainly by the Jacobeans, for all of their more routine entrances and exits. I once even claimed that, when De Witt visited the Swan, the whole stage front must have been hung with curtains reaching across the entire *frons*, so that, being most concerned to show the physical structure (the hardware) of the playhouse, the sketcher had to guess at the entrance doorways mainly from the fact that, for the play that he saw there, the players entered only from one section or other of the hangings fronting the *frons*.[4] Excluding any soft furnishings from his drawing, De Witt could only deduce what was behind the curtains fronting the stage facade by watching where the actors entered through the hangings. The play he might have seen there, this argument goes, made no use of the Swan's central opening. He therefore showed no such feature in the playhouse's hardware. Ignoring its soft hangings, he depicted only the hard features that he could identify. Thanks to the obscuring presence of the stage curtains, he omitted the key central feature of the *frons*. That does

---

[4] See for instance Gurr, "DeWitt's Sketch of the Swan," *Notes & Queries* 7 (1960), 328, and *The Shakespearean Stage 1574–1642*, 4th edn, Cambridge University Press, 2009, p. 167.

seem a rather fanciful conclusion, especially since De Witt certainly did include in his sketch the fairly soft outlines of the figures who sit watching the play from the balcony over the stage, and the distinctly imprecise outline of what might have been hangings round the edges of the stage.

In general, the use of three doors in the *frons scenae* did offer a fairly simple choice of dramatic options for the early players. It could clearly identify which characters are on the opposing sides, while the central position shows who stands in authority over them. It commonly does take three to make, and to settle, a stage quarrel. Against this are the views held by Tim Fitzpatrick and others, that two doors are all the early stages needed for entrances and exits. Fitzpatrick asserts the primacy of the first of these two pictures we have of the early stages, with its sole access to the stage by the pair of double doors that stand as the dominant feature of the *frons*.[5]

Some of the earlier plays themselves do seem to make it evident that they had no need for a central opening. Plays routinely used two opposed parties, accessing the stage through a pair of flanking doors, sometimes slanted so that they partly face each other. These would have been a distinctive feature of the stage, at least the Rose on Bankside. Mariko Ichikawa has debated extensively the problem of which of the two doors might the players have chosen for their entrances, especially since, as was so appallingly routine, the original playbooks tell us nothing about which of the three possible points of entry should be used.[6]

The two flanking doors made some choices inevitable. Knowing which of the two to enter by was essential, both to prevent those on stage from looking the wrong way when a new entrant appeared and to be consistent in other movements. The very fact that they were on the flanks of the *frons*, and that the central opening between them was, at least in Jones's design, twice the width and with the authority of its own centrality, makes such usage almost inevitable.

So it is a real puzzle why no stage directions should specify which door a character ought to enter by. In most instances other than scene openings, the players on stage had to know which door they could expect a new entrant to appear from. The total absence of specifications in playbook stage directions over which was to be used may be a remnant feature of the standardised use of the opposed doorways for each opposing side, but there are still far too many variants on that pattern to make such a choreography

---

[5] See Tim Fitzpatrick, *Playwright, Space, and Place in Early Modern Performance: Shakespeare and Company*, Farnham: Ashgate, 2011.
[6] Mariko Ichikawa, *Shakespearean Entrances*, Basingstoke and New York: Palgrave, 2002.

self-evident. Still, the very absence of specifying stage directions does suggest that a norm existed, and players, if not audience, would always have known which doors to use.

An archetypal pattern of some sort is evident from many of the earlier plays. I have argued before that *Romeo and Juliet* must have the Montagues entering by one flanking door and the Capulets by the other, with their fight in the first scene halted by the authority figure of the Duke, who enters through the central opening to separate the brawlers. Similarly, the second *Tamburlaine* has just one ceremonial entry, for the Soldan of Egypt to his 'state', which must have been from the central authority position. That stands in contrast to almost all of Tamburlaine's own entries. They are in pursuit of war, and on the march, which suggests that he must normally have entered from one flanking door and left through the other. That would emphasise the play's most obvious inference, that Tamburlaine stood for conflict, while the central opening signalled the order and control that he keeps subverting. Such a three-way pattern is self-evident in most of the earlier plays.

Coriolanus largely conforms to this disposition of entrances. Use of the flanking doors by the two opposing parties illustrates the power conflict between patricians and plebeians. Menenius and Gaius Coriolanus enter from the upper-class side, and the citizens, misled by their tribunes, through the other. This underpins the battle between the two sides, and the accession, and deposition, of Coriolanus as pretender to authority in Rome. Perhaps Shakespeare took the subject on just because it showed the ultimate aspects of one-sided authority.

In the Shakespeare corpus, of all the plays this one should have had no use for the *locus*. In their conflict, the two sides have the choice either of making patrician Coriolanus their leader or leaving the tribunes to lead the hungry plebeians against the Senate, the patricians who were withholding the grain from them. The chief use of the central opening in this play was to admit Coriolanus's assault and intrusion, unaccompanied by the Roman soldiery, through the gates of Corioli. That one violent intrusion was enacted as a symbol, almost parodic in its own way, of the only means by which, in this exceptional play, any character could establish a central authority. Such knowing re-utilisations of *locus* and *platea* tell us something of how the traditional positioning of authority developed and became transformed through those years.

Perhaps because of that, or possibly for some other inevitably complex reason, Shakespeare evidently found this early story before the days of imperial Rome worth the re-telling. The hero's ambivalent status, and the great metaphor of the body politic which Menenius so cunningly misrepresents to the mob, was a not unfamiliar tale to Jacobeans. A couple of years before, in a book about the body politic and other concepts of the state, Edward Forset had highlighted it, much more innocently than Shakespeare's version.

> This similitude was both fitly and fortunatly enforced by *Menenius Agrippa*, who being imployed in the appeasing and persuading of the seditious revoulting commons of Rome, did by a very tale of this proportionable respectiveness of the parts in mans body, and the mutualitie of kindnes and ayd afforded from each to other, so sensibly shew them their errour, that surseasing their malignant envy wherewith they were inraged against their rulers (whom they accounted as the idle belly that swallowed the labors of their hands) they discerned at the last, that their repining against, and their pining of that belly, whence was distributed to them their bloud and nourishment, necessarily tended to their owne destruction; and were thereuppon forthwith reclaymed into their bounds of obedience.

Shakespeare subtly and adroitly undermines such a one-sided reading. He turns Menenius's speech into a calculated distraction, a delaying action, holding the mob until the militant Gaius arrives to quell them with his power, as he exultantly declares when his hero arrives. His florid version of the body politic metaphor lists 'the kingly crowned head' as an integral part of the body, in spite of the fact that Rome has just expelled its line of kingly rulers. The power conflict between patricians and plebeians, with Menenius and Gaius Coriolanus on the upper-class side and the citizens on the other, underpins the accession to power, and then the deposition, of Coriolanus as pretender to authority in Rome. Perhaps Shakespeare took the subject on just because it showed some of the more complex aspects of divided authority.

But why did he choose a story from the other end of the republic, its very first days? Both *Julius Caesar* and *Antony and Cleopatra* were set in the last days of Rome's republic, the troubled years when it first became great, and returned to monarchy with the empire. That great time was the subject of the other Roman plays. *Coriolanus* is set at the republic's beginning, when Rome was struggling to find a means of governing its people that excluded monarchs. Coriolanus, as the play declares, was one of the nobles who had expelled the last of its seven kings. It must have been the nature of this a troubled political moment that made Shakespeare choose to put such a divided and divisive figure on stage.

We know that Shakespeare reread his Plutarch while middle England, including his home at Stratford, was afflicted with riots over the price of food. The Members of Parliament who spoke up on behalf of the riotous and hungry citizenry against the dearth, Yelverton and Hyde, were then openly called the tribunes of the people, in explicit reference to Rome's troublesome division. When patrician Menenius asserts that the "Helmes o'th state" care for the citizenry like fathers, the second citizen has a harsh and highly explicit reply:

> Care for us? True indeed, they nere car'd for us yet. Suffer us to famish, and their Store-houses cramm'd with Graine: Make edicts for Usurie, to support Usurers; repeale daily any wholsome Act established against the rich, and provide more piercing Statutes daily, to chaine up and restraine the poore. If the Warres eate us not uppe, they will; and theres all the love they beare us.

A sharp, and to most Londoners of the time, an utterly familiar outcry. The Usury Act of 1605 tried to set a limit of ten per cent on interest rates, without any effect. The social crises over grain shortages that had run for seven years through the previous decade were now re-appearing. The price of bread, the staple food for everyone, was soaring again. There were shortages of every major commodity. Authority in London was being loudly challenged by the poor just when Shakespeare chose to write about the similar crisis in ancient Rome.

The first Act of the play has flocks of characters entering by separate flanking doors. We must assume that the patricians would have been identified by their use of one, and the plebeians by the other. As the Folio text has it, the first entrants comprise '*a Company of Mutinous Citizens with Staves, Clubs, and other weapons*'. To meet them comes Menenius, entering through the other door. He addresses them in order to hold them there on stage until the arrogantly militant Caius Martius arrives to join him, through the same patrician door. He is followed by '*Sicinius Velutus, Junius Brutus Cominius, Titus Lartius, with other Senators*'. Such an assembly of patricians clearly identifies their door as marking where the opposition to the plebeians should always emerge. Caius, soon to be named Coriolanus for his victory, is firmly positioned on one side of the political quarrel. The *locus* remains inert and unused.

In the next scene Aufidius and the Senators of Corioli enter, probably by the door formerly used by the plebeians, the other opposition to Martius. The third scene has the women with their sewing, most likely entering through the patrician door. Then comes the first battle scene, Martius with the Roman soldiers confronting the gates of Corioli. Evidently this was staged in the traditional manner, the figures on stage confronting the *frons scenae*, where the door they have entered through becomes part of the besieged city's walls. The central opening becomes the city's main entrance. Martius and his army must turn when they enter through a flanking door, to stand '*as before the City Corialus*'. They confront the central opening, a pair of heavy doors, closed as they are to them. A messenger comes through the other door to tell Martius of the situation of the main Roman army with 'our Generall', Cominius. Martius orders the trumpeter to '*Sound a Parley*' to the Volscians, and in response two Senators appear on '*the walls of Corialus*', standing on the stage balcony above the central opening. Noises off signal Aufidius leading the offstage battle, and Volscian soldiers emerge from the central opening. After some toing and froing, Martius cursing his own soldiers, he advances to the '*gates, and is shut in*'. The stage directions are imprecise, but do show the intention.[7] While the trumpets are still sounding, his followers retreat, leaving Martius alone inside the gates with the Volscian enemy. Lartius arrives by a flanking door, is told what has happened, and laments until Martius reappears through the central opening, '*bleeding, assaulted by the Enemy*'. A pair of perhaps too-concise stage directions then say '*They fight, and all enter the City. Enter certaine Romanes with spoiles.*' The Act ends with Aufidius promising to take revenge on Martius.

This was almost certainly not the only section of the play to make use of the central opening. In the second Act, Volumnia, Virgilia and Valeria join Menenius to watch Martius get his award, the '*Oaken Garland*' and the title of Coriolanus.[8] The ladies must enter by the patrician door, where Menenius greets them. They must then all stand on the flanks of the stage, presumably by the patrician door, to observe the ceremonial entry. This must be by the centre: '*A sennet. Trumpets sound. Enter Cominius the Generall, and Titus Lartius: betweene them Coriolanus, crown'd with an Oaken Garland, with Captives and Souldiers, and a Herauld.*' Not only the Herald's announcement but also the position of Martius between the two generals, three abreast, signals the ceremonial aspect of this entry, and the need for

---

[7] Charles Edelman, questioning the idea of the '*trenches*' that the Romans retreat into while on stage, offers an intriguing coverage of the various conjectures by Empson and others about how this whole scene might have been staged originally (*Brawl Ridiculous. Swordfighting in Shakespeare's Plays*, Manchester University Press, 1992, pp.140–1).

[8] Anthony Miller, *Roman Triumphs and Early Modern English Culture*, Basingstoke: Palgrave, 2001, notes (p.137) that *Coriolanus* 'makes the politics of triumph its problematic centre'.

the centre's wider-spaced opening. At the end of the scene the procession departs through the same opening, '*in State, as before*'. This is where the authority position fits well with the action.

The same pattern would have fitted the next ceremonial scene, '*in the Capitoll*', when the stage direction brings each division in the realm together, though their final stances are apart: '*A Sennet. Enter the Patricians, and the Tribunes of the People, Lictors before them: Coriolanus, Menenius, Cominius the Consul: Sicinius and Brutus take their places by themselves: Coriolanus stands.*' This separates the two sides of Rome, with Coriolanus alone on his feet in the centre. What follows reflects these divisions. Patrician Coriolanus will not do what his fellows urge him to, and the Act ends with citizens mutinying against his becoming the next consul. In Act 3 the mutiny is brutally mishandled, and Coriolanus is provoked to the point where he exiles himself from Rome. No further use is made in the play of the central opening, the *locus* with its authoritative status. Rome's chance of returning to a single ruler seems to have gone.

It has been suggested that for the last scenes, Coriolanus occupies what is usually thought to be a tent. For the long supplication scene itself (5.3) he has been said, and directed, to sit in a golden chair of state. No stage direction, nor any set of words, gives any reason for making such assumptions. The confrontations all are matters of standing, and some kneeling, but they all are in confrontation with a vertical Coriolanus. In the crucial scene where he reverses his stance, Aufidius remains present in the background throughout, to witness his reversal. He would not have merely stood behind him or to one side while Coriolanus sat in central state. The central figure may have remained standing in front of the *locus* of authority to face all who come to plead with him, the prime authoritative position. But he cannot be seated while they go on their knees and make their pleas to him. As the final scenes and his murder show, his occupation of the *locus* is transient, no more than the temporary effect of a warrior's short-term power. He never becomes the consul or ruler that his mother expected of him.

This transient use of the authority position affirms what I have elsewhere called 'a symbolic choreography', the use of opposing doors and a central space not only for spectacular 'discoveries' but also for entrances by Weimann's authority figures. Given how readily the early plays could be staged at different venues with diverse kinds of resource, often in the halls of great houses while travelling round the country, or at individual great men's houses in London, or at Court, we should not too readily assume that any single ideal shape for any stage and its entrances would have been fixed in the minds of the writers. We have a regrettable compulsion to look too hard for fixity in such fluid conditions. Some form of archetypal stage design must have existed in the writers' minds while they were composing their plays, and in those of the players doing the staging. A (however post-Weimann) version of this concept does seem to offer a good match for that.

CHAPTER 13

Rethinking Shylock

In the winter of 1596–97 Richard Burbage got into desperate financial trouble. It came from his father, who died in February 1597, bequeathing his first major source of income, the Theatre, to his elder son Cuthbert, and the new venue, the Blackfriars, to Richard. Both properties were costly gifts. The Theatre's lease was due to expire in April 1597, and its landlord, Giles Allen, had sworn that he would turn his property to better use than a playhouse. As Cuthbert reported of his half of the inheritance, the Theatre, in 1635, "The father of us . . . built this house upon leased ground, by which meanes the Landlord & Hee had a great suite in law & by his death, the like troubles fell on us, his sonnes."[1] Richard suffered the like troubles to Cuthbert's conflict with Allen over the Theatre with his own inheritance, the Blackfriars, since his father in 1596 had borrowed nearly a thousand pounds to buy its freehold and build the playhouse, and in November had lost any means of repaying his creditors when the Privy Council banned performing there. That was when Shakespeare started writing his play about Shylock the moneylender.

Shylock is distinctive in the Shakespeare canon in quite a number of ways. In *Shakespeare and the Geography of Difference*, John Gillies points out how many times Shakespeare made use of exotic characters who are alien to the society of the plays they appear in.[2] All of them are at first tolerated, but later generate disaster. Such notable aliens as Tamora and Aaron, Othello, and Cleopatra can be allied with Shylock as figures whose acts prove to be what Gillies calls 'innately transgressive'. Shakespeare took a lot of trouble to identify Shylock as not just a resident of Venice but an alien there, one whose 'tribe' made him the archetypal outsider, in Venice

---

Original publication: "Rethinking Shylock," *Shakespeare International Yearbook* 12 (2012), 153–66.
[1] Quoted from the "Sharers' Papers" in Andrew Gurr, *The Shakespeare Company, 1594–1642* (Cambridge: Cambridge University Press, 2004), 278.
[2] John Gillies, *Shakespeare and the Geography of Difference* (Cambridge: Cambridge University Press, 1994), 99ff.

as much as in Belmont's Christian society. His alien role in *The Merchant of Venice* has attracted a massive cloud of commentary, and yet nothing has been said about the likelihood of his role being applied to the immediately dire and local circumstances of the Shakespeare company just when it was written.

Shylock as moneylender was a distinctly inconspicuous but far from insignificant link between the play's story and the players it was written for in the winter of 1596–97. There is ample evidence that this activity became a potent source of hostility for the performers of the play in its early showings on the Theatre's stage, and to its leading player in particular.[3] By the end of 1596, when the play was being written,[4] the company's financier, James Burbage, was in precisely the situation that Antonio finds himself in when he went to Shylock for his loan and then became bound to repay it without the means to do so. By February of the next year, after Burbage died and his younger son inherited the new playhouse, it was Richard who the hostile creditors besieged. Shylock has attracted an enormous amount of attention for his alien character. The highlighting of the non-Venetian with which Shakespeare so wonderfully camouflaged his villain has prevented us from seeing the immediate and entirely current London-based reason he had for incorporating such a potent story in the heart of a romantic comedy set in that remote and mythical great city and seaport, so unlike familiar London.

Close behind this feature of Shakespeare's play stands the Lord Chamberlain, Henry Carey. On 8 October 1594, as the new company's patron, he sent a strange letter to the Lord Mayor. Written when the first winter of the year that he set up the Shakespeare company was approaching, on the face of it his letter simply asked the Lord Mayor to let his new company perform through the coming season of cold weather at an indoor venue. Carey cited the old practices, asking:

> where my nowe companie of Players have byn accustomed for the better use of their qualities, & for the service of her Majestie if need soe require

---

[3] Studies such as John Gross, *Shylock: A Legend and Its Legacy* (New York: Simon and Schuster, 1992), and James Shapiro, *Shakespeare and the Jews* (New York: Columbia University Press, 1996), are brilliant at identifying the effects of the invention of Shylock, but ignore its immediate cause.

[4] The date of *Merchant* is generally seen as determined chiefly by the reference in line 27 of the first scene to a ship that Salarino calls 'my wealthy Andrew', a prize captured from the Spanish at Cadiz and brought to England in June 1596. Composition in late 1596 and staging in 1597 fits the time of the Blackfriars crisis perfectly. We might even use that dreadful fiasco as a determining factor for dating the play. The story from Ser Giovanni's *Il Pecorone* on which the whole play is based must have come into Shakespeare's mind as its apposite basis only after the petition went to the Privy Council in November 1596.

to plaie this winter time within the Citye at the Crosse kayes in Gracious street. These are to require & praye your Lordship the time beinge such as thankes be to god there is nowe no danger of the sicknes) to permit & suffer them soe to doe.

In an article I wrote some years ago about this letter,[5] I suggested that the Lord Mayor who came into office at the end of that month, Michaelmas 1594, Sir John Spencer, who was an alderman particularly hostile to playing, would have refused Carey's request. That refusal, I argued, was why early in 1596 Burbage bought a property in the 'liberty' of the Blackfriars, and converted it into a new roofed playhouse. We know that Carey helped Burbage to acquire the Blackfriars property. He wrote about it to Sir George More, owner of part of the site that included a section Carey himself had once owned. On 9 February 1596, he wrote saying, knowingly, 'you have all redie parted with part of your howse to somme that meanes to make a playe howse in yt'. Such a comment implies Carey's approval of the project. His previous letter of 1594 to the Lord Mayor shows that he wanted to help his new company establish its playing venues, one for summer and one for winter. In view of the Mayor's rejection, James Burbage must have assumed that the Blackfriars, located in a precinct independent of his authority, would make an admirable replacement inside the city for the Cross Keys inn.

Carey's son, however, whose own dwelling-place was a set of chambers literally underneath the new playhouse, took a different view. He became the second signatory on the petition of the residents which that November asked the Privy Council to stop the project. The first was Elizabeth Russell, sister-in-law to Lord Cecil who chaired the Council. These Blackfriars residents had plenty of clout, and the Council immediately approved what they asked for. Carey himself had died on 22 July of that year. Soon after his death Thomas Nashe reported that the company, 'however in their old Lords tyme they thought there state setled, it is now so uncertayne they cannot build upon it'.[6] All too soon that proved to be an appallingly appropriate pun.

Burbage bought the Upper Frater of the Blackfriars site on 4 February 1596 for £600, to which he added the cost of constructing a completely new playhouse inside it. The total price of his commitment to build the playhouse must have been well over £1,000, far more money than he could

---

[5] Andrew Gurr, "Henry Carey's Peculiar Letter," *Shakespeare Quarterly* 56 (2005) 51–75 reproduced as Chapter 2 in this volume.
[6] *Thomas Nashe, Works*, ed. R. B. McKerrow, revised edn (Oxford: Oxford University Press, 1958), vol. 5, 194. The addressee of Nashe's letter was most likely William Cotton, one of Carey's many servants.

possibly have possessed within his personal resources. Of his debts entailed by the later Blackfriars, Cuthbert Burbage's 1635 declaration went on to say that 'our father purchased it at extreame rates & made it into a play house with great charge & trouble'. Such charge and trouble at 'extreame rates' meant going to London's moneylenders, securing massive loans taken up at extortionate rates of interest. William Ingram has noted how the revised terms of the interest chargeable by moneylenders laid out in the Usury Act of 1571 helped to precipitate the flood of money that went into theatre-building from 1575 onwards.[7] Moneylending at high rates of interest was routine by the 1590s, and London's venture capitalists saw building playhouses as a thoroughly profitable activity. In November 1594, once the Privy Council's new regulations about playing meant that only suburban playhouses could be used for plays and the mayoralty ignored Carey's letter asking for the Cross Keys, two venture capitalists, Francis Langley and Oliver Woodliffe, neither of them previously involved with playing, each started building a playhouse in London's suburbs. On the south bank of the Thames Langley built the Swan, and in the east Woodliffe converted the Boar's Head in Stepney from an inn to a playhouse. Clearly they both expected to make good profits from their ventures. The recurrent phrase 'take interest', used in *The Merchant*'s first exchange between Shylock and Antonio (1.3.43, 67, 68, 86), was applicable to their involvement in two ways.

Shakespeare started writing his play at the end of 1596, and the company first staged it early in 1597. That was precisely when James Burbage – and after he died in February his son Richard – would have come under

---

[7] William Ingram, "The Economics of Playing," in *A Companion to Shakespeare*, ed. David Scott Kastan (Oxford: Blackwell, 1999), 31.5–16. The law of 1571, which coincided with the completion of Gresham's Royal Exchange, redefined the terms for lending at interest, condemning usury but accepting interest charges so long as they ran at a level set by the state, initially 10 per cent; this led to a surge of money for new building becoming available from then on. The issue was essentially one of interpreting the Bible's injunction over usury. Thomas Wilson's *Discourse of Usury*, a dialogue published in 1572 but written before the revisions announced in the 1571 Act were passed, makes his Merchant declare as his last words: 'It had been my part, having had such wealth, to have vysited the prisons, where men lie long for smal debt, and have beene oppressed wyth usurye to their utter undoing: to have ayded the pooore householders, the fatherlesse chyldren and the widowes. But hereafter I will vysite Christ more often in hys afflicted members, and lend freely by gods grace to suche and so many as I shalbe able and know to be honest, godly men, and relieve them chieflye, and make also restytucyon unto them whom I have most oppressed, and get my goods hereafter by lawfull means' (p. 380) Wilson's *Discourse* was edited by R. H. Tawney in 1925; his Introduction provides an extensive account of many aspects of moneylending at the time, in face of the much-exercised biblical declaration that usury is a damnable sin. The law about chargeable interest was an ass that bore heavy burdens. Charles Edelman has sensible things to say about the Elizabethan definitions of usury, in "Which is the Jew that Shakespeare Knew? Shylock on the Elizabethan Stage," *Shakespeare Survey* 52 (1999), 103–4.

direct attack from the loan sharks who had financed his new theatre. They of course found, once it was completely blocked from use, that they were equally blocked from taking any profit out of their investments. We can only imagine how much pressure these investors immediately applied to the old man to get their money back. Richard already knew such pressure at first hand. He is recorded back in 1591, in a lawsuit laid against him by the widow of Burbage's brother-in-law and financier John Brayne, which demanded payment of arrears on Brayne's loans to old Burbage. The testimony claimed that he defended his father's holdings against his creditors by wielding a fierce broomstick and twisting one complainant's nose in defence of his father's profits.

The events surrounding the Blackfriars crisis – from the residents' petition, sent to the Privy Council in November 1596, to the death of James Burbage in mid-February 1597 – make the *Merchant of Venice* composition and first staging at such a time almost certain, and certainly apposite to its leading player's misfortunes. What is perhaps most intriguing is whether it was being prepared while James Burbage was still alive but coming near to his death, or whether Richard's subsequent inheritance prompted its composition. At either time, Portia's fortunate rescue of both Antonio and Bassanio was an act largely of wish-fulfillment, one that both the dying James Burbage and his younger son would have welcomed through that dire period.

The longer-term consequences of the Blackfriars disaster on the Burbages, with its largely fortuitous replication of Portia's rescue, should hardly surprise us. But its reality was distinctly less than an act of good fortune, except in the most material sense. One substantial consequence of James Burbage's argosy-like and ineffective venture of 1596 revealed its impact on his sons two years later, at the end of 1598. As part of their hopeful because underfunded project to build a new playhouse for the company on Bankside out of the stolen remains of the old Theatre, Cuthbert and Richard needed a major injection of cash to help them redeploy the retrieved timbers to make the Globe. It must have been as a direct result of their father's unhappy experience over his loans for the Blackfriars that they turned for their funding not to London's loan sharks but to their fellow players. As company sharers, the interests of Heminges, Shakespeare, Phillips, Pope, and Kempe were already sunk deep in its activities, so they were the best source of new cash free from loan-shark pressure to supply the funds for the new playhouse. All of them would profit equally from the company's collective success. *The Merchant of Venice* was there in the company repertory as a reminder of the troubles James and Richard had suffered from London's moneylenders. Within less than a year the play was in print as a quarto. In February 1599 it must have been in clear and potent recall of the sunken Burbage argosy of two years before that Shakespeare and four other sharers signed up to each of them giving the Burbage sons £100 to build the company's new home. Such a request can hardly have startled them, since they had all been sharing in the performances of the *Merchant* through most of the previous two years.

As sharers in the new building and in the company whose future they were gambling on, this act did not turn the players into moneylenders themselves. In any case, as company sharers they were clearly confident that they would soon get their money back. That, of course, they did, and more. The unique new deal that got the Globe built soon proved so successful, with a majority of the company sharers owning the playhouse they performed in, that when in 1608 Richard Burbage did finally retrieve his expensive inheritance, the Blackfriars, for the company's own use, he allocated its shares equally among the Globe's sharing housekeepers, mostly to the same owners. That sharing became the ultimate guarantee of the Shakespeare company's unique success as a commercial theatre enterprise. Other companies tried to imitate their financial structure, but rarely with any success.

Such a reading of the immediate background to the Shylock play raises many questions. Given the stressful conditions of moneylending in London, and the Burbages' experience of the perils that came from usurous borrowing, we have first to ask why Shakespeare should have taken such care to convert his model from a local London moneylender to someone as thoroughly exotic as the Jewish Shylock. The play is packed with information emphasising the local colour of mythical Venice, the great Mediterranean trading and shipping centre that so easily outshone London with its Rialto and its synagogue. The wholly alien character of Shylock's culture, his ally Tubal, his daughter Jessica, his hatred of the Christian Antonio, his emphasis on having the prosperity of the heirs of Jacob, all his moneys and usances as Antonio describes them, make such elaborate colorification into a comprehensive disguise. It seems that Shakespeare would not do what Jonson might have opted to try, making his Shylock into a version of what many of London's citizenry such as Langley and Woodliffe were practising routinely at London's Rialto, the Royal Exchange.

We do, of course, know something about the Shakespeare family's own familiarity with usury. As Charles Edelman notes, both John Shakespeare and his eldest son were quite used to charging exorbitant rates of interest in Stratford when they lent their fellow-citizens money. We also know that one of Shakespeare's Stratford friends and business contacts was the venture capitalist John Combe. Shakespeare's own financial dealings were extensive, and even as early as 1596 we can assume he knew at first hand some of the processes of venture capitalism. It is a major pity that we lack much detailed information about his London contacts and possible dealings, so cannot know how familiar he was with some of the capitalists of that time. The few items of hard information we do have, such as the court order that William Wayte took out in 1596 to protect himself from Langley, Shakespeare, and two women, are tantalising, but what the order imports is quite obscure. Although the date of Wayte's order is intriguing, and seems significantly close in time to the Blackfriars affair, we have no idea why he should have named Shakespeare along with the loan shark Langley as the people against whom he took out his surety of the peace. We do know that Wayte's stepfather, William Gardiner, was a justice for the South Bank area including the Swan's Paris Garden, which was enough to make Leslie Hotson think Shakespeare made him the model for Justice Shallow in 1597. Few scholars now take that seriously, but the fact that Wayte took out his surety indicates that Shakespeare had got himself involved in a fracas in a part of the suburbs of London that three years later was to accept the Globe, but where he had no obvious interest in 1596.[8] Langley had recently completed the Swan and filled it with a new company of Pembroke's Men. Shakespeare seems to have been involved with a former company under the same patron around 1593, but we know no more than that. As with Hotson, this almost empty terrain is ripe for planting with wild conjecture.

If we refuse to speculate over why Shakespeare chose to set his play in Venice, the location for the old tale he was dramatising, and not in London, we still have to face the perennial question of the story's more likely applications. Using a tale in which moneylending was only one relatively minor element for what was essentially a love-romance did offer the company a wish-fulfilling diversion from its current crisis. But even in such a routine view Shylock still stands out as an exceptional creation. At its crudest, we might fit melancholy Antonio to the dying James Burbage, father-figure to his son's Bassanio, while the outsider Shylock deliberately misrepresents the thwarted moneylenders now pestering old Burbage for repayment of their bonds. Such applications must have been in the author's mind, certainly in the minds of at least some of the players, and just conceivably in the minds of a few audience members familiar with the company's financial

---

[8] Hotson's theories about this are described with some vigour and a lot of conjecture in *Shakespeare Versus Shallow* (Boston: Little, Brown and Company, 1931), 9–83. See Park Honan, *Shakespeare. A Life* (Oxford: Oxford University Press, 1998), 260.

struggles at the end of 1596. The success of the residents' petition against the Blackfriars playhouse must have been a talking-point for many Londoners besides Thomas Nashe and his contacts.

Given Richard Burbage's close personal commitment to his father's financial troubles, the question which part he might have taken in the play, or been expected by the author to take in the first performances, is another intriguing question that, regretfully, can promote only speculative answers. Nothing survives to say who took which parts originally. Richard is usually assumed to have played Bassanio, the romantic hero. Who played the first Shylock we have no idea. Counting the number of lines spoken by the main characters, Tom King found that Shylock has 335 against Bassanio's 329 (Portia's is the largest part, with 557).[9] It is almost too easy a presumption that Richard would have taken Bassanio's role rather than playing Shylock. Playing Bassanio would have been a dangerous stimulus to make people apply the story to local circumstances. If the pressure from the debt collectors had any direct impact at the end of 1596, Richard might have played Antonio, who has only 188 lines but is generally thought to warrant the title role as Venice's merchant. On the other hand, Richard's opposite Edward Alleyn did play the bottle-nosed Barabbas in *The Jew of Malta* for the other duopoly company, and it is possible that Burbage might have found taking the part of Shylock in his own play an ironically apt inversion of his father's recent experiences. On this issue we are left with guesswork at best.

A possibly more rewarding question is what else in the theatrical culture of the time might signal the aftereffect of the players staging this radical parable about their collective experience as a shipwrecked company. Much has been made in the past of Marlowe's precedent for Shylock in *The Jew of Malta*'s Barabbas, and the public uproar in July 1594 over the trial and execution of the Portuguese Jewish doctor Ruy or Roderigo Lopez, which may have prompted the Admiral's Men to revive Marlowe's play. We can see Shakespeare openly diverging from Marlowe in his portrait of Shylock, and especially, despite the two similar balcony scenes with their caskets of gold and jewels, his use of Jessica as one of the sets of lovers in the finale, in contrast to Barabbas who poisons his own Abigail. For all its punishment of Shylock, Shakespeare's play was an overt comedy, not at all what T. S. Eliot called the "terrible farce" of Marlowe's ostensible tragedy.

One oblique hint survives to suggest an effect the portrayal of Shylock by the Chamberlain's might have had on the Admiral's company and its

---

[9] Tom King, *Casting Shakespeare's Plays. London Actors and Their Roles, 1590–1642* (Cambridge: Cambridge University Press, 1992), 184–5.

writers, and whether they showed any sign of knowing its immediate and local application to the Burbage troubles. This is linked to the choice of the Venetian setting for Shylock, and more broadly with the distinctly gradual acceptance by both companies that London itself was a respectable setting for their comedies. Shakespeare's avoidance of the possibility of any direct application of Shylock to James Burbage's financial troubles is easily read as a tribute to his tact and general discretion over the popular but mostly crude business of making satirical applications. He may have been following company policy, which seems to have been discreet enough to avoid overt use of local conditions and settings except where it was unavoidable, as in the English history plays with their scenes at Court and in Eastcheap. That was not the common response, though. Early in 1598 Jonson did choose to locate *Every Man in his Humour*, written for the Chamberlain's, in a version of Italy's Florence, however obviously it was London-set, and which he changed openly to London in the 1616 Folio version. Some time before that the Chamberlain's Men had performed what was probably their first and almost only surviving play largely set in London, the tragedy *A Warning for Fair Women*, published in 1599. It had to use the London setting, since it dramatised a known murder story about Londoners, one previously told at length by Holinshed, like *Arden of Feversham*. As such, the company had no choice but to maintain the original London location, as did Arden with its town in Kent. Otherwise, both of the duopoly companies, at least before 1598, seem to have avoided setting any of their plays explicitly in London. The fact that Shakespeare wrote the Eastcheap scenes of the two Henry IV plays through 1596–97 at roughly the same time as he wrote *The Merchant*, and that subsequently he never set any comedy closer to London than Windsor, could be read in two ways – either as a show of his innate discretion, or as a more positive tactic of avoidance. That would mean he emphasised Shylock's alien status precisely in order to avert direct applicability to the Blackfriars catastrophe. The fact that no scholar has seen Shylock as a possible allusion to James Burbage's crisis at the end of 1596 might be seen as a tribute to such discretion.

The other dominant company of the time was less cautious. William Haughton was the first known writer who does seem to have openly used a London setting for a comedy, and he did so in a strikingly close rewrite of Shakespeare's play. He was an inventive playwright, starting the fashion for comedies in which the Devil visited London in 1600, a fashion imitated by several others, including Jonson with *The Devil is an Ass* in 1616. Late in 1597, not long after *Merchant*, Haughton wrote *Englishmen for my Money*, set explicitly and firmly in the city, and staged in February 1598. Full of overt references to the Exchange, Crotched Friars, Leadenhall, and other sites in the city of London, it borrows many features from *The Merchant*. Its central figure is a Portuguese financier Pisaro, an alien moneylender, rich from trading usurously in the city. The avaricious but ultimately defeated father of not one but three English daughters, he boasts in the play's opening speech that he owns thirty-two ships all coming successfully to London from Spain, and declares that he has become rich 'by the sweet lovde trade of Usurie, / Letting for Interest, and on Morgages'.[10] Though not specified as a Jew, on stage he wore the same bottle nose that Alleyn had worn when he played Barabbas in Marlowe's play and the usurer Leon in the parodic *Blind Beggar of Alexandria*.[11] Shylock-like, he tells the audience that three English lovers of his daughters

> Have pawnde to mee their Livings and their Lands:
> Each severall hoping, though their hopes are vaine,
> By mariage of my Daughters, to possesse
> Their Patrimonies and their Landes againe.
> (TLN 23–7)

That is the basis for Haughton's plot. Pisaro adds that they are deceiving themselves, and 'though I guild my Temples with a smile, / It is but Judas-like, to worke their endes'.

Haughton found Shylock's alien character a good starting-point for his own comedy, openly set in London. His play reflects his company's own *Jew of Malta* by making Pisaro a Portuguese as Lopez was, although Haughton seems to have avoided any extra anti-Semitism by making his appeal to his audiences entirely through exploitation of xenophobia. Besides Pisaro himself, outwitted by the three young English gentry who are his daughters' lovers, he made Pisaro's own favoured candidates for their hands three other foreign merchants, a Dutchman, an Italian, and a Frenchman. Like Pisaro himself, all three are fooled by the ingenuity of the three English lovers and the trio of daughters, who prefer their English suitors to the aliens. One of them charges Pisaro with precisely what the 1571 Usury Act forbade: 'You take Tenn in the hundred more then Law', he says (TLN 1948). Later Pisaro himself admits 'I take two and twenty in the hundred, / When

---

[10] Quotations are taken from the Malone Society text of the 1616 edition of the play, entitled 'ENGLISHMEN For my Money, OR, A pleasant Comedy, called, A Woman will have her Will'. The MS edition was edited by W. W. Greg and published in 1912. This is TLN 19–20.

[11] At TLN 1424 the English lover Harvey calls him 'signor bottle-nose'. By 1598 Alleyn himself had withdrawn from acting, but the player of Pisaro could still have worn his familiar fake nose. See Andrew Gurr, *Shakespeare's Opposites. The Admiral's Company 1594–1625*, Cambridge: Cambridge University Press, 2009, esp. 38, 232–3.

the Law gives but ten' (TLN 2395–6). Such practices define him as the play's comic villain, much as was Shylock in contemporary views. Unlike Shylock, though, while also making him an alien Haughton openly located his work at London's Royal Exchange, and explicitly inflated Shylock's moneys and usances into Royal Exchange-based usury.

Haughton's plot develops the element represented in *Merchant* by the love between Shylock's Jessica and the Venetian Lorenzo. Like Jessica, Pisaro's daughters betray their father by marrying their English lovers. In the process they succeed in achieving what Pisaro announces in his first speech that he will prevent, returning to their husbands the wealth they had mortgaged to Pisaro before the play begins. At the end, a London citizen, Mr Moore, a pleader to Pisaro at the Exchange and witness to all the turmoil of the play's finale, tells him that fretting about his loss is pointless:

> These Gentlemen have with your Daughters helpe.
> Outstript you in your subtile enterprises:
> And therefore, seeing they are well descended,
> Turn hate to love, and let them have their Loves.
> (TLN 2668–71)

Pisaro accepts the inevitable, and all ends happily. Like *Merry Wives*, the core of the romantic plot has young gallants achieving financial gain by marrying the daughters of a rich citizen, a means of getting money that anticipated the practices in the boy company plays of the next decade, mostly staged, ironically for us and the Burbages, at the Blackfriars.

In its English setting Haughton's play, besides trebling the number of the alien's daughters, suffers none of the Shakespeare play's problems with Jessica's disloyalty to her father. Their own Englishness eliminates her sense of cultural distance. It is the four foreigners – Pisaro and the suitors with their comically poor command of English – who suffer as the play's fools. Xenophobia is a familiar knee-jerk reaction for most crowds, whether Elizabethan playgoers or the gatherings who bay at modern World Cup matches. Haughton's farcical treatment strips out the awkward corners from Shakespeare's play. The Admiral's play takes for granted the inherent xenophobia of Venetian attitudes to Shylock as something that could readily be exploited as a feature of contemporary London. Pisaro's pleasure in his gains from usury is only one part of what he loses at the conclusion. In his London setting Haughton found ample evidence for the hatred of such greed that his play expects his audiences to share and to boo at.

Haughton, perhaps knowingly, gives no direct sign of any possible application of Shakespeare's play to the Burbage crisis of 1596–97. He marks its differences quite clearly. Whereas at 1.3.27 Shylock rejects the idea of dining with Bassanio and having to 'smell pork', Pisaro's guest, the Frenchman Delion, says he will relish eating Pisaro's beef and his bacon when he dines at his house (TLN 421). In one major scene characterising Pisaro's business practices at the Exchange there is much talk of shipping being seized off Italy by Spanish galleys. Later in the same scene the Italian suitor asks Pisaro why he is so melancholy, and when he answers that it is because his ships are in peril replies that the galleys were set back by the wind, and Pisaro's ships are safe. His dealings with London citizens at the Exchange show him sharp and selfish with his money. The comic post who brings him information about his argosies arriving safely in Plymouth gets no payment for his good news. Haughton used the most notable elements in *The Merchant* while ignoring its most immediate local application. This avoidance might be seen as unhelpfully negative, but it fits the case quite as well as the idea that Shakespeare chose to set his play in Venice in order to avoid any charge of application to local people. If *Englishmen*'s author knew of the pressure that the Blackfriars catastrophe laid on the Burbages, he was evidently discreet enough to avoid any mention of it in his own play.

Some of Shakespeare's variations on the moneylending theme in *Merchant* need pursuing, if only to meet a few other likely targets for company hostility. Only forty lines into the play Antonio declares 'my ventures are not in one bottom trusted'. He has three argosies at sea, and he does not expect what Graziano in his blunt epistrophe twice calls the 'strumpet wind' (2.6.17 and 20) to block their successful passage. James Burbage had two ventures, the Theatre as well as the Blackfriars, for his own argosies, leaving one of them to each of his sons. By April 1597 both of them were hopelessly lost. The sons' and their company's consequent financial troubles must have become known to many people besides Thomas Nashe. This calls to mind, however obliquely, the sharpness of Shylock's assurance to Antonio that he will 'take no doit / Of usance for my monies' (1.3.133–4). Taking no interest other than the pound of flesh is one thing. When the playing company's whole concern was for a place they could use for playing, the Privy Council, which banned its use of the Blackfriars, might have taken no doit of interest from it but they certainly got the equivalent pound of flesh by killing the work of the most interested party. The players participating in *The Merchant* had no magical Portia to wave her legal or financial wand and rescue them from their troubles.

Portia's rescue of Antonio from the knife came from Shakespeare's source, as did the forfeit the Duke lays on Shylock. Antonio then asks that Shylock be required to convert himself into a Christian, and give all his remaining wealth to his daughter. This double punishment seems a curiously oblique way of punishing Shylock as a Jew for his use of usury. Only in this, perhaps, was Shakespeare emphasising the English law that Haughton later chose to underline as Pisaro's chief fault. The fact that in Shakespeare's play it clears Shylock out of the way in Act 4, so that the lovers at Belmont, above all Lorenzo and his Jessica, are free to indulge themselves, in their lengthy self-indulgence released from all that Bassanio was fraught by in the earlier Acts, is part of the comforting process the final Act so thoroughly provides.

In a larger perspective, Antonio's insistence that Shylock convert himself into a Christian consorts well with Portia's rescue of Antonio and Bassanio from the hateful loan shark. If nothing else, it can be seen as a comfort Shakespeare gave his company, a trick of wish-fulfillment. It does not touch on one of the worst features of the current issue. When Nashe wrote his wry pun about the company not being able to build after Henry Carey's death it was the entire working group, the company, that he recorded as the victim, not James Burbage in person. Nashe must have known that Carey's son George, the company's new patron, did not share his father's position over supporting the idea of the Blackfriars playhouse. As second signatory of the hostile petition, George Carey was active, if not instrumental, in blocking the playhouse from use by what with his father's death had become his own company as its patron. He did, after all, live directly under the new playhouse. Haughton picked out Pisaro the usurous moneylender from *The Merchant* as his victim without making any acknowledgement, or possibly not realising, that there was a further reason for the company playing at the Theatre to grieve over the loss of the Blackfriars besides the pressure from the moneylenders.

In an extreme view, Shylock might even be seen as not just a London loan shark but also an even more oblique target, the company's new patron himself. Shylock was a substitute, a straw man that they could thwack with their double grievances. Beyond his identity as an alien, the man with the vengeful knife might have been imagined not just as a London loan shark but also as their own new patron. Shakespeare himself did not view all the signatories of the petition with much personal animosity, since he maintained regular contact with another of them, his fellow-countryman Richard Field. He stayed in touch with him well enough to read copies of a number of Field's later publications, at least up to 1599, and lodged in Silver Street with a Huguenot family, the Mountjoys, who he must have met through Field's wife Jacqueline Vautrollier. But the company as a whole can hardly have ignored the heavy implication of George Carey's signature on the petition. He was not going to help them in the many ways that his father did.

Essentially all that the portrait of Shylock in Shakespeare's play offered the company, and especially Richard Burbage, was an outlet for their anger. Perhaps even more than the pressures applied by the sharks swimming round their leader, Shylock could have given them a self-comforting means of expressing on stage the grievance that they felt over George Carey's hostile action in November 1596. If the latent identity of Shylock as straw man can be applied to the London loan sharks, he might with equally good reason be applied to the company's new patron.

CHAPTER 14

Measure for Measure's *Hoods and Masks*
The Duke, Isabella, and Liberty

Start with five basic assumptions. First, that Shakespeare's original scripts, of which the text of *Measure for Measure* is a copy at two or more removes, did not contain many directions about how to stage the plays (as opposed to stage directions) simply because the writer was on the spot to say what he wanted, and did not have to record it in his manuscript. Developing out of that is the second assumption, that he did have fairly precise ideas about what he envisaged for the stage. The fact that *Measure for Measure*, together with more than half of his other surviving plays, did not reach print until seven years after he died shows that he made the stage publication his main and indeed his only concern. Hence my third assumption, that if we stay content with what we can make of the text on the page, we miss a great deal of the original concept. And my fourth assumption, one that runs counter to many current theories, from Barthes's death of the author to the freedom given the reader by hypertext on computers, that seek to diminish the status and the authority of the author, and his or her individuality, is that Shakespeare's own thinking is peculiar and striking enough to be well worth careful pursuit. The currently strong point that plays as staged are the product of a collaborative process, an endeavour to which the author is only one contributor, has a lot less force when applied to the plays of an author like Shakespeare, who had considerable experience working with the team who produced his plays and even with the audiences who first saw them.[1] Therefore, as my final assumption, I would claim that we have a lot to learn from trying to reconstruct not just his words on the page, as

---

Original publication: "*Measure for Measure*'s Hoods and Masks: the Duke, Isabella, and Liberty." *ELR* 27 (1997), 89–105.

[1] Besides the allegiance of the New Oxford editors, who in their edition have tried to freeze the production process at the moment of first staging, the case has been strongly argued and widely adopted since it was first put by G. Thomas Tanselle in "Historicism and Critical Editing," *Studies in Bibliography* 29 (1976), 167–211.

centuries of editors have been trying to do, but his playscript as he might have meant it to translate onto his original stage. It is this that prompts my concern for the role of hoods and masks in one of Shakespeare's more debated and I think misread plays.

One of the many visual features of the intended staging that was largely ignored in the written scripts is what the players wore for the original performances. Some visual effects are made explicit in the texts, such as the colour of Othello's, Morocco's and Aaron's faces, and possibly of Cleopatra's too. We know that one of the two boys who originally played Hermia and Helena, Rosalind and Celia, and Beatrice and Hero, was expected to be small and fair, whereas the other had to be tall and dark. We can even guess at the kind of dress Rosalind wore, as a duke's daughter and as a page. We do know roughly what Hamlet wore, and what colour. We can be confident about the monk's gown and hood that various friars wore, including the Duke in *Measure for Measure*. But there is nothing comparably helpful that tells us what the Duke's opposite, Isabella, would have worn, and it matters.

Measure for Measure has been greatly argued over, with commentators jousting over just about every question from whether the Duke is a quasi-divine figure or a fool to whether Isabella's silence in answer to his offer of marriage at the end indicates acceptance or rejection.[2] The details of costume in the play, not least the monk's hood with which the Duke disguises himself, may throw a little light on some of the more central of these questions.

An easy handle for the play's major concern is built into the word 'liberty'. The chronic struggle between excessive freedom and excess of law is evident in *Measure for Measure*, which deploys the ambivalence of the Elizabethan sense of liberty as a metaphor or exemplar meaning not freedom generally, as the Roman citizens use it in *Julius Caesar* and *Coriolanus*, but sexual freedom. One extreme, sexual liberty or libertinism, is represented by Lucio, while the law that seeks to repress sexual freedom is represented by the Duke. As he says at the opening Vienna is too free in its sexual

---

[2] See Richard Levin's sharply dismissive assault on the claims for the Duke as King James in the "Historical Readings" chapter of his *New Readings vs. Old Plays* (Chicago, 1979), pp. 171–93. One article among the many that assume a nunlike Isabella is Amy Lechter-Siegel's "Isabella's Silence: The Consolidation of Power in *Measure for Measure*" in *Reconsidering the Renaissance*, ed. Mario A. di Cesare (New York, 1992), pp. 371–80. In *The Literary Use of the Psychoanalytic Process* (New Haven, 1981), Meredith Ann Skura calls the match at the end 'an arbitrary device' (p. 244). Another psychoanalytic critic, Carolyn E. Brown, uses the bed-trick to downrate the closing betrothal as an issue. See "The Wooing of Duke Vincentio and Isabella in *Measure for Measure*: 'The Image of It Gives [Them] Content'", *Shakespeare Studies* 22 (1994), 189–219.

habits, 'libertie, plucks Justice by the nose'. Claudio has already broached the pun, complaining that he is being taken to prison for the crime of 'too much liberty, (my Lucio), liberty', namely, the lechery and sexual freedom that made Juliet pregnant.[3]

As a solution to the problem of finding a middle way between sexual freedom and the law, the end of the play offers that wonderfully all-embracing bag marriage. Each of the four pairs set up to be married at the close represents a point across the scale that runs between the extremes of liberty and the law. Lucio is to be married to the whore Kate Keepdown, who has already had a child by him. Claudio is to be married to Juliet, whom he made pregnant before the legal bond of marriage was completed. Angelo is to be married to Mariana, whom he slept with in the bed trick. And the Duke offers (twice, being shy) to marry Isabella, who has only pretended (although in public, for all her shyness) to sleep with someone. Marriages, the customary happy ending for romantic comedies, are used to satisfy, if that's the word, all the different positions across the scale from absolute liberty to absolute law.

The word that stands against 'liberty' in the play is 'licence'. With its legal connotations, in its sexual application it means the freedom to be licentious.[4] Licence in its second meaning of freedom from restraint, the antonym to law, is what Lucio represents most fully, as Escalus notes over the child he has had by Kate Keepdown. 'That fellow', says Escalus, 'is a fellow of much License' (3.2.217). The word is also there in Isabella's first innocent comment when Angelo reveals his sexual blackmail: 'Plainlie conceive I love you,' he tells her. Her reply, more true than she knows, is 'I know your vertue hath a licence in 't'. She thinks he is making himself seem fouler than he is to pluck on those who might be tempted. Like liberty, licence is a word twisted into opposite directions. Marriage is the legal 'licence' that must restrain the licentious impulses of both Lucio and Angelo.

If you see the play in such a diagrammatic way, then of course the fourth marriage between the Duke and Isabella has to be included to complete this not very musical scale. But it is notoriously not specified in the written text of the play. First the Duke contrives to propose to Isabella while she is still staring dumbstruck at her brother, in wonder that he is alive after all. The

---

[3] My text is the New Variorum edition of *Measure for Measure*, ed. Mark Eccles (New York, 1980). Other Shakespeare plays are cited from *William Shakespeare: The Complete Works*, ed. Stanley Wells et al. (Oxford, 1986).

[4] Ian Donaldson notes that *Bartholomew* Fair uses 'license' similarly as 'a kind of unifying pun', in *The World Turned Upside-down. Comedy from Jonson to Fielding* (Oxford, 1970), p. 50.

Duke's clumsiness is marvellously comic: 'If he be like your brother, for his sake / Is he pardon'd, and for your lovelie sake / Give me your hand, and say you will be mine, / He is my brother too.' And then he has to turn away with an embarrassed mumble: 'But fitter time for that' (5.1.495–97). Isabella says not a word to that ham-fisted proposal, which in the circumstances is understandable. But nor does she speak when he renews his offer at the close. This is where Shakespeare's taciturnity over the stage directions that he would probably have inserted if he had been more remote from the actual rehearsals of his play-scripts becomes a real challenge. Different productions over the last twenty years have given Isabella a wide variety of reactions to the Duke's offer of his hand to lead her off into marriage at the close, ranging from total and scornful rejection to delighted surprise. What, though, we might, not quite idly, ask, did Shakespeare want?

In the critical structuring of the play it has been more common to pair Isabella with Angelo than with the Duke. Bernard Beckerman said she is first introduced as 'a female counterpart to Angelo'.[5] That view follows from the two magnificent confrontations she has with Angelo in Act 2, and fits the absence of any steam of love rising in either of their bloods at the outset. They are also matched if we believe the recent claim that both of them are erotic religious flagellants.[6] But such an opposition elevates Angelo beyond his role as the Duke's shadow. The Duke, too, has used his dark corners not for what Lucio claims but to keep himself away from the temptations of the blood. And like Angelo, the sight of Isabella draws him out of his former seclusion. Unlike Angelo he does not use his position of power to force himself on her, but his proposal of marriage at the end of the play is a law-abiding version of what Angelo has tried to lay on her in the middle. His first proposal, crassly offered as she is still staring at the vision that she now sees of Claudio alive after all, can be made on stage to look dangerously like a request for a pay-off, a reward for the judicial service he has rendered her, of preserving Claudio's life, her maidenhead for Claudio's head.[7] Angelo's experience is a violent parody of

---

[5] Bernard Beckerman, "A Shakespearean Experiment: The Dramaturgy of *Measure for Measure*," *Elizabethan Theatre 2*, ed. David Galloway (Toronto, 1970), p. 121.

[6] See Carolyn E. Brown, "Erotic Religious Flagellation and Shakespeare's *Measure for Measure*," *English Literary Renaissance* 16 (1986), 139–65.

[7] Robert N. Watson, "False Immortality in *Measure for Measure:* Comic Means, Tragic Ends," *Shakespeare Quarterly* 41 (1990), makes the point that the play is indifferent to bodies, as witnessed by the dual substitutions, Ragozine's head for Claudio's and Mariana's maidenhead for Isabella's (429). It is not clear where that leaves Elbow or Pompey the Bum.

the temptation that the Duke goes through more quietly, and with better restraint.

Structurally, it has to be the Duke who is the counterpart to Isabella, not Angelo. This counterparting, this equivalence between the Duke and Isabella in the different manifestations of their initial concern that the law should govern and even deny the temptations of the blood, is shown most clearly, for those who care to lift their eyes from the page, in the patterning of their visual appearance and the comments that the other characters make on their appearance in the opening act. You also have to see the play as a learning process for the sexually alert characters, in which every expectation is collapsed into the central commitment of marriage. Lucio at one extreme has it laid on him as a punishment. At the other extreme, both the Duke and Isabella go through a learning process that draws them away from the anti-sexual rigour of the absolute law they are both clinging to at the outset. The Duke's proposal to Isabella is the final mark of his redemption from his fourteen years of dark and anti-social corners. Isabella's acceptance of his offer marks her final transformation from the rigours of St Clare, the last step in her progress along the path of the bed trick and her induced plea of mercy for Angelo. This matching of the Duke to Isabella is underwritten in the play by their clothes and their different disguises.

The wandering friars, usually Franciscan, with their simple robes and large hoods that concealed the face, had an obvious theatrical value. Shakespeare's plays have many friars and men of the (Catholic) church in them, but he made substantial use of the friar's hood and its capacity to conceal the face in only this one play. That was his main theatrical contribution to the fashion for disguised-ruler plays that grew up in about 1603. What is most striking about his use of the friar disguise in *Measure for Measure* is that he apparently had a disconcertingly intimate knowledge of the Franciscans, and in particular of the minor order of women Franciscans, the nuns of St Clare.

Up to the dissolution of the English monasteries in the Reformation, the Clares or Minoresses had a large nunnery in London, in an area near the Tower still known as the Minories. There, along with the two other Franciscan abbeys for women in England, they followed the regime not of St Clare herself, their founder, but of her later follower, Isabella of Este. The so-called 'Isabella Rule' by which the later Minoresses were governed, an English version of which survives in manuscript from the fifteenth century, may well in some oblique way have given *Measure for Measure*'s heroine her name.[8] The "Isabella Rule" certainly fits the play more neatly than the only other given explanation for the heroine's name, that Shakespeare had a great-aunt called Isabella who became a nun.

There was a means for Shakespeare to have learned about London's Poor Clares, too. The Franciscan nunnery called the Minories was located in Aldgate Without, just to the east of the Tower, a little way south of St Botolph's in Aldgate. St Botolph's was a church and parish with which Shakespeare had a long neighbourly connection through the 1590s, and again before 1604 when he came back from Southwark to lodge with the Huguenot Mountjoys. The nunnery was in fact closed in March 1539, a good fifty years before Shakespeare arrived in that part of London. By 1590 the building was being used as a storehouse for arms from the Tower.[9] Twelve of its nuns, however, were still living in the local parish as pensioners in 1555, and some survived into the 1570s. How much Shakespeare might have learned about the Poor Clares from people in the neighbourhood we cannot tell, but local gossip would be the easiest form of access to the knowledge Shakespeare seems to have had when writing *Measure for Measure*. Whether that might have led him on to consult the Lord Admiral's copy of the 'Isabella Rule' before it was given to the Bodleian in 1604 is an even more remote conjecture.

Isabella, when she arrives on stage in 1.4, enters along with what the stage direction calls 'Francisca a Nun'. That was another reasonable choice of name, since the Poor Clares were a Franciscan order. It must indicate her dress, since the name 'Francisca' is not used in the dialogue. Isabella is about to become a probationer, a new novice in an order of nuns, as we already know from her brother's statement in 1.2 to Lucio that 'This day, my sister should the Cloyster enter, / And there receive her approbation.' This raises a not-so-small question about her precise status in this scene and subsequently. Holman Hunt's famous painting in the Tate Gallery shows Claudio and Isabella standing at a prison window in contention, with Isabella wearing the white robe of a novice in a Benedictine nunnery. This image has fixed many people's ideas of Isabella, and not a few stage productions.

---

[8] This idea was mooted by G. K. Hunter, "Six Notes on *Measure for Measure*," *Shakespeare Quarterly* 15 (1964), 168–69. Darryl J. Gless, "*Measure for Measure*", *the Law, and the Convent* (Princeton, 1979), p. 262, points out that the 'Isabella Rule' manuscript was in the possession of Charles Howard, the Lord Admiral, in the 1590s. Howard gave it to the Bodleian Library along with 16 other manuscripts and 34 printed books in the year of *Measure for Measure*'s first staging, 1604. (See *A Fifteenth-Century Courtesy Book and Two Franciscan Rules*, ed. R. W. Chambers and W. W. Seton, EETS No. 148 [London, 1914], pp. 75–76.) Gless lists some of the rules cited by Francisca in the play (p. 263).

[9] See A. F. C. Bourdillon, *The Order of Minoresses in England* (Manchester, 1926), p. 87.

But it is not a plausible form of dress for the original staging. Her brother Claudio says she has not yet received the status of probationer or novice. Lucio, when he comes to the nunnery asking for Isabella, assumes that she is already sworn and inquires about her as 'A Novice of this place'. But his assumption is premature.[10]

The scene opens with Isabella talking to Francisca the nun as a visitor to the nunnery, and asking her about the rules of the order. Francisca relates them, and when Isabella asks if there are not any more than she recites, protests that they are surely quite severe enough. It is then that Isabella reveals that the order she proposes to enter is the order of St Clare. In response to Francisca's defensiveness, Isabella protests in return that she was asking because she wanted what she worshipfully calls not less severe rules but 'a more strict restraint / Upon the sisterhood, the votarists of St Clare' (1.4.4–5). The long 'o's that run through that last phrase and the drawn-out vowel of the last word suggest a wonderfully comic devoted breathlessness in the heroine. The Poor Clares were famous, and to some people notorious, for the extreme rigour of their rules and the intensity of their devotion to poverty. Hence the adjective in their common name. The rigour was notorious enough for the order to insist on a minimum of a year's probation before candidates could be sure that they could stand the life of poverty. You did not 'receive your approbation' until you had endured the poverty of the order for a year.

For all her eagerness, Isabella has certainly not yet been sworn into the order, as Francisca acknowledges when they hear Lucio knocking:

> Turn <u>you</u> the key, and know his businesse of him;
> <u>You</u> may; <u>I</u> may not; <u>you</u> are yet unsworne:
> When <u>you</u> have vowd, you must not speake with men,
> But in the presence of the *Prioresse*;
> Then if you speake, you must not show your face;
> Or if you show your face, you must not speake
> (1.4.8–13; my emphasis)

She speaks with a wonderfully comic combination of haste and precision. So Lucio arrives in what might be thought of as the nick of time to distract Isabella from entering the nunnery and swearing herself to St Francis, St Clare, and St Isabella.

Shakespeare's direct knowledge of the Isabella Rule may not have been so precise, or may have been adapted to heighten the drama of the moment

---

[10] See Margaret Hotine, "*Measure for Measure:* Further Contemporary Notes," *Notes and Queries* 37 (1990), 184–86.

of Lucio's arrival. Under the Isabella Rule in England, Minoresses spent a year as postulants or novices, under the guidance of a sworn nun, and they did not take their vows until they had spent a whole year proving their capacity to live in silence and poverty. The fifteenth-century English translation of the Rule specifies that postulants should be warned, and should not take the vow until 'it be wel declarid to hem the hardnessis and the scherpenessis by whoche they cometh to Joye of Paradise'.[11] Either Isabella expects to skip this first year's postulancy, since she is on the verge of taking the vow, or Shakespeare chose to discount the preliminary year because it did not suit the play's need for absolute commitment on entry to the nunnery.

Isabella in fact cannot yet be even a postulant. So for this first scene at the nunnery door we have to ask whether she is already wearing the humble garb of the postulant, or whether she is still dressed in the gentlewoman's attire that she is trying to discard. The traditional dress of the Poor Clares was rough and plain. They wore a grey or brown habit with a similarly drab mantle over it. In an early fifteenth-century French picture of ten Minoresses in a choir, seven are wearing grey mantles over grey habits, two wear grey over brown, and one brown over grey. The headdress was a white coif with a black veil. St Clare herself in the Sforza *Book of Hours* is shown wearing a dark grey habit under a brown mantle, and a black veil over her coif.

In the play Francisca must be dressed as a nun, with the veil of the Clares that would conceal her face from a man's view. Isabella certainly does not yet have this veil. That would not be given her until she took her probationer's oath. In 1.4 not only can she speak to Lucio but also he can see her face. We know he does, because he greets her with a comment on her blushing: "Haile Virgin, (if you be) as those cheeke-Roses / Pro-claime you are no lesse" (1.4.16–17), and goes on to call her a saint. She is not yet 'a Novice of this place', or her face would be hidden and she would not be able to speak to him, as by the rules of the Order Francisca cannot. At this point Isabella is, as Lucio again states, a 'Sister' only to Claudio, not to the Clares. She wants the hood that Francisca wears, as the Duke wants Father Thomas'. But she never secures it, because Lucio arrives in the nick of time to draw her back into the city.

After Lucio's appearance at the nunnery door, the events of the play, starting with Angelo's sentence on her brother, draw her away from her

---

[11] Quoted by Bourdillon, p. 36.

self-imposed imprisonment in the nunnery and further and further into the raw life of Vienna, in a precise parallel to the Duke's reluctant abandonment of his fourteen years of withdrawal from social life.

This last-minute failure to draw the Franciscan veil over Isabella's face is in a way a negative form of headgear. Its negative aspect is made positive by the scene that immediately precedes it, because there the Duke has asked his 'holy Father' to supply him with the equivalent monkish hood that will allow him to share Vienna's raw life without being identified.

> I will, as 'twere a brother of your Order,
> Visit both Prince, and People: Therefore I pre 'thee
> Supply me with the habit, and instruct me
> How I may formally in person beare
> Like a true Frier.
>
> (1.3.44–48)

There is no direct indication which of the many orders of wandering friars, Dominican or Franciscan, the Duke's holy Friar Thomas belongs to, but with Isabella as a would-be Poor Clare, symmetry demands that Thomas should have been dressed like a Franciscan monk. Duke Vincentio puts on his monastic pretence of holy poverty just as Isabella is deprived of hers. The visuals of staging require them to be the same kind of holy order. Friar Thomas is a match for Sister Francisca.

To this point we should attach the game played with Isabella as a sister. *Measure for Measure* consistently and insistently plays on the religious and the family meanings of brotherhood and sisterhood, not just the monastic one. Lucio identifies Isabella in 1.4 as caught between two sisterhoods, 'A Novice of this place, and the faire Sister / To her unhappie brother Claudio'. In 2.2 Angelo is told that Claudio has a sister who is 'to be shortlie of a Sister-hood'. In 5.1 she is not only 'the sister of one Claudio' (69), but (three lines later) also 'in probation of a sisterhood'. She starts with a double sisterhood, from one of which she is withdrawn by the threat to her brother. The other she thinks she loses when she is told that Claudio has been executed. Once the Duke has restored her to one of her sisterhoods by revealing Claudio to be alive, he follows that magic with his double invitation to her to renounce the other sisterhood by marrying him. Her would-be sisterhood as a nun of St Clare, and the duty of wearing the face-concealing veil that Sister Francisca wears in 1.4, is lost to her when she is drawn away from the nunnery gates by Lucio. The Duke's adoption of a hood of the same Order at the same time plays a neat visual game, setting himself in disguise as opposite to Isabella, stuck with the gentlewoman's dress she had hoped to abandon at the nunnery door, and so lacking the veil that was the female equivalent of the Duke's hood.

Hoods of course are always a disguise. The Duke's adopted 'habit' ironically proves the validity of Lucio's quoted adage 'Cucullus non facit Monachum' (5.1.264), the hood does not make the monk.[12] When the Duke tells Isabella in the final scene that he was 'holy to your businesse, / (Not changing heart with habit)' (5.1.389–90), we know that he is lying, a fine action for a judge and ruler (although, of course, he is also speaking a disguised truth). We know from several references in the text that the Duke wore a friar's gown roped at the waist, and the hood. It would have been a help if Shakespeare had bothered to tell us what signs of the religious habit Isabella wore at her first appearance at the nunnery door. His presence at rehearsal made it unnecessary for him to specify in his script what he wanted Isabella to wear, but that omission is a major loss for us. As a would-be but still unsworn probationer, she could not wear the Franciscan order's grey or brown, with black and white headgear, but neither do we usually expect to see her dressed in the opposite mode, the extravagant attire of a rich gentlewoman, the fleshly clothing of the young of the city such as the pregnant Juliet. What could she have worn?

The text does provide some hints. The Provost announces her to Angelo punningly in 2.2 as Claudio's sister, and 'to be shortlie of a Sister-hood, / If not alreadie'. In 2.4 (after a scene when the Duke has appeared disguised as 'a good Frier' who is 'bound by my charity, and my blest order'), Isabella is again announced as 'One Isabell, a Sister'. These have been read as signals that she is dressed as a nun, but they cannot be. They are simply extensions of the punning game on her dual sisterhood. At this point she must be dressed recognisably as Claudio's sister, a lady, rather than as a sworn-in novice. Indeed, instead of the veil she aspires to, Shakespeare seems to have expected that in the original performances she would wear a mask of the fully concealing kind that was standard for court ladies. Having appeared barefaced to Lucio, with the prospect of Francisca's visible black veil before her, there is more than a little aptness in her appearing subsequently to Angelo in the secular equivalent, the Tudor gentlewoman's familiar outdoor wear, a black velvet mask.

That point is supported by the significantly possessive adjective that Angelo uses when he speaks to her of 'these blacke Masques' which

---

[12] Feste's use of the same adage in *Twelfth Night* has been invoked to suggest that Robert Armin played both parts. I think it more plausible to see the coincidence reflecting how standard it was to use monkish disguises in the theatre of the time.

'Proclaime an en-shield beauty ten times louder / Then beauty could displaied' (2.4.79–81). If we can rely on this possessive, Isabella must arrive to plead with Angelo not veiled like a nun but masked like any gentlewoman out of doors. Angelo later says she looks like a woman:

> Be that you are,
> That is a woman; if you be more, you'r none.
> If you be one (as you are well exprest
> By all external warrants) shew it now,
> By putting on the destin'd liverie.
>
> (134–38)

Her livery as a woman, or as a nun? I think that her dress for this encounter should be, would have been in the original production, similar to what Mariana wears in the final scene, when she appears in a gentlewoman's mask to conceal her identity from Angelo.

Masks were routine outdoor wear for ladies. Stubbes in his *Anatomie of Abuses* in 1583 declared that 'when they use to ride abrod they have invisories or visors made of velvet, wherwith they cover all their faces, having holes made in them against their eyes, whereout they look'.[13]

Such masks were common on the early stages. In the second scene of *Woodstock* the Earl urges his wife to ride with him: 'On with thy cloak and mask! To horse, to horse!'[14] A citizen's wife in *The Roaring Girl* defends them to her husband, who voices an eloquent attack on them as thieves to beauty. In reply, Mrs Openwork says 'May wee not cover our bare faces with maskes / As well as you cover your bald heads with hats?' Face-masks or visors were certainly not worn only at balls by men as in *Romeo and Juliet* and *Much Ado*. In *Othello*, 4.2.9, Othello asks Emilia about his wife, and whether when she was talking to Cassio she might not have sent Emilia off 'To fetch her fan, her gloves, her mask nor nothing?' In *Two Gentlemen of Verona*, 4.4.150, the disguised Julia talks to Silvia about forlorn Julia grieving back in Verona: 'But since she did neglect her looking-glass, / And threw her sun-expelling mask away, / The air hath starved the roses in her cheeks.' They had of course many functions besides protecting complexions from the sun. In *Cymbeline* 5.3.21, Posthumus describes the two valiant and sunburned country boys in the battle, with 'faces fit for masks, or rather fairer / Than those for preservation cased, or shame'.

Masks were an efficient form of concealment for any face, female or male, whether for the preservation of the complexion or for modesty and

---

[13] Philip Stubbes, *The Anatomie of Abuses* (1583), sig. G2.
[14] *Woodstock a moral history*, ed. A. P. Rossiter (London, 1946), p. 230.

shamefastness. Concealment had many possible motives. The robbers at Gadshill wear them, in *1 Henry IV*, 2.3, where they are told 'Case ye, case ye, on with your visors!' For women their function was usually routine. As Cressida says (*Troilus and Cressida*, 1.2.256), she depends 'Upon my back to defend my belly, upon my wit to defend my wiles, upon my secrecy to defend mine honesty, my mask to defend my beauty'. Wearing masks was standard for women, and especially, I would conjecture, for the boys who played the women's parts on the Shakespearean stages. In the final Act Mariana, standing in the public street with Isabella for her encounter with the returned Duke, wears the standard lady's black velvet mask to conceal her identity from Angelo. The question is whether Isabella as a gentlewoman is also masked in the same scene, and whether when she first confronts Angelo she wears a mask to defend her modesty along with her complexion.

    She certainly meets him having first travelled the streets of Vienna, so she might have been expected to wear a mask for her complexion. She might equally have worn it out of modesty. She is insistently called a saint, by men as widely variant in their outlooks as Lucio and Angelo. Lucio's first greeting to her at the nunnery door is a naughty parody of Gabriel's first words at the Annunciation: "Hail, Virgin" ("Ave, virgo"), although his next words question whether she is fit for that role.[15] The audience here knows better than Lucio which kind of nunnery she is aiming at. Whether by his second meeting with her Angelo knows any better than Lucio is rather more in question. The 'destin'd liverie' that he urges on her in his seduction speech is the frailty she has just acknowledged to be a characteristic of women. He sees her livery as the dress of a gentlewoman familiar with the sins of the flesh rather than a novitiate nun. He offers her the transformation of liveries and allegiance that he has observed in himself at the beginning of the scene, his own change from angel to devil. In the next scene Isabella tells her brother that Angelo wears 'the cunning liverie of hell' (3.1.95). For his judicial function when meeting Isabella he wore a black gown with fur trimming. Furred robes hide all, as Lear was to say. Clothing is now explicitly to be dissociated from the wearer, and Angelo is no angel, for all his judicial appearance. Nor is Isabella the loose-legged lady of the town that her dress might seem to make her. By now in the play the Duke's own disguise is beginning to reveal that his subjects' dress can be more incongruous to their character than their appearance would suggest. His shadow Angelo is one proof of the point, with his transformation under

---

[15] Robert N. Watson makes this point adroitly, p. 425.

his judicial robes. The Duke's disguise is equally misleading. And so, we might argue, is Isabella's.

Act 3, scene 1, where the Duke insists ambiguously on 'my holie Order', ostensibly his monastery but more really the law and order of his dukedom, is a model of the way appearances front the reality of the scene's actors. This scene, usually acknowledged as the play's turning-point, sets the language, if not the dress, of courts against the appearance of the monastic life. The Duke in his Franciscan disguise calls Isabella fraternally 'yong sister' (3.1.153), when we know that her choice between being Claudio's sister or the Poor Clares' sister is still in the balance. He affirms his own rejection of Vienna's raw sexual life when he assures the Provost that he can be safely left with Isabella, on the grounds that 'my minde promises with my habit', although we are in a position to know that whatever his real mind is now, his habit is assumed. Is his promise true? In the immediate wake of Angelo's change under his own judicial livery into the livery of hell, the audience might well doubt the Duke's assurance much more than the Provost does. He speaks to the Provost with tongue in cheek, as he does later to Isabella when he assures her 'trust not my holie Order / If I pervert your course' (4.3.152–53). Which course, and which sisterhood, he does not specify. In the peculiar rhyming verse with which he ends Act 3, he compresses his own game into a paradox that seeks to justify his deception. 'So disguise shall by th' disguised / Pay with falsehood, false exacting, / And performe an olde contracting' (3.2.94–96). Lies and deceit are to be used against the deceiver. Disguise will work for good. Dressed in his monkish habit, of course, the Duke could hardly say anything else.

In the long final scene the Duke's first appearance, as a hooded friar, is falsely modest again. He maintains the posture of monkish humility. In disguise he has always kept his hood well over his face – he tells Lucio 'I remember you Sir, by the sound of your voice (5.1.331)', an indication that his head has usually been bowed in religious humility and his face invisible. When Lucio tears off the Duke's hood he learns what we have known, that the monk is not, as he says, 'honest in nothing but in his Clothes'. Disguise now becomes openly a means to everyone's uncasing. And that brings us back to some consequences of my earlier question. When the Duke uncases himself, and reveals himself in the dress of the ruling Duke, what does Isabella wear?

For the visual effect of the play's finale, this question is absolutely crucial. All the Duke's elaborate stage-managing of Isabella in order to put her to the test, making her enact her simulated shame in public, and then to beg for mercy for Angelo, is made apparent when he sheds his own Franciscan grey. That is only one of a whole series of uncasings in this scene. First Mariana uncases her face to show Angelo his mistake. A bit later Lucio uncases the Duke and learns the error of his ways. And finally the Duke uncases Claudio to show Isabella what he has to give her. That is the last of what I think may possibly be not three but four uncasings in the finale. Isabella stands by Mariana throughout this scene. Mariana's disguise that she sheds for Angelo is the gentlewoman's mask. Isabella must be dressed like Mariana, not as a nun, and she may have arrived on the stage wearing a similar mask, the one she originally wore to visit Angelo. She would then be the first of the disguisers to uncase herself, at the beginning when she kneels to ask the Duke for her revenge on Angelo.

But is she dressed like Mariana? What Isabella wears for the final scene and its sequence of uncasings and for the Duke's final proposal of marriage to her is the visual crux of the play. We know about the Duke's livery. We need also to identify what we think Isabella's livery was. When first she kneels to the Duke pleading (falsely) for justice as a woman dishonoured, and later when she stands to receive his twice-run offer of marriage, her attire has to be the ultimate test of honesty in clothing. She is dishonest at the outset of the scene, when she plays her part by claiming to have been dishonoured by Angelo. That is the first point where her dress becomes crucial. For such a gesture the grey garb of the Poor Clares, emblem of purity and virtuous poverty, would hardly suit a fallen woman. For the whole of the finale she must wear the gentlewoman's garb, perhaps still with the visor or mask that Angelo mentions in 2.4. The mask is really the only doubtful element. She cannot change her courtly dress subsequently, since she is onstage throughout the scene. For the whole of the finale there is a strong case for seeing Isabella still dressed in the riches, including the gentlewoman's mask, with all the freedom it offered to display wealth and lechery, that she was trying to shed when she first appeared on stage in 1.4.

It seems, therefore, if you read the inadequate hints in this way, that Isabella must at the end receive the Duke's proposal of marriage in her colourful gentlewoman's dress and not, as so many productions have had it, in the humble dress of a votarist of St Clare. She never matches the Duke in the pretence, the disguise, of being a religious. She is a sister only to Claudio, and so she keeps her courtly lady's attire throughout. In this, and for all her double deceptions, of Angelo with the bed-trick and of the Duke with her claim that Angelo seduced her, she is being at least a little more honest than the Duke. Her dishonesties are part of her learning process in the service of good, paying with falsehood false exacting. In the end both of the leading learners are freed from their devotion to rigorous law. Both of them, I think, end the play in their full city costume, finally abandoning their different pretences to deserve the protective rigour of monkish attire. That conclusion leaves us to ask whether they must also affirm their visual equivalence, one to the other in their costume, and finally join hands to exit together, for all Isabella's silence in response to the Duke's two proposals.

The visual impact of costume is distinctive throughout this play. The Duke starts and ends as a ruler, donning his grey gown and hood through the play's middle action as his disguise for his honesty. His dress through the middle of the play is a knowing piece of concealment. Isabella on the other hand starts as a would-be novice, dressing in a kind of disguise, the flesh-conscious attire of a gentlewoman, up to the place where she has truly to disguise her real self by acting the part of a dishonoured lady on her knees to the returned ruler. False monks are in. True nuns are out. The Duke sheds his monkish garb when Lucio uncovers him. Isabella never gets hers on. As half of such a pair of opposites, can she indeed fail to take the Duke's hand when they walk off the stage at the end?

All this has to stand only as a set of conjectures, of course, rather than direct hits on the ostensible target of the original staging of the play. Behind this analysis of the function of the hoods and masks in the play, which is no more than one illustration of what we might be able to find to augment the more narrowly linguistic analyses of the text, I have been trying rather more to define the kinds of question we ought to be asking than providing firm answers about the original staging. It is fresh and fertile territory, even if it doesn't tell us exactly what sort of colour Isabella might have worn in her dress as a gentlewoman. White, for virginity? Black, for a modest puritanism? A discreet and humble grey, like the friar's robe? A noble scarlet like Hester or O'Hara? There is plenty of room for guesswork.

And there is still the question whether using the original staging concept that we can identify as Shakespeare's own is not in itself, to invoke the current pejorative that denies all real benefit from literature, too likely to prove reductive. Having Shakespeare's own concept of how the play should be staged still gives us only one of a multitude of possible ways of staging it. It might be preferable to retain the freedom to read a law-abiding Isabella dressed as a nun throughout who does not unmask and take the de-hooded or unfrocked Duke's hand at the end, and to ignore the original reductive stage design. Confining yourself to the words on the page and their multiple possibilities, and ignoring the precise and monovalent readings that staging insists on, might be a richer way with the text, if you buy Harry Berger's argument that staging is reductive because it insists on a single interpretation.[16] That way, I think, lie the indeterminate and interminable games with hypertext and the business of writing or rewriting your own texts, and doing your own editing. It may be the way into the future. But I do believe that it is also worth holding to the value of finding a little bit more about the Shakespearean concepts than we can find if we confine ourselves to study of the flat words on the flat page. They give us more, you might say, to play with. There is a lot in the past and in Shakespeare's own concepts that we can still learn from.

[16] See Harry Berger, Jr., *Imaginary Audition: Shakespeare on Page and Stage* (Berkeley, 1989).

CHAPTER 15

The Transforming of Henry V

Shakespeare never took his work for the Chamberlain's Men as seriously as we do now. Nor did his company. They did not hesitate to revise his manuscripts to make them suit their needs for staging. The evidence for that is there in *Henry V.* It was the only play from the nearly forty he wrote alone or in collaboration that survives in two versions, one close to his original manuscript and the other what the company revised it into. In my view they had good reasons for their revision, because the manuscript as he wrote it has never been fully realised on stage.

The *Henry V* that we all know was the Folio text, printed from the manuscript that Shakespeare sold to his company in 1599. In my view Shakespeare knew that his authorial version, so well known and widely used, would be impossible to stage as he wrote it, for many reasons besides its known ambivalence, the notorious 'rabbit and duck' aspect. Such a view means, if you extend it to the infinite number of attempts to put it on stage that have been made since 1623, when the Folio text was first published, that they are all contorted attempts at doing the impossible. That is a large and pretentious claim to make, especially since the play has proved so popular in the theatre, at least in times of war. Nicholas Hytner's production at the National in London, an Iraqi war version starring Adrian Lester, with spin-doctoring of the war speeches projected on television, and jeeps and humvees driven on stage, was acclaimed by some as the best show of 2003 in London. Hytner's jeeps, and Henry's speeches shown on television, were obvious ways of restaging a sixteenth-century play in the twenty-first century, but as in every production from 1599 on it was still necessary to make drastic cuts and alterations to the shape of the Folio play. Every stage and film production has deviated from the text we read on the page.

Original publication: "The Transforming of *Henry V*," *Shakespeare International Yearbook* 5 (2005), 303–13.

This affirms how necessary it has always been to rewrite the Folio text. So we need to recognise why the original text in the Folio version is unstageable.

First and last there is the rabbit and duck issue. The version first composed in 1599 is distinct for its Chorus that tells you before each act begins exactly how you should feel about what it is going to show. The Chorus that precedes Act 2, for instance, says

> Now all the youth of England are on fire
> And silken dalliance in the wardrobe lies.
> Now thrive the armourers, and honour's thought
> Lies solely in the breast of every man.

But in the act that follows this claim the first thing we get is the Eastcheap crew arguing amongst themselves as they give themselves military titles – Lieutenant Bardolph, Ancient or Ensign Pistol, Corporal Nym. Moreover their reasons for arming are that, as Pistol says, 'I shall sutler be unto the camp, and profits will accrue.' It is not honour that reigns in their minds. Then we move straight to the three conspirators at Southampton, once again hardly a demonstration of honour's thought being solely in every man's breast. The Prologue itself had been immediately followed by the Archbishop of Canterbury, preparing his speech about the Salic Law, telling his bishop of the need to preserve the church's wealth by getting Henry to go to war. We are presented from the outset with a problem in juxtaposing what the Chorus tells us to see, and what is then actually staged.

Similarly in Act 4 and that celebrated 'little touch of Harry in the night' to his soldiers before Agincourt. All we see on stage is Henry walking round in disguise, and getting himself into an argument with his soldiers, those characters who uniquely in Shakespeare get ordinary names, John Bates, Alexander Court and Michael Williams – no Mouldy or Bullcalf there. That is one of the few scenes in the whole play entirely invented and inserted by Shakespeare, and the argument is one that many readers say Henry loses, ending with him feeling furiously resentful that his soldiers lay all the responsibility for their coming deaths on their leader. In spite of the Chorus's heroic claim about Harry cheering everyone up that night, the long scene that follows gives absolutely no evidence of such an action. It is the soldiers themselves who resolve to fight bravely, not knowing that they are saying so in Henry's presence. Only after sunrise does he inspire them with the 'We few, we happy few' speech. This constant contrast between the Chorus and what follows is at its best in Act 3, the Harfleur siege, which I shall come to shortly.

In the Introduction to my edition of the Folio text[1] I called the Chorus 'coercive' because all of its speeches offer a single 'heroic Henry' reading of his character, while the play itself gives us an alternative story. That Shakespeare knew what he was doing using the Chorus in this way is made obvious by the episode of the killing of the French prisoners, a feature of the play which both the Olivier and the Branagh films cut away. In the Folio text we see Henry, during a pause for him to orate over the deaths of York and Suffolk, hear an offstage '*Alarum*'. He immediately says

> But hearke, what new alarum is this same?
> The French have re-enforc'd their scatter'd men:
> Then every soldiour kill his Prisoners.
> Give the word through.

They all exit, and immediately Llewellyn and Gower tumble onstage to misrepresent what we have just witnessed. 'Kill the poyes and the luggage.' roars Llewellyn, and Gower reports, wrongly, 'they have burned and carried away all that was in the King's tent, wherefore the King most worthily hath caused every soldiour to cut his prisoner's throat. O, 'tis a gallant King.' That is not what we have just heard. When the offstage '*Alarum*' sounds Henry assumes the French are about to renew their attack, so he gives the order to free more English soldiers for fighting.

That the author knew what he was doing here cannot be doubted. The French attack on the baggage train kills the Eastcheap Boy, and Henry's order to cut the prisoners' throats deprives Ancient Pistol of his 'egregious ransom' from Monsieur Le Fer, which is why he is still penniless when he meets Llewellyn in Act 5. These, however, are tiny and generally unobserved incidentals – no director to my knowledge has ever made use of the discrepancy between what the Folio has Henry say and Gower's conclusion about it. What has ruled with most directors (and critics) is Gower's misrepresentation of Henry's reason for giving the order. To cut the actual order leaves us with only Gower's error. It was not given in a hot spirit of revenge but out of cold calculation, to ensure victory. Modern productions, if they keep the order at all, almost all choose to prefer Gower's misinterpretation and therefore lay the killing of the boys as a piece of involuntary camouflage over the quick and ruthless order to kill the prisoners,

---

[1] The New Cambridge *King Henry V* (Cambridge: Cambridge University Press, 1992).

concealing Henry's real motive and letting Gower's assumption that the order was given in revenge disguise the King's political calculation.[2]

That was Shakespeare's own doing. It justifies what most critics nowadays see in the Folio text, quite rightly, as a *gestalt* exercise, a phenomenon that changes according to how you see it, a shape that looks like a rabbit at one moment and a duck at another. The playwright John Arden said there is a secret play inside the official play, one that questions all the jingoism and the militant heroics that the Chorus lays on its audiences. Is Henry a great hero, or a cold calculator out for his personal interest? My point is that because this ambivalent presentation was written into the Folio text, it cannot be put on stage.

We might even conclude that Shakespeare well knew that his version would not reach the stage. The difficulty of staging such a two-faced text was a problem the Shakespeare company itself had to face as early as 1599, when Shakespeare sold them the manuscript which they much later gave to the printer of the First Folio. As they read what Shakespeare wrote, they must have seen that the manuscript which became our Folio text was a bit of a mess. Not only did it show the dark side of Henry, it also had quite a few contradictions in it. The Chorus for one thing was a unique and unfashionable intrusion. The text confused Southampton and Dover as the port for the English army's embarkation, and it cited even in the stage directions a lot more noble names, English and French, than it supplied speaking parts for. It gave the Dauphin some lines to speak at Agincourt, but nothing at the closing scene in the French Court in Act 5, where he should have but did not confirm his loss of accession to the French throne by kneeling to Henry, as earlier versions of the play made him do. It mentioned the threat from the Scots, traditional allies of the French, yet it included a Scots captain along with the Irish, Welsh and English captains. The third Chorus mentioned the French offer of the dukedoms in France that the English claimed together with the hand of Katherine the French king's daughter in marriage, but 'the offer likes not', not, that is, until Act 5 when Henry's victorious counsellors and of course Henry himself accepted precisely that deal.

We cannot doubt that Shakespeare knew what he was doing with the image of Henry. The Folio text as we have it inescapably gives us a play that shows him in two forms, one a hero, greatly boosted by the misleading

---

[2] Graham Bradshaw, in *Misrepresentations: Shakespeare and the Materialists* (Ithaca: Cornell University Press, 1993), ch. 1, gives an outstandingly thorough résumé of the bivalent readings of the Folio text.

Chorus, the other the cold-blooded politician that we first met at the beginning of *1 Henry IV*, when he plays his games with Falstaff and the others at the tavern and declares 'I know you all, and will *awhile* uphold / The unyoked humour of your idleness.' Falstaff is the cloud that the sun-king is allowing to dull the glow of the prince before he casts it off to stand in his full regal glory. Such a plan utterly discards the prodigal son aspect that features so strongly in *The Famous Victories of Henry V*. The same ambitious prince when he is military victor after Agincourt tells Princess Katherine while he is asking her to marry him that 'in loving me you shall love the friend of France, for I love France so well that I will not part with a village of it'. Marriage to Katherine, scorned earlier according to the Chorus, he knows will ensure that he inherits the French crown in place of the Dauphin. The wooing scene is not an amorous love-match but a diplomatic alliance.

This two-faced play has never been staged as its author wrote it. I have never seen a version that succeeds in presenting both sides of Henry, even though Peter Hall tried hard with his production of 1964. In performance, such a bivalent play cannot present a clearly ambivalent and self-contradictory image for its central character, especially with the loading of heroic victoriousness it has acquired over the years. Only one of the twenty-six actors I have seen play the part has ever allowed Henry to appear thoroughly two-faced. Throughout the last fifty years, for all the multitude of anti-war versions, every director and every actor of Henry has found it essential to make him sympathetic as a war-leader. We might excuse the versions done in time of actual war, like Olivier's streamlined film made at the time of the D-Day landings, which copied the 1930s Old Vic stage version in preferring Gower's explanation of the reason for killing the prisoners, and even Branagh's weeping Henry personally carrying the body of the boy off the field of battle. Hytner's Iraqi invasion version at the National Theatre showed Henry doing his word-spinning in television broadcasts, and himself impatiently shooting Bardolph in the head, but it still made Henry a hero.

Hence my claim that the play as composed in Shakespeare's own Folio version cannot be staged in all its contradictory ambivalence. Readers may find it two-faced, but, as mediated by stage production and audience expectation, not playgoers. One example will show how impossible the original text as printed in the Folio is to stage with any precision. Its difficulty appears from the very first adaptation of the text into a more playable form, the version that Shakespeare's own company made and staged out of the Folio version after they first bought it from him in 1599, in the first Quarto text of 1600, made by the company out of Shakespeare's original manuscript.

My example is the siege of Harfleur and its conclusion. The Shakespeare company took only forty lines out of the whole of the Folio manuscript's Act 3 Chorus and scenes 1 to 4. Here is the complete Quarto text of scene 6, as modernised in my edition of the Quarto:[3]

Enter Nim, Bardolph, Pistol, Boy

NIM Before God, here is hot service.
PISTOL 'Tis hot indeed.
    Blows go and come, God's vassals drop and die.
NIM 'Tis honour, and there's the humour of it.
BOY Would I were in London, I'd give all my honour for a pot of ale.
PISTOL And I. If wishes would prevail,
    I would not stay, but thither would I hie.
        Enter LLEWELLYN, *and beats them in*
LLEWELLYN God's plut, up to the breaches, you rascals, will you not up to the breaches?
NIM Abate thy rage, sweet knight, abate thy rage!
BOY Well, I would I were once from them. They would have me as familiar with men's pockets as their gloves and their handkerchiefs. They will steal anything. Bardolph stole a lute case, carried it three mile, and sold it for three ha'pence. Nim stole a fire shovel. I knew by that they meant to carry coals. Well, if they will not leave me, I mean to leave them.
        Exit Nim, Bardolph, Pistol, *and the* Boy

        Enter GOWER
GOWER Captain Llewellyn, you must come straight to the mines, to the Duke of Gloucester.
LLEWELLYN Look you, tell the Duke it is not so good to come to the mines. The concavities is otherwise. You may discuss to the Duke, the enemy is digged himself five yards under the countermines. By Jesus, I think he'll blow up all if there be no better direction.
        Enter the KING *and his lords. Alarum*
KING How yet resolves the Governor of the town?
    This is the latest parley we'll admit,
    Defy us to our worst. For as I am a soldier,
    A name that in my thoughts becomes me best,
    If we begin the battery once again
    I will not leave the half-achieved Harfleur
    Till in her ashes she be buried.

[3] *The First Quarto of King Henry V*, The New Cambridge Shakespeare (Cambridge University Press: Cambridge, 2000), pp. 50–51.

            The gates of mercy are all shut up.
            What say you, will you yield and this avoid,
            Or, guilty in defence, be thus destroyed?
                Enter Governor
GOVERNOR Our expectation hath this day an end.
            The Dauphin, whom of succour we entreated,
            Returns us word his powers are not yet ready
            To raise so great a siege. Therefore, dread King,
            We yield our town and lives to thy soft mercy.
            Enter our gates, dispose of us and ours,
            For we no longer are defensive now.
                                                    [*Exeunt*]

The Quarto text is a streamlined version that removes, I think quite knowingly, several features of the Folio text that cast doubt on Henry's leadership. From the four scenes in the Folio text it cuts the Chorus and all of Henry's famous speech of exhortation, 'Once more unto the breach, dear friends, once more, / Or close the wall up with our English dead!' It uses only the reluctant Eastcheap soldiers, with Llewellyn in his first appearance beating them offstage as dilatory cowards. Then comes a very brief exchange between Llewellyn and Gower about the mines. The siege is not proving very successful. Then the Quarto text goes directly to Henry ordering the Governor of Harfleur to surrender or else, and the Governor announces that he will surrender the town because the Dauphin has not brought any help.

In all, the Quarto version shortens the Folio's 214 lines of dialogue (249 including the Chorus) to 40. Most surprisingly to Folio devotees it eliminates the whole of Henry's most famous speech, 'Once more unto the breach, dear friends!' It cuts out the lengthy debate over the mines along with the new Britons, Irish Macmorris and Scottish Jamy, it shortens Henry's long speech threatening Harfleur, and it cuts his final speech about how weary the soldiers are before they all enter the gates of Harfleur.

Removing what is probably Shakespeare's most memorable speech for moderns is one feature of the Quarto which has demoted it in most people's eyes, and the cut needs careful explanation. The chief justification for the Quarto version is its decision to cut not only Henry's rabble-rousing speech in the Folio but also the action accompanying that extraordinary entry stage direction which precedes it, the direction calling for '*scaling ladders at Harfleur*'. The reason for that should be a revelation to every male actor who has ever tried to exhibit his aptitude by reciting 'Once more unto the breach', including Olivier, Branagh and every other player of the Henry part. It calls for a form of staging which would have showed its first audiences unequivocally that the attack on the breach that followed Henry's exhortation was a failure.

We have to think about how Shakespeare would have expected the opening scene of the Folio *Henry V* Act 3 to be staged at the Globe with those scaling ladders. At the outset we would watch the soldiers run onstage carrying short wooden ladders. After they and we have listened to Henry's 'Once more unto the breach' speech, the soldiers would set their ladders against the stage front, and climb up them to disappear inside the tiring house. Henry himself then leads the others offstage brandishing their swords. The Eastcheap group stay behind to do their swaggering until Llewellyn enters to scourge them into battle, at which they flee through the flanking doors. Llewellyn and Gower then discuss the problems the siege is having with the mines, till Macmorris enters with Jamy, and Llewellyn has his lengthy quarrel with Macmorris. Shakespeare probably expected that the scaling ladders would be taken offstage during this long debate, though he might have expected that they could be left there propped against the tiring-house wall, with intriguing possibilities for the staging. Either way, in the Folio and the Quarto this sequence ends with Henry and his soldiers returning on stage so that Henry can summon the Governor of Harfleur to hear his speech ordering him to surrender.

Some idea of the original staging intended for the Globe is crucial here. The Governor appears to reply to Henry on the stage balcony over the central opening. The tiring-house front now represents the town gates through which the English army will exit to close the scene. When the Governor surrenders the town to Henry it will be opened so that Henry and the others can enter the town in triumph. What nobody, in any production I have ever seen or heard of, nor any editor or critic of the play has pointed out, is that the Governor's appearance on the walls shows that the attack which opened the Act, and which Henry inspired with his famous speech, was a failure. The soldiers who we see scaling the walls of the stage balcony on their ladders must all have been killed when they entered the town. We know that, because the Governor is now standing on the very walls that we saw them climb. For Shakespeare to insert his '*scaling ladders at Harfleur*' direction meant he wanted to show visually what we ought to conclude subsequently from Henry's speech ordering the Governor to surrender, that the famous attack on the breach was not successful.

Not a single director or editor or critic has ever made that rather obvious deduction from the fact that the Folio text of the play shows Henry in 3.4 standing in front of the town gates telling the Governor, still safe on his town walls, to surrender. The 'Once more unto the breach' speech has seduced all minds, jingoistic or not, into assuming like the Chorus that after such heroic rhetoric the charge must succeed, and that filling the wall up with our English dead was not an option. For the staging he envisaged, Shakespeare inserted the device of the ladders as his own tacit affirmation of a failure that we in our wisdom have never let ourselves acknowledge.

The players who first revised the Folio text for the stage, and whose work is evident in the 1600 Quarto text, must have known very well what effect such a staging would have. They knew enough to cut out the scaling ladders along with Henry's entire speech of exhortation, showing a better understanding of what Shakespeare had in mind than the many directors who subsequently got their hands on the Folio version. In the much briefer version that the original players composed for the Quarto we go straight into the scuffle onstage between the Eastcheap braggarts and Llewellyn, before Henry returns with his soldiers to a trumpet or drum-roll '*alarum*', at which the Governor appears on the balcony to hear Henry threaten mayhem if they do not surrender. The governor on the balcony then surrenders, and everyone disappears offstage through the town gates below him. No problem, no ambiguity, no sign of Henry as a failure. Forty lines in place of the Folio's 249. These cuts remove the ambivalence of Shakespeare's presentation, shrinking the Harfleur encounter to a minimal siege and leaving the war to its proper climax at Agincourt.

The company's reluctance to admit, unlike their author, that Henry could fail is a consistent feature of the Quarto version. The evidence of its text, printed less than a year after the play was first staged in the summer of 1599, and almost certainly the version that the company revised from the manuscript used much later to print our Folio text, cuts out almost every suggestion that Henry was a two-faced rabbit and/or duck. It cuts the Choruses too, altogether shortening the verbose Shakespeare text by half, from 3,400 lines to 1,700. The revisers made sure that the heroic victory at Agincourt was the play's highlight, and that its victor was truly a military hero. They cut the entire opening scene where the two bishops reveal their self-interested plot to seduce the king into forgetting Parliament's threat to sequester church property by offering him a huge bribe towards the war with France. With the Choruses they remove the third Chorus's reference to the French offer which Henry ignored but later accepted along with Princess Katherine: they also cut the speech which killed the soldiers and the use of scaling ladders at Harfleur. As part of the same hero-making process they cut out all the references to the king having killed Falstaff by rejecting him in 2 *Henry IV*. The result was a much cleaner and simpler 'heroic Henry' version of the original Shakespeare text.

The revisers were of course far from perfect in their reading of the complex Folio text. They kept the order to kill the prisoners, for instance, and Gower's outraged misrepresentation of his motive, as so many directors have done subsequently. Further, they showed a limited grasp of what Shakespeare was doing with that order by inserting Pistol on stage so that he hears the king say 'Bid every soldier kill his prisoner' and exclaims in bloodthirsty glee 'Couple gorge!' Such enthusiastic support for the order did give the clown playing Pistol an additional opportunity to use the comic catchphrase he reiterates elsewhere, but it ignores the fact, carefully exploited by Shakespeare, that the cutting lost Pistol his promise of 'egregious ransom', which is why he appears still short of money when Llewellyn meets him later and forces him to eat the leek. That comic interchange stood in both versions.

The players who seem to have made the Quarto revision did a lot of sensible rewriting. The role of the Dauphin, for instance, whose gift of tennis balls features in Henry's decision to invade France in both versions, shows in the Folio signs that Shakespeare was uncertain what to do with the French prince. The Quarto tidied the uncertainty away. In the Folio the Dauphin speaks to Exeter when he comes as ambassador to the French king, but is then forbidden by his father the king to go to Agincourt. That was what happened in Holinshed, Shakespeare's main sourcebook. Despite that, in the Folio he reappears before the battle, being mocked by his own French colleagues, but fails to appear in the final scene, when his lawful inheritance, the French crown, is passed on to Henry by the marriage to Katherine. An earlier version of the play definitely made the Dauphin appear in that scene, and kneel to swear fealty to Henry. It seems that while he was writing the play Shakespeare decided to minimise the Dauphin's role as antagonist, but only made his mind up after completing the Agincourt scene. It was possibly with his help that the Quarto revisers became more decisive, taking the Dauphin out of Agincourt and the conclusion, and reallocating his boastful speeches before Agincourt to the Duke of Bourbon.

As we all know, you can do a lot to a play on stage even if you do not change the words or make the cuts the Quarto revisers did in slimming down their Shakespeare manuscript. In 1964 the Royal Shakespeare Company produced Peter Hall's version, with Henry played by Ian Holm, who later became Fluellen in Branagh's film (Branagh played Henry V at the RSC twenty years after Holm). Holm's was an icy king, his wooing of

Katherine a calculating game, hilarious to the audience because the staging made it clear that both lovers knew all too well the sole reason for the alliance was diplomatic. That was underlined by the attendant Lady Alice, who was utterly charmed by the romance of the occasion, fluttering round them with sighs and romantic gestures to the intense irritation of both. In Hall's version the killing of the prisoners was ordered at the sound of the '*Alarum*' with ruthless speed, plain evidence of Henry's utter determination to secure victory at any cost. It did keep in 'Once more unto the breach' – how could it not these days? – but otherwise throughout the play laid emphasis on Henry as a coldly calculating, self-serving politician. Other attempts to show the anti-Henry side of the Folio text have been less successful. None have departed anything like as far from the Folio text as does the 1600 Quarto.

The play Shakespeare originally sold to his company in 1599 had to be simplified quite drastically. It was the company that changed Henry from a two-faced pursuer of his personal interest in securing the crown ('No king of England if not king of France!') into a plain hero figure, inspiring his doubtful soldiers with his speech at Agincourt ('We few, we happy few, we band of brothers'), and making him, as the Chorus says, into 'the mirror of all Christian kings'. That simplification in its way justifies all the other changes that twenty generations of directors and actors have made in the nearly four centuries since the Folio text was first published. Perhaps Shakespeare knew what he was doing, writing a play that he realised could not be staged in all its ambivalent complexity. He certainly knew that the play was no longer his once he handed it over to his company and retreated to being just one of its players (my guess is Westmorland, the king's cousin who wishes they had more men at Agincourt and is proved wrong). The central claim, that Shakespeare wrote the complex Folio text we brood over these days knowing it would never be staged in the form he conceived, suggests above all that he recognised very clearly the distance between what he wrote for his company and the use they would put it to. He was obviously a very private man.

There are many, many implications in all this. The most evident point is that we should never trust the printed texts to give us precisely what the Shakespeare company put on stage. Another is that some plays were written less coherently than others. We might find some reassurance about the authorial presence from the fine-tuning of the image patterns in *King Lear* and *Macbeth*, or the clever inversion of the soldier and black machiavel stereotypes in *Othello*. Even the tongue-in-cheek precision with which every little plot detail is tied up in that endless concluding scene of

Cymbeline can give us some reassurance that Shakespeare knew exactly what he was doing. But we ought also to give a lot more credit to the local and immediate pressures on the production and re-scripting of the plays.

And one final point. If Shakespeare's own company revamped the text he gave them before staging *Henry V*, we might count that as a liberation, justifying whatever any director or film-maker subsequently might choose to make of it. What we must be careful of, though, is to recognise just what Shakespeare was doing, and to make sure that we present the play in the sort of detail that is not self-contradictory. Could this herald the rebirth of the author?

CHAPTER 16

Headgear as a Paralinguistic Signifier in King Lear

Ophelia's identification of Hamlet as mad because when he visited her in her chamber he was not wearing a hat suggests strongly that in the original performances he had one on his head at least for his opening scenes. His urgings to Osric in Act 5 to put his own hat to its proper use indicate that he was wearing it again by the play's last act. Our current neglect of headgear with its multiple functions as what the specialists in body language like to call a paralinguistic signifier has lost us several potent features not only of the original staging of *Hamlet* but also of *King Lear* with its panoply of regal and ducal crowns and their varying status, and Lear's own progressive shedding of all his headgear. That loss is accompanied by an even bigger one: access to what actually happened in the original performances of the two divergent versions of its conclusion. The evidence about the wearing and not-wearing of headgear in the first performances of *King Lear* repays careful study.[1] We have regrettably little evidence about what the original players of *Lear* might have worn, but the indications about headgear in the text strongly suggest that the author expected it to be used significantly. The play's choice to open the 1606 Christmas entertainments at Court argues, if nothing else, that the players took considerable care over the correctness of their royal and courtly regalia.

Two substantial features in the first stagings of *King Lear* would have affected the early audiences more than they have current critical readings, in large part because both would have been far more conspicuous in the original staging than they are in the written text. The first visible feature was Albany's attempt at the end of the play to repeat Lear's own mistake

---

Original publication: "Headgear as a Paralinguistic Signifier in *King Lear*," *Shakespeare Survey* 55 (2002), 43–52.
[1] The chief contributors to the questions about the crowns and coronets in *King Lear* are G. P. Shand, 'Lear's Coronet: Playing the Moment', *Shakespeare Quarterly* 38 (1987), 78–82; and R. A. Foakes, 'King Lear: Monarch or Senior Citizen?', in *Elizabethan Theater: Essays in Honor of S. Schoenbaum*, ed. Brian Parker and Sheldon P. Zitner (Newark, NJ, 1996), pp. 271–89.

by offering to divide his rule between the two surviving earls, a reminder of and contrast with the play's opening, marked by the ducal coronet on Albany's head. The second was the way that the headgear of the three participants in that closing moment signalled Albany's intention to continue the decline in the social ranking of Albion's rulers that Lear had initiated. Albany with his ducal coronet, addressing the two earls, should have set himself in the same posture as Lear with his crown addressing the two dukes at the opening. In the original production Kent and the new Earl of Gloucester, to whom Albany offers his coronet, wore the headgear marking their rank, velvet bonnets. Their presence was marked contrast to the coronets that Cornwall and Albany wore when they were with crowned Lear at the opening.

The decline in headgear through the play is a feature reminding the early audiences of Albion's fall into its old disunity: small realms, governed by minor nobles, each at odds with its neighbours. King James had hailed the glorious new unity of Britain in his first speech to the English Parliament in 1604: 'Do we not yet remember', he asked, 'that this Kingdome was divided into seven little King-domes, besides Wales? And is it not stronger now by their union? And hath not the union of Wales to England added a great strength thereto? Which though it was a great Principalitie, was nothing comparable in greatnesse and power to the ancient and famous Kingdome of Scotland . . . And now in the end and fulnesse of time united, the right and title of both in my Person, alike lineally descended of both the Crownes, whereby it is now become like a little World within it selfe.'[2]

Albany's offer to re-divide the kingdom, distributed once already between the two son-in-law dukes by Lear, to an even lower-ranked pair of earls, is no testimony to his grasp of the events he has witnessed. Such a process of continued division was recognisably taking Albion back to its ancient 'little Kingdomes'. Kent's withdrawal from the share-out makes only a minor amendment to Albany's uncomprehending repetition of Lear's act of division. The way this last incident in the play was reflected in the possible games with the headgear worn for it by the original performers offers some peculiar perspectives on the different versions the variant texts offer for the actual conclusion.

On St Stephen's Night in 1606 in the great chamber at Whitehall the King's Men staged a very dangerous game.[3] Their usual ploy of showing

---

[2] Speech to the Upper House of Parliament, 19 March 1604, quoted in Charles Howard McIlwain, *The Political Works of James I* (Cambridge, Mass., 1918), pp. 271–2. '*The Kings Majesties Speech in Parliament, 19 March 1603*' was made available in print from Robert Barker, the King's printer, soon after the speech was given.

[3] The King's Men performed nine plays at Court in the 1606–7 season. *King Lear* was given pride of place on the opening night of the festivities, St Stephen's Night (now Boxing Day). For a full account

their king and patron the modesty of their attempts to simulate the reality of kings and their courts on stage was intensified for the court performance of *King Lear* by a local allusion laid out for deliberate shock-effect in the opening words. For the two play-earls to specify rivalry between the two named play-dukes Albany and Cornwall in the presence of the two real dukes, Prince Henry, who had just been made Duke of Cornwall, and his young brother, who had been the Duke of Albany since 1601,[4] and to do so explicitly in the context of a disunited kingdom, was an audacious and extremely risky attempt to make the courtiers sit up and take note of how the old *King Leir* had been rewritten in order to emphasise its application to the current debate over the union of the two kingdoms of England and Scotland. On the face of it, in the players' thinking this story about 'the division of the kingdoms' was designed to make an explicit exhibition of the dystopia that must follow disunification. Its very first lines made it a blatant piece of propaganda supporting the policy currently being urged on the two Parliaments by the company's own royal patron, who was there at the performance.[5] That daring piece of politics raises two questions. First, how assertively was the royal status of dukedom declared at the court performance by the ducal coronets that feature in the play? Secondly, what version did the court see of the several alternative stagings with the ducal headgear that might have been offered at the end of the play?

When the play's first lines were spoken on St Stephen's Night a lot of eyes would have turned immediately to the Master of the Revels, Sir Edmund Tilney, if he was present for the performance that he had chosen for that prime day of festivity ('Have you heard the argument? Is there no offence in't?' There was little likelihood of Tilney being seen as a Hamlet figure).[6]

---

of performances at Court, and a summary of the evidence for the staging of the St Stephen's Night performance of *King Lear*, see John H. Astington, *English Court Theatre 1558–1642* (Cambridge, 1999), p. 240.

[4] For the general context of the Boxing Day performance, see Leah Marcus, *Local Reading and its Discontents* (Berkeley, 1988), pp. 148–59.

[5] The thought that the young princes might have become rivals for the king's crown was evidently not a problem in 1606. It might have been more troublesome later, since there is a record of James being greatly upset by a play that Prince Charles's Men staged at court on 10 January 1620. According to the Venetian Ambassador, 'the comedians of the prince, in the presence of the king his father, played a drama... in which a king with his two sons has one of them put to death, simply upon suspicion that he wished to deprive him of his crown, and the other son actually did deprive him of it afterwards. This moved the king in an extraordinary manner, both inwardly and outwardly.' Quoted in G. E. Bentley, *The Jacobean and Caroline Stage*, 7 vols. (Oxford, 1940–68), vol. I, p. 214.

[6] James was there, but there is no evidence for either prince nor any record of anyone else who attended the performance. See W. R. Streitberger, ed. *Jacobean and Caroline Revels Accounts, 1603–1642*, Malone Society Collections xiii (Oxford, 1986), p. 20, and Astington, *English Court Theatre*, p. 240. The Duke of Lennox is not specified as going either, though he was more likely to have been a spectator than the coronetted princes.

The Master, explicitly enjoined to allow no living persons to be represented on stage, and having allowed this play to be shown at the royal court, must have known he was prompting a *frisson* at the very outset of the performance. For the first two speakers to mention the Dukes of Albany and Cornwall must have seemed to be sailing very close to the wind. James's two young sons, the twelve-year-old Henry, newly created as Duke of Cornwall and his six-year-old brother Charles, the Duke of Albany, were not actually in attendance that night, but the players could not have known that in advance, and their titles were familiar to all. Moreover, Charles's title 'Albany' was recognised as referring explicitly to his Scottish origins, since it was his original Scottish dukedom. He had been made the Duke of England's York on 6 January 1605, but his Scottish title remained in use. When he was given an acting company to patronise in 1608 it was registered in the provincial records at Norwich, Leicester and even at York itself as 'the lord Albones players'.

A little quick consideration must have reassured the watching courtiers. Tilney at least must have been confident that it was free of offence. Indeed, we might speculate about his prior awareness of how the play's subject could be put to 'application'[7] about the not-yet united state of England and Scotland at that moment. The very obviousness of its application must have been, on second thoughts to the listening courtiers, a guarantee that it was properly licensed. The mythical ancient British kingdom of Albion, created by Brutus of Troy, and affirmed in the play by its antique setting and the use of 'British' instead of 'English' at 3.4.172 in F and 11.169 in Q, and Scene 20.242 in Q (where the Folio text has 'English'),[8] was a vision that well suited James's political hopes. On the face of it the ancient Albion of *King Lear* provided the perfect precedent for his wish to unite his two crowns, his dual paralinguistic signifiers, and enjoy the renewal of the mythical single united kingdom.

We know that King James was present for the performance of *King Lear* at Court on 26 December 1606, the first play of the season, as he was for

---

[7] Jonson may well have had the court performance of *King Lear* in mind when he noted in his 1607 epistle to *Volpone* that 'application . . . is grown a trade'. *Volpone* is closely related to *King Lear* in its images of monstrosity as well as its time of composition for the same company of players. A play viewed as propaganda for the royal policy in a play by the King's servants would expect its applications to be licensed, unlike Jonson's earlier games with *Sejanus* for the same company. Jonson might well consider such a practice as a workmanlike exploit, part of the royal servants' trade.

[8] Line references are from the Norton Shakespeare. Quotations from the Quarto or Folio texts of *King Lear* are from the facsimile edition, *The Complete King Lear 1608–1623*, prepared by Michael Warren (Berkeley, 1989). In either text of *King Lear* 'British', and 'Britain' or 'Briton', were used far less frequently than they were in *Cymbeline*.

all nine of the King's Men's plays that winter. If the young dukes had also been present[9] the pointedness of the ducal names announced by the first speakers would have been prominent visually as well as verbally, by their coronets. We have lost today much sense of how blatantly obvious was the application of the names of the two dukes, and the way their titles were affirmed by their visual signifiers, the headgear paraded at court from 1603 onwards. Dukes and ducal coronets were a novel feature at James's court. First established in England by Richard II, all ducal titles had disappeared by the thirteenth year of Elizabeth's reign. She executed her last Duke (Norfolk) in 1571, and never renewed any of the other old ducal titles. None of Elizabeth's most eminent and senior grandees was ever more than an earl. By contrast James had made his sons dukes while they were still in Scotland, and he gave his cousin Lennox an English dukedom in 1603. Lennox and the two princes with their ducal robes and coronets were the most conspicuous feature of the Jacobean court that emphasised its difference from the Elizabethan.[10] The relief felt nationally that the childless Elizabeth had been replaced by a monarch with two sons made them and their princely status into a substantial prop to James's English crown.

Headgear as a feature of social status was the most prominent way of signalling a man's rank. In staging *King Lear*, what modern productions and modern study even of the original staging tend to miss is how potently the headgear worn in 1606 would have supported that view. In the first scene of the original production a lot of hats were on stage putting out signals about the relative eminence of their wearers: one royal crown, three ducal coronets, two earl's velvet hats, along with a variety of other signifiers. On St Stephen's Night 1606 the golden headgear of rulers monarchic and ducal was on show both on stage and in the audience at Whitehall. What happened to the stage versions, including the declining succession of hats worn by Lear, is well worth registering.

The Tudor sumptuary laws, which prevailed against all the violations that new fashions as well as social climbing introduced until James

---

[9] In 1605–6 James went to forty-nine Court performances, eleven-year-old Henry to nineteen (including all those staged by his own players), and five-year-old Charles, who was not yet the patron of a company of players, to two. Princess Elizabeth, ten at the end of 1606, was not made patron of a company until a year after her younger brother, and is not on record as attending plays in these years.

[10] Shakespeare knew very clearly the distinction between a crown and a coronet. In *The Tempest*, Prospero makes the differentiation when at 1.2.135 he tells Miranda that part of his brother Antonio's deal with King Alonso was to make Milan a subordinate dukedom to the kingdom of Naples, and to 'subject his [Antonio's] coronet to his [Alonso's] crown'.

abolished them in 1604, were most scrupulous and detailed in specifying what the different ranks of the aristocracy were allowed to wear. Only kings and dukes could wear golden crowns on their heads, and ducal coronets were markedly smaller and less elevated than the 'archée' royal crown. Earls wore a less distinct costume, differentiated from dukes chiefly by the absence of gold, except for a single ornament on their velvet hats, although the rest of their clothing could be similar: 'Earls and above that rank and Knights of the Garter in their purple mantles' were permitted to wear 'cloth of gold, sylver tissued, silke of purple color'.[11] The golden circlet of a duke's or prince's headgear was a mark of his proximity to the throne. Elizabeth's abolition of her dukedoms may have reflected her instinctual dislike of the visible features of ducal wear as much as her fear of rivalry and rebellion from those eminences nearest her own rank.

In the original staging of *King Lear* at the Globe one of the strongest visual marks of the play's progress and its point as royalist propaganda was the decline or declension of the headgear that its authority figures wore. At the outset King Lear entered wearing his crown, followed by his two sons-in-law wearing their ducal coronets, and a third coronet was carried onstage ready to be presented to the new duke, whichever between France or Burgundy was to be Cordelia's husband. It was borne ahead of Lear at his entry, as specified in the Quarto stage direction.[12] In contrast to such golden signifiers of authority, Kent and Gloucester, the two earls who begin the play with their discussion about the ducal succession to Lear, wore velvet hats with no more gold on them than the medals or ornaments that the Sumptuary Laws prescribed for that level of Elizabethan nobility. Albany's and Cornwall's princely coronets were visibly shrunken versions of Lear's own elevated and substantial circlet. More gold was on show on the players' heads for this scene than anywhere else in Shakespeare. Lear's gesture in dismissively handing the third coronet to the two dukes heightened the spectacle's garish colours still more.

In this early production the headgear changed through the play as authority shifted. For Lear's second appearance after the opening throne-room scene, in 1.4, he must have worn a hunting hat. The flourish ('Sennet') of trumpets that announced his initial entry was echoed in parody for

---

[11] Under the original sumptuary laws earls were permitted to wear, besides their cloth of gold and purple silks and their gentlemanly velvet, merely a golden ornament on their velvet hats. The laws are listed in diagrammatic form by Frances Elizabeth Baldwin, *Sumptuary Legislation and Personal Regulation in England* (Baltimore, 1926), pp. 228–9.

[12] Directors and editors have taken different views about the coronet. R. A. Foakes, in his Arden 3 edition, pp. 14–16, notes the distinctiveness of James's 'archée' crown, and accepts the idea that the third coronet was intended for Cordelia's new husband.

this second entry by the more ordinary brass of hunting horns, marked in the Folio text's stage direction '*Hornes within*'. This was an entry in more relaxed mode, escorted by his knights, from a day given over to King James's favourite pastime. By the time the storm scene blew up the original Lear had lost even the hunter's protection against bad weather, since at Scene 8.13 in Q the Gentleman tells Kent that 'unbonneted he runnes' (cut in F). His loss of headgear in the storm became his version of Poor Tom's nakedness, the concluding item in his loss of all material possessions. In the last section of the play all Lear secured for his head was the parodic crown of flowers with which he returned to Cordelia, and which he may have kept on until he died at the end of the play.[13] This decline in his headgear, from the golden crown of the opening, to the hunting cap that James himself always preferred for his outdoor activities, to a nominal nudity like Tom's in the storm, bareheaded while he raged against the hurricanoes, and on to the flowery parody of what Kent still insisted on seeing in his face before he went mad, was designed to mark the shifts in Lear's mind and his status as the story developed, and perhaps the matching declension of national authority and control.

By the end of that production Lear lay dead, and the sole remaining wearer of a golden circlet, Albany, offered to resign his authority to the two remaining earls, Kent and the new Gloucester. The headgear of this surviving trio provided a visual marker for the decline in power of a divided kingdom, from royal crown to ducal coronets and now to the earls' velvet bonnets. It is a nice question, which we must come to later, whether it was the Duke Albany or the Earl Gloucester who was chosen to make the final authoritative speech in these first productions of the play, at the Globe and then before King James. Certainly whichever speaker it was who spoke of this sad time was registering the question whether the shrinkage of authority that runs progressively through the play (or regressively, if you see the play as propaganda for James's desire to unite his two kingdoms) was to be seen continuing through to the present time and the divided kingdoms which were James's preoccupation in 1605.

When Shakespeare rewrote the old *King Leir* for the King's Men[14] the most conspicuous change was to make the old play's sons-in-law not the

---

[13] Foakes, 'King Lear: Monarch or Senior Citizen?', 283, considers that he might have regained his crown by this point, through a complex process of acquisition from Edmund to Edgar to himself. No stage directions or indications in the dialogue give any support to this idea.

[14] The likelihood that several of the Queen's Men's plays were allocated to the Lord Chamberlain's Men in 1594, when the new duopoly was established, notably *The Troublesome Reign of King John*, *The Famous Victories of Henry V* and the ur-*Hamlet*, all of which Shakespeare had rewritten by 1600, gives his decision to rewrite *King Leir* in 1605 an immediate reason that intensifies its 'application' to

'King of Cornwall' but a duke, and to transform the 'King of Cambria', or Wales, into the Duke of Albany, or Scotland. Since Henry had been made Prince of Wales in 1606 as well as Duke of Cornwall, the change was as obvious as it was pointed. The old Queen's Men's play ignored Scotland altogether as a part of the united kingdom that King Leir ruled over, but the times and political circumstances had changed since then. In Shakespeare's revision the names suggest that the Duke of Cornwall was given Wales and the west, while Albany was given Scotland, leaving the third part, England, by far the most opulent of the three (as James's presence in London testified), to be awarded to the husband of the third daughter, Cordelia, recipient of the third coronet, and hence of course to Lear himself.

That is why the third ducal coronet was such a feature of the play's opening. The Pied Bull Quarto of 1608 supplies this stage direction for Lear's regal entry in 1.1: '*Sound a Sennet. Enter one bearing a Coronet, then Lear, then the Dukes of Albany, and Cornwall, next Gonorill, Regan, Cordelia, with followers.*' If the 1608 quarto text does give any indication of the version staged at Court in 1606, this third coronet was the central exhibit of the ceremony that Lear then conducted. He explains his plan to the speculating nobles with evident glee at his secrecy, telling them that he is not going to divide the kingdom into two, as they had been thinking and perhaps fearing, but into three. There will now be a third duke to enjoy the share-out, and the third and so-far unoccupied coronet is intended for him. That is why Lear has ordered France and Burgundy to be fetched into the royal presence. One of the two lords of the great lands south of England is to get Cordelia, and with her the third British dukedom and the best share of Lear's to-be-disunited kingdom. He has it all, quite literally, mapped out.

Cordelia's refusal to follow his plan, and his consequent denial of the third coronet to her husband, turns the vacant circlet of gold into a neat visual indication of the impossibility of Lear's original scheme. After Cordelia has upset it, he dismissively tenders that now-redundant emblem of partial authority to Cornwall and Albany, saying 'This Coronet part betwixt you.' (Q; '... betweene you' F). The golden circlet, an unbreakable image of the circle that to Aristotle signified perfection, dangles idly between them. Neither duke can take it up: nobody could wear half a crown. Lear's angry and dismissive gesture destroys with it, all

James's political interests in that year. For his adaptation he consulted a number of sources, perhaps most notably Holinshed, where he would have found a more searching history of the legend. But I have little doubt that for his contemporaries, the names Cornwall and Albany would give the play its most immediate 'application'.

unknowing, his own expectation that he will keep his crown when he delegates authority to the two wearers of the lesser golden emblems. The king's crown now vanishes from the stage along with Lear's authority. In the succeeding scenes both Albany and Cornwall wear their coronets, and are called dukes by loyal Gloucester, but Lear never recovers his signifier of authority. The declension of his headgear through the rest of the play registers the inadequacy of his expectation that, while giving up the labour of government to the dukes, he could retain 'The name and all the addicions to a King'.

Other hints beside the shifts in his headgear uphold the view that after the opening scene Lear is recognisably unkinged. Gloucester still insists on calling him king, and there are other references to his former status. But Goneril in 1.3 simply calls him 'my Father', and in the next scene the disguised Kent, for all his view of the authority in Lear's face, can only call him 'Master', like the servant to any lord. Lear's own knight in this scene calls him merely 'my Lord'. Oswald draws attention to his reduced status by naming him to his face 'my Ladies Father'. This scene lays more emphasis on his loss of status than later scenes, when he is again addressed by his royal title, and it also calls in question Albany's new power as Lear's successor. The confrontation between downgraded parent and contemptuous daughter intensifies when Albany joins the scene with his visible new authority as coronet-wearer, to find Lear raging at Goneril's decision to strip him of his trappings. Lear turns on him, demanding, with resonant emphasis on this manifestation of female control, 'Is it *your* will?' Albany's evident lack of knowledge about what is going on shows his poor command of what the disguised Kent said he still saw in Lear's face. 'My Lord, I am guiltlesse, as I am ignorant', he protests (F adds the half-redemptive qualifier 'Of what hath moved you.'). It is Goneril who is in control. She overrides Albany's attempts to find out what is going on. A ducal yet uncomprehending authority figure adds a touch of incongruous colour to a scene swelling with black fury. His lack of comprehension – in utter contrast to the gross likemindedness of the other husband and wife, Regan and Cornwall, in a later scene – stands as a first example of the losses that Lear's forsaking of his crown are leading to. The two texts of the play present distinctly different Albanys, the earlier of whom it is thought might have been played by Shakespeare himself.[15] It is the stage presentation of Albany, the senior

---

[15] I have some difficulty with the methodology of Donald Foster's *Shaxicon*, which identifies the sequence of Shakespeare's parts by the distinctive recurrence of their vocabulary in later plays, and particularly in Foster's identification of Albany as one of his parts in 1605. Albany's role in the play

survivor, and the level of his comprehension of the events by the end of the play, that is the last and largest of the issues considered here.

The other coronetted figure, Cornwall, on his reappearance in 2.2, makes a strong contrast to Albany. This is a powerful scene. For the first time since Scene 1 the word 'King' recurs, and each time it is applied to Lear, not Albany or Cornwall. Old Gloucester refers to Lear as 'King' and Cornwall as 'the Duke', possibly in a direct indication that Cornwall continues to wear his coronet, and certainly a reminder of the lowering of the new ruler's rank. Cornwall is the figure of power now. He enters accompanied by his host Gloucester to find Kent fighting with Oswald and Edmund, and promptly imposes his power by putting Kent in the stocks. This second authority figure is as ignorant as Albany of what is going on, but his reaction is manifestly an unjust one. The contrasting injustices of Albany's submission to his wife's control and Cornwall's brutish (British) and summary punishment of Kent give graphic testimony to the changes in authority. Moreover, the prior show of Albany's lack of control or comprehension offers little reassurance about any return to unity once Cornwall is killed. If the invasion by the might-have-been third duke, France, were not enough evidence of division, we have seen that Albany has a lot to learn if he is to replace Lear as an authority figure. What he tries to do in the final scene with his by now singular authority colours all the different possible versions of the play's ending profoundly, both as components in the propaganda game, and in the larger philosophical and theological implications. In both texts of the final scene he makes two attempts to exert the control that his coronet should give him, with Cornwall dead, France defeated and all three daughters beyond remarriage, and twice the ex-king Lear checks him. The whole scene is redolent with the King's Men's point about the chaos that comes from the forsaking of single authority. Its ostensible function as pro-royalist propaganda is qualified chiefly by Albany's behaviour as the sole heir to rule. That behaviour appears to shift drastically in its presentation between the two texts.

The difference between the two versions of *King Lear*, the first version as reflected in the Quarto of 1608 and the distinct version in the Folio of 1623 (from a revision made in 1611?), where the final speech moves from Duke Albany to Earl Edgar, if it was a calculated change (a necessary consideration: there is no sign of any preparation for the transfer in the section leading up to it), presents us with too many alternative ways of reading the

as the only authority figure who survives to the end is so central to its conclusion that any revisions, such as those claimed for the Folio text, must have been given special attention. The *Shaxicon* evidence here comes close to being whirled in a circular argument.

staging of the conclusion for comfort. Like any frayed rope, there are so many loose strands that no single strong re-connection can be possible.

In both texts Albany employs the royal 'we' to issue the first of his attempts to be authoritative. Q in its entry direction and speech headings calls him 'Duke'. The coronet on his head asserts his right to take control (I quote from the F version; Q is identical, although set as prose):

> You Lords and Noble Friends, know our intent,
> What comfort to this great decay may come,
> Shall be appli'd. For us we will resign,
> During the life of this old Majesty
> To him our absolute power.
>
> (5.3.271–5)

The status quo will be restored. Before he beats that redemptive retreat, though, he singles out the old Earl of Kent and the new Earl of Gloucester, Edgar, for particular reward, restoring their lost titles and territories to them. Then he goes on to a general proclamation, extending his restoration of justice to the entire kingdom.

> All Friends shall
> Taste the wages of their vertue, and all Foes
> The cup of their deservings.
>
> (5.3.277–9)

But Lear breaks in on that hopeful proclamation of restored order with his bleak assertion that no such earthly reimposition of justice is possible. He sums everything up in those wonderfully allusive and denying words 'And my poore Foole is hang'd' (5.3.280). Every word in that simple countervention is telling. 'And' is the effect of injustice that discounts Albany's hope; 'my' reasserts Lear's own responsibility for the disaster; 'poor' echoes France's valuation that Lear so signally failed to understand earlier, that Cordelia is 'most rich being poor', the spiritual overriding the material; 'fool' links paternal love and simplicity with Lear's other sheltered speaker of truth; and she is hanged, the fate of the criminal and, since crucifixion was a Roman form of hanging, of Christ. This gratuitous alteration of the ending to the old play, where Cordelia lives on, united to 'the Gallian king' (a kindlier conclusion affirmed in Tate's sentimental union of Cordelia with Edgar), is set here against Albany's attempt at making a return to the normality of the status quo out of which Lear broke at the beginning of the play. In the face of that appalling fact, his well-meaning rewards and punishments have no value. Hanging is a judicial punishment, a curious choice of means for Edmund's murder. Applying the connotations of such a distinct form of killing to Cordelia's death makes a fool of any coronet-wearer, however well-meaning. Albany's innocent and well-intentioned desire to restore the old order shows no growth of stature either in his authority or in his understanding.

Shakespeare uses Albany to underline the enormity of Cordelia's murder. His helplessness is a mark of how inadequate earthly attempts at justice must be (and, in the process, perhaps, how unimportant the play was as royalist propaganda). The point carries through to the very end of the play, because there, in the second of his attempts to control events, Albany does it again. As the sole surviving authority figure, with Lear dead at his feet, he offers to repeat quite exactly Lear's own original mistake that started the trail of destruction. He tries to divide the kingdom a second time. In a woefully diminished version of Lear the king's giving his authority to two dukes, Albany the duke now offers it to two earls. It is a distinctly unimpressive demonstration of his grasp of what has been going on. Then, in spite of all the visible evidence in the bodies on stage of what happened when control was handed down from a king to two dukes, he is prepared to allow it to descend further from himself as the one surviving duke to a pair of earls. Dualism runs throughout the play as the enemy of unity. The singular Cordelia is said by the anonymous Gentleman to redeem mankind from the general curse of 'twaine', and although Albany calls the two earls his friends, 'you twaine', their duality as much as their lack of golden headgear signals a further decline from the unified regal control that the play started with. That is the negation of Albany's timid attempt to renew Lear's initial error. The offer does him no credit, and gives little hope of future unification, as any rough survey of England's history through the time of James's 'seven little Kingdomes' would have affirmed to Jacobean listeners.

There is a particularly tantalising question about Albany's last gesture for which no evidence survives, either from the 1606 version of the play as it is represented in the Quarto text or from the alternative Folio text. It would be logical for Albany to accompany his offer of authority with its emblem, that paralinguistic signal on his head. If he was imitating Lear's own initial announcement, he would keep his coronet on his own head, as Lear kept his crown. But it is possible that the act of making a wholesale renunciation required him to do more, and to offer the surrender of his signifying headgear too. If he was making a serious proposal of renunciation, as he surely was, a gesture offering his coronet to the two earls would be a kindlier, infinitely shrunken version of Lear's angry gesture with the third coronet to Cornwall and Albany in the opening scene. The two earls were being offered half a coronet each. Then Kent's immediate rejection of the offer would have left the signifier dangling, as it leaves us. We are stranded in utterly conjectural territory, wondering whether, if Albany's offer of the golden circlet was a literal one, Kent's refusal would have left it in Albany's hands, so that it went back onto his head, or whether it then found its singular way into Edgar's hands, and stayed there. This is where we have to curse Shakespeare's chronic economy in writing his stage directions. This question, about who might have held or worn the remaining coronet, raises in its most acute form one of the trickiest aspects of the two-texts problem. The presence of Albany's coronet as a feature of the play's closure leaves us with not just two possible and alternative resolutions to the play but four.

If at the Court performance in 1606 Edgar was left with the coronet in his hands or on his head, such a posture would look very different from the later version, since the earlier text gives the last speech to Albany, while the Folio allocates it to Edgar. The last four ponderous lines sound quite different if delivered by a coronet-wearing Albany. They are different again if given by Albany while Edgar holds the coronet, and even more different if delivered by Edgar without the golden headgear. The fourth option, Edgar speaking while holding the coronet, is the only choice possible for those who need to see some expression of hope for the future expressed by a single and fully comprehending speaker in the last speech (I quote F again; Q gives the plural 'have' in the third line):

> The waight of this sad time we must obey,
> Speake what we feele, not what we ought to say:
> The oldest hath borne most, we that are yong,
> Shall never see so much, nor live so long.
> (5.3.298–301)

The second line, about putting what we feel ahead of what we ought to say, sounds in Albany's mouth like a self-reproof, an expression of regret that he had tried to issue rewards and punishments in the face of what Lear held up to him. It works against his attempt to re-divide the newly united kingdom, and could be read as a sign that he now has a better understanding. In Edgar's mouth, on the other hand, it sounds more like a reproof to the fumbling and uncomprehending Albany, and a fatalistic acceptance of the foolishness of this great stage. If Albany speaks it while holding or wearing the coronet, the lines become a reluctant acceptance of his responsibility, now with the clearer knowledge that his offer of the coronet had ignored, although nothing has occurred in between to open his eyes. If he speaks them while Edgar holds the emblem of authority, it would mark his recognition of what the play has at last taught him. Edgar is the sole heir, and the kingdom will not be re-divided. If as in the Folio text Edgar says the last words, and does so while holding the coronet, they indicate both his recognition and the general shrinkage marked by the headgear that takes authority from kings down to earls. If he speaks them while Albany still retains the coronet, he is expressing the resignation of the lesser beings who survive, and his words direct attention away from the survivors to dead Lear and the on-stage corpses of his three daughters. The four choices each mark a distinct point in the huge gamut, from religious hope to pessimistic nihilism, that so many critics have distinguished in the play's conclusion.

There is one possible, and easy if not comforting, solution to this multi-choice dilemma, which in these variable forms surely entertains more alternatives than the original players would have bothered to canvass. This solution requires us to see the change in the last speech-heading between the Quarto and Folio texts as accidental, and allows us to set up Edgar as the single heir to a united Britain, and the speaker of the final words. A version of the play starting with Lear as king, passing authority to the two sons-in-law as dukes, and finally making Albany as the surviving duke offer it to the two earls has a striking consistency. The symmetry of the declension in rank argues that the golden token of authority should end up in Edgar's hands. The steps down from king to dukes and duke to earl collapse if Albany retains the coronet and speaks the last words, as he does in the Quarto text. So the Folio version should rule. This explanation has the convenience of reducing the final difference between Q and F to a compositorial slip in Q. The case for the F text's being, at least in this one instance, a distinct revision, however discreet, of the play's now-embarrassing 'application' to the defunct politics of 1605–6 lapses. And having a single version of the play simplifies life beautifully. The Folio version might be upheld as the nearest thing we have to a non-variable authorial input, identical in 1605, at court in 1606, and consistent thereafter.

But however convenient that may be, it is still outweighed by the predominant likelihood that *King Lear* was designed in 1605 to be judged as a token of support for James's desire to unify his kingdoms. The fact that the play texts survive in multiple forms, the record of a flow rather than a fixity, is a mark of how quickly the local readings could be displaced. Even the two surviving versions of the text understate the multitude of ways the early stagings might have presented the play. Those four or more ways of playing the closure might well reflect distinct versions of the early performances. Which, if any, was the author's own original preference and which of them might show any changes he or his fellow-players might have introduced in later years we have no way of knowing. Certainly as performed at court in December 1606 the play was meant to appear, at least on the surface, as a blatant piece of propaganda upholding the desire of the players' patron to make his two crowns into one, and the strengths of a united kingdom under a single head. Tilney's approval of the text as performed with the names cited in the very first line is ample testimony for that. The versions of the conclusion that most intensify the dystopia of the final act might be seen as concomitants of that work of propaganda, readings of the play whose urgency disappeared when the two Parliaments denied James his hope. The choice, for instance, of having Cordelia murdered so gratuitously, the most emphatic of all the changes that Shakespeare made from the Queen's Men's *King Leir*, its familiar (recently published)[16] precedent, might, if we were determinedly reductive, simply be seen as the most graphic of the many examples that the play provides of the horrors that come from de-unifying the state. Seeing the two earls in their hats being offered the surviving coronet as a parody of the initial gift of authority to Albany and Cornwall would have renewed that grim vision. As propaganda the play has to indicate that there is no hope that could possibly emerge from its dystopian image of a dualistic future.

Such a local reading brings little content to the modern reader, since the original circumstances were so transient. Moreover this reconstruction of the staging has inevitably in crucial areas to be inferential. The hard evidence of headgear-wearing is no more than hinted at in the dialogue and stage directions. The fixity of one's idea about the rest depends on how far one expects the Jacobean Court to have been thorough in following its own sumptuary expectations over the clothing that went with social rank. Readings of the moment when Albany tries to reproduce Lear's original error in dividing his kingdom are made no easier by the multitude of possible stagings of the responses to that idea, and the degrees of generosity which they leave for our opinions of Albany and Edgar as re-unifying rulers. Still less do they give much guidance to the reading or readings which the play's original author might have given to the weighty philosophical and religious connotations that derive from Cordelia's murder and its impact on the play's conclusion.

The pits of idle speculation go very deep here. They do give a distinct deep resonance to the differences between studying Shakespeare on the

---

[16] *King Leir* was first entered in the Stationers' Register in May 1594, re-entered to the eventual printers in May 1605 and published in the summer of that year.

page and on stage. On the page we can hold all these possible conclusions at the same time, and make our personal choices, leaving, if we can bear to (though critics rarely manage to do that) the ending as problematic, contingent, or even simply unclear. On stage the choices are made for us, and they might well have been altered more than once between 1605 and 1611, or whenever the last speech was reattributed to Edgar, if not by a compositor happy to be coming to the end of his stint of type-setting.

The Cause is in My Will: A Bibliography

Acts of the Privy Council of England, New Series, ed. John Roche Dasent. 32 vols. London: HMSO, 1890–.
Adams, Simon. "Eliza Enthroned? The Court and its Politics," in *The Reign of Elizabeth I*, ed. Christopher Haigh. Athens: University of Georgia Press, 1985, pp. 55–77.
Allen, Michael J. B. and Muir, Kenneth, eds., *Shakespeare's Plays in Quarto*. Berkeley: University of California Press, 1981.
Altman, Joel B. *The Tudor Play of Mind: Rhetorical Inquiry and the Development of Elizabethan Drama*. Berkeley: University of California Press, 1978.
Astington, John H. *English Court Theatre 1558–1642*. Cambridge University Press, 1999.
  Actors and Acting in Shakespeare's Time. The Art of Stage Playing. Cambridge University Press, 2010.
Baldwin, Frances Elizabeth. *Sumptuary Legislation and Personal Regulation in England*. Baltimore, MA: Johns Hopkins University Press, 1926.
Barish, Jonas. *The Antitheatrical Prejudice*. Berkeley: University of California Press, 1981.
Barroll, J. Leeds. "Drama and the Court," in *The Revels History of Drama in English*, ed. Lois Potter, Clifford Leech, and T. W. Craik, 8 vols. London and New York: Methuen, 1975–83.
  "A New History for Shakespeare and his Time," *Shakespeare Quarterly* 39 (1988), 441–64.
Baskervill, Charles Read. *The Elizabethan Jig*. University of Chicago Press, 1928.
Bawcutt, N. W. *The Control and Censorship of Caroline Drama. The Records of Sir Henry Herbert, Master of the Revels 1623–73*. Oxford: Clarendon Press, 1996.
Bayer, Mark. *Theatre, Community, and Civic Engagement in Jacobean London*. University of Iowa Press, 1988.
Beckerman, Bernard. "A Shakespearean Experiment: The Dramaturgy of *Measure for Measure*," in *Elizabethan Theatre 2*, ed. David Galloway. Toronto: Archon Books, 1970, 108–23.
Bennett, Paul E. "The Word 'Goths' in 'A Knack to Know a Knave'," *N&Q*, 200 (1955), 462–3.
Bentley, Gerald Eades. *The Jacobean and Caroline Stage*, 7 vols. Oxford: Clarendon Press, 1942–68.

The Profession of Player in Shakespeare's Time, 1590–1642. Princeton University Press, 1984.
Berger, Harry, Jr. *Imaginary Audition: Shakespeare on Page and Stage*. Berkeley: University of California Press, 1989.
Bergeron, David. "Women as Patrons of English Renaissance Drama," in *Patronage in the Renaissance*, ed. Guy Fitch Lytle and Stephen Orgel. Washington, DC: The Folger Shakespeare Library; London and Toronto: Associated University Presses, 1981, pp. 274–90.
Berry, Herbert. "The Globe Bewitched and *El Hombre Fiel*," *Medieval & Renaissance Drama in England* 1 (1984), 211–30.
The Boar's Head Playhouse. Washington, DC: Folger Books, 1986.
Booth, Stephen. *Shakespeare's Sonnets*. New Haven, CT: Yale University Press, 1977.
Born, Hanspeter. "The Date of 2, 3 *Henry VI*," *SQ*, 25(1974), 324–6.
Bourdillon, A. F. C. *The Order of Minoresses in England*. Manchester University Press, 1926.
Bowsher, Julian and Miller, Pat. *The Rose and the Globe – Playhouses of Shakespeare's Bankside, Southwark. Excavations 1988–90*. MoLA Monograph 482009. London: Museum of London Archaeology, 2009.
Bradshaw, Graham. *Misrepresentations: Shakespeare and the Materialists*. Ithaca, NY: Cornell University Press, 1993.
Brennan, Michael. *Literary Patronage in the English Renaissance: The Pembroke Family*. London and New York: Routledge, 1988.
Brown, Carolyn E. "Erotic Religious Flagellation and Shakespeare's *Measure for Measure*," *English Literary Renaissance* 16 (1986), 139–65.
"The Wooing of Duke Vincentio and Isabella in *Measure for Measure*: 'The Image of It Gives [Them] Content'," *Shakespeare Studies* 22 (1994), 189–219.
Bruster, Douglas. "On a Certain Tendency in Economic Criticism of Shakespeare," in *Money and the Age of Shakespeare: Essays in New Economic Criticism*, ed. Linda Woodbridge. Basingstoke: Palgrave Macmillan, 2003, pp. 67–79.
Calendar of State Papers, Domestic Series, of the Reign of . . . Elizabeth, 1581–90, ed. Robert Lemon and Mary Ann Everett Green, 12 vols. London: Longman, 1856–72.
Carson, Neil. "John Webster: The Apprentice Years," *Elizabethan Theatre* 6 (1978), 76–87.
Cerasano, S. P. "New Renaissance Players' Wills," *Modern Philology* 82 (1985), 299–304.
"Competition for the King's Men? Alleyn's Blackfriars Venture," *Medieval and Renaissance Drama in England* 4 (1989), 173–86.
Chambers, E. K. *Notes on the History of the Revels Office under the Tudors*. London: A. H. Bullen, 1907.
The Elizabethan Stage, 4 vols. Oxford: Clarendon Press, 1923.
William Shakespeare, 2 vols. Oxford: Clarendon Press, 1930.

Cheney, Patrick. *Shakespeare, National Poet-Playwright*. Cambridge University Press, 2004.
  Shakespeare's Literary Authorship. Cambridge University Press, 2008.
Clopper, L. M. "London and the Problem of the Clerkenwell Plays," *Comparative Drama* 34 (2000), 291–303.
The Complete Works of William Shakespeare, ed. Stanley Wells and Gary Taylor. Oxford University Press, 1986.
The Complete Works of Thomas Nashe, ed. R. B. McKerrow, 5 vols. London: A. H. Bullen, 1904–10.
The Complete Works of Shakespeare, ed. David Bevington, 4th edn. New York: HarperCollins, 1992.
Dekker, Thomas. *The Gull's Hornbook*. London, 1610.
  The Shoemaker's Holiday, ed. R. L. Smallwood and Stanley Wells. Manchester University Press; Baltimore: Johns Hopkins University Press, 1979.
Digges, Leonard. "Poets are borne not made." 1640, in *The Riverside Shakespeare*, ed. G. Blakemore Evans. Boston: Houghton Mifflin, 1974, pp. 1845–6.
The Dramatic Records of Sir Henry Herbert, 1622–1673, ed. J. Q. Adams. New Haven, CT: Yale University Press, 1917.
Donaldson, Ian. *The World Turned Upside-down. Comedy from Jonson to Fielding*. Oxford University Press, 1970.
Drayton, Michael. *Idea*, Sonnet 47, in *The Works of Michael Drayton*, ed. J. William Hebel. Oxford: Blackwell, 1931–41.
Dutton, Richard. *Mastering the Revels. The Regulation and Censorship of English Renaissance Drama*. University of Iowa Press, 1991.
  Licensing, Censorship and Authorship in Early Modern England: Buggeswords. Basingstoke: Palgrave, 2000.
Eccles, Mark. *Christopher Marlowe in London*. Cambridge, MA: Harvard University Press, 1934.
  "Elizabethan Actors I, A–D," *Notes & Queries* 236 (1991), 58–49.
  "Elizabethan Actors II, E–J," *Notes & Queries* 236 (1991), 454–61.
Edelman, Charles. *Brawl Ridiculous. Swordfighting in Shakespeare's Plays*. Manchester University Press, 1992.
  "Which is the Jew that Shakespeare Knew? Shylock on the Elizabethan Stage," *Shakespeare Survey* 52 (1999), 99–106.
Edwardes, Richard. *Damon and Pithias*. London, 1565.
English Professional Theatre, 1530–1660, ed. Glynne Wickham, Herbert Berry and William Ingram. Cambridge University Press, 2000.
Erne, Lukas. *Shakespeare as a Literary Dramatist*. Cambridge University Press, 2003.
Es, Bart van. "'*Johannes fac Totum*'? Shakespeare's First Contact with the Acting Companies," *Shakespeare Quarterly* 61 (2010), 551–77.
Evans, Robert C. *Ben Jonson and the Poetics of Patronage*. Lewisburg, PA: Bucknell University Press, 1989.
Feuillerat, Albert. *Documents Relating to the Office of the Revels in the Time of Queen Elizabeth, ed. with Notes and Indexes*. Louvain: A. Uystpruyst, 1908.

A Fifteenth-Century Courtesy Book and Two Franciscan Rules, ed. R. W. Chambers and W. W. Seton, EETS No. 148. London, 1914.

Finkelpearl, Philip J. "'The Comedians' Liberty': Censorship of the Jacobean Stage Reconsidered," *English Literary Renaissance* 16 (1986), 123–38.

The First Quarto of King Henry V, The New Cambridge Shakespeare. Cambridge University Press, 2000.

Fitzpatrick, Tim. *Playwright, Space and Place in Early Modern Performance. Shakespeare and Company*. Farnham: Ashgate, 2011.

Foakes, R. A. "King Lear: Monarch or Senior Citizen?" in *Elizabethan Theater: Essays in Honor of S. Schoenbaum*, ed. Brian Parker and Sheldon Zitner. Newark, NJ: University of Delaware Press, 1996.

Gabriel Harvey's Marginalia, ed. G. C. Moore Smith, Stratford upon Avon, 1913.

George, David. "Shakespeare and Pembroke's Men," *Shakespeare Quarterly* 32 (1981), 305–23.

Gieskes, Edward. *Representing the Professions. Administration, Law, and Theater in Early Modern England*. Newark, NJ: University of Delaware Press, 2006.

Gillies, John. *Shakespeare and the Geography of Distance*. Cambridge University Press, 1994.

Gless, Daryl J. *'Measure for Measure', the Law, and the Convent*. Princeton University Press, 1979.

Gosson, Stephen. *The Shoole of Abuse, Conteining a Pleasaunt Invective against Poets, Pipers, Plaiers, JESTERS, and Such Like Caterpillers of a Comonwelth*. London, 1579.

 Playes Confuted in Five Actions, 1582, in *Markets of Bawdrie*, ed. Arthur F. Kinney. University of Salzburg, 1974.

Gras, Henk. *Studies in Elizabethan Audience Response to the Theatre*, 2 vols. New York: Peter Lang, 1993.

Greenblatt, Stephen. "Shakespeare and the Exorcists," in *Shakespeare and the Question of Theory*, ed. Patricia Parker and Geoffrey H. Hartman. London: Taylor and Francis, 1985.

 "Murdering Peasants: Status, Genre, and the Representation of Rebellion," in *Learning to Curse: Essays in Modern Culture*. London: Routledge, 1990, pp. 99–130.

Greene, Robert. *The Second Part of Conny-catching*, 1592, ed. G. B. Harrison. London: The Bodley Head Quartos, 1926.

 The Thirde & Last Part of Conny-catching, 1592, ed. G. B. Harrison. London: The Bodley Head Quartos, 1926.

Gross, John. *Shylock: A Legend and its Legacy*. New York: Simon & Schuster, 1992.

Gurr, Andrew. "DeWitt's Sketch of the Swan," *Notes & Queries* 7 (1960), 328.

 The Shakespearean Stage. Cambridge University Press, 1970, revised 1980, 1992, 2009.

 "Shakespeare's First Poem," *Essays in Criticism* 21 (1971), 222–6.

 "Shakespeare's Many-headed Audience," *Essays in Theatre* 1 (1982), 52–62.

 Playgoing in Shakespeare's London. Cambridge University Press, 1987.

"Money or Audiences: The Choice of Shakespeare's Globe," *Theatre Notebook* 42 (1988), 3–14.
"The Tempest's *Tempest* at Blackfriars," *Shakespeare Survey* 41 (1988), 91–102.
The New Cambridge King Henry V. Cambridge University Press, 1992.
"The Chimera of Amalgamation," *Theatre Research International* 18 (1993), 85–93.
"Three Reluctant Patrons and Early Shakespeare," *Shakespeare Quarterly* 44 (1993), 159–74.
"The Loss of Records for the Travelling Companies in Stuart Times," *REED Newsletter* 19 (1994), 2–19.
"The Date and Expected Venue of *Romeo and Juliet*," *Shakespeare Survey* 49 (1996), 15–25.
Playgoing in Shakespeare's London, 2nd edn. Cambridge University Press, 1996.
The Shakespearian Playing Companies. Oxford: Clarendon Press, 1996.
"Privy Councillors as Theatre Patrons," in *Shakespeare and Theatrical Patronage in Early Modern England*, ed. Paul Whitfield White and Suzanne R. Westfall. Cambridge University Press, 2002, pp. 221–45.
"The Great Divide of 1594," in *Words that Count: Essays on Early Modern Authorship in Honor of MacDonald P. Jackson*, ed. Brian Boyd. Newark, NJ: University of Delaware Press, 2004, pp. 29–50.
The Shakespeare Company 1594–1642. Cambridge University Press, 2004.
"Henry Carey's Peculiar Letter," *Shakespeare Quarterly* 56 (2005), 51–75.
"Shakespeare in Three Dimensions," in *In the Footsteps of William Shakespeare*, ed. Christa Jansohn. Munster: Lit Verlag, 2005, pp. 73–85.
"The Work of Elizabethan Plotters, and *2 The Seven Deadly Sins*," *Early Theatre* 10 (2006), 67–87.
"Did Shakespeare Own his Own Playbooks?" *Review of English Studies* 60 (2009), 206–29.
Shakespeare's Opposites. The Admiral's Company 1594–1625. Cambridge University Press, 2009.
The Shakespearean Stage 1574–1642, 4th edn. Cambridge University Press, 2009.
"In-jokes about Spear-shakers," *Notes and Queries* 257 (2011), 237–41.
"Rethinking Shylock," *Shakespeare International Yearbook* 12 (2012).
Gurr, Andrew and Mariko Ichikawa. *Staging in Shakespeare's Theatres*. Oxford University Press, 2000.
Gurr, Andrew and Farah Karim-Cooper, eds. *Moving Shakespeare Indoors. Performance and Repertoire in the Jacobean Playhouse*. Cambridge University Press, 2014.
Hall, Joseph. *Virgidemiarum*. London, 1597.
Hannay, Margaret P. *Philip's Phoenix: Mary Sidney, Countess of Pembroke*. New York: Oxford University Press, 1990.
Hay, Millicent V. *The Life of Robert Sidney, Earl of Leicester (1563–1626)*. Washington, DC: The Folger Shakespeare Library; London and Toronto: Associated University Presses, 1984.

Heinemann, Margot. "Rebel Lords, Popular Playwrights, and Political Culture: Notes on the Jacobean Patronage of the Earl of Southampton," *Yearbook of English Studies* 21 (1991), 63–86.

Henslowe's Diary, ed. R. A. Foakes and R. T. Rickert. Cambridge University Press, 1961.

Heywood, Thomas. *An Apology for Actors*, 1612.

Hobgood, Alison P. *Passionate Playgoing in Early Modern England*. Cambridge University Press, 2014.

Honan, Park. *Shakespeare. A Life*. Oxford University Press, 1998.

Hosley, Richard. "Three Renaissance English Indoor Playhouses," *English Literary Renaissance* 3 (1973), 166–82.

Hotine, Margaret. "*Measure for Measure*: Further Contemporary Notes," *Notes & Queries* 37 (1990), 184–6.

"The Politics of Anti-Semitism: *The Jew of Malta* and *The Merchant of Venice*," *Notes & Queries* 236 (1991), 35–8.

Hotson, Leslie. *Shakespeare versus Shallow*. Boston: Little, Brown & Co, 1931.

Hunter, G. K. "Six Notes on *Measure for Measure*," *Shakespeare Quarterly* 15 (1964), 168–9.

Hyland, Peter. "'A Kind of Woman': The Elizabethan Boy-Actor and the Kabuki Onnagata," *Theatre Research International* xii (1987), 1–8.

Disguise on the Early Modern English Stage. Farnham: Ashgate, 2011.

Ichikawa, Mariko. *Shakespearean Entrances*. Basingstoke and New York: Palgrave, 2002.

Ingram, William. "The Closing of the Theaters in 1597: A Dissenting View," *Modern Philology* 69 (1971–2), 105–15.

A London Life in the Brazen Age. Cambridge, MA: Harvard University Press, 1978.

"The Economics of Playing," in *A Companion to Shakespeare*, ed. David Scott Kastan. Oxford: Blackwell, 1999, pp. 315–16.

Jackson, MacDonald D. "Three Old Ballads and the Date of *Doctor Faustus*," *Journal of the Australasian Universities Language and Literature Association* 36 (1971), 187–200.

Jewell, Simon. "The Lords President, Their Activities and Companies: Evidence from Shropshire," *Elizabethan Theatre*, 10 (1988), 93–111.

Jonson, Benjamin. *Discoveries 1641. Conversations with William Drummond of Hawthornden*, ed. G. B. Harrison. London: Bodley Head Quartos, 1923.

Works, ed. C. H. Herford and Percy and Evelyn Simpson, 11 vols. Oxford: Clarendon Press, 1925–47.

Kenny, Robert W. *Elizabeth's Admiral: The Political Career of Charles Howard, Earl of Nottingham 1536–1624*. Baltimore, MA: Johns Hopkins Press, 1970.

King, Tom. *Casting Shakespeare's Plays. London Actors and Their Roles, 1590–1642*. Cambridge University Press, 1992.

Knutson, Roslyn L. "Henslowe's Naming of Parts: Entries in the *Diary* for *Tamar Cham*, 1592–3, and *Godfrey of Bulloigne*, 1594–5," *N&Q*, 30 (1983), 157–60.

"Evidence for the Assignment of Plays to the Repertory of Shakespeare's Company," *Medieval and Renaissance Drama in England* 4 (1989), 75–89.

The Repertory of Shakespeare's Company, 1594–1613. Fayetteville: University of Arkansas Press, 1991.

Lamb, Mary Ellen. "The Myth of the Countess of Pembroke: The Dramatic Circle," *YES*, 11 (1981), 194–202.

Lechter-Siegel, Amy. "Isabella's Silence: The Consolidation of Power in Measure for Measure," in *Reconsidering the Renaissance*, ed. Mario A. di Cesare. New York: Medieval and Renaissance Texts and Studies, 1992, pp. 371–80.

Leggatt, Alexander. *Jacobean Public Theatre.* London: Routledge, 1992.

Leinwand, Theodore. *Theatre, Finance and Society in Early Modern England.* Cambridge University Press, 1999.

The Letters and Epigrams of Sir John Harington, ed. Norman Egbert McClure. Philadelphia: University of Pennsylvania Press, 1930.

The Letters of John Chamberlain, ed. Norman Egbert McClure, 2 vols. Philadelphia: The American Philosophical Society, 1939.

Levin, Richard. *New Readings vs. Old Plays.* Chicago University Press, 1979.

"The Contemporary Perception of Marlowe's *Tamburlaine*," *Medieval and Renaissance Drama in England* 1 (1984), 51–70.

Lin, Erike T. "Performance Practice and Theatrical Privilege: Rethinking Weimann's Concepts of *Locus* and *Platea*," *New Theatre Quarterly* 22 (2006), 283–98.

Lindley, David. *The Trials of Frances Howard and Fiction at the Court of King James.* Basingstoke: Palgrave Macmillan, 1993.

Shakespeare and the Materiality of Performance. New York: Palgrave Macmillan, 2012.

Loewenstein, Joseph. *Ben Jonson and Possessive Authorship.* Cambridge University Press, 2002.

Lublin, Robert I. *Costuming the Shakespearean Stage. Visual Codes of Representation in Early Modern Theatre and Culture.* Farnham: Ashgate, 2011.

Lyly, John. *The Complete Works of John Lyly*, ed. R. Warwick Bond, 3 vols. London, 1902.

M., T. *The Black Book.* London, 1604.

Macintosh, Iain. "Inigo Jones – Theatre Architect," *TABS* 31 (1973), 6–15.

McIlwain, Charles Howard. *The Political Works of James I.* Cambridge, MA: Yale University Press, 1918.

McLure, Millar. *Marlowe. The Critical Heritage.* London: Routledge, 1979.

McMillin, Scott. "Casting for Pembroke's Men: The *Henry VI* Quartos and *The Taming of A Shrew*," *Shakespeare Quarterly* 23 (1972), 141–59.

The Elizabethan Theatre and "The Book of Sir Thomas More". Ithaca, NY: Cornell University Press, 1987.

"The Queen's Men and the London Theatre of 1583," *Elizabethan Theatre* 10 (1988), 1–17.

"Building Stories: Greg, Fleay, and the Plot of *2 Seven Deadly Sins*," *Medieval and Renaissance Drama in England* 4 (1989), 53–89.

McMillin, Scott and MacLean, Sally-Beth. *The Queen's Men and their Plays.* Cambridge University Press, 1999.
Malone Society Collections. Oxford: The Malone Society.
Manley, Lawrence. "Why did London Inns Function as Theaters?", *Huntington Library Quarterly* 71 (2008), 181–97. Special Issue, "Spaces and Places of Early Modern London", ed. Jean Howard and Deborah Harkness.
Manley, Lawrence and MacLean, Sally-Beth. *Lord Strange's Men and their Plays.* New Haven, CT: Yale University Press, 2014.
Marcus, Leah. *Local Reading and its Discontents.* Berkeley: University of California Press, 1988.
Marino, James J. *Owning William Shakespeare. The King's Men and Their Intellectual Property.* Philadelphia: University of Pennsylvania Press, 2011.
Marlowe, Christopher. *Faustus,* ed. J. D. Jump. London: Methuen, 1962.
  The Jew of Malta, ed. N. W. Bawcutt. Manchester University Press, 1978.
  Tamburlaine, ed. J. S. Cunningham. Manchester University Press, 1981.
Marston, John. *The Scourge of Villanie.* London, 1598.
Menzer, Paul. "'The Tragedians of the City?' Q1 *Hamlet* and the Settlements of the 1590s," *Shakespeare Quarterly* 57 (2006), 162–82.
Miller, Anthony. *Roman Triumphs and Early Modern English Culture.* Basingstoke: Palgrave, 2001.
Murray, J. T. *English Dramatic Companies,* 2 vols. London: 1910.
Naunton, Robert. *Fragmenta Regalia or Observations on Queen Elizabth, Her Times & Favourites,* ed. John S. Cerovski. London and Toronto: The Folger Shakespeare Library Presses, 1985.
Neill, Michael. "'Exeunt with a Dead March': Funeral Pageantry on the Shakespearean Stage," in *Pageantry in the Shakespearean Theater,* ed. David M. Bergeron. Athens, GA: University of Georgia Press, 1985.
Nungezer, Edwin. *A Dictionary of Actors and Other Persons Associated with the Public Representation of Plays in England before 1642.* New Haven: Yale University Press, 1929.
Oliver, H. J., ed. Dido Queen of Carthage *and* The Massacre at Paris. London: Methuen, 1968.
Orgel, Stephen. *Impersonations: The Performance of Gender in Shakespeare's England.* Cambridge University Press, 1996.
Orrell, John. "The London Stage in the Florentine Correspondence, 1604–1618," *Theatre Research International* 3 (1977–8).
  The Theatres of Inigo Jones and John Webb. Cambridge University Press, 1985.
Oxford Dictionary of National Biography, ed. H. C. G. Matthew and Brian Harrison, 60 vols. Oxford University Press, 2004.
Parker, Patricia and Quint, David, eds. *Literary Theory/Renaissance Texts.* Baltimore: Johns Hopkins University Press, 1986.
Patterson, Annabel. *Censorship and Interpretation: The Conditions of Reading and Writing in Early Modern England.* Madison: University of Wisconsin Press, 1984.

P[eacham], H[enry]. *The Mastive, or Young-Whelpe of the Olde-Dogge. Epigrams and Satyrs*. London, 1615.
Perkins, William. *The Works of that Famous and Worthie Minister of Christ, in the Universitie of Cambridge, M. W. Perkins*. Cambridge, 1603.
Pinciss, G. M. "The Queen's Men, 1583–1592," *Theatre Survey* 11 (1970), 50–65.
The Plays of Henry Medwall, ed. Alan H. Nelson. Cambridge: D. S. Brewer, 1980.
Rainolds, John. *Th' Overthrow of Stage Playes*. London, 1599.
Raleigh, Walter. *Selections from His Historie of the World, His Letters, etc*. Oxford: Clarendon Press, 1917.
Records of Early English Drama. Cambridge, ed. Alan Nelson, 2 vols. University of Toronto Press, 1989.
Records of Early English Drama. Norwich 1540–1642, ed. David Galloway. University of Toronto Press, 1984.
Rochester, Joanne. *Staging Spectatorship in the Plays of Philip Massinger*. Farnham: Ashgate, 2010.
Rokison, Abigail. *Shakespearean Verse Speaking: Text and Theatre Practice*. Cambridge University Press, 2009.
Rosador, Tetzeli von. "The Sacralizing Sign: Religion and Magic in Bale, Greene, and the Early Shakespeare," *Yearbook of English Studies* 23 (1993).
Rowland, Richard. *Thomas Heywood's Theatre, 1598–1639. Locations, Translations, and Conflict*. Farnham: Ashgate, 2010.
Rowlands, Samuel. *The Knave of Clubbes*. London, 1609.
Rutter, Carol Chillington. *Documents of the Rose Playhouse*. Manchester University Press, 1984.
Rutter, Tom. "Adult Playing Companies, 1603–1613," in *The Oxford Handbook of Early Modern Theatre*, Oxford University Press, 2008, pp. 72–87.
  Work and Play on the Shakespearean Stage. Cambridge University Press, 2008.
Sales, Roger, ed. *Shakespeare in Perspective II*, Harmondsworth: Penguin, 1985.
Salkeld, Duncan. "New Allusions to London 'Shewes' and Playhouses, 1575–1605," *Early Theatre* 8 (2005), 101–7.
Schanzer, Ernest. "Thomas Platter's Observations on the Elizabethan Stage," *Notes & Queries* 201 (1956), 465–7.
Schoenbaum, Samuel. *William Shakespeare. A Compact Documentary Life*. Oxford: Clarendon Press, 1977.
Schoone-Jongen, Terence. *Shakespeare's Companies. William Shakespeare's Early Career and the Acting Companies, 1577–1594*. Farnham: Ashgate, 2008.
Shakespeare's Poems, ed. Katherine Duncan-Jones and H. R. Woudhuysen. London: Arden, 2007.
Shakespeare, William. *The Riverside Shakespeare*, ed. G. Blakemore Evans. Boston: Houghton Mifflin, 1974.
Shand, G. B. "Lear's Coronet: Playing the Moment," *Shakespeare Quarterly* 38 (1987), 78–82.
Shapiro, James. *Shakespeare and the Jews*. New York: Columbia University Press, 1996.

Sheen, Erica. *Shakespeare and the Institution of Theatre*. Basingstoke: Palgrave Macmillan, 2009.

Shochet, Lauren. *The English Masque and Public Culture in the Seventeenth Century*. Oxford University Press, 2010.

Sidney, Philip. "The Defence of Poesie," in *The Prose Works of Sir Philip Sidney*, ed. Albert Feuillerat, 4 vols. Cambridge University Press, 1963.

Skura, Meredith Ann. *The Literary Use of the Psychoanalytic Process*. New Haven: Yale University Press, 1981.

Sloane, Barney and Malcolm, Gordon. *Excavations at the Priory of the Order of the Hospital of St John of Jerusalem, Clerkenwell, London*. MoLAS Monograph 20. London: Museum of London Archaeology, 2004.

Smith, Mary E. "Staging Marlowe's *Dido Queen of Carthage*," *Studies in English Literature* 17 (1977), 177–90.

Smout, Clare. "Actor, Playwright, Sharer ... Rival? Shakespeare and Heywood, 1603–4," *Early Theatre* 13 (2010), 175–89.

Stephens, J. *Satyrical Essayes*. London, 1615.

Stern, Tiffany. *Documents of Performance in Early Modern England*. Cambridge University Press, 2009.

Streitberger, W. R., ed. *Jacobean and Caroline Revels Accounts, 1603–1642*. Oxford: Malone Society Collections, 1986.

Stubbes, Philip. *The Anatomie of Abuses*. London, 1583.

Talvacchia, Bette. "The Rare Italian Master and the Posture of Hermione in *The Winter's Tale*," *Lit: Literature Interpretation Theory* 3 (1992), 163–74.

Taking Positions: On the Erotic in Renaissance Culture. Princeton University Press, 1999.

Tanselle, G. Thomas. "Historicism and Critical Editing," *Studies in Bibliography* 29 (1976), 167–211.

Taylor, Gary. "The Fortunes of Oldcastle," *Shakespeare Survey* 38 (1985), 85–100.

Thomson, Leslie. "'With patient ears attend': *Romeo and Juliet* on the Elizabethan Stage," *Studies in Philology* 92 (1995), 230–47.

Tricomi, A. H. "Phillip, Earl of Pembroke, and the Analogical Way of Reading Political Tragedy," *Journal of English and Germanic Philology* 85 (1986), 332–45.

Vendler, Helen. *The Art of Shakespeare's Sonnets*. Cambridge, MA: Harvard University Press, 1997.

Wallace, Charles W. "Shakespeare and his London Associates as Revealed in Recently Discovered Documents," *University Studies of the University of Nebraska* 10 (1910), 47–76.

Warren, Michael. *The Complete King Lear 1608–1623*. Berkeley: University of California Press, 1989.

Watson, Robert N. "False Immortality in *Measure for Measure*: Comic Means, Tragic Ends," *Shakespeare Quarterly* 41 (1990), 411–32.

Weimann, Robert. "Bifold Authority in Shakespeare's Theatre," *Shakespeare Quarterly* 39 (1988), 401–17.

Author's Pen and Actor's Voice. Playing and Writing in Shakespeare's Theatre. Cambridge University Press, 2000.
Wernham, R. B. "Christopher Marlowe at Flushing in 1592," *English Language Renaisssance* 6 (1976), 344–5.
"Where Medway greetes old Thamesis silver streams." Manuscript poem. Oxford: Bodleian Library.
Whetstone, George. *Epistle Dedicatory, Promos and Cassandra*. London, 1578.
White, Paul Whitfield. "Patronage, Protestantism, and Stage Propaganda in Early Elizabethan England," *Yearbook of English Studies* 21 (1991), 39–52.
  "Theater and Religious Culture," in *A New History of Early English Drama*, ed. John D. Cox and David Scott Kastan. New York: Columbia University Press, 1997.
Whitney, Charles. "'Usually in the werking Daies': Playgoing Journeymen, Apprentices, and Servants in Guild Records, 1582–92," *Shakespeare Quarterly* 50 (1999), 433–58.
  "The Devil his Due: Mayor John Spencer, Elizabethan Civic Antitheatricalism, and *The Shoemaker's Holiday*," *Medieval and Renaissance Drama in England* 14 (2001), 168–84.
Wickham, G. W. *Early English Stages, 1300–1660*, 3 vols. London: Routledge and Kegan Paul, 1959–81.
Wilson, F. P. *The Plague in Shakespeare's London*. Oxford: Clarendon Press, 1927.
Wilson, Luke. *Theaters of Intention: Drama and the Law in Early Modern England*. Stanford University Press, 2000.
Wilson, Richard. *Will Power: Essays on Shakespearean Authority*. Detroit: Wayne State University Press, 1993.
  "'A Stringless Instrument': Richard II and the Defeat of Poetry," in *Shakespeare's Book. Essays in Reading, Writing and Reception*, ed. Richard Meek, Jane Rickard and Richard Wilson. Manchester University Press, 2008.
Wittek, Stephen. *The Media Players: Shakespeare, Middleton, Jonson and the Idea of News*. Ann Arbor, MI: University of Michigan Press, 2015.
Woodstock a Moral History, ed. A. P. Rossiter. London: Chatto Windus, 1946.

Index

Ackroyd, Peter, 5
Acts of the Privy Council of England, 55–9
Admiral's Men, 25, 37, 47, 64–7, 70, 75–7, 78–98, 107, 109, 127, 164, 214
Agamemnon, 128
Albany, Duke of, 249–52, 254–63
Alchemist, The, 108, 178
All's Well that Ends Well, 162
Allen, Giles, 207
Alleyn, Edward, 6, 15, 16, 22, 25, 36, 43–4, 47, 53–4, 56, 66–77, 81, 85–96, 134, 139, 158, 214, 216
Alleyn, Richard, 94
Altman, Joel, 185
Anatomie of Abuses, 231
Anatomy of Abuses, 149
Ancient Pistol (*Henry V*), 238, 239, 242, 246
Angelo (*Measure for Measure*), 223, 225, 228–31, 232–4
Anne, Queen, 105–6, 141
anti-realism, 145, 148, 153, 155, 158–9, 165
anti-semitism, 186
Antonio (*Merchant of Venice*), 208, 210–11, 212, 213–14, 218–19
Antony and Cleopatra, 102, 160, 202
Apology for Actors, An, 106, 125, 154
applause, 162–3
application, the art of, 181–7, 192–5
apprentice riots, 17, 21, 24, 27–31, 137–8
Arden of Feversham, 215
Arden, John, 240
As You Like It, 78
Astington, John, 3, 128
Astrophel and Stella, 103
Attewell, George, 164
Aubigny, Lord, 123
audiences, 181–95

Baines, Richard, 89
Bardolph, Lieutenant (*Henry V*), 238, 241–2
Barish, Jonas, 151

Barnes, Barnabe, 111
Barroll, J. Leeds, 61
Bartholomew Fair, 155
Bassanio (*Merchant of Venice*), 211, 213–14, 218, 219
Bassano, Antonio, 19
Bath, 84, 93
bear baitings, 24, 31
Bear Garden playhouse (Hope playhouse), 47
Beaumont, Francis, 155
Beckerman, Bernard, 224
Beeston, Christopher, 46, 68, 92, 106, 133, 134, 137–8
Believe As You List, 118
Bell inn, 31, 41
Bellendon, 76, 96
Benger, Sir Thomas, 122
Bentley, John, 83
Berger, Harry, 235
Berry, Herbert, 60
Billingsley, Henry, 33
Blackfriars (Revels Office site), 121–2
Blackfriars Children, 105
Blackfriars petitioners, 10–16
Blackfriars playhouse, 3, 7, 11, 24–5, 35–6, 37–49, 59, 65, 121, 133, 135, 136, 138, 169–70, 171, 177–9, 199, 207–15, 217, 219
Blackfriars residents, 209, 213
Blind Beggar of Alexandria, 216
Boar's Head company, 51
Boar's Head inn, 37, 50, 51, 210
bodies, removal from stage, 159–62
boy companies, 32, 65–6, 79–80, 108, 110, 138, 156–9, 187
Boyd, Michael, 180
Branagh, Kenneth, 239, 241, 243, 246
Brayne, John, 211
Brecht, Bertolt, 158
Bristol, 136, 141
Brooke, William, Lord Cobham, 11
Bruster, Douglas, 38, 48

276

Bryan, George, 56, 67, 68, 91
Buc, George, 118, 141
Buckhurst, Lord. *See* Sackville, Robert, Lord Buckhurst
Buckle, Cuthbert, 22–3, 26, 27, 32, 54, 57–8
Bull inn, 31, 41
Burbage, Cuthbert, 43, 44, 46, 48, 102, 207, 210, 211
Burbage, James, 5–6, 10, 16, 22, 24–5, 35–6, 37–43, 52–4, 59, 62–3, 65, 72, 90, 92, 110, 121, 135, 188, 207–9, 210–12, 213–15, 218–19
Burbage, Richard, 6, 15, 25, 39, 43–6, 48, 67–8, 70, 72–3, 90, 91, 100, 102, 110, 133, 207, 208, 210–14, 220
Burghley, Lord. *See* Cecil, William, Lord Burghley

Caesar, Sir Julius, 124–5
Canterbury, 142
Capulets, 201
Carey, George, second Lord Hunsdon, 2, 11, 34–5, 65, 71, 209, 219–20
Carey, Henry, first Lord Hunsdon, Lord Chamberlain, 2, 5–6, 10–36, 37, 40–1, 43, 44, 48–9, 52–9, 60–7, 70–1, 78, 95, 103, 208–10, 219
Carey, Katherine, 61
Carleton, Dudley, 20
Carwarden, Sir Thomas, 42, 121–2
Catholicism, 152, 157
Catiline, 108
Cecil, Sir Robert, 54, 57
Cecil, William, Lord Burghley, 10, 26–7, 54–8, 90, 105
censorship, 112, 115–29, 141, 142, 182, 192–4
Chamberlain, John, 20–1
Chamberlain's Men, 37, 41, 44, 64, 68, 76–7, 78, 100, 102, 104, 107–9, 155, 164, 214–15, 237
Chambers, E. K., 163
Chapel Children, 42, 79–80
Chapman, George, 183
Cheney, Patrick, 114
Chester, 132
Chettle, Henry, 127
Christie, Agatha, 178
Civil Wars, The, 104
Claudio (*Measure for Measure*), 223, 224, 226, 228–9, 234
Cleopatra, 104, 207, 222
Clifford, Lady Anne, 104
Clifford, Margaret, 104
Cobham, Lord, 55, 57, 65
Cocke, John, 46, 147

Cockpit playhouse, 46, 47, 135, 136–8, 169
Colin Clout, 104
Combe, John, 213
Complaint of Rosamond, The, 103
Compton, William second Lord, 20–1
Condell, Henry, 39, 44–6, 48, 68, 92
Conspiracy and Tragedy of Byron, 183
Contention, The, 73, 112
Cordelia (*King Lear*), 254–6, 259–60, 263
Coriolanus, 3, 102, 196, 201–5, 222
Coriolanus, Gaius, 201
Cornwall, Duke of, 250–2, 254, 255–8, 260, 263
Corpus Christi plays, 132, 142
counterfeiting, 147–8
Court of Aldermen, 19, 22–4
Court performances, 90, 92–3, 120–9, 250–3, 261
Coventry, 84
Cowley, Richard, 67, 91
Cromwell, Thomas, 55
Cross Keys inn, 13, 18, 24–5, 31, 33, 35–6, 40–3, 48
cross-dressing, 148, 152–3, 158
crowns and coronets, 2, 249–64
Curtain playhouse, 31, 51, 62, 133, 134, 139, 188
curtain-calls, 162
curtains, 199–200
Cutlack, 75–7, 96–7
Cymbeline, 231, 248
Cynthia's Revels, 108

Damon and Pithias, 189
Daniel, Samuel, 103–5, 107, 108
Daniell, John, 141–2
Dauphin, the (*Henry V*), 240, 241, 243, 246
Davenant, William, 109, 169
Davies, John, 102
Dead Men's Fortune, The, 67
deception, 146–51, 158–9
Defence of Poesie, 187, 189
Dekker, Thomas, 20–1, 86, 127–9, 138, 170
Delia sonnets, 103
Derby, Earl of, 55, 57
Derby, Lady, 51
Derby's Men, 66–7, 77
Dering, Sir Edward, 192
Devil is an Ass, The, 158, 184, 215
Devil's Charter, The, 111
Dido Queen of Carthage, 79–80, 87, 98
Digges, Leonard, 192
Doctor Faustus. See Faustus
Donne, John, 86
Downton, Thomas, 66, 67, 94, 127, 128, 129, 133
Drayton, Michael, 86, 162

dress, 146–7, 148–9, 151, 152–3, 161, 164, 222, 226–7, 228–31, 232–5
Drummond, William, 184
Duchess of Malfi, The, 111
Duke of York's Men, 133
Duke, John, 67, 91
Duke, the (*Measure for Measure*), 222–5, 228–30, 232–5
Dulwich College, 43, 139
Dutton, Edward, 67, 94
Dutton, Richard, 95
Dymoke, Sir Edward, 103

E.S. (satirist), 86
Edelman, Charles, 212
Edgar (*King Lear*), 258–9, 261–4
Edward I, 110
Edward II, 69, 74, 78, 79, 88–9, 98
Edward IV, 187
Edward IV, King, 126
Edwards, Richard, 189
Elizabeth I, Queen, 55, 56–9, 61–2, 106, 136, 142, 144, 186, 193, 253
English Traveller, 106
Englishmen for my Money, 215
Erne, Lucas, 45
Essex, Earl of, 55–7
Every Man in his Humour, 102, 215
Every Man Out of his Humour, 107, 111
evil, 150
Exeter, 84
Eyre, Simon, 20, 21

Faerie Queen, 184
Fair Maid of Italy, The, 75, 96
Famous Victories of Henry V, The, 76, 241
Farrant, Richard, 42, 121
Faustus, 77, 79, 80, 81, 82, 87, 94, 98, 157, 183
Faversham, 93
Field, Richard, 10, 45, 100, 219
Fitzpatrick, Tim, 200
Fleetwood, William, 52, 62–3, 188
Fletcher, Giles, 13, 24
Florio, John, 103, 104
Fluellen. *See* Llewellyn
Folkestone, 93
food riots, 203
Foot out of the Snare with a detection of sundry late practices . . . of the Priests and Jesuites of England, The, 148
Forman, Simon, 186, 192
Fortescue, Sir John, 54, 56, 58
Fortunatus, 128–9
Fortune playhouse, 15, 34–5, 47, 66, 123, 128, 133, 135, 138

Francisca (*Measure for Measure*), 226–30
Friar Bacon and Friar Bungay, 75, 77, 96, 98
Friar Francis, 75, 96
Frith, Moll, 158
frons scenae, 172, 174–5, 177–8, 198–200, 203–4
Fulgens and Lucrece, 151

Gager, William, 71, 153
Game at Chesse, A, 127, 148, 193
Gardiner, William, 213
Garnier, Robert, 104
Gasser, A. P., 81–2
Gawdy, Philip, 84
Gee, John, 148
Gentili, Alberico, 153
George a Greene, 75, 96
Gillies, John, 207
Globe playhouse, 3, 7–8, 15, 25, 35, 36, 38–40, 43–8, 59, 66, 102, 133, 138, 145, 164–5, 170, 171, 177, 179–80, 181–2, 183, 195, 196, 199, 211–12, 213, 244, 254
Gloucester, 93
Gloucester, Earl of (*King Lear*), 254–9
Goneril (*King Lear*), 257
Goodale, Thomas, 67
Goodall, Thomas, 92
Gosson, Stephen, 147
Gower (*Henry V*), 239–40, 241, 242–4, 246
Greenblatt, Stephen, 191
Greene, Robert, 31, 73, 81, 85, 99
Greg, W. W., 118
Greville, Fulke, 104, 183
Groatsworth of Wit, 99
Guildhall, 10, 12, 18–19, 21, 22, 23, 28, 35
Guilpin, Everard, 75, 96
Gull's Hornbook, The, 170
Gunaikeion, or, Nine Books of Various History Concerning Women, 106
Gunnell, Richard, 133

Haec Vir, 148
Hall, Joseph, 86, 189–90, 192
Hall, Peter, 241, 246–7
Hamlet, 76, 96, 102, 112, 150, 158, 161, 165, 174–5, 187, 191, 193–5, 249
Harington, Sir John, 146–7
Hart, John (Sir John Harte), 24, 90
Harvey, Gabriel, 81–2, 86
Hathaway, Anne, 99
hats. *See* headgear
Hatton, Christopher, 62
Haughton, William, 215–19
headgear, 1, 2, 249–64. *See also* hoods
Heinemann, Margot, 60

Heminges, John, 39, 44–6, 48, 56, 67, 68, 102, 133, 211
Heneage, Sir Thomas, 54, 57
Henrietta Maria, Queen, 107
Henry IV plays, 102, 215
  1 Henry IV, 110, 232, 241
  2 Henry IV, 163–4, 246
Henry V, 78, 102, 112, 113, 159, 162, 174, 237–48
Henry VI plays, 73–4, 78, 97, 111–13
  1 Henry VI, 74, 86, 94, 97
  2 Henry VI, 73–4, 88, 97, 111
  3 Henry VI, 69, 88, 97, 112, 147
Henry VIII, 154, 162
Henry VIII, King, 121
Henslowe, Philip, 6, 14, 25, 43, 47, 66–70, 73, 74–7, 80, 85, 86–8, 91, 96–8, 105, 107, 109, 117, 119, 127–8
Herbert, Henry, Earl of Pembroke, 2, 51, 60, 67, 71–2, 118–19, 126–7, 131, 193
Herbert, Mary, 72
Herbert, Philip, 4th Earl of Pembroke, 183
Herbert, William, 71, 139
Hertford's Men, 92
Hester and Ahasuerus, 76, 96
Heywood, Thomas, 45, 75, 86, 96, 105–7, 120, 125–6, 138, 154
Hic Mulier, 148
Hierarchy of the Blessed Angels, The, 107
Historiarum et Chronicorum totius Mundi Epitome, 81
History of the World, 181
Holinshed, Raphael, 215
Holland, John, 68, 69–70, 92
Holm, Ian, 246
Honan, Park, 5
hoods, 221–2, 225, 228–30, 233, 235
Hope playhouse, 134–5, 138
Hotine, Margaret, 186
Hotson, Leslie, 213
Howard, Charles, Lord Admiral, 2, 11, 16, 22–4, 27, 33–5, 51–9, 60–4, 74, 76, 78, 95, 122, 136
Howard, Francis, 157
Hunt, Holman, 226
Hyland, Peter, 3
Hythe, 142–4
Hytner, Nicholas, 237, 241

Iago, 197
Ichikawa, Mariko, 200
illusion/illusionism, 145–56, 158, 159–60, 163, 165
Ingram, William, 210
inns for playing, 13–15, 18, 21–5, 31–5, 142
Inns of Court, 137, 147, 164, 185

Ipswich, 84, 93
Isabella (*Measure for Measure*), 222–35
Isabella Rule, 225–8
Isle of Dogs crisis, 51

James I, King, 51, 123, 130, 132, 136, 137, 142, 155, 170, 250–6, 260, 262–3
Jeffes, Humphrey, 133
Jew of Malta, The, 75–7, 78, 79, 86–9, 93, 94, 96–8, 107, 183, 186, 190, 214, 216
jigs, 164–5
Jones, Inigo, 8, 137, 169–70, 172, 175, 178, 197, 200
Jones, Katherine Duncan, 5
Jones, Richard, 66, 92, 94
Jonson, Ben, 25, 86, 98, 107–8, 111, 112, 151–2, 155, 158, 171, 178–9, 184–5, 191, 192, 212, 215
Juby, Edward, 67, 94
Julius Caesar, 1, 102, 162, 164–5, 195, 202, 222

Kemp, Will, 56, 67, 68, 91, 100, 102, 164, 165, 211
Kent, Earl of (*King Lear*), 250, 254–5, 257–8, 259, 261
King John, 102
King Lear, 1, 2, 57–8, 102, 160, 174, 247
King Leir, 75, 96, 97, 255, 263
King, Tom, 214
King's Children, 141
King's Men, 25, 36, 39, 46, 108, 111, 112, 118, 133–5, 136, 138–9, 250, 253, 255, 258
Kirkham, Edward, 123
Knack to Know a Knave, A, 164
Knell, William, 83
Knight of the Burning Pestle, The, 155
Knollys, Sir Francis, 55, 57
Kyd, Thomas, 89, 190

Lady Elizabeth's Men, 131, 133, 138, 140
Lady's Tragedy of 1611, The, 118
Laneham, John, 68
Langley, Francis, 26, 37, 49–52, 210, 212–13
Lanier, Aemilia, 19
Lansdowne MSS 86, Article 10, 122
laughter, 189–92, 193
Lee, Robert, 133
Lee, Sidney, 113
Legge, Thomas, 82
Leicester, 84, 142
Leicester, Earl of. See Sidney, Robert, Earl of Leicester
Leicester's Men, 72, 83, 164
Leinwand, Theodore, 38, 48
Lennox, Duke of, 253
Lester, Adrian, 237

Leveson, Sir Walter, 58
liberty, 222–3
licence, 223
Llewellyn (*Henry V*), 239, 242–6
London, 215–18
Lopez, Ruy/Roderigo, trial of, 76, 96, 186, 214
Lord Chamberlain's Men. *See* Chamberlain's Men
Lord Mayor, 10–36, 37, 40–3, 48–52, 54, 57, 58–9, 63, 64–5, 83, 90, 136, 188, 208–9
Lord Strange's Men. *See* Strange's Men
Love's Labours Lost, 176
Lowin, John, 46
Lucio (*Measure for Measure*), 222–3, 224, 225, 226–30, 232, 233–4, 235
Lydd, 93
Lyly, John, 32, 187–8

Macbeth, 247
Malcolm, Gordon, 122, 124
Manningham, John, 186, 192
Mariana (*Measure for Measure*), 223, 231, 232, 234
Marlowe, Christopher, 5–6, 22, 75, 78–90, 92–5, 97–8, 107, 147, 186, 190, 193, 214, 216
Marprelate pamphlets, 32
Marston, John, 86, 111
Martin, Sir Richard, 13, 16, 21, 23–6, 32, 35, 37, 41–2, 54, 57–8
Martin, William, 57
masks, 222, 231–2, 234–5
Massacre at Paris, The, 79, 87–9, 94, 97
Massinger, Philip, 118–19
McCurdy, Peter, 8
McMillin, Scott, 90
Measure for Measure, 1, 2, 221–7
Medwall, Henry, 151
Meleager, 71
Menenius, 201–4
Merchant of Venice, The, 3, 38, 43, 76, 78, 110, 176, 186, 187, 207–20
Meres, Francis, 106, 111
Merry Wives of Windsor, The, 102, 110, 112
metatheatre, 150–66
Middleton, Thomas, 157, 174
Midsummer Night's Dream, A, 115, 117, 155, 162, 164, 176
moneylending, 1, 210, 211–14, 218–19
Montagues, 201
Montaigne, Michel de, 104
Moore, Joseph, 139–40
More, Sir Thomas, 119, 126
Mountjoy, Lord, 104, 105
Much Ado About Nothing, 231

Mulcaster, Richard, 157
Munday, Antony, 107, 128, 187
Musophilus, 104

Nashe, Thomas, 65, 80, 83, 86, 209, 214, 218–19
Naunton, Robert, 61
Neill, Michael, 159
New Romney, 93
New Shreds of the Old Snare, 148
Newington Butts playhouse, 30, 31, 75, 96
Newton, John, 133
Norwich, 84, 93, 130–1, 132, 135, 139–41

Oatley, Sir Roger, 20–1
Octavia, 104
Oenone and Paris, 106
Olivier, Laurence, 159, 239, 241, 243
Ophelia, 249
Orgel, Stephen, 158
Orrell, John, 169
Othello, 53, 160, 174, 231, 247
Othello (character), 150, 197, 207, 222, 231
Oxford's Men, 83

Palladis Tamia, 106
Pallant, Robert, 68, 92
Palsgrave's Men, 133
Paul's company, 32
Paul's/Chapel boy company, 79
Peele, George, 85, 110
Pembroke, Earl of. *See* Herbert, Henry, Earl of Pembroke
Pembroke's Men, 66, 68–77, 88–92, 95, 96–8, 102
Percy, Thomas, Earl of Northumberland, 89
Perimedes the Blacke-Smith, 81
Perkins, William, 146
Phillips, Augustine, 39, 56, 67, 68, 91, 102, 211
Philotas, 105
Phoenix and the Turtle, The (poem), 114
Pierce Penilesse, 86
Pisaro (*Merchant of Venice*), 216–19
Pitcher, John, 104–5
plague, 12, 23, 24, 27–9, 30–3, 40, 56, 57, 59
Plato, 154
Platter, Thomas, 164
play endings, 162–5
Playes Confuted in Five Actions, 147
Playgoing in Shakespeare's London, 2
Poetical Essays, The, 104
Poliakoff, Stephen, 146
Pope, Alexander, 113, 211
Pope, Thomas, 56, 67, 68, 91, 102
Porter's Hall, 134, 136–7, 139
Portia (*Merchant of Venice*), 211, 214, 218–19

Prince Charles's Men, 132–3
Privy Council, 130–1, 132–7, 143, 207, 209–11, 218
  regulation of playgoing, 10–36
Promos and Cassandra, 187
prose, 105–7, 159
Protestantism, 152
Puckering, Sir John, 54, 57, 58
Puritanism, 146–7

Queen Anne's Men, 51, 74, 98, 105, 106, 109, 133, 138
Queen's Men, 6, 22–3, 31, 41, 52, 53, 59, 60–2, 63–4, 68, 72, 75–7, 82–4, 87, 92, 94–8, 102, 154–5, 164, 256, 263
Queen's Revels Children, 133

Rainolds, John, 152–3
Raleigh, Walter, 181, 183, 184
Ranger's Comedy, The, 75, 96
Rape of Lucrece, The, 5, 49, 70, 100, 101–2, 106
Read, Timothy, 177
Reason, Gilbert, 140
Red Bull playhouse, 9, 46, 51, 74, 123, 133, 135, 138
Remembrancia, 12–13, 15, 17, 24, 26, 32, 58, 63
Revels Office, 115–29, 133, 139, 142
Revels, Master of the, 3, 5, 6, 17, 34, 84, 92, 103, 111, 115–29, 131, 133, 139, 141, 193
Revenger's Tragedy, The, 174
Rialto, 212
Ricardus Tertius, 82
Richard Crookback, 76
Richard Duke of Yorke, 69, 73
Richard II, 77, 78, 104, 111, 186, 193–4
Richard II, King, 42, 253
Richard III, 76, 113, 149–50, 158, 173–4
Richardson, Ian, 150
Richmond Palace, 128
Roaring Girl, The, 231
Romeo and Juliet, 107, 111, 176, 201, 231
Rosamund, 104
Rose playhouse, 5, 9, 11, 14–15, 17, 25, 27, 29, 31, 32, 34, 36, 37, 47, 51, 53, 64–77, 85, 87–98, 128, 172, 176, 200
Rosseter, Philip, 134
Rowe, Nicholas, 109
Rowley, William, 133, 138
Royal Exchange, 212, 217
Royal Shakespeare Company, 246
Russell, Lady Elizabeth, 10, 13
Rutter, Tom, 38, 48

Sackford, Henry, 122
Sackville, Robert, Lord Buckhurst, 54–5, 57, 58
Salisbury Court playhouse, 47, 123, 133
Sam Wanamaker Playhouse, 8, 199
Sapho and Phao, 187
Schoenbaum, Samuel, 5, 113
school plays, 152–3, 156–7, 185
Scourge of Villainy, 111
Sejanus, 108
Seven Deadly Sins, 2 The, 44, 67, 69, 90–2
sexual freedom, 222–3
Shakespeare and the Geography of Difference, 207
Shakespeare company, 25, 48, 208, 212, 237, 240, 242, 247
Shakespeare Company 1594–1642, The, 3
Shakespeare, John, 212
Shakespeare, William, 37, 39, 44–6, 49, 54, 59, 67, 78–9, 86, 92, 95, 96–8, 99–114, 147, 155, 172, 184, 196, 201–3, 207–20, 221–4, 225–6, 227–8, 230, 235–6, 237–42, 243–8
Shakespeare's Opposites, The Admiral's Company 1594–1625, 3
Shakespearean moment, 1
Shakespearean Stage, The, 8
Shoemaker's Holiday, 20
Shoreditch, 5
Shrewsbury, 93
Shylock (*Merchant of Venice*), 43, 110, 186, 187, 207–20
Sidney, Mary, 103
Sidney, Robert, Earl of Leicester, 71–2
Sidney, Sir Philip, 103, 152, 154, 187, 189–92
Sincler, John, 68, 69–70, 92
Singer, John, 66, 94
Slater, Martin, 67, 94
Sloane, Barney, 122, 124
Sly, Will, 68, 91
Sonnet 99, 145
Southampton, 84
Southampton, Earl of, 100, 109
Spanish Contract, The, 131
Spencer, Elizabeth, 20–1
Spencer, John, 19–22, 23, 26–34, 37, 42
Spenser, Edmund, 5, 6, 104, 107, 184
St Paul's choir school, 157
St Clare, Order of (Poor Clares), 225–30, 233, 234
St John's (Revels Office site), 115, 119–26, 128
stage doors, 201, 203–6
staging, 196–206
staging, non-realistic, 158–9
Stanley, Ferdinando, 67
Stern, Tiffany, 119
Strange, Lord, 89, 95
Strange's Men, 15, 41, 44, 56, 66–77, 85, 87–98
Streitberger, W. R., 120, 128
Stubbes, Philip, 149, 231
Summer's Last Will and Testament, 79

sumptuary laws, 253–4
Sussex, Earl of, 60–2, 95
Sussex's Men, 68–71, 73, 83, 87, 92, 95–7
Swan playhouse, 26–7, 30, 32, 37, 50, 51, 58, 133, 173, 197–200

Tamburlaine, 77, 79, 80–8, 93, 94, 98, 185, 186, 189–90, 201
Taming of A Shrew, The, 96, 112, 145
Taming of the Shrew, The, 69, 74, 76, 102, 112
Tarlton, Richard, 22, 83–4, 177
Taylor, Anne, 104
Tempest, The, 6, 7, 162, 177, 178–9
Tethys' Festival, 105
'theatre of estrangement', 157–8
Theatre playhouse, 11, 16, 27, 31, 32, 36, 37, 42, 43, 51, 53, 54, 62, 64, 68, 72–3, 92, 95, 188, 207–8, 211, 218, 219
Tilney, Sir Edmund, 23–4, 53–4, 103, 115–29, 251–2, 263
Titus and Vespasian, 75, 96
Titus Andronicus, 2, 68–70, 74–6, 78, 94, 96–7, 160
Towne, Thomas, 67, 94
Townsend, John, 131
Tragedy of Anthony, 104
transvestism, 152, 158
Treatise on Play, 147
Troia Britannica, 106
Troublesome Reign of King John, The, 76, 97
True Tragedie of Richard the Third, The, 112, 154
Tunstall, James, 66, 92, 94
Turner, Ann, 157
Twelfth Night, 164
Two Gentlemen of Verona, 231
Two Wise Men and All the Rest Fools, 164

universities, playing at, 153–4
Usury Act (1571), 210, 216
Usury Act (1605), 203

van Es, Bart, 99
Vautrollier, Jacqueline, 219

Venice, 212–13, 215, 218
Venus and Adonis, 49, 100–1, 106
Verfremdungseffekt, 158
Volpone, 108, 184

Walkley, Thomas, 53
Walsingham, Francis, 67, 84
Wambus, Francis, 130–1, 139, 144
Wanamaker, Sam, 7, 8
Warning for Fair Women, A, 215
Warwick's Men, 83
Wayte, William, 213
Webb, John, 8, 167–70, 172, 175, 197
Webbe, Sir William, 17, 21, 24, 29, 31, 33
Webster, John, 111
Weimann, Robert, 150, 174, 196–7
Westcott, Sebastian, 157
Westminster, 137
Whetstone, George, 187–90, 192
White Horse inn, 131
Whitefriars (Revels Office site), 123
Whitefriars playhouse, 123, 133
Whitgift, John, Archbishop, 17, 23, 31–3, 54–8, 79
Whitney, Charles, 19, 28, 33–4
Wickham, Glynne, 156
William Shakespeare
    A Documentary Life, 5
Winter's Tale, The, 6–7, 177–8
witchcraft, 146–8
Witt, Johannes de, 197–200
Witter, John, 39, 44
Wolley, Sir John, 54, 55, 57
Woodliffe, Oliver, 37, 49–51, 210, 212
Woodstock, 231
Woodward, Edward, 150
Worcester College drawings, 167–72, 198
Worcester, Earl of, 120
Worcester's Men, 47, 51, 53, 106
Works of Samuel Daniel, The, 104
Wren, Christopher, 167

York, 84, 136, 141